Stealth Fighter

Stealth Fighter

A Year in the Life of
an F-117 Pilot

Lt. Col. William B. O'Connor,
USAF (ret.)

ZENITH PRESS

First published in 2012 by Zenith Press, an imprint of MBI Publishing Company, 400 First Avenue North, Suite 300, Minneapolis, MN 55401 USA

Zenith Press titles are also available at discounts in bulk quantity for industrial or sales-promotional use. For details write to Special Sales Manager at MBI Publishing Company, 400 First Avenue North, Suite 300, Minneapolis, MN 55401 USA.

To find out more about our books, join us online at www.zenithpress.com.

Library of Congress Cataloging-in-Publication Data

O'Connor, William B., 1958–

Stealth fighter : a year in the life of an F-117 pilot / William B. O'Connor.

    p. cm.

Includes bibliographical references.

ISBN 978-0-7603-4135-3 (hardbound with jacket)

1. O'Connor, William B., 1958- 2. Operation Allied Force, 1999. 3. Kosovo War, 1998–1999—Aerial operations, American. 4. Kosovo War, 1998–1999—Personal narratives, American. 5. Fighter pilots—United States—Biography. 6. F-117 (Jet attack plane) I. Title.

DR2087.5O25 2012

949.7103'1548092—dc23

2011042101

Credits:

All photographs are from the author's collection unless noted otherwise.

Front cover photo montage: F-117. *Photo courtesy of Lockheed Martin*; desert landscape *Tim Roberts Photography/Shutterstock.com*

Spine: F-117A patch. *Author's collection*

Back cover: (top) *Photo by Judson Brohmer courtesy of Lockheed Martin;* (bottom) F-117 Nighthawks of the 8th Fighter Squadron, 49th Fighter Wing, Holloman Air Force Base, New Mexico, hold for takeoff at Al Jaber Air Base, Kuwait, March 13, 1998. *U.S. Air Force*

Printed in the United States of America

Contents

Prologue

Night-1

I'M LATE, I'M LATE, I'M LATE. That nagging little thought in the back of my mind just won't go away.

It's a few hours past midnight early on March 25, 1999. I am somewhere over Hungary at 18,200 feet on a coal-black night in an F-117 Stealth Fighter with all its external lights turned off. Loaded within the belly of my jet is a pair of 2,000-pound laser-guided bombs. The communication antennae that I would rely on for a recall have been retracted, and I'm racing as fast as I can toward a hostile border to enter my first real combat. This is the second wave of attacks on Night-1 against the country I grew up calling Yugoslavia, and I'm desperate.

The guys in the first wave had some semblance of surprise and met little resistance, but that was hours ago. There won't be any more surprises tonight—anyone with access to CNN watched me take off from Italy's Aviano Air Base about an hour before, and all the targets we'd attacked so far fell into very distinct categories. The Serbs know exactly what we're interested in, and our politically allowed routing into and out of Serbia is ridiculously constrained.

They know I'm on my way. They know approximately where I'm going and what I plan to do with my pair of bombs. They know the tiny little corridor I'll have to fly through to get there, and with the few hours they've had to regroup after absorbing our first wave of attacks, I'm guessing they're pissed off and ready to battle.

I methodically run through the pre-combat checklists for the tenth time, confirming that all my cockpit controls are set properly. Nothing is amiss. After a few seconds I run them again—it gives me something to do.

I've already received the code words authorizing me to cross the Serbian border and attack my assigned targets. I won't speak to another human until I'm ready to land. The last obstacle holding me back is the requirement to cross the Serbian border within plus or minus sixty seconds of a very specific time. The *minus* part hasn't been a factor all night—the first jet I'd started had to be aborted at the last possible moment, sending me running to a spare aircraft. The *plus* part is going to be tight.

For the past hour, my jet, tail number 840-828, and I have been desperately scrambling to make up the twenty-one minutes I was late in taking off. Hoping that our carefully planned deconfliction routing is as good as it needs to be tonight, I've been cutting a few corners. Normally, doing this isn't too dangerous, provided there isn't someone out there in the dark too far off their time line—someone like me, for instance.

Peering out into the night reveals nothing, of course. Anyone who might be in the area as a potential collision risk is also blacked out. I look anyway.

There's no need to do anything with the throttles. They've been pushed up against the stops in the far left corner of the cockpit for some time now. Pushing on them harder won't make the slightest difference in my speed. I push anyway. Just checking.

Finally, as I watch the moving map display in my cockpit, the small white symbol representing my jet crosses the northern border of Serbia. I'm fifty-five seconds past the middle of my timing window, so there's a whole five seconds to spare before I'd have to turn around. Not bad. I can easily make up the difference during the next three or four legs on the way to my first target. More importantly, I'm allowed to continue.

This is it. I've just violated a sovereign national border with the intent, and my government's authorization, to commit acts of war. I also accept that my opposition, in the course of their duty to protect their homeland, is fully entitled to try to kill me in return. Finally, I can relax.

Yes, relax. The irony of that thought isn't lost even as it occurs to me. It's only going to take about a half hour to blow up a couple heavily defended buildings and dodge a few missiles and anti-aircraft cannon shells. But that's the easy part. While the actual mission isn't going to take long, it had taken me seventeen years to make it past that border.

Previously, in my life as an aviator and warrior, being left behind had always been the problem. Before this moment I'd always been in the wrong place at the wrong time. When I had been in combat units, peace had prevailed. All the actual shooting wars had occurred while I had been assigned to training or test units. The Libya raid, Grenada, Panama, the Gulf War—I'd watched them all on TV while tracking the adventures of friends from previous assignments.

My family, of course, didn't see it this way at all. In their eyes, this was the first time I wasn't fortunate enough to have been elsewhere when war broke out. But in the fraternity of warriors, few things are more painful than watching your brethren go off to battle while you stay behind. To wish for diplomatic efforts to fail is inexcusable, but not to be in on the action once hostilities have commenced is equally unthinkable for a warrior.

A warrior's first combat is an experience for which he or she can never be truly ready. We were trained, we had the most sophisticated aircraft in the world, and we were more than willing to leap into the breach. But the whole *baptism by fire* thing was still an unknown, which wasn't helped by the fact that none of our squadron-mates who had already been there seemed able to describe the experience. Even Winston Churchill, who was rarely at a loss for words, came up a little short: "There is nothing more exhilarating than to be shot at without result"—a phrase that will no doubt make perfect sense . . . tomorrow.

In any case, I had held the uncertainty in check for years. Now, as I race invisibly *(I hope)* into harm's way, I am finally going to get my chance.

I love flying. I also love to read just about everything related to aviation, whether they be histories, biographies, war stories, or tales of exploration. So after becoming a combat veteran and witness to history in an odd little conflict, I waited for the stories to come forth so that I could read all about *my* war. With few exceptions, I'm still waiting. After several years, I decided to step up to the plate and offer my version of events during the air war over the former Yugoslavia.

This isn't a history of the F-117 or even of the Kosovo War.* The firsthand experiences that follow simply relate the day-to-day

---

* I'll point you to Ben Rich's *Skunk Works* and Benjamin Lambeth's *NATO's Air War for Kosovo* for those subjects. The best history of conflict in the area I've found is Andre Gerolymatos' *The Balkan Wars*. For political analysis, the gold standard is *War in a Time of Peace* by David Halberstam.

events of one pilot over the course of a year. I have always been known as a fairly calm and dispassionate observer (by the admittedly skewed standards of the fighter pilot community, anyway). Hopefully I can do some small justice in recording a fraction of the service performed by the men and women of the 8th and 9th Expeditionary Fighter Squadrons. My recollection of events will almost certainly differ from those of others who were there, and I look forward to reading their stories someday—but this is the way I saw it.

CHAPTER 1

Farewell to the Raven

Plan for the worst, hope for the best, then do what
you can with what you've got.

IN THE SPRING OF 1998, I was finishing a tour with the 429th
Electronic Combat Squadron (ECS) at Cannon Air Force Base,
just west of Clovis, New Mexico. To eyes more accustomed to rolling
hills covered by green fields and dense forest, Clovis wasn't even
the slightest bit lovely—just tabletop-flat farmland comprised of the
leftovers from the creation of West Texas. When I asked my wife
where we should go next, she said, "I don't really care. Just as long as
it isn't south, or west, of here." She swore that she could see the curve
of the earth from our backyard. Among air force brats, Cannon was
known as the only base where you could watch your dog run away
for three days.

Without so much as a hill or a natural tree between us and
the Rockies, the wind would *blow*. The direction never seemed

to matter. In the spring, after the farmers had plowed their fields, visibility could go down to well under a hundred yards due to the blowing dust. The sky became a gritty beige fog as cubic miles of topsoil attempted to migrate to another state. They never made it though, because the next day the wind would be blowing just as hard from the opposite direction and all the dust would come back.

The town and the airfield owed their existence almost exclusively to location. The only reason the town had grown up there, versus any other spot north, east, south, or west, was because it had been the location of a watering stop by a railroad siding. The airfield was there because the land was flat and cheap and because there were relatively uninhabited square counties of it around. We never got any noise complaints, and we never lost a gunnery range to vacation home encroachment.

People from elsewhere didn't move to Clovis for the scenery or to retire. The town's most notable boast is that it was once the site of a storefront studio where Buddy Holly recorded some songs in the late 1950s. It also has a higher percentage of churches-to-population than any other town its size in the country. (A bored young lieutenant commented that was because they had so much more to pray for than other towns their size.) But the people made up for it. The sense of community was tangible, and if I had to deploy overseas and leave my family behind, it would have been tough to come up with a more supportive town than Clovis.

Before this assignment I'd had no experience with any of the F-111 communities. My previous tours had been flying the T-33 in upstate New York with Air Defense Command before the air-defense mission was disbanded, followed by F-16s at Homestead AFB in Florida before Hurricane Andrew blew the base into the Everglades. In 1989 I did a tour test flying and delivering brand new F-16s coming out of the factory in Fort Worth (the best job I would ever have) and then a year as a military advisor and F-16 instructor pilot to the Egyptian Air Force at Abu Suwayr Air Base near the Suez Canal. Prior to Cannon I had been assigned as an exchange officer and instructor pilot to the U.S. Navy's Training Command, where I became the only USAF pilot at that time to carrier-qualify in both the T-2 and the TA-4.

I had been flying the EF-111 Raven for two years, and it was time to move on. Normally, a tour is supposed to last about three years, but the EF-111 was being retired. I had been one of three pilots and three electronic warfare officers (EWOs) to go through the very last F-111 training class in the U.S. Air Force. And now the 429th, the last tactical electronic combat squadron in the air force, was being disbanded.

The F-111's history is famous, or infamous, as a case study in how aircraft procurement should *not* be done. In the early 1960s, Robert McNamara, President Kennedy's secretary of defense, unilaterally decreed that the age of manned aircraft was just about over. He killed off the heavy bomber programs designed to replace the B-52 and the advanced interceptor programs designed to counter Soviet manned bombers (assuming that the Russians would obviously follow his lead and cancel their own manned programs—they didn't), but figured there was a need for one more fighter. To economize, he decided that the heavy bomber, medium bomber, tactical fighter, and naval interceptor missions could all be wrapped up in one package. The F-111 was supposed to have been the last manned combat aircraft ever built—designed to do *everything* for *everybody*! Just some of the F-111's "necessary accoutrements," besides manually swept wings, fold-up nuclear blast curtains, and spring-loaded coffee-thermos dispensers, included a space-age ejection capsule equipped with enormous landing bags, inflatable flotation pontoons, and a manually operated bilge pump (yes, a bilge pump!) for when the capsule was being used as a boat.

By the time both services' (mostly incompatible) requirements had been packed into the design, the plane was wildly overweight, unmaneuverable, and, well, a medium bomber. The navy bravely attempted some carrier trials with their version before calling it quits and starting over with what eventually became the F-14 Tomcat.

The EF-111 airframes were all between thirty and thirty-five years old and had begun life in the early 1960s as F-111A models. As A-models, they had participated in the first hurried deployment of the type to Vietnam in 1968, dubbed Operation Combat Lancer. At the time, great hopes had been placed upon the jet's ability to fly alone at night, in any weather conditions, hugging the earth using onboard terrain-following radar (TFR) and employing the first generation of laser-guided bombs against high-value targets. This stuff was cutting edge in 1968—just a little *too* cutting edge, as it turned out.

Just nine days after completion of the first training class for combat aircrew, six jets were deployed to Takhli Royal Thai Air Base. One day after arriving in-country, tail number 66-0016 successfully flew the model's first combat mission. The target was a "suspected" truck park. Unfortunately, this mission was pretty much the high point of the jets' combat debut. During the following week, two of the original six aircraft crashed. A few weeks later, one of the two replacement jets disappeared—neither the aircraft nor the crew were ever found. Operations were suspended, and the surviving jets returned to the States. From start to finish, combat operations only ran from March 18 to April 22 for a loss rate of almost 40 percent in just five weeks.

The F-111A wouldn't return to combat until the fall of 1972, and on that occasion some foolish person decided to create a bit of PR fodder by attempting to set a record for the shortest time between the deployment order and actual combat operations. The 429th TFS (Tactical Fighter Squadron, back then) was the "lucky" unit accorded this honor and actually did set the record—only thirty-three hours elapsed between the first aircraft's departure from the United States and bombs impacting a target northeast of Hanoi.

The longer version of the story, which is usually left out, is that the first strike package had been planned for six aircraft and the combat launch was scheduled to occur only four hours after hitting the ground from their trans-Pacific ferry. Of those six, three aircraft aborted on the ground with equipment failures, the fourth aborted in the air with equipment failure and returned to base, the fifth couldn't get to its primary target due to weather and was forced to bomb an alternate, and the sixth jet never returned. After that loss on the first night, the 429th stood down for five days while the aircraft systems were thoroughly, and properly, checked out as they hadn't been before.

Combat missions resumed on October 5, 1972, and the F-111A finally began to hit its stride. First striking from medium altitude, the jets progressed to single-ship, night, and low-altitude missions in weather conditions that grounded other aircraft. Through those storied last months of 1972, and through the end of the Linebacker II campaign, eighteen F-111As flew over four thousand combat sorties with an additional six losses to enemy action (and four non-combat losses). Their final blow, on May 14, 1975, sank one of the Cambodian gunboats that had hijacked the SS *Mayaguez*.

Over the years, the technical kinks were worked out and subsequent models of the F-111 were gradually improved until the ultimate incarnation, the F-111F, arguably became the finest strike aircraft the U.S. Air Force ever deployed. Modern F-15E Strike Eagle drivers will contest that last point in respect to their aircraft's admitted sophistication and accuracy, but they can't pretend to have the range, payload, or speed an F-111 possessed decades before the first Strike Eagle ever rolled out of a factory. Though officially classified as a fighter, the F-111 was in actuality the meanest kick-ass medium bomber in the world. As a fighter it sucked.

One of the many lessons of Vietnam was the need for more sophisticated and capable electronic combat aircraft. Older versions of electronic warfare (EW) platforms used over Vietnam, such as the EB-66 or pod-equipped F-4s, had lacked the combination of speed, range, payload, maneuverability, and self-protection capability necessary to be effective (and survive).

The F-111 airframe was a natural choice. Its huge internal weapons bay, originally designed to carry nuclear weapons, was redesigned to house ten separate jamming transmitters weighing in at 20,000 pounds total. Each transmitter was optimized to counter specific Soviet surface-to-air missiles (SAMs) and radar systems within a particular frequency band and broadcast its signal via individual horn-shaped antennas. Each antenna could be independently steered through 360 degrees of motion. The EWO could assign each of the ten transmitters to ten separate locations, and the antennas would automatically pivot and rotate so they could continually point toward their assigned targets regardless of how the pilot was maneuvering the plane. These broadcast antennas were all lined up in a single row along the belly of the aircraft housed in a structure that we called the canoe. A jamming signal might take the form of a subtle deception, to flood a radar scope with hundreds of false targets or, via sheer power, to just cook the innards out of whatever radar was pissing us off.

Hostile signals that were processed for intelligence purposes, or to be countered, were received through a separate set of antennas housed atop the vertical stabilizer in a structure called the football. Though the smaller of the two structures, the football was actually the size of a rowboat, at more than nine feet long and weighing over two thousand pounds. Its location was designed to be as far away from the broadcast antennas as possible without unbalancing the aircraft and have the bulk of the aircraft placed between the canoe and the football. This design helped minimize interference between the two systems.

The fact that the crew compartment was also located between these two electronic behemoths, and that we straddled the free world's largest mobile source of electrons, and that supposedly, as a "joke," one of the transmitters had once been used to cook a bag of microwave popcorn set on the ramp fifty yards away, and . . . well, the cockpit was purportedly shielded, but you get the point. We treated the lady with all the respect we could muster, but to this day all of us still faintly glow in the dark.

The EF-111 was a Frankenstein monster of a jet—big without being pretty, powerful without being graceful, put together with too many bits and parts that didn't always seem to match. F-111s were the world's first aircraft where the wings could be repositioned while in flight. She was just shy of seventy-seven feet long and had a wingspan that ranged from less than thirty-two feet wide with the wings fully swept (smaller than an F-16) to more than sixty-three feet wide with the wings fully deployed. The wings could also be manually swept from 16 to an amazing 72.5 degrees aft—so far back that they could no longer be seen from the cockpit. Her empty weight, at about 57,000 pounds, was almost identical to that of a Boeing 737 airliner (a plane designed to carry more than 130 passengers). Fully fueled and equipped to gross takeoff weight, we might trundle along at 89,000 pounds.

She carried a dizzying 32,000 pounds of fuel internally. By comparison, an entire F-16 with fuel weighs 25,000 pounds; a car weighs about 3,000 pounds, with a fuel weight of maybe 100 pounds. At low altitude with the wings swept back, the F-111 could flat-out outrun anything ever built—which was good for us since she couldn't turn worth a damn and was completely unarmed.

Another notable oddity was it being the only aircraft I've ever flown that didn't really list a maximum speed, though in theory that was up in the Mach-2.5 range. For all practical purposes, you could go just as fast as the plane would let you until a sensor mounted on top of the canopy told you that parts of the plane were beginning to melt due to skin friction—the jet could literally go the speed of heat. The actual wording in the manual went along the lines of this:

> The maximum <u>sustained</u> speed coincides with a skin-temperature of 308°F. Any speed faster (hotter) than 308°F must be limited to no more than 5 minutes duration, or a peak skin-temperature of 418°F, whichever comes first. Before this maximum speed is achieved blistered external paint and partial delamination of the honeycomb panels can be expected.

While I'm not exactly sure what a "partially delaminated honeycomb panel" was going to do to me while flying at more than twice the speed of sound, it certainly didn't sound good. The fact that I would be sitting in an enclosed metal object heated to a hundred degrees hotter than the temperature necessary to bake a Thanksgiving turkey didn't sound very sensible either. Letting the bird run for all she was worth might sound cool, but you would blister and scorch most of the paint, and the skin of the aircraft would be hot enough to boil spit.

In addition to this external heat, we also had to deal with the waste heat generated internally by those ten JSS units in the weapons bay. Engine-driven generators pumped a combined total of 180KVA of power into those jammers, and only electrons were coming out. So the jet carried over 400 pounds of coolant fluid just to keep that system from melting down. Even that wasn't enough: When the coolant fluid itself became too hot, it was in turn cooled with fuel that had been bypassed before being fed to the engines. Using jet fuel to cool off components that were already too hot to be safe was something else that didn't sound quite right to me.

Years after Vietnam, three of those first six F-111s deployed for Combat Lancer survived to be rebuilt by the Grumman Corporation as EF-111s. Tail number 66-0016 (known as "Sixty-Sixteen" due to an abbreviated version of its number being painted on the aircraft), which flew that first combat sortie in Vietnam, became the only F-111 of any variant to claim an air-to-air kill. It happened during the first night of Desert Storm. The EF-111 was being chased by a French-built Iraqi F-1 Mirage. When jumped by the Mirage, the Raven pilot lit the afterburners, swept the wings fully back, and pitched the plane nose down into the black desert night, inviting the Mirage to follow. No other aircraft was ever going to keep up with a Raven going downhill, but the Mirage pilot also knew that "downhill" doesn't last forever; eventually the Raven would have to level off. What the Mirage pilot *didn't* know was that the Raven crew had engaged the TFR system and had set the autopilot to perform a maximum-g pullout that would bottom out only a hundred feet above the pitch-black desert floor. One hundred feet would be cutting it ridiculously close for a human in daylight and downright suicidal at night, but the computer worked perfectly. The Raven pulled up at the last millisecond. The Mirage didn't, and it impacted the desert floor. Sixty-Sixteen, most famous of all the F-111s, is now on static display as a "gate guard" at Cannon AFB.

In the spring of 1996, as a newly pinned major, I took the EF-111 assignment to avoid a desk job and, frankly, because there just wasn't anything else to fly. At that period during the Clinton drawdown, officers coming right out of pilot training were being assigned desk jobs. Airframes just weren't available, but since the EF-111 was scheduled to be retired in a mere two years, most pilots didn't want to invest the time and effort required to be trained in a dying system. I didn't care.

By any conventional wisdom I should have been chasing after a "good" staff job, whatever the hell that was. But I had joined up to fly, and if choosing airplanes over a Pentagon office job was going to negatively affect my career, so be it.

During my two years with the 429th ECS, I spent a full seven months in training. Since the EF-111 only had flight controls for the pilot in the left seat, the last existing F-111F squadron on base had held back four jets. The F-model had controls for both the pilot in the left seat and an instructor in the right. The jets' trip to the boneyard had been delayed long enough for each of the three of us to get a half-dozen landings with an instructor pilot. For the rest of our training, the instructors were just going to have to trust us since they were now only "along for the ride."

Seven months of training left just seventeen months of operational service with which to "pay back" our education. Suffice to say, the U.S. Air Force got its money's worth: during those seventeen months, I was deployed on four separate rotations to Saudi Arabia to participate in Operation Southern Watch, where the United States and its coalition of allies had been effectively occupying the airspace of Iraq, 24/7, since the end of the Gulf War.

This hot-and-cold combat had been going on for almost eight years by the time I arrived, and the administration had absolutely no intention of ever bringing the U.S. Air Force home. When I finally left for the last time in April 1998, our squadron had tallied 2,780 consecutive days in theater. My share of that was a bit over two hundred days, spent living in eight-man tents at Al Kharj Air Base, Kingdom of Saudi Arabia. Living in tent city (we averaged about five thousand people there at any given time) was a bit monotonous, but the flying was interesting, and there certainly was a lot of it.

The Iraqi border was almost an hour's flying time away, and from takeoff to landing a typical mission could last anywhere from three to ten hours. The longer ones occurred during a memorable couple of weeks in October 1997. Saddam Hussein had done something provocative along the border, and our detachment was ordered to provide a twenty-four-hours-a-day presence over Iraq.

Unfortunately, at that time we had only four aircraft in-country, and one of them was hard-broke and awaiting parts. With our three remaining jets, we set up a rotation where a single jet would launch for the border. An hour later it would have pushed into Iraq to monitor whatever threat system was of interest that day. Every two hours or so we'd wander south to the Saudi border to top off with fuel from the orbiting tanker fleet before returning to our assigned areas. After eight hours, a replacement would launch to fly north, and over the radio we'd hand off responsibility to him for his shift "in the box." If it were practical, we'd arrange to pass head-to-head on our way out for an aerial "high-five" as we left.

For my shift, I woke up around midnight, flew for several hours before the sun came up, then returned to land around noon. After a week of this routine, we were beat. During peacetime, aircrews are normally limited to seventy-five flying hours per month. Anything beyond that requires a hard-to-come-by waiver. In seventeen years of flying, I had been grounded by the seventy-five-hour rule a grand total of twice, and waivers hadn't even been considered. In Saudi, however, our waivers were rubber-stamped on the sixth of the month.

During just the first week or so of that particular flare-up, my logbook shows sixty-six hours of total flight time, twenty-eight aerial refuelings, a border incident involving an Iraqi MiG-23, and one in-flight emergency over enemy territory (a throttle linkage had become disconnected from the fuel control, so I had to come back single engine).

Things then calmed down a little. The cavalry arrived in the form of four extra flight crews to share the load. As usually happens, the pace of operations slacked off as soon as they were in place, briefed, and rested up enough to be of use. For the remainder of that deployment, we then had too many people for too little work. Sortie durations went back down to the two-and-a-half- to three-and-a-half-hour range, and now twice the number of people had to share them. So, after an impressive start, I ended up with only eighty-five hours total for the month. The maintenance guys really needed the slowdown, though. We had beaten their jets to death.

There have always been cliques and rivalries within the air force, as there have been within all the services. The more famous contests were between Tactical Air Command (TAC) and Strategic Air Command, TAC and Air Defense Command, and the majority of TAC versus what little had survived of the medium-bomber community—the B-57 and F-111. TAC won them all by absorbing or eliminating its rivals. Eventually only TAC remained and was rechristened Air Combat Command (ACC).

Once the last wing of F-111Fs had been disbanded, ACC called for a cost analysis of the EF-111, as measured against the navy's EA-6B Prowler (a plane the U.S. Air Force had rejected as obsolete before the first EF had even been built more than twenty years previously). The publicly stated motivation for the analysis was to see which airframe would be cheaper to support while waiting for the stealth aircraft that would eventually replace conventional fighters. The game was rigged though. In considering the EF-111, the U.S. Air Force studied the cost of hourly operations, engine cycle replacement, proposed equipment upgrades, and long-term maintenance issues that were now exacerbated by the absence of other F-111 airframes in the inventory. The navy ignored these details in their own analysis and essentially only considered the cost of the EA-6B's hourly fuel and oil burn. Surprise, surprise, the EF-111 lost.

With the F-4G Wild Weasels already disbanded after the Gulf War, the U.S. Air Force was now deliberately abandoning much of its hard-earned electronic combat capabilities. Our training and corporate knowledge would be discarded. Even the last few experienced EWOs who couldn't be absorbed as F-15E Strike Eagle back-seaters were seconded to the navy as EA-6B crew.

The U.S. Air Force did convert some F-16s into high-speed anti-radiation missile (HARM) shooters with bolt-on avionics pods to replace a few of the F-4Gs. The new variant was known as the Block-50, and its pilots stepped up to the plate as fighter pilots always do and did the best they could with what they were provided. But the Block-50 was only intended to be an interim solution to the lack of a fully integrated electronic combat policy. A decade later this "interim solution" was still the only game in town. The fact that the answer to the EC puzzle—a combat fleet comprised solely of stealth aircraft—was, at best, several decades away, was intentionally ignored. Also ignored was the simple fact that our entire support fleet of tankers, transports, AWACS, EC-135s, RC-135s, U-2s, and so on would *always* need EW protection and would *never* be stealthy.

In one respect, there weren't many other options available. When the Clinton administration took office in 1993 it was determined to harvest the "peace dividend" that the end of the Cold War had suggested. Inconveniently, the world was still a dangerous place and had yielded no such dividend. A study, called the Bottom-Up Review, was commissioned, with the bottom-line goal of forcing the services to fit the funding allocated by the new administration instead of funding the services to meet the threat. Defense spending as a percentage of the national GDP, which had fallen from 9.7 percent in 1962 to the 4.7 percent of the "Hollow Force" Carter years—where fully a third of our combat aircraft on the ramp couldn't fly because they didn't even have engines—was slashed to 3.2 percent and falling.

More than 30 percent of U.S. combat aircraft, almost 1,800, were eliminated. The number of fighters alone eliminated by the Clinton administration, by some weird coincidence, just exceeded 1,737, the total number of U.S. Air Force aircraft (of all types) shot down by the North Vietnamese during the Kennedy, Johnson, Nixon, and Ford administrations—combined. We were shrinking hard and fast.

Only forty-two Ravens were ever built. Thirty-six survived. Of those, just thirty-two made it to the boneyard under their own power. They were "replaced" by exactly half their number, sixteen previously retired EA-6Bs that were removed from the boneyard to be refurbished. Though we didn't know it at the time, the Raven was going to be missed much sooner than anyone would have guessed.

CHAPTER 2

FIGMO

Old USAF-speak for Finally (or F*#!),
I've Got My Orders

THE EF-111 WAS ON ITS way out. When a squadron is thought to be getting the short end of the stick by being disbanded, Air Force Personnel Command (AFPC) often takes care of the remaining people with a process referred to as block assignments.

In ACC, personnel assignments are handled by a small unit of officers working out of the Porch at Randolph Air Force Base near San Antonio, Texas. Many years ago, a long, narrow walkway, about ten by eighty feet, along the front of a building had been windowed-in to create extra workspace. The room has about eight desks lined up along the inside wall, and each desk is responsible for the comings and goings of personnel to the various combat aircraft in the inventory. Officially their title is the Fighter-Bomber Officer's Assignment Branch of the Air Force Personnel Center, but FBOABAFPC is unpronounceable as an acronym, so they needed another name. In deference to its architectural origins, this skinny little room where career paths are determined has always been known as, simply, "the Porch."

Bad attitudes weren't uncommon among the Porch guys, largely because they were fighter pilots themselves temporarily performing staff jobs. Being on a staff would be bad enough, I suppose, but they also had the misfortune of having to hand out the very cockpit assignments they had been taken away from and presumably still wanted for themselves.

In addition to ensuring that all the "good" assignments were properly manned, they also had the responsibility of making sure that the less desirable slots were filled. Every fighter pilot who learned that his next assignment was a desk job or driving a jeep for the army as an air liaison officer in Korea or some other nasty surprise got the word through his Porch handler. Naturally, good assignments were accepted as "due." Bad assignments involved lots of fights, cursing, and arguing over the phone—before you went to them anyway.

The handlers developed thick skins and had a morbid sense of humor about it all. For a long time their unofficial unit-patch was a rendering of an old-fashioned telephone with a large woodscrew impaling it from top to bottom. When a squadron-mate passed you in the hallway muttering that he had just been "screwed over the phone" you pretty much knew that he had been talking to the Porch. (I don't know what the promised follow-on payback was for a handler, but it must have been substantial. No one I met ever admitted to wanting to work there.)

But for every bad deal there was often a good one. And for those of us who hadn't been on station for a full three years, block assignments generally fell into the good-deal category. Instead of each individual in the unit having to negotiate with his handler on the Porch, one guy would represent us all. In this case, it was Cootch, a friend and fellow New Englander, who held similar ideas about flying. He'd once been an F-117 pilot, and we'd talked about the plane often.

One day Cootch came to me saying that he was compiling a tentative wish list of assignments. Some major at Randolph had called, trying to figure out how to deal with the sudden influx of pilots when our unit was disbanded. "Nothing formal," Cootch said. "Just something to get an idea of what you might be interested in."

There had been on-and-off talk about our assignments for a while, but no one had thought much of it. I hadn't, anyway. I was also a bit distracted by another project at that moment, so I didn't have a ready answer for him.

"I'm just looking for rough ideas," he prompted. "What do you think you might want?"

In no particular order I told him that I'd always been intrigued by novel aircraft like the F-117, but that I'd also enjoyed my time with the navy and thought that another exchange assignment, this time to Pensacola, Florida, would be interesting too. Realistically though, I was still less than five years out of the F-16, so I'd probably be sent back to that, assuming I'd even get another flying assignment. After all, by that point in 1998 I was a passed-over major who had been in the cockpit for sixteen years straight—it wasn't too likely I'd get to see the inside of another jet.

After our brief exchange, I didn't think any more on the subject. Or maybe I just hadn't been paying attention. Negotiations with the Porch can take months, and based on my previous experience, we hadn't even started yet. But not long afterward, Cootch came to me with a big smile on his face. "Congratulations, you got your F-117."

"I got my what?"

"You know, the Black Jet that you asked for a while ago. It's yours." (For obvious reasons, the F-117 was often referred to as the "Black Jet.")

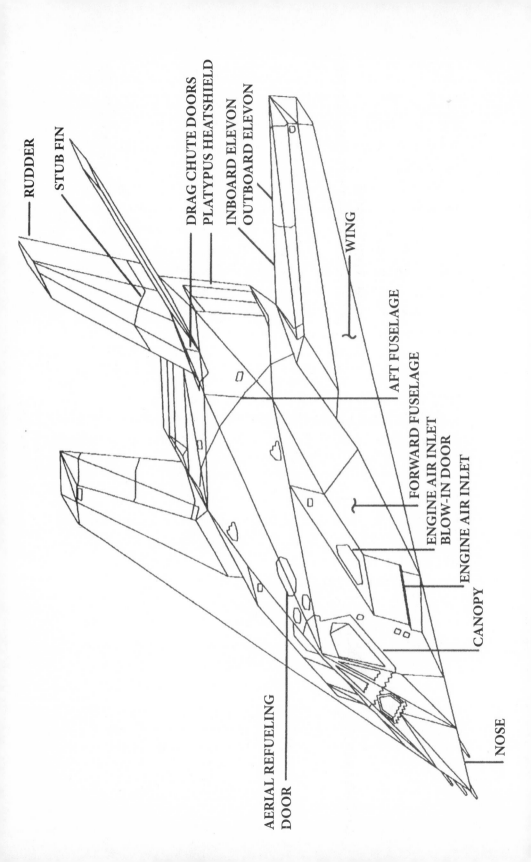

RUDDER

STUB FIN

DRAG CHUTE DOORS
PLATYPUS HEATSHIELD
INBOARD ELEVON
OUTBOARD ELEVON

WING

AFT FUSELAGE

FORWARD FUSELAGE

ENGINE AIR INLET
BLOW-IN DOOR

ENGINE AIR INLET

CANOPY

NOSE

AERIAL REFUELING
DOOR

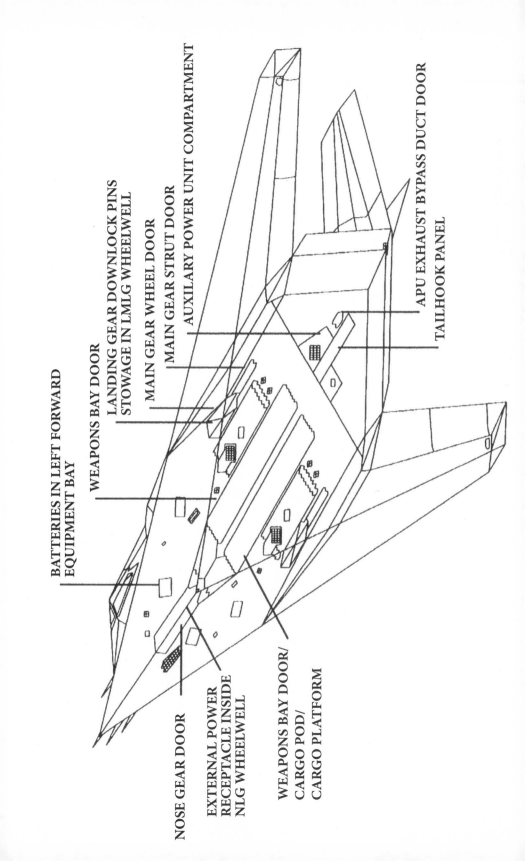

BATTERIES IN LEFT FORWARD
EQUIPMENT BAY

WEAPONS BAY DOOR

LANDING GEAR DOWNLOCK PINS
STOWAGE IN LMLG WHEELWELL

MAIN GEAR WHEEL DOOR

MAIN GEAR STRUT DOOR

AUXILIARY POWER UNIT COMPARTMENT

APU EXHAUST BYPASS DUCT DOOR

TAILHOOK PANEL

NOSE GEAR DOOR

EXTERNAL POWER
RECEPTACLE INSIDE
NLG WHEELWELL

WEAPONS BAY DOOR/
CARGO POD/
CARGO PLATFORM

"Uh, yeah . . . really? Cool . . . you know, I thought we were just talking. Uh, that's great, I guess." After almost seventeen years in the U.S. Air Force, the concept of simply asking for something and then actually getting it a few days later just wasn't registering. Not that I was displeased. The thought of flying an F-117 was exciting, but now I had to go home to explain this to my wife. Normally getting an assignment was a lengthy process where the pros and cons could be weighed. You might not end up where you wanted, but at least there were no sudden surprises.

My perspective on an assignment had always been centered on the plane and the mission. Location, while a small consideration, was mostly secondary. For my wife, it's all about the town, schools, houses, neighborhoods, and all the other details that I didn't have any clue about yet. The one thing I knew for sure was her unequiv-ocal "Just as long as it isn't south, or west, of here." And that's exactly where we were headed. All that was left was to wrap up opera-tions, retire the jets to the boneyard, and give the 429th a proper send-off.

The 429th spent an entire weekend celebrating and saying goodbye. On Friday evening, April 17, the entire squadron dressed up for a formal "Dining Out" celebration at the officer's club. Since we were all getting ready to transfer at more or less the same time, it made for a loud and rowdy evening. The next afternoon, after attending my kids' morning soccer games along with all of the other party-weary parents, I gathered up some gear and drove south to the pig roast at my friend Nordo's ostrich ranch outside of Portales. Nordo was an EWO who had begun his career as a marine. He was on exchange to Cannon when he decided to transfer to the air force. How he got into part-time ostrich ranching was a mystery, as that particular get-rich-quick craze had peaked several years before. In any case, we dug a huge pit, split some wood, and spit a 180-pound pig.

This was an ATF party—alcohol, tobacco, and firearms. You were supposed to bring at least two of the three to attend. Most pilots have a little bit of "gun-nut" in them, and we weren't any different. At an adjoining sand pit we blazed away for several hours with every rifle, shotgun, and pistol we owned.

I was trying out a very old, beautifully engraved, double-barreled, open-hammer shotgun that had been in my family for at least four generations. My best guess was that it had been carried over from Ireland by an immigrating great-great-grandfather. It was about 120 years old. Because it was made of Damascus-Steel, and therefore unsafe to use with modern powders, I had spent a small fortune having the barrels internally sleeved and strengthened. Regardless of these improvements, most of the more knowledgeable shooters in our group chose not to stand anywhere near me the first few times I fired it off.

We made a huge mistake with the pig (nicknamed "Ed" by then). For some reason we had shaved off a lot of the outer hide thinking that it would cook better that way. When we lowered the spit over the red-hot coal pit the exposed fat instantaneously melted into the fire, and the whole thing damn near exploded. There wasn't much we could do about it by then except to turn it every half hour and not stand too close. There were songs and toasts and lots of stories around the fire as we watched Ed slowly turn black.

Sunday morning was family day, and I brought the kids with me for a glorious day out back at the ranch. All the kids chased the ostriches around for a while before settling down to eat a lot of pork and various other meats left over from the previous night. In the afternoon, my friend Hodgie, his son, my kids, and I did some shooting. The kids fired .22-caliber rifles for about an hour before the adults brought out bigger toys. I had my M1903 Springfield that day, and we used it to pop bricks set on end about a hundred yards out.

We couldn't stay at the ranch too long that night, however. We had to get ready for a house-hunting trip to Holloman AFB, near the town of Alamogordo, New Mexico, the next day.

CHAPTER 3

PCS to Holloman

Permanent Change of Station

THE DRIVE FROM CLOVIS TO Alamogordo (all south and west) took about four hours. It had been a busy weekend, we were worn out, and I wasn't optimistic about what my wife's reaction to the town would be.

The last time I'd been posted to Holloman had been a dozen years earlier for AT-38 LIFT. LIFT stood for lead-in fighter training. It was the basic course all prospective fighter pilots attended before continuing on to the formal training for whatever fighter they were assigned to. It was a short and abusive introduction to the fighter pilot culture. The intent was to teach some of the fundamentals of tactical maneuvering and ground attack while giving a jump-start to the aggressive attitude the fighter pilot would be expected to carry on throughout his career.

My wife had visited me briefly back then and favorably remembered the dunes of the White Sands and the mountain forests; she had forgotten—or had blocked out—everything else. I remembered it in detail though and, like most pilots, hadn't liked it at all. Our unofficial class patch for LIFT had been a rendering of a car's rearview mirror with a reverse image of the "Welcome to Holloman" highway sign receding into the distance. The caption read *"Happiness is . . ."*

Holloman had been built just before the U.S. entry into World War II as a training base for the British. They hadn't liked it either. Not just because of the heat, dust, mesquite, and yucca. Not just because of the thorny ocotillo, prickly pear, devil fingers, scorpions, and rattlesnake-infested lava beds. They had disliked the place because they thought the weather was "too good" to train pilots headed for Europe.

Shortly after Pearl Harbor had been attacked, the air corps commandeered the base for its own use. The United States appreciated the base for exactly the same reason the British didn't. Where the RAF hadn't believed that the desert climate was conducive to training pilots to fly in Europe, the United States observed that it was perfect for training personnel en route to the deserts of North Africa. Over the years, the remote base has been home to a wide variety of fighters and classified test programs.

Most importantly, it is adjacent to the army's White Sands Missile Range. This massive forty-by-one-hundred-mile–wide chunk of airspace has been used at various times to test captured German V-2 rockets after the war, first-generation cruise missiles, almost every U.S. surface-to-air and surface-to-surface missile, and the first pre-Hiroshima atomic bomb at the Trinity Site. It still hosts a NASA contingent because the dry lake by the White Sands is an alternate space shuttle runway. The famous rocket-sled track where Col. John Paul Stapp had ridden an open seat to supersonic speeds in the early 1950s continues in operation. "Star Wars" experiments still dot the surrounding hills. Another unit flies remotely controlled unmanned fighters as target drones for weapons testing, and the German Luftwaffe base their F-4 and Tornado training units here. Many other small units, classified to various degrees, are scattered throughout the surrounding desert.

Holloman wasn't always a forthcoming and considerate neighbor. In the late 1940s, V-2 rocket tests would occasionally go wildly astray (one took out a cemetery in Juarez, Mexico). Some rockets carried chimpanzees in primitive capsules wearing little simian spacesuits. In 1947, a classified experiment to fly a manned extreme-altitude balloon from New Mexico to the Eastern Seaboard barely got over the Sacramento Mountains before crashing north of Roswell. The embarrassed team quickly scooped up the debris to keep the whole thing quiet, and the pilot's name was never released. During the decade leading up to the Mercury program, anthropomorphic dummies dressed in experimental spacesuits and parachutes were regularly pitched out of a variety of planes and balloons.

The original UFO stories all center around this area and seem to derive directly from the testing that often went astray during the 1940s and 1950s, the infamous "Roswell incident" being the more famous. I suppose that it really isn't a mystery why the alien myths started right here. In retrospect, with all the secretive A-bomb, experimental aircraft, V-2, rocket-sled, extreme-altitude balloon, spacesuit, and ejection-seat testing performed here (virtually none of it acknowledged at the time), it would have been more surprising if a UFO phenomenon *hadn't* sprung up.

In any case, for a pilot interested in the unusual, Holloman was definitely the place to be. In time, it became the perfect location to base the pseudo-secret F-117.

The first part of our drive went alright, and the mountain passes through Lincoln National Forest and Ruidoso were gorgeous. I was beginning to think that this might be better than what I remembered from my last posting. As we passed over the crest of the Sacramento Mountains, we could see all the way across to the Organ Mountain Range. It was about forty miles away, but looked closer due to the clear, dry air. The space between is called the Tularosa Basin. The area took its name from the little mission village of Tularosa, which had been one of the original Spanish outposts centuries ago.

Like Death Valley or the Dead Sea, water could flow into the Tularosa Basin, but there was no exit. The most spectacular result of this geological circumstance was the White Sands National Monument, a vast 275-square-mile area of pure sugar-white gypsum, easily visible from outer space. The beautiful rolling dunes look exactly like what people think the Sahara Desert ought to—probably because so many movies have been filmed here instead of the actual Sahara.

As we descended down into the basin, the land dried up and lost its picturesque beauty as perceived from a distance (down into "the uglies," as one of the kids described it). Like many small towns, Alamogordo looks its worst when seen from the highway. Unfortunately, that's the first impression everyone gets.

I could tell my family was thinking, *What have you gotten us into this time?* This was just a house-hunting trip, supposedly an opportunity to set something up for the family to look forward to. But it had been a long and tiring weekend followed by a long and tiring drive. Tears were being suppressed. I definitely had my work cut out for me.

I drove right out to the base to visit the squadron and sign out a Dash-1, the pilot's manual that details the systems, procedures, and performance data for any given aircraft. The F-117s and glossy black T-38s taxiing around impressed my ten-year-old son a little, anyway. The girls were still wary. Our next stop was the housing office to see if there was anything available on base. Most bases have waiting lists that usually stretch for months, but there was an empty house for us to look at right away. We quickly figured out why.

If this place was at all representative, then base housing was a disgrace. The advertised 1,700 square feet was really about 1,400 feet, the difference being the footage of the backyard patio and carport. The sliding doors to the back were broken, the screens were ripped, and there was dust, dirt, and gravel strewn across the living room floor. The door to the bathroom wouldn't open fully without hitting the toilet. The landscaping consisted of dirt—period. I hightailed it back to the squadron to ask where in town people really lived.

The first neighborhood we came to as we drove back toward Alamogordo was near the golf course. The neighborhood looked nice. Everything was neat and reasonably green as we drove around collecting flyers from the houses with "for sale" signs out front. One owner saw us and waved us down from his front yard. He flew F-117s and was preparing to PCS. His family was selling their house and took the opportunity to show us around. As luck would have it, our wives and kids all got along and traded stories about the town and schools. We were impressed by how nice the place was and were bowled over by the view of the Sacramento Mountains right out back as the sunset cast an orange glow on the cliff faces. The mood that evening was definitely improving.

The next morning we drove around with a realtor without seeing any areas much better. There were several other nice places around town, but most had at least one major drawback. There was one excellent rental that sorely tempted us. It was a two-story overhanging a corner of the golf course with big balconies, lots of room, and a western view out across the basin. The drawback? It was pink. And I mean *pink*! Pink marble floors and carpets, pink stone counter tops, pink walls, drapes, and cabinets. Even the ceiling was painted pink. I have nothing against colors, but who paints *everything* pink? It looked as if God had picked up the house in his two hands, poured in 2,000 gallons of Pepto-Bismol, and then shook.

We asked if the owner would repaint. No. We asked if we could repaint. No. We asked if we could repaint with the promise to return it to its pink color after we had left. No. The owner was afraid that we'd be unable to match that original shade of pink later on. So we got back in the car to keep looking. (After the house sat vacant and neglected for several years, I drove by one day to see the owner in the driveway giving directions to a crew of painters. Of the dozens of cans being unloaded from the van not a single can of pink paint was in sight. It sold the next week.)

Another house in the same neighborhood, on Desert Hills Drive, had the best combination of landscaping, floor plan, and view of the mountains. We made an offer and it was accepted. The drive back to Cannon was made in much better spirits.

For every service family, wrapping up the odds and ends of a move become practiced, but rarely welcome. The packing, school transfer arrangements, dealing with utilities at both ends, collecting medical records, making the rounds through seemingly every office on base to out-process, and closing up business in the old squadron when your mind is really on the next are all just a pain.

On the other hand, the F-117 Dash-1 I'd signed out from Holloman was encouraging. Compared with the EF-111, the systems in the Dash-1 were simple and certainly far fewer in number. The F-117 was a relatively uncomplicated jet as far as the day-to-day flying was going to be concerned. The mission was going to be more difficult, but I'd be able to deal with that later.

I still had chores on Cannon to do, mostly collecting flight and personnel records. In the afternoon, I met with my wing commander to pick up a copy of my promotion recommendation form (PRF). Even though I'd already been passed over for promotion and the odds of a subsequent promotion were virtually nil, everyone had to go through the formalities of pretending that I was still in the game.

There are three possible recommendations on a PRF. "Don't Promote"—self-explanatory and a certain kiss of death for any career. An officer is probably already in, or on his way to, Leavenworth prison to rate one of these, and it's rarely used. Well over half of a year-group being considered for promotion will receive a straight "P" recommendation—"Promote." It sounds nice, but it's really the consolation prize. The real prize is a "DP"—"Definitely Promote." Maybe 30 to 40 percent of a group competing for lieutenant colonel will get DPs, and the success rate for promotion is over 99 percent. If promotion slots are still available after exhausting the pool of officers with DPs, then the officers with Ps will be considered. The success rate for promotion to lieutenant colonel with a P over the years has varied from 20 to 30 percent. Playing a round of Russian roulette with *four* bullets in the gun gives better odds of survival than getting promoted to lieutenant colonel with a "Promote" recommendation. And that is only during your primary zone, which for me had ended the previous year. Once you have been passed over, the probability of getting a promotion with a P in any subsequent year above-the-zone (ABZ) is a statistical anomaly measured in fractions of well under 1 percent.

DPs to the rank of lieutenant colonel are allocated directly by the wing commander. The politics of garnering one has been the cause of much speculation over the years. Clearly superior officers who work hard and are respected by the people under them often get DPs, of course, but square-fillers, the connected, and suck-ups consume far more than their due. Those of the latter variety aren't hard to spot. They've volunteered to leave the cockpit for a high-visibility staff job or to become a general's aide even when there is a shortage of pilots in the field. In a squadron of single-seat aircraft, they make it to squadron command without ever having risen above two-ship flight lead, but have briefed more brass at staff meetings than they can remember. They always seem to have an excuse to not fly, but death itself couldn't keep them away if a high-ranking general were visiting.

Throughout my career I had been advised by well-meaning individuals that I was screwing up in my career planning. I was told that I shouldn't take a job test-flying brand-new F-16s out of the factory and that I shouldn't fly with the Egyptian Air Force as a military adviser for a year, but instead should be looking for staff jobs. I was told that flying as an exchange officer with the navy, and carrier-qualifying in two different jets, was a complete waste of time and that I should really be bucking for a spot as a general's aide. But I had disagreed and chased my jets around the world, and that was right for me.

It's an odd but true fact that you can serve as a lawyer, an accountant, a dentist, or a doctor for your entire career in the air force, but remaining an active pilot isn't an approved option. For the masses like me, who once reveled in the slogans painted on almost every wall screaming "The Mission of the United States Air Force is to Fly and to Fight, and Don't You Ever Forget It" and believed it . . . we still believed that, even after the slogans were painted over, and as long as we can keep flying and get in on the fight, we'll be around.

On this particular day, as expected, my PRF was marked with a P. No surprise there. The air force has always been an up-or-out organization. And since the *up* part had been dealt with, it looked like the *out* part would be coming along soon. Majors are separated from the service after twenty years, meaning that three years from that day, I would be forty-two years old, with two kids in school and looking for a job.

Tuesday, May 5, 1998, was my last flight with 429th, and I was performing a sad duty. We had an easy launch, then flew to the boneyard at Davis-Monthan Air Force Base in Arizona to deliver another pair of Ravens to oblivion. There, some jets are supposed to be mothballed, while the rest will be shelled out for usable parts to be given to the navy's EA-6B fleet. The leftover hulks will eventually be sold for scrap metal. That short one-and-a-third-hour hop in aircraft number 66-036 completed my brief EF-111 career.

Along the way, the pilot in the lead aircraft had mentioned that he might "torch" down initial approach once we arrived as a final tribute to the jets. Torching is a very cool—and way illegal—stunt that involves dumping fuel from a stand-pipe just over and between the engines. Simultaneously, the pilot will ignite the afterburners and kick the rudder to force the stream of raw fuel into the hot exhaust. The lick of orange-yellow flame can extend for more than twice the length of the plane and be seen for miles. The *very cool* part is obvious. The *illegal* part stems from the inconvenient detail that the fire doesn't always go out right away.

Torching is not supposed to happen, but an awful lot of pictures of it are posted on the Internet, so clearly not everyone has been following the letter of the law. In any case, the pilot either thought better of the idea or got talked out of it by his very proper EWO. I had another flying assignment waiting for me, so I wouldn't even consider it . . . certainly not in front of that many witnesses, anyway.

My EWO was Grinch, and I think that he was a bit teary-eyed in the final turn before landing. This was his actual fini-flight—his final flight—in the air force. He was a passed-over major like me and was headed to Nellis Air Force Base in Nevada for a staff job running one of the Red Flag Exercise offices. His twenty years would run out before he got a chance to fly again.

Squish, the EWO from the jet that had gotten there first, tossed some water around our feet as a token "wetting" after we had climbed down the ladder our last time. I had dropped many aircraft at the boneyard over the years and was familiar with the drill. As soon as the engines spool down, workers are hovering over you. The natural temptation for a crew is to secure some last souvenir: the data plate with the plane's identity, the eight-day clock (wind-up and built by the hundreds of thousands during World War II), or the real prize, the grip from the control stick. In any case, the boneyard workers have seen it all before and are there to make sure nothing disappears.

Our only souvenirs were the small oxygen regulators that clip onto the end of the hose opposite our masks. They weren't considered to be "aircraft equipment," and there were no other units flying F-111s in the U.S. Air Force to turn them over to, so we got to keep them. After processing the paperwork and actually receiving a hand receipt for the jet (this is a government organization, after all), we asked for a tour of the place.

Tours of the boneyard are pretty hard to come by, but this was far and away the best I'd ever received. One of the workers had a free afternoon and did a superb job showing us around. We passed literally thousands of old pickled F-4s, early-model F-16s, T-2s, TA-4Js, F-111s, T-33s, C-130s, C-141s, and absolute forests of B-52s. About twenty of my old T-Birds were in flyable storage, but many were little more than parted-out hulks waiting to be sold for their scrap value. They were sad-looking old ladies. I wished that I were rich enough to rescue a few of these old birds from their fate.

Squish let out a shout when he spotted an F-111E that he had flown in during Desert Storm. He leapt out of the van and charged across the field (to shouts from the driver to watch out for rattlesnakes). He emerged from under the plane a few moments later wrestling the nose-gear door on which we could still make out his and his pilot's names.

No, they didn't let him keep the door. Though since it had already been separated from the aircraft and its scrap-metal value was maybe a dime, I can't imagine who would have valued it more than he would have.

The following week, back at Holloman, I packed the Jeep and drove to Alamogordo in time to go through our new house with an inspector for the preliminary walk-through. Not quite perfect, but very workable. I was looking forward to this plane and assignment—one last adventure. I began the in-processing drill at Holloman, the reverse of what I had just finished at Cannon. The bulk of it was boring and inconsequential. The rest wasn't even *that* interesting.

I met the other two guys in my F-117 class. Both were also majors. One, Mauler, had been an RF-4 pilot before the U.S. Air Force disbanded the manned tactical-reconnaissance community. He then flew F-16s during the Gulf War. He already had a line number for promotion to lieutenant colonel.

On Thursday, following a series of useless newcomer briefings that treated us as if we were new to the air force instead of just being new to the base, the three of us went to the 7th squadron for a Bandit party at the Goat Sucker Bar. The 7th was the training squadron for the F-117. A Bandit party is where individuals are recognized and inducted into the fraternity after completing their first F-117 flights.

The squadron's nickname was the Bunyaps; at first I'd thought that "goat sucker" was a rough translation of this strange word. But it turned out that a Bunyap was an aboriginal death-demon, a mythical creature in the folklore of a Burmese tribe. The 7th had been stationed there during World War II when those first P-40 pilots had been casting about for a squadron name, and as a result the face of a Bunyap was depicted on the original World War II patch. The term goat sucker was actually the common name for the class of raptors that includes the Nighthawk—the F-117's official, though rarely used, nickname.

The 7th was a hard-partying bunch. The next morning I attended a few more briefings before hitting the road.

* * *

Two days later, on Saturday, I was back at Cannon cashing a mutual fund to raise enough capital for the down payment on the house. One of the age-old problems in the military is the constant moving; with moves roughly every two years (Clovis was our ninth mailing address in seventeen years), you never got to build any home equity. Every time we sold a house, we were set back at least 6 percent in realtor fees and so were constantly starting over. Opting for base housing usually involved living out of a suitcase for months before there was an opening and, contrary to popular belief, isn't free. Instead of paying rent, you paid a "housing allowance," which varied with rank. The allowance I'd have to pay for that 1,400-square-foot dump we'd looked at on base would be several hundreds of dollars a month in excess of what my mortgage was to buy a house twice its size in Alamogordo.

By the following week, living two lives in two towns was becoming an interesting juggling act. I was back and forth every other day, it seemed. While driving by the 429th on my way off base for the last time, I counted only seven EF-111s remaining on the ramp.

Back at Holloman, I drove to the 7th squadron for a T-38 sandbag sortie. On a sandbag sortie, you sit in the back (usually referred to as "the pit"), as the sortie really belongs to the guy up front. You're just along for the ride, taking up space and weight (like a bag of sand), trying to pick up a little information.

The T-38 was smaller than I remembered, but its lines still evoked admiration. It had been the air force's advanced trainer for about a third of a century then, and there was nothing on the horizon to replace it. Upgrades were being planned that wouldn't even be installed for another decade. With tandem seats and twin afterburning engines, the jet is (just) capable of supersonic speeds and is extremely maneuverable. For a while it held the world time-to-climb record, wrested from the vastly more powerful F-104 Star

Fighter. Officially it is named the Talon. Though a fitting name, no one ever calls it that. It is almost exclusively referred to as the "38." First flown in 1959, it is one of those classic designs, such as the P-38 Lightning, T-33 Shooting Star, and F-86 Sabre, where they just got it right the first time. It's a sleek, sculptured, glossy black stiletto of a jet and just about the coolest toy any overgrown kid could wish to play with.

I flew with a guy who at first meeting seemed to be hyperactive, animated, and fast-talking. Later on I realized that he must have been tired that day, because he was usually even more wired than that. His accent sounded like it was from knee-deep in the Ozarks. You'd think that exposure to college and the outside world would have tempered it more, but he was a good pilot and a nice guy in any case.

We were supposed to have been acting as the chase ship for an F-117 training sortie for one of the guys in the senior class. Unfortunately the weather didn't allow for that, so we flew a single-ship acro ride instead. Wearing a parachute again for the first time in years wasn't very comfortable. The Raven's ejection capsule had spoiled me, I suppose.

The next morning, we had a T-38 cockpit refresher class taught by Norm, one of our civilian instructors. I remembered Norm from when he was a lieutenant colonel and the squadron operations officer (Opso) for the 434th when I was going through LIFT in 1986. Back then, he was one of the designated "fire and brimstone" types trying to whip us into TAC warriors, seemingly more marine drill instructor than USAF instructor pilot. But he had mellowed nicely since then and looked and acted more like the character Norm from the show *Cheers* than a drill instructor.

The instructions we received were just the very basics of how to climb into and out of the jet, how to strap in, how to arm and de-arm the ejection seat and explosive canopy jettison system, and how to start the engines—essentially how not to embarrass ourselves right away. We even received our first mission grade sheets for the event. Mine, for mission CFT-1, had a checkmark in the box labeled "Effective" with an exhaustive write-up in the remarks section that consisted in its entirety of "Accomplished in accordance with Syllabus." The overall grade was a "2," which essentially meant I passed. Contractors are rather binary people: It's either pass or fail with them, with few shades of gray in between.

The ACC system grades are simple: "D," dangerous—self explanatory; "0," unable; "1," poor—you were safe, with some minimal competence, but below what is expected by the end of training; "2," good—the average skill level expected for that task; "3," excellent—above average (you expect a few of these toward the end, but not so many as to throw off your ego); and finally "4," which has no real verbal equivalent and is almost never given out by any fighter instructor pilot. To do so may imply that the student is better than he is, and it isn't even humanly possible for another pilot to be better than he is, just ask him. So "4"s don't happen.

Afterward, mission accomplished, instead of wandering off for lunch, we decided to walk over to the training squadron just to check in and see what was going on. That turned out to be lucky, as we found that all three of us had been scheduled on short notice for front seat sorties in the T-38 that afternoon. After some frantic hustling, signing off on local regulations we hadn't actually read yet, checking that we had flight gear inspected and ready, and (hardest of all) filling out a boldface sheet for a plane that none of us had touched in a dozen years, we flew.

A boldface sheet contains a series of responses to a list of the most time-critical emergencies an aircraft is liable to experience. The responses must be memorized word-for-word, letter-for-letter, punctuation-for-punctuation, perfectly. If you misplace a single comma in a single sentence, you will be grounded for the day.

The instructors had seen it all before and were just laughing. The IPs—the instructor pilots—didn't expect to see much more than basic safety and that we could land a jet without breaking anything—our first flights in the F-117 would be solo, after all.

Out at the jet, I strapped right in as if I knew what I was doing. Then progress more or less came to a grinding halt as I'd exhausted the "extensive" training I'd received that morning. My IP in the rear cockpit talked me through the ground operations, radio calls, taxi routing, and pretty much everything else for the next sixty-five minutes. The takeoff was a muscle-memory thing, as all of my old ingrained pilot training habits began re-emerging. After a few moments airborne, it felt as if I'd been out of the front cockpit only a few days instead of a dozen years. That was just for the hands though. The book knowledge and local procedures didn't exist.

Surprisingly, the departure procedure cost me my only write-up. That sole grade sheet comment was "Turned to 205 degrees heading instead of 220 degrees after takeoff." That made me laugh afterward to think I'd guessed even that closely to begin with.

The area work included some standard aerobatics, stalls, and high-g turns—basic stuff. Then we returned for a visual straight-in approach and several touch-and-go landings from the overhead pattern before quitting with a grand total of 1.1 flight hours.

Unlike the EF-111, where I'd have to dump several thousand pounds of fuel to land safely after only an hour in the air, the T-38 lands quickly because it's about ten minutes away from a fuel-starvation flame-out. Another mindset I'd have to readjust. The next morning (after reading up on the systems and departure procedures), we went out and did it again.

CHAPTER 4

Stealth 101

Always try to look unimportant—the enemy may be
running low on ammo.

FRIDAY, MAY 29, WAS OUR first full day of F-117 academics. Because there was only one F-117 base in the world, all of our training was done "in-house" at Holloman. The training squadron owned four F-117s (Black Jets) and about a dozen T-38s. The T-38s were used by the instructors to chase the Black Jets during student sorties, primarily to help preserve the F-117 fleet by limiting the jets' flight time, but also because the T-38's operating costs were about a tenth of using another Black Jet as a chase aircraft.

Since every F-117 had been built as a single-seater, a student's first ride would, of course, also be his first solo. That was one of several reasons why pilots had to be on at least their second tour of duty before applying for the program. While most pilots came from fighter backgrounds, we usually also had a half dozen or so from the bomber and U-2 communities. The idea was that with this more seasoned corps, the training program could be radically abbreviated. For the most part, the abbreviated training concept worked well, but there were occasionally washouts from the program. At only seven weeks long, versus seven or eight months for an F-16 or F-15 course, you pretty much had to have your act together right from the beginning.

Our class—all three of us—was officially designated as Class 98-HTH (I have no idea what the HTH stood for). Like every other program, our training began in a classroom. The job of providing the academic and simulator instruction had long since been subcontracted by the USAF to a civilian corporation. Our instructors were a small cadre of former fighter pilots who had either been F-117 pilots themselves or just happened to be at Holloman when it came time to retire. Leading the group was Klaus, an immigrant from Germany as a child and the son of a Luftwaffe ME-109 pilot. He flew F-4s early in his USAF career and had credit for one MiG kill over Vietnam. Later on, he became the operations group commander (OG) of the 49th Fighter Wing and flew F-117s during the Gulf War. Our other instructors included T. J., who also flew F-4s and had been an AT-38 squadron commander at Holloman before retiring here. Norm, for me, anyway, was a fixture at Holloman since he had been my Opso while going through fighter lead-in a dozen years earlier. I also had history with Butch. His background was mostly in F-16s, and he had been one of my instructors at MacDill Air Force Base, Florida, when I going through initial F-16 training. Soups had flown A-10s during the Gulf War and was in the process of writing a book about the history of close air support as a thesis for his PhD in history.

Klaus was the first speaker, and he warmed us up with a collection of Gulf War videos. These were the original cockpit videos from a few of those first attacks. Unlike the stuff that has been released to the public, these hadn't been declassified by having the audio portion deleted and the data windows blacked out. From there, he launched right into the origins of the F-117.

Since the introduction of radar during World War II, engineers have been trying to develop technologies to defeat it. Early attempts could be as crude as "chaff"—bundles of stripped foil pitched out a hatch by hand, the idea being to create several blurry false targets hopefully to confuse the enemy. Early ventures at frequency jamming were also attempted, but took a few decades to become more effective. Endeavors to build non-metal planes (gliders, really) entirely of wood, fabric, and glue to make them transparent to radar had also been tried with little success. Unfortunately, the obvious solution, the technology to absorb radar energy directly, simply didn't exist on a practical level. The material needed already existed, but covering a conventional aircraft with a thick enough layer of radar-absorbent material (RAM) to achieve any useful effect made it essentially unable to fly.

So, to counter the increasing radar and SAM threats being developed over the years, the U.S. Air Force deployed a variety of technologies. Most combat aircraft carried some sort of chaff. Stand-off jammer aircraft such as the EB-66 and EF-111 were developed. Individually carried electronic countermeasure (ECM) pods were fitted to fighters, and anti-radiation missiles, such as the AGM-45 SHRIKE and AGM-88 HARM, were employed—with varying degrees of success. The best technique in those early days— which the pilots preferred because it was also the most fun—was flying at extremely low altitudes to get under enemy radar coverage. To that end, aircraft such as the F-111 and B-1 had been designed with terrain-following radar to function solely in the low-altitude arena. This was a tradeoff tactic though, as it also brought the aircraft down into the heart of the anti-aircraft artillery (AAA) threat. Flying low worked reasonably well against the early Soviet SA-2 systems encountered over Vietnam and was the intended tactic to be used in the event of World War III. But the 1973 Yom Kippur War put an end to those delusions.

In 1973, the Israelis, flying state-of-the-art U.S. aircraft with world-class pilots, had their butts handed to them by the new SA-6 being employed by not always well-trained Syrian and Egyptian operators. The Israelis lost 109 jets over the Sinai and Golan Heights in a bit over two weeks.

It was a simple exercise in arithmetic to compare the numbers from the Yom Kippur War with our own air force and the expected Soviet systems in Europe. One sobering study (kept quiet for years) predicted that during a future World War III, the bulk of our air force could be annihilated in seventeen days, leaving only the nuclear option to prevent Western Europe from being overrun.

While the United States had never embraced a defensive mindset and had only fielded one strategic SAM system to that point, the Nike-Hercules dating from the 1950s, and one real medium-range tactical system, the HAWK (homing all the way killer), the Soviets had fielded over fifteen different systems. One Soviet SAM system was even armed with nuclear warheads.

It had become clear that there had to be a better way. So in 1974, the U.S. Defense Advanced Research Projects Agency (DARPA) initiated a program known as Project Harvey (named after the 6 feet 3 1/2 inches tall invisible white rabbit from the play of the same name). The ultimate goal was to develop a combat aircraft with as low a radar signature as possible. Five aerospace corporations had been contracted a million dollars each to give it their best shot. Surprisingly, Lockheed hadn't been among them. It was only an accidental tip-off that allowed Lockheed's Ben Rich to lobby for inclusion. Rich had been an engineer on the secret U-2 and SR-71 reconnaissance aircraft and had by then advanced to become

Lockheed's successor to the famous Kelly Johnson as director of the Skunk Works. The "Skunk Works" is the official alias for the department responsible for all of Lockheed's highly secret advanced development projects. It was formed in 1943 to build America's first jet fighter, the P-80, and numerous other projects that belong to the shadow world of military operations.

By the time Rich had gotten wind of Project Harvey, there was no money left for another developmental contract. So Lockheed was offered a shot—for a dollar. But Rich wanted in and wisely turned down the token dollar. He knew that any new technologies developed with company funds would then be proprietary. Lockheed was famous for building small fleets of extremely advanced aircraft—often used for highly secretive missions. During World War II, they had built the United States' first operational subsonic jet fighter, the P-80. They skipped the Mach-1 era altogether and jumped right to fielding the United States' first fighter capable of speeds in excess of Mach 2, the F-104 Star Fighter. Along the way came the high-flying U-2, the higher-flying SR-71, the hypersonic D-21 drone (which would ride piggyback on an SR-71 until released), and other things not yet named.

In Rich's own words, the unsung hero of Lockheed's effort was an anonymous staff mathematician and electrical engineer named Denys Overholser. Overholser and his mentor, another mathematician named Bill Schroeder, had discussed the possibilities of utilizing some of the equations associated with optical scattering (how electromagnetic waves bounce off variously shaped objects) on this project. Both had the rather odd hobby of reading obscure Russian mathematics papers and had made the ultimate "nerd's nerd" discovery. They had stumbled across a paper published in Moscow a decade earlier titled "Method of Edge Waves in the Physical Theory of Diffraction." It had been written by Pyotr Ufimtsev, the Soviet's chief scientist at the Moscow Institute of Radio Engineering and the last in a long line of scientists developing a long series of wave equations originally derived centuries ago by the Scottish physicist James Clerk Maxwell.

The U.S. intelligence community had helped translate this research and brought it to the West. The paper was in no way classified or related to weapons development at all. It was purely theoretical math. Years later, Ufimtsev immigrated to the United States to teach at the University of California, Los Angeles, and only then discovered his inadvertent contribution to the development of stealth aircraft.

The equations that Ufimtsev had developed made the reflections of radio waves off hard surfaces predictable. Not invisible, transparent, or tactical in any way—just predictable. The problem for Lockheed was that the calculations were so ferociously difficult that the most advanced supercomputers in the world at the time could only compute results for flat surfaces. Any attempt to perform the calculations for the curved surfaces you would find on a conventional aircraft—well, those machines would still be grinding away toward a solution today.

Schroeder recognized how these equations could be applied to Lockheed's current project. The solution was not even to attempt to design an aircraft with any curved surfaces, but to build one with dozens, or perhaps hundreds, of individual flat triangular and rectangular plates. Then the challenge was to compute the reflection from each and every flat surface before adding them all together to build a picture of the aircraft's total radar signature. Once you knew where every bit of radar reflection was coming from, you could then reorient those individual plates so that the reflection would go off in a direction away from the radar looking at it.

The process became known as "faceting." And that became the real secret—not to absorb all the radar or make the plane somehow transparent, but to make the plane's signature predictable. That predictability could then be used to shape a tactically useful aircraft. The jet would also be covered in thin sheets of RAM, but the bulk of the stealth effect was achieved by its shape.

Traditionally, a single engineering specialty will take the lead during the design of a new aircraft. An aerodynamicist may be in charge of pushing through a new wing or fuselage shape, as happened with the early delta wings and area-ruled fuselages of the "Century Series" of interceptors. Sometimes it may be the power-plant guy: "Here's the engine we're going to use, build us a jet fighter for it." This is how the P-80 came about. Occasionally it may be the armaments people—the A-10 is fundamentally a massive 30mm Gatling cannon with a plane built around it. In this particular case, this was the first time the lead was owned by an electrical engineer.

The computer program designed by Overholser's team to make these calculations was called Echo-1. Armed with that tool, the first test subject, the Hopeless Diamond, was built. It was described as a diamond for obvious reasons and "hopeless" for its aerodynamic qualities (or rather, its complete lack thereof).

Early radar testing of the Hopeless Diamond turned out to be staggeringly successful. The White Sands experimental radar range near Holloman AFB was used. When the radar was fired up for the initial testing, the only thing that showed up was the reflection of the pole on which the test model was supposed to be mounted. Assuming that the model had fallen off the pole, the radar operators sent technicians downrange to fix the problem. To their surprise, the ten-foot model was still in place.

To test the model at all, Lockheed then had to design an invisible "stealth pole" to mount the model utilizing the same technology as the proposed fighter. The results were once again astounding, and incredulous USAF officials were called in to witness and verify the data.

The first opportunity to impress these officials almost resulted in embarrassment. When the radars were turned on, the reflections, while still very small by airplane standards, were orders of magnitude larger than what the USAF officials had been led to expect. They could still clearly see a small radar return from where the model was mounted.

While the Lockheed engineers were trying to explain this discrepancy, a radio call came in from a technician downrange. He reported that a bird was perched on the ten-foot model. The quick reply was an order to blow the horn of the pickup truck the guy was sitting in. As the startled bird flew away, the radar reflection on the test scope disappeared.

The very idea that a combat aircraft could be made so invisible as to hide behind a bird was an opportunity that couldn't be passed up. Everything associated with the program became classified at the highest levels. The program was transferred from DARPA to the USAF special projects office. The word "stealth" was forbidden to be mentioned in any unclassified document. And in April 1976, the Ford administration gave Lockheed the go-ahead for a full-scale aircraft. The Skunk Works was officially in the stealth fighter business.

Northrop was the other finalist in the design competition and also employed some faceting but had opted for more of a curved-body design. Their model, while promising, was slower, and appeared ten times larger on radar than the Lockheed design. Eventually, with the advent of vastly more powerful computers in the 1980s, Northrop perfected their more elegant curved-body approach to design the B-2 Stealth Bomber.

The first attempt to make this interesting science project into something like a real aircraft was code-named Have Blue. The code name was chosen because it meant absolutely nothing. But proving that a model was stealthy was meaningless until you could make it fly—and reshaping the original diamond into something that could sorta-kinda-maybe fly was a daunting task. Lockheed didn't even attempt to go right to a final design, but first concentrated on an intermediate proof-of-concept aircraft.

Two developmental aircraft, Have Blue 1001 and Have Blue 1002, were built. They were about two-thirds the size of the intended F-117 and looked like something Wile E. Coyote might have ordered from the *Acme Super-Duper-Secret-Airplane Catalog*. Shaped approximately like a chipped obsidian arrowhead, it was said that if you saw it being built on the factory floor before the wings had been installed, you could tell right away that it was some sort of a vehicle. A few minutes' further study would probably reveal in which direction the vehicle was supposed to travel. But that it was an aircraft, or of what possible use it could be, was not in evidence.

Its existence, like that of an earlier monster—created by Doctor Frankenstein—depended on the donation of body parts originally intended for others. The General Electric J-85 engines had been borrowed from a pair of navy T-2 trainers. The fly-by-wire flight control system had been lifted from General Dynamic's F-16A fighter. The landing gear, ejection seat, and most of the cockpit instruments had been taken from a Northrop F-5 fighter.

The wings were swept at an amazing 72.5 degrees. The exhaust ports, called platypus nozzles, had been flattened and spread out to help disguise the heat signature of the aircraft from infrared sensors on the ground and then tiled over with the same material used on the belly of the space shuttle. The control fins had been canted inward in a further attempt to hide the exhaust heat. The intakes were covered by grilles.

Needless to say, the aerodynamics of these things was suspect. So much so that the first Have Blue prototype wasn't even covered in RAM. Its sole purpose was to prove that the thing could even fly and be controlled at all.

The F-16 is said to be so dynamically unstable that it can only fly with the aid of its flight control computers. The truth is that it's closer to being dynamically neutral. On the other hand, the Have Blues were, and subsequent F-117 aircraft still are, wildly unstable. Any appearance of controlled flight is purely an illusion created by four separate computer systems continuously bringing the jet back from an uncontrollable tumble *fifty times per second*. The natural flight path an F-117 would take without this computer quadruple redundancy would more closely resemble a poorly kicked football tumbling end over end than that of a conventional airplane.

The first flight was on December 1, 1977, and the plane, to most people's surprise, handled reasonably well, within expectations of course. That first Have Blue only lasted until its thirty-seventh flight before suffering a fatally damaged landing gear during an attempted touch-and-go. The pilot, Bill Park, ejected but was permanently disabled, ending his test pilot career.

The second Have Blue was a little more refined and was used to complete the flight test program and, more importantly, was covered in RAM to validate the radar predictions. This second part went extremely well. Small anomalies in its radar reflections could be traced to individual screw heads that hadn't been tightened all the way and were sticking up a few millimeters. As for the flying qualities of the jet, it lasted almost a year, until its fifty-second flight, before crashing. This time the pilot got out uninjured.

For security reasons, the remains of both jets were bulldozed into the desert where they had fallen, and on the vast test ranges, the precise locations weren't marked. It is said that no one knows exactly where they are now.

The final design, code-named Senior Trend, was scaled up, given bigger engines and a weapons capability. The wings' sweep changed from 72.5 degrees to a slightly less extreme 67.5 degrees, and they were extended a few feet. Most obviously, the fins were now canted outward. It turned out that the inward canted fins didn't actually hide the exhaust very well and from some angles reflected it down toward the ground. After a few test flights, the size of the fins was increased by 50 percent after one had departed its jet due to flutter.

All in all, these changes didn't affect the stealth of the aircraft, but stability improved greatly. It was during these transitional days that the jet acquired the "Wobbly Goblin" moniker. Like its predecessors, the Senior Trend aircraft borrowed heavily from the success of others. The cockpit equipment, including the heads-up display (HUD), attack sensor display (SD), and switches on both the control stick and throttles, came from the navy's McDonnell-Douglas F/A-18. Other displays came from the army's OV-10 Bronco and the navy's P-3C Orion ocean patrol aircraft. The inertial navigation system was copied from the B-52 bomber, and various other components came from the Lockheed stable of the SR-71 spy plane, C-130 transport, F-104 Star Fighter, and the L-1011 airliner. The ejection seat was a standard ACES-II, identical to those in F-16s, F-15s, and A-10s.

Like the previous Have Blue jets, the intakes were covered by radar-reflecting grilles. They looked like huge ice cube trays. For them not to act like ice cube makers, which would be disastrous for the engines, they were equipped with an automatic wiper system. The ice sensors could even detect the difference between hard ice and mushy ice accumulations and would automatically squirt alcohol from pores in the wipers as they swung back and forth.

Whether all of this was evidence of genius or occasionally crossed the line into just weird was a frequent topic of conversation. Because the production run was so small, everything was essentially handmade and ridiculously expensive. The tolerances were exacting and went far beyond skin-deep.

Not everyone was impressed. Inglorious names have been attached to the jet, such as Cockroach, Wobbly Goblin, and Stinkbug, to name a few. Real F-117 pilots have always called it the

Black Jet. This dated back to the early days when the first F-117 pilots also flew A-7s as part of their cover story. The A-7s were painted gray. The F-117s were painted black. So a pilot checking the flying schedule would have to note whether he was going to fly the gray jet or the Black Jet that night.

Lockheed's legendary designer Kelly Johnson, by then semi-retired, hated it. He supposedly remarked that "no aircraft that looked that ugly could possibly be any good." His original idea had been along the lines of a flying saucer–shaped design. The problem is that saucers (unless spinning like a Frisbee) are even more inherently unstable than the Have Blue/F-117 designs. No one at Lockheed could figure out how to make a saucer fly, and as Ben Rich commented, "The Martians wouldn't tell us."

Aesthetics aside, the air force was so impressed by the final product that instead of the original order for a "silver bullet" force of a dozen or so aircraft, it ordered a complement of fifty-nine aircraft to equip a combat short wing of just over two squadrons (a normal wing is three squadrons; four squadrons would be a long wing). One caveat was that the aircraft had to be painted black. A few studies had shown that black wasn't actually the optimum color—the first Have Blue was painted a mottled gray. But in aviation the Golden Rule is "He who has the gold gets to make the rule," so the jets were painted black.

In any case, Ben Rich, who had taken a huge gamble on this venture, had been vindicated. He had recognized the value of an emerging technology before anyone else and had hung his career on the line in support of the jet. Even if he had done nothing else at Lockheed, he will always be known in the air force as the "Father of Stealth."

Back in our training class, Klaus went on to describe the early "black" days up at Tonopah, Nevada. For a long time the F-117s were forbidden to fly off range in case one were to crash or be forced down by an emergency. For years, hangar doors would never be opened until after dark. Flying would even be canceled if the moon was going to be too bright. The wing's personnel lived at Nellis AFB and would commute each Monday morning to Tonopah. Each Friday, they would return to their families and be unable to say where they had been or what they had been doing all week. Relationships and family life suffered tremendously. This went on for a decade.

In those days, wing commanders within range of Tonopah had been warned that "some night an odd-looking jet might drop in. If that happens, secure the jet in an isolated hangar, confiscate every camera around, and follow any instructions that the pilot gives. The cavalry will already be on its way." The word *extreme* doesn't even begin to describe the level of security that existed then. And just to add one last bit of fodder for the conspiracy nuts who are convinced that there are aliens from outer space at Area 51, the map designation that contains Tonopah airfield is right next door at Area 52.

After the existence of the jet had been revealed in late 1988, the rules loosened up a bit, though the jet still wasn't publicly displayed until 1990. During these ensuing "gray" days, the F-117 still operated out of Tonopah, but could now fly day sorties, and the pilots could live slightly more normal lifestyles. Of course, the bulk of the flying would always be in the dark. Klaus' advice to us was that we would have to "learn to be comfortable with the night."

Over the next couple of weeks, I settled into a routine. My class had simulators each morning and academics every afternoon during the first week of June. The systems were slowly becoming more familiar. A small mockup of the cockpit was in our classroom where we could familiarize ourselves with the location of the switches and controls. When you're in training, you can spend hours running through the various checklists until, without looking, the controls fall into your hands as easily as the light switches in your home. Every aircraft has a checklist "flow" designed to make the starting procedures more logical. Most fighters, including the F-117, have a flow that starts in the back left side panel and works forward. After the gear has been checked (always in the forward left corner), the flow zigzags across the forward panel before finishing down the right side panel. Eventually all of this becomes second nature. Training in the real simulator is better. In there (when you can scrounge the time), the lights and systems react appropriately and you get a better feel for the pacing.

The base had only one F-117 simulator (sim) to support our admittedly small training classes and the rest of the wing's continuation training. It was an impressive piece of technology and could mimic every conceivable flight condition except motion. Every switch, control, and instrument was identical to those in the aircraft. In fact, spare parts were occasionally cannibalized from the sim to repair an aircraft. The operator could dial in the time of day, season of the year, snow cover, rain, lightning, clouds, fog. . . . The visual presentations were good enough that you could "take off," stay low, and follow the roads to your neighborhood. During one sim, I "landed" at Cannon AFB, taxied to where the 429th operations building had been, taxied through the parking lot, and pulled into the front door (the virtual world ended at that point). After the Gulf War, realistic anti-aircraft fire and surface-to-air missile shots could also be programmed into what you'd see "outside."

The sim was a great tool to practice ground procedures, switchology, and basic attacks. But we'd eventually be able to practice those in the actual jet. The real benefit was in being able to dial in any conceivable emergency on which to train. Engine fires, fuel leaks, electrical failures, midair collisions, and thunderstorms were all in there. There was a list of every emergency anyone ever dreamed up waiting for us. Before we'd be allowed to touch a real jet we would experience and successfully deal with all of them. And until we were perfect, the instructor would hit "reset" and we'd do it over and over and over. No pilot particularly cares much for sims, but the huge training advantage they offer can't be ignored. One of the guys labeled the whole experience "panic-in-a-can."

We were also given tours of the jet out on the flight line. The RAM coatings felt rough, something like hard rubber, though we were warned not to touch the jet with our bare hands too much. The earlier rumors that the coatings were carcinogenic supposedly aren't true, but everyone continued to act paranoid enough to make me wonder. And after all, gloves can't hurt. Just walking around the jet was hazardous enough all by itself. All sorts of probes and sharp edges were waiting for us at forehead level, and since everything was painted dull black, every hazard lurked in a perpetual shadow.

The jet was an odd conglomeration of the fabulous and the seemingly sloppy. The cockpit layout wasn't horrible, but could have been more efficient. Standard Lockheed, I guess. The old cliché about Lockheed products (at least among General Dynamics engineers, who are justifiably famous for their brilliant cockpit designs) was that they were built to achieve some very specific performance criteria, such as speed, extreme altitude, or, in this case, stealth. Once that single data point of performance was achieved, the engineers would slap their foreheads as they realized they had forgotten to include a cockpit in the design. So they'd quietly and quickly cut a hole in the top, weld in a seat, and randomly mash in whatever instruments might be lying around. On the whole, the cockpit was comfortable enough. It would be a good office for the next three years.

On Thursday, June 5, I tried to call the family up in Clovis, but the cleaning people answered from our old house. Even though the house was scheduled to be gutted and renovated after we were gone, we still had to pay for it to be cleaned and repainted, just like everyone else, before it was torn apart (bureaucrats!). Bets and the kids were living in the Cannon transient quarters while the house was being dealt with.

That afternoon we finished up an instrument refresher course (IRC) and completed the open book test. The IRC is a bit of a pain. The test, required each year, is deliberately designed to make us dig through volumes of regulations to pry out the answers. They aren't hard, but take hours to do properly.

The following Friday evening, the family coasted in and we all camped on the floor for the next few days. The kids had decided to try to save our tropical fish after they couldn't find anyone in Clovis to take them. They brought the fish tank down with only about four inches of water left in the bottom to minimize sloshing and an ice pack floating in there to stun the fish down to something like suspended animation. Most were floating in a belly-up position by the time they got here. I thought that they were all dead, but, surprisingly, all but two survived the trip.

Saturday evening we drove to a house on base for a dinner party. It was for the families of both the senior and junior classes. We had a nice time, and the house was a lot better than expected after the one we'd been offered. The mood was a little awkward, though, since the party had been scheduled before the announcement that our senior class host was being washed out of training.

The following Monday, I was in class while Bets caught the moving van. All of the dismantled furniture was scattered across the floors, and boxes were stacked up to the garage ceiling by the time I got home. I spent the entire week doing graded sims by day and unpacking by night.

The sims weren't too bad—far better than when I was in pilot training and never knew what to expect. Back then my most memorable session had occurred during an emergency procedures mission in the T-37 simulator. I was alone in the cockpit with an instructor on the console throwing different emergencies at me every minute. It was the classic challenge: "I bet you can't start the engines!"; "I bet you can't taxi!"; "I bet you can't take off!"; and on and on and on. I was barely holding my own when a long quiet period began. That was bad.

Obviously, the instructor had set up something nefarious such as a slowly leaking hydraulic system, a low oil pressure, an engine gauge just barely out of tolerance—something subtle and sneaky. And I couldn't find it. I sweated out five or ten of the longest minutes of my life as my imagination began to invent emergencies that weren't even there. I was convinced that I was blowing this one royally and would be washed out of pilot training before I even got to solo. Then the instructor came back up on the intercom to say, "Okay, I've got my coffee now. Where were we?"

The F-117 world was a different sort of community than I was used to. We rarely, if ever, expected to employ as a formation, so individual action was pretty much all that counted. This was a significant change from the more traditional squadrons I'd been assigned to. But that's why only experienced pilots, with at least one fighter or bomber tour under their belts, were accepted for training.

Unfortunately, even then a few didn't make it—like our host from the previous weekend. The other two guys in his class graduated a few days later while he was still awaiting his fate. From the IPs, I gathered that his situational awareness is what did him in. When the missions didn't go as planned, he couldn't improvise and adjust quickly enough and his performance fell off. There was no real cure for that at this stage of the game.

During this week, a dozen F-117s returned from their most recent deployment to Kuwait. They had deployed there last October—during the same period we had been flying our butts off with three EF-111s out of Al-Kharj.

On Monday, June 15, I had another sim and did some studying at work. Our unpacking was about 90 percent complete at this point. This is the dangerous stage of a move, where progress begins easing to a halt. It's usually that last percentage that takes months to sort out. Many an air force family has leaned a picture against an out of the way wall at this stage *temporarily*, only not to touch it until it was time to move again. And every family has at least one unopened shipping box up in the attic with the stickers from three different moving companies over the sealing tape.

I ran into Nordo, from Cannon, at work. His family had put their ostrich ranch up for sale and he was settling in to his new assignment with the test wing here. His group was doing some interesting work with the new GPS systems coming online.

I also ran into Pete. Pete had been my first flight commander in T-33s at Griffiss Air Force Base after I'd arrived as a new second lieutenant fresh out of pilot training. He was retired from the U.S. Air Force now and was doing some serious technical work on base as a contractor. He also raised livestock on his ranch up near Tularosa in his free time. He looked a little ragged with a bit of a beer belly and bed-head hair (always did) and couldn't have cared less. He always knew his stuff and could fly a jet with the best of them. It was great to see him again.

One of my early "Oh, shit!" aviation experiences had occurred with Pete. He and I were flying a low-level navigation route over much of the Adirondacks through some very marginal visibility and had finally spilled out over Lake Ontario. At that time I was flying at 300 feet above ground level (AGL, as opposed to MSL, which stands for mean sea level—which is what an altimeter reads). But the fog and glassy calm water of the lake made it impossible to judge our altitude visually. And without anything to focus on, we couldn't tell how low the visibility was becoming. As the new guy that I was, I asked his advice back there in the pit.

He said something like, "Don't worry, we're in protected airspace so just fly three hundred on the gauge." No problem. And off we went, zorching through the murk with exactly 300 feet on the altimeter and 360 knots on the airspeed indicator. I'd only just been cleared down from 500 to 300 feet on the previous sortie, so I was trying extra hard to be precise. Somewhere in our peripheral vision we both thought we saw something zip by, pretty much at our level.

"Did you just see something?" came from the back.

"Yeah, but it was just kind of a shadow," I responded.

Dead ahead another shadow began to materialize. It was about twelve feet long, beige fiberglass, and had a metallic blue lump on the back end that read *Evinrude*. Simultaneously three sets of eyes got very wide—mine and the two guys in the boat.

I uttered a very spontaneous and honest exclamation of "Crap!" as I yanked the control stick into my lap to gain some altitude.

"What was that all about?" Pete shot at me.

"A boat, it was a boat!" I sputtered. "We were level with a damn boat!"

He had been looking back in the direction of that first "shadow" at the moment and hadn't seen a thing.

"Come on. We were never below three hundred feet the whole time. I was watching." Then there was a pause, and through the rearview mirror I saw him fumbling with the route map. "Uh, I just realized something," he said.

"Yeah, what's that?"

Pete has a tendency to laugh at inopportune moments. So, beginning to chuckle, he said, "The surface of the lake is listed at two hundred forty-six feet on my chart." He sounded like this was the funniest thing he'd heard in days. "We were only fifty-four feet off the water all that time, and we didn't even know it." He had to struggle through his laughter as he reminded me that the tolerance on our altimeters was plus or minus 75 feet before he broke up completely.

I eventually learned to appreciate Pete's skills as a pilot and his sense of humor. He is one of the most curious guys regarding anything scientific I know and a great friend to this day. He still denies that he was in the jet with me that day. Maybe he's right. But he can't seem to deny it without laughing at the same time.

That week we had sim missions every day except for Friday, when we took our written tests. I got 100 percent on the closed book exam, which was all by memory, but missed two questions on the open book exam, which was the reverse of what would be expected. I missed one for not reading the full question and the other because the publications I had been issued for the exam hadn't been updated. The first hit was a fair kill, but dinging me for that second question was a cheap shot.

That afternoon the newly promoted majors hosted a party at the club. It was fun to get back into that atmosphere for a while. Nordo was one of those selected for advancement. Back at Cannon we had been worried that his transfer from the marines to the air force might have left a trail of unintelligible records and hurt his promotion chances, so I was happy to drink his beer.

The next morning I drove the family up to the mountain village of Cloudcroft, where there was a small parade and an Old West–themed festival with damsels-in-distress and mock cowboy shootouts in the street. The very steep road paralleled an old railroad track built at the turn of the century to haul logs down from the mountains to be shipped off toward El Paso and Albuquerque. It's mind-numbing to think of the loaded trains barreling down that grade after the inevitable brake failures. Even the roads have runaway gravel ramps every mile or so for out-of-control trucks headed downhill.

Cloudcroft was great. One boast is that at 9,200 feet above sea level, they have the highest golf course in the country. Whether that would make it easier to whack a ball because of the thin air or harder because you'd never catch your breath wasn't elaborated on. The town subsists to a large degree on the tourist trade, but the trees, greenery, and clear cold air make it a wonderful change from the desert floor. Even during the worst of the summer, the temperature rarely gets above the low 70s, and the sound the wind makes while passing through the tall pine trees reminded me of camping in New Hampshire as a kid.

We drove along the western rim of the Sacramento Mountains to the Sunspot National Solar Observatory, taking note of all the good camping and hiking spots along the way. The location of some good trout streams would have completed the picture, but there didn't seem to be any open water.

Halfway down the mountain, in the hamlet of High Rolls, we stopped for an excellent lunch at the Silver Spring BBQ. There was a hokey-looking teepee out by the road to draw attention to the place, and the restaurant itself was built into the side of a hill. Plywood walls, gallons of homemade cherry cider for sale, vinyl red and white checkered tablecloths, and no three chairs matching. It appeared to be a family-run deal with Mom at the register, an enthusiastic high-school girl running around waiting tables, and gravely voiced Dad in back running the kitchen. It was easily among the top three places I've had BBQ in either the United States or Canada, and we'd only stopped by accident.

The upcoming week was going to be busy. We'd have a few more practice sims to prepare for our taxi rides in the actual jet the following week—and then our first flights.

CHAPTER 5

Bandit Number 545

Wars are not won by diplomacy, fine
speech, or impeccable table manners. After all
has been said and done, the contest will have
been decided by fire and steel, on target, on
time—period!

MONDAY, JUNE 29, 1998. For the seventh time in my career
since graduating from pilot training, I walked out to climb the
ladder of a new jet. First introductions can be important.

Our F-117s were sheltered in two long parallel rows of individual hangar bays, all facing inward. This area was known as the
canyon. While standing in front of my assigned aircraft's shelter,
horns blared as the massive doors slowly rumbled aside. A gentle
flutter of brightly colored and familiar cloth caught my eye first.
Suspended high over each and every F-117 was an American
flag. The doors continued opening to grudgingly admit more light.

There it was.

Matte black. Hulking. It seemed to be clutching the floor rather than just resting upon it. The wings, what little there were of them, swept back from the nose at an impossibly sharp angle in two razor-straight lines. Not a single curve, or any other concession toward "normal" aerodynamics, was visible—nothing but black facets. This was obviously the product of a demented diamond cutter who had taken it upon himself to carve a plane from a very large chunk of coal.

Not for the first—or the last—time, I wondered how this thing could possibly fly. Of grace or beauty, it engendered no feelings whatsoever. Those would come later. Of sheer power, it needed to make no statement at all. It just stood there to be recognized and respected. Here was an aircraft created to do just one thing and to do it better than anything else in the world. And it seemed to know it.

It occurred to me that I had been thinking of it as an "it," when normally an aircraft is a "she." That, too, would come later. For a moment I just stood and stared. Unblinking and uncaring, it seemed to stare right back. Somehow, it was as if the F-117 was sizing me up rather than the other way around.

We were going to get along just fine.

This wouldn't be a real sortie. I'd get to preflight the jet, strap in, start her up, and then taxi down the runway. Chasing along like a puppy would be a small pickup truck driven by my instructor, Beav. The point of this exercise was to combine all the academics and ground procedures that had only been artificial to this point.

By the time I arrived at the shelter, the jet had been under power for almost an hour via an external power cart. This procedure allowed the jet's ancient B-52 inertial navigation system (INS) to align. Once the new RNIP—ring-laser-gyro navigation improvement program—modifications were complete, which would replace the old INS, we'd be able to do away with that part of the preflight and walk out to a cold jet.

As I walked around the aircraft with checklist in hand, the crew chief followed to answer questions and make any adjustments that might be necessary. The cockpit was entered via a long bent ladder specifically designed for this jet. An ordinary boarding ladder would touch the sides of the jet and damage the RAM coatings, so a Rube Goldberg contraption had been designed that arched up and over the side of the canopy rail. The angles were funny, and it wasn't an easy ladder to climb. The crew chief followed me up to the cockpit to help me strap in and get situated. Then he descended before carefully swinging the ladder away. It would be a ten- to twelve-foot jump down to the concrete to get out now.

Most of the cockpit checks would be familiar to any fighter pilot. Parachute harness connected, lap and shoulder straps attached, oxygen and intercom leads connected, systems and armament-panel switches off, circuit breakers checked in, throttles and fuel-dumps off, ejection, emergency gear extension, and dragchute deployment handles stowed . . . and so on. To help ensure the ground crew's safety, before starting the engines I'd doublecheck that the throttles were off, the landing gear handle was down, the tail-hook deploy switch was guarded, the bomb bay door controls were set to the AUTO/CLOSE position, and the lasers were off.

The only thing outside the cockpit I needed to look at was my crew chief, stationed about fifteen feet to the right and front of my jet. His job was to monitor the start and the ground crew swarming around under the jet—all of whom were out of my view. We spoke through an intercom system and umbilical plugged into a receptacle in the nose wheelwell of my jet. Until

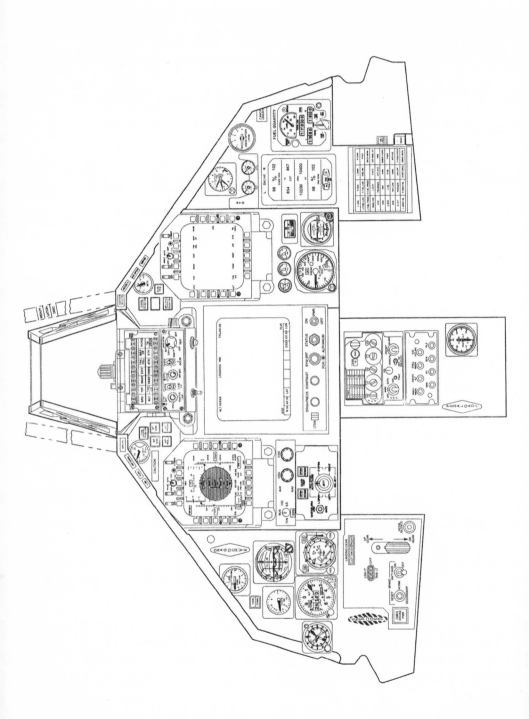

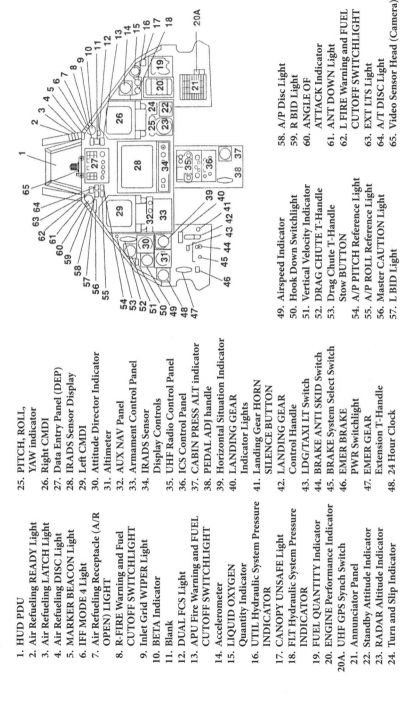

1. HUD PDU
2. Air Refueling READY Light
3. Air Refueling LATCH Light
4. Air Refueling DISC Light
5. MARKER BEACON Light
6. IFF MODE 4 Light
7. Air Refueling Receptacle (A/R OPEN) LIGHT
8. R-FIRE Warning and Fuel CUTOFF SWITCHLIGHT
9. Inlet Grid WIPER Light
10. BETA Indicator
11. Blank
12. DUAL FCS Light
13. APU Fire Warning and FUEL CUTOFF SWITCHLIGHT
14. Accelerometer
15. LIQUID OXYGEN Quantity Indicator
16. UTIL Hydraulic System Pressure INDICATOR
17. CANOPY UNSAFE Light
18. FLT Hydraulic System Pressure INDICATOR
19. FUEL QUANTITY Indicator
20. ENGINE Performance Indicator
20A. UHF GPS Synch Switch
21. Annunciator Panel
22. Standby Attitude Indicator
23. RADAR Altitude Indicator
24. Turn and Slip Indicator

25. PITCH, ROLL, YAW indicator
26. Right CMDI
27. Data Entry Panel (DEP)
28. IRADS Sensor Display
29. Left CMDI
30. Attitude Director Indicator
31. Altimeter
32. AUX NAV Panel
33. Armament Control Panel
34. IRADS Sensor Display Controls
35. UHF Radio Control Panel
36. ICS Control Panel
37. CABIN PRESS ALT indicator
38. PEDAL ADJ handle
39. Horizontal Situation Indicator
40. LANDING GEAR Indicator Lights
41. Landing Gear HORN SILENCE BUTTON
42. LANDING GEAR Control Handle
43. LDG/TAXI LT Switch
44. BRAKE ANTI SKID Switch
45. BRAKE System Select Switch
46. EMER BRAKE PWR Switchlight
47. EMER GEAR Extension T-Handle
48. 24 Hour Clock

49. Airspeed Indicator
50. Hook Down Switchlight
51. Vertical Velocity Indicator
52. DRAG CHUTE T-Handle
53. Drag Chute T-Handle Stow BUTTON
54. A/P PITCH Reference Light
55. A/P ROLL Reference Light
56. Master CAUTION Light
57. L BID Light

58. A/P Disc Light
59. R BID Light
60. ANGLE OF ATTACK Indicator
61. ANT DOWN Light
62. L FIRE Warning and FUEL CUTOFF SWITCHLIGHT
63. EXT LTS Light
64. A/T DISC Light
65. Video Sensor Head (Camera)

I taxied out of the canyon, he had veto power over everything I did.

Once everything was ready, I flipped on the battery toggle switch, made one last check of all the warning lights and panels, and called "antennas clear" over the intercom. Then I threw another switch that extended the communication and navigation antennas. Once those antennas had finished slowly bristling out the sides and belly of the fuselage, I started the onboard auxiliary power unit (APU), itself a small jet engine, to begin the engine start sequence.

I called to my crew chief through the intercom: "Fire bottle posted, fore and aft areas clear, ready right."

He crouched down on one knee to sweep the area visually one last time then parroted my words before raising an arm with two fingers extended. Then he made a circling motion over his head, which let me know that it was safe to start the number two engine. I pushed the right engine's RUN switch to the START position, and a high-pitched whining noise spooled up. Once the core engine rpm exceeded 10 percent, I bumped the right throttle forward to the idle position.

The General Electric F-404 engine starts up very predictably and smoothly compared with others. I ran my eyes down the engine's instrument stack to confirm that the core rpm, fan rpm, exhaust gas temperature, hydraulic pressure, fuel flow, and oil pressure were all within limits. Then I checked that the engine-driven generator had kicked on before turning the auxiliary generator off. The EDTM (electronic data transfer module), an over-large, antique, and clunky portable hard drive containing the mission's flight plan, was then set and locked into its receptacle.

The left engine started just as easily before I spent almost ten minutes powering up the aircraft systems, running their self-diagnostic functions, and checking the flight controls and brakes for proper operation. Extra attention was paid to the flight control systems (FLCS). The self-test functions are a bit finicky and require that a pilot input appropriate control stick and rudder deflections at various points in the test. Doing this allows the system to compare what the pilot is doing with his controls with where the aircraft's sensors believe that the control surfaces are positioned. Any hesitation or misstep by the pilot will cause the test to fail, and he will have to reset the system and start over. While all of this is going on, the entire jet will be lurching and rocking about as the 100-pound control surfaces slam around under the influence of 3,000 pounds of hydraulic pressure. For obvious safety reasons, all ground crew need to be well clear of the aircraft until the test is concluded.

Once I was satisfied and ready for taxi, I called over the intercom, "Clear power and air, traps and doors, glareshields down, canopy coming down."

I could see the ground crew hustling around to drag the last power and cooling-air umbilicals attached to my jet off to the sides as I carefully pulled two glare shields, called "elephant ears," toward me before lowering the canopy. If I were to forget those and leave them flipped forward, they would be easily crushed by the more than 400-pound canopy slowly motoring down. Once the canopy was down, I swung a massive lever on the right side of the cockpit forward to lock the canopy in place. Improbably, I then folded a tiny little strap of Velcro up over the locking lever to hold the lever in place.

With the canopy finally closed and locked, the shrieking noise coming off the engine inlets just off my shoulders blissfully faded away and the cockpit was surprisingly quiet. After requesting and receiving clearance from ground control to taxi, I raised both my fists to the crew chief and then swung my thumbs outward for the

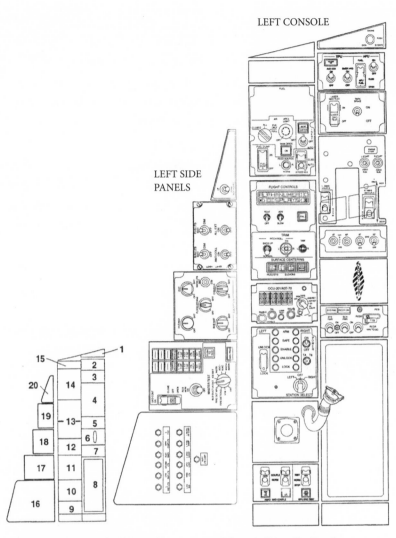

LEFT CONSOLE

LEFT SIDE
PANELS

1. **ENGINE DATA EVENTS Switch**
2. **EPU/APU Control Panel**
3. **LASER GND Test Panel**
4. **Throttle Panel**
5. **A/P A/T Control Panel**
6. **CANOPY/SEAT Emergency
   Jettison T Handle**
7. **RCS Control Panel**
8. **Map and Let Down Book Container**
9. **AMAD/EPU Ground Control Panel**
10. **Anti G Suit Hookup**
11. **Weapons Interface Panel**
12. **Weapons Controller Panel
    (PAL/AMAC)**
13. **FLIGHT CONTROLS (FCS) Panel**
14. **Fuel System Control Panel**
15. **Blank**
16. **Left Circuit Breaker Panel**
17. **MASTER TEST Panel/Weapons Bay
    GRD CONT DOOR Switch**
18. **COCKPIT LTS Control Panel**
19. **EXT LTS Control Panel**
20. **SEAT ADJUST Switch**

RIGHT CONSOLE

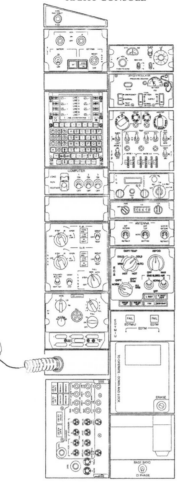

RIGHT SIDE PANELS

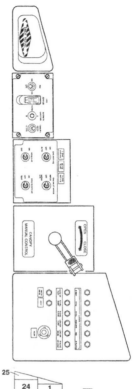

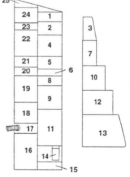

1. AHRS Control Panel
2. OXYGEN REGULATOR Panel
3. EMER REFUEL T-Handle
4. IFF Control Panel
5. TACAN Control Panel
6. ILS Control Panel
7. Miscellaneous Switch Panel
8. ANTENNA Control Panel
9. Ecs Control Panel
10. Anti-ice/De-ice Panel
11. EDTMIU Panel
12. CANOPY MANUAL
    CONTROL Handle
13. Right Circuit Breaker Panel
14. Utility Light
15. DI PHASE/BASE BAND Switch
16. Electrical Fault Indicator Panel
17. Oxygen Hose

18. KY-58 Control Panel (Provision Only)
19. IRADS Control Panel
20. Blank
21. COMPUTER Control Panel
22. CDNU Panel
23. Blank
24. ELEC Control Panel
25. AHRS Fast Erect Panel

signal to pull the wheel chocks. Once the chocks were clear, the crew chief backed out toward the center of the canyon with his arms crossed over his chest to establish that there were no other aircraft or vehicles in the way. Then he began waving me forward. With just a little power the plane began to roll out into the sun. I tapped the top of each rudder pedal with the toe of my boots to make the plane nod slightly. This was one last test of the wheel brakes before I pressed the nose wheel steering button to start my turn out of the canyon.

The plane taxied normally, the steering was responsive, and the forward visibility wasn't as horrendous as I'd expected. At the end of the runway one last check was waiting for me. Called "last chance," a separate crew from the one in the aircraft shelter was waiting to give my jet another inspection to confirm that nothing had come loose or begun to leak during the taxi out. Every panel was double-checked closed, landing gear safety pins were pulled, and tires were still in good shape. These guys were the masters of their domain. All it takes is for one nineteen-year-old on the crew to give a thumbs down on any critical component and the mission will be scrubbed with no questions asked. The pilot, whether he's a lieutenant or a general, doesn't get a vote. But my jet was in good shape that day, and I received a thumbs up and a sharp salute.

I called the tower for clearance onto the runway, and Beav in his little blue pickup truck tagged along beside me. Once on the runway I ran up the engines to feel the real vibrations and hear the real noise as I scanned the engine instruments one last time. Then I released pressure from the toe brakes to begin my takeoff roll.

And after all that work, the game was over. The throttles came back to idle and I slowed the jet to practice the drag chute release procedures before taxiing back to the hangar.

Not very satisfying. My first flight wouldn't happen until the next day.

A first flight in any plane is always significant; this was a little more so. In addition to it being my first flight, and my first solo, I had an unusual pair of observers. As soon as I showed up at the squadron, the commander walked in to ask Beav and me if we'd be comfortable with a reporter sitting in. We were introduced to a writer and his photographer. They were from what the writer described as Sweden's equivalent of *Popular Mechanics*. He had gotten clearance from the U.S. Air Force to write an article on our aircraft and thought a first flight would be a point of interest for his story. So we spent a half hour or so being interviewed and photographed before kicking them out to do the real brief. The reporter promised to send a copy of the magazine with the article to us when it was published—of course, it would be in Swedish and therefore not very useful to me.

The plan was to do a repeat of the taxi ride we had practiced the day before, followed by an actual takeoff and flight to the local training airspace for a few maneuvers before returning to land. Beav would be chasing in a T-38 instead of a pickup truck this time, so the entire sortie could only be a little over an hour long.

The crew chief helped me into the cockpit again. It is said that some planes are "put on" rather than just climbed into—that the plane becomes an extension of yourself. With the F-117, it is more a case of you becoming part of the plane. Once strapped down, connected, and sealed in, all of my interactions with the outside world became artificial. I saw only through gold-tinted panels and infrared displays. I heard only through the intercom system. I could speak only through the radio. I moved not with muscles, but with engines. As far as the external world was concerned, once the canopy was sealed, the jet and I had become one entity.

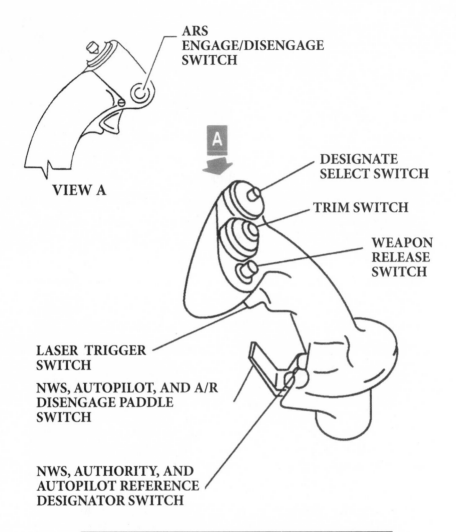

ARS
ENGAGE/DISENGAGE
SWITCH

VIEW A

A

DESIGNATE
SELECT SWITCH

TRIM SWITCH

WEAPON
RELEASE
SWITCH

LASER TRIGGER
SWITCH

NWS, AUTOPILOT, AND A/R
DISENGAGE PADDLE
SWITCH

NWS, AUTHORITY, AND
AUTOPILOT REFERENCE
DESIGNATOR SWITCH

DESIGNATE SELECT SWITCH OPERATION	
SWITCH POSITION	DISPLAY SELECTED
CENTER	IRADS
UP	HUD
DOWN	NOT USED
LEFT	LEFT CMDI
RIGHT	RIGHT CMDI

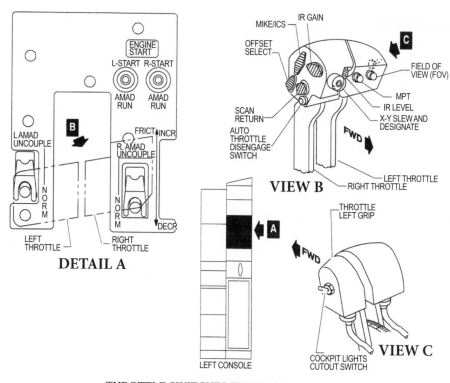

DETAIL A

VIEW B

VIEW C

THROTTLE SWITCHES FUNCTION

SWITCH	POSITION	RESULTS
IR LEVEL	UP DOWN CENTER	INCREASES IR LEVEL DECREASES IR LEVEL OFF LEVEL REMAINS AS SET
X-Y SLEW AND DESIGNATE	CENTER UP DOWN RIGHT LEFT	NO SLEW SLEWS UPWARD SLEWS DOWNWARD SLEWS RIGHT SLEWS LEFT
COCKPIT LIGHTS CUTOUT	DESIGNATE	WHEN PRESSED, DISPLAYS TRACKING GATE WHEN RELEASED, COMMANDS TRACKING
MPT	FORWARD AFT	COCKPIT LIGHTS ON COCKPIT LIGHTS OFF
OFFSET SELECT	PRESSED	FORCES IRADS TO MPT IN CERTAIN MODES (MEMORY POINT TRACKING)
FIELD OF VIEW (FOV)	UP DOWN CENTER	OAP-1 DESIGNATED OAP-2 DESIGNATED CURRENT DESTINATION SELECTED
SCAN RETURN	PRESSED	ALTERNATELY SELECTS WIDE OR NARROW FIELD OF VIEW
IR GAIN	FORWARD AFT CENTER	DECREASES IRAD GAIN INCREASES IRAD GAIN OFF
MIKE/ICS	UP NEUTRAL DOWN	TRANSMIT UHF COMMUNICATION RECEIVE UHF AND INTERCOM TRANSMIT INTERCOM
AUTO THROTTLE DISENGAGE SWITCH	PRESSED	DISENGAGES AUTO THROTTLE

The start and taxi were normal, and Beav was waiting in his T-38 at the end of the runway by the time I got there. After the ground crew had completed their last chance inspection I called for takeoff, and we both pulled out onto the hold position. The takeoff speeds and characteristics of the two jets were too different to take off in formation. So Beav took off first and flew a closed traffic pattern. The idea was for him to get airborne before me so that he could watch the entire takeoff roll and be immediately in position to offer help if there were any problems.

As he approached the perch, he called "Abeam," which was my signal to run the engines up to full power and check the instruments one last time. Then he began a diving turn toward the runway. Halfway through the turn he called "Ten seconds," and I released the brakes. My concentration was focused out front as I accelerated toward the watery sheen of the mirage shimmering along those two miles of hot concrete in front of me. The acceleration to takeoff speed in this thing took longer than anything I'd flown before. Depending on weights and temperatures, the takeoff roll in an F-117 can last as long as a minute. This one seemed longer. Finally I made speed and rotated away from the ground.

Once the landing gear came up in a series of clunks I stole a glance out to the left. Our timing had been perfect and I'd gotten airborne just as Beav had swooped down alongside my aircraft into formation on the left wing. Before this flight I had thought that the whole parallel takeoff act was perhaps a bit excessive, but it certainly looked cool.

In the meantime, the jet was flying just fine. She didn't have any oddities worth noting other than very restricted forward visibility compared with other jets—cluttered by way too much framing. Visibility to the rear was as bad, or maybe even a little worse, than the F-111s. The view out the sides was okay, but up, there was a roof, an actual roof. To a non-pilot that doesn't sound like a big deal, but in any turn beyond about 30 degrees of bank, that is where the horizon is. From the seat you really couldn't see any of the plane outside. It was very much like the cockpit was just floating in space without other references. It occurred to me that flying formation as a wingman in this thing might present a few challenges.

The area work was easy enough, but one of my first impressions was how little the plane "talked" to me. There really wasn't any of the perceptual feedback that occurs in a conventional jet. Fast or slow, accelerating or decelerating, everything felt the same. It didn't get louder or quieter, and almost no pitch or trim change was evident with changing speed. In some ways it was like I was still in the sim. Traditional stability is mostly just a vague, and mostly missed, intention. It all felt very artificial. No big deal, just something else to get used to.

The return consisted of radar vectors to a couple of instrument approaches. (During peacetime several radar reflectors, called "blisters," are bolted to the exterior of the F-117 so that it can be seen by the air traffic control radar system.) These approaches terminated in low approaches over the runway—no touch-and-goes allowed. ACC has always, as had TAC before it, forbidden practice touch-and-go landings in fighter aircraft unless an IP is on board. One of the reasons for this policy was to help preserve the tires (a set of main-gear tires on a T-38 in training command has a life expectancy of about four and a half days). So the Catch-22 for us was that because there was only one seat and we could never have an IP on board, we never got to practice touch-and-goes. Every landing had to be a full stop.

The actual landing turned out to be easy. The huge flat bottom of the jet seemed to catch a large volume of air between it and the runway. Sort of like dropping a large sheet of plywood on a flat surface—that last bit of the fall was cushioned. So touchdown on the main gear, though fast, was relatively smooth.

As soon as the nose gear fell through and I had all three wheels on the ground, I reached up with my left hand to grab the gray drag chute T-handle (not to be confused with the identically shaped canopy jettison T-handle or the alternate landing gear extension T-handle). A sharp pull of 3 to 4 inches opened two small doors way back on the spine of the jet. A small spring-loaded drogue was then ejected into the airstream and drew the main chute out to be inflated. A few seconds later I felt the large and unmistakable tug of a B-52 drag chute deploying. A B-52 uses three of these chutes to stop its third of a million pounds, so the single one attached to my approximately 35,000 pounds was more than enough. Stopping was easy. A much harder thing would be having to taxi forward with that thing inflated back there, so I had to get rid of it.

The trick is that the chute rests in a dangerous place. The risers pass through a narrow notch between the two fairly delicate and RAM-covered rudders. The recommended procedure to jettison the chute is to very gently ease the plane to the left side of the runway and then turn back at about a 45-degree angle toward the center line. From there I ran up the engines to fully inflate the chute and paused a few seconds to allow the rudders and canopy to stabilize. Then I turned the T-handle clockwise 90 degrees and sharply tugged it back another 3 to 4 inches. The chute released, and the heavy metal attachment lug at the base of the risers went flying back toward the rudder notch.

If everything had been done just right, the metal lug wouldn't hit anything expensive as it went whizzing by with a few inches to spare. Another possibility would be having one of the heavy nylon straps getting caught between a rudder and the rudder's base, called a chute wrap. If that happened the natural movement of the rudders, aided by 3,000 psi of hydraulic pressure, would cause the straps to saw through other expensive parts. But today was a good day and everything worked as advertised. I'd had a ball.

Traditionally, every solo pilot provides his IP with a bottle of his choice. Some liquors are deliberately chosen for their scarcity and require a good deal of hunting to track down. Beav asked for a case of Fresca! I hadn't heard that brand name since the 1970s and didn't know the stuff was still being made. I got off cheap.

By July 1, our simulator check rides were complete. Mine went well except for one brief moment of embarrassment.

I'd found that after starting my fourth RTU—replacement training unit—in a four-and-a-half-year span (the T-2, A-4, EF-111, and now the F-117, not even counting the short T-38 spin-up), all the information in my head was starting to blend together. Four entirely different sets of systems, specifications, and collections of boldface procedures were crowding my tiny brain, and I wasn't always able to keep all of that information separate.

While rolling along the simulated taxiway, the instructor induced a brake failure situation. No big deal. I maintained directional control with the nose wheel steering while analyzing why I lost the brakes in the first place, then engaged the alternate systems to bring the jet safely to a halt before hitting anything or encroaching on the active runway. The checklist procedures (if I'd actually had time to reference them) went like this:

Drag Chute—Deploy (not applicable)

HOOK—DOWN (also not applicable)

If no braking action evident:

ANTI-SKID switch—Off

EMER BRAKE PWR switchlight—Press

If still no braking action:

EMER BRAKE PWR switchlight—Press off
AUX GEN switch—On
After aircraft comes to a halt, *and* if generators are inop:
BATTERY switch—Off

I did all of that in a reasonably quick manner and stopped the jet without running off the taxiway. Success!

The instructor's comment was something to the effect of this: "Well, good job handling the situation and getting the jet stopped, but what was that with the number-one engine?"

Without even realizing it I had automatically shut down the left engine while analyzing the brake problem to cut down on excess thrust. While that technique certainly worked for the T-2 and EF-111, it wasn't designed for the F-117.

That afternoon I flew an even better aircraft sortie than my first—until the end at least. The takeoff roll of this thing was impressively long, and you didn't even rotate the nose gear off the runway to set the takeoff attitude until over 180 knots. The jet wouldn't finally break ground until it was going over 200 knots (and that's without any ordnance loaded). But as I eased back on the stick and felt the world fall away, I was back in my element. This was only my second flight, but I had become acclimated enough to absorb a lot more of the experience.

A takeoff in a multi-engine jet is a busy time for the pilot, not in terms of physical action, but in the constant mental sifting of options. The rituals of an obtuse, but critical, science (known as TOLD—takeoff and landing data) must be observed at every speed during that roll. Based upon the aircraft's weight, runway length and slope, density altitude of the field, ambient temperature, runway condition (wet, dry, icy, etc.), and wind at every speed during the takeoff roll there is a distinct reaction required by the pilot if a malfunction occurs. And each reaction is modified by the presence (or absence) of wheel brakes, the anti-skid function of those brakes, runway arresting cable, tail hook, drag chute, functional hydraulic system, and departure end barrier.

With all of the data calculated and in consideration of any malfunction that can occur, two very basic questions come up in the event of an emergency: Should I stop or go? And how can I accomplish that without breaking anything or killing myself? Only seconds separate the various phases and appropriate options before the variables make one reaction not only wrong, but dangerous. There isn't enough time to figure out what to do as events are unfolding—you need to have a plan in place beforehand.

An abbreviated version of the process goes something like this: After I've pushed up the throttles to ensure that every engine gauge is within parameters, I release the toe brakes to begin my roll. A few moments later I call out "Airspeed is alive" once the airspeed indicator has begun to function (they generally don't work at all until you are going 40 to 50 knots, so this is the first time you can check). At these slow speeds I'm using nose wheel steering to keep the jet tracking straight down the runway. As the speed increases I gradually use less nose wheel steering by proportionally blending in more rudder deflection. Any malfunctions at these slower "highway speeds" of 80 to 100 knots can be dealt with by simply pulling the throttles to idle and gently applying wheel brakes, and the jet will stop in a half mile or so.

The next milestone is called MACS (minimum acceleration check speed), abeam some easily identifiable reference point such as a tower, runway remaining marker, or barrier stanchion where a precalculated speed must be met. Usually at about 2,000 to 3,000 feet down the runway, this speed is in the vicinity of 100 to 120 knots. This check validates that the engines are producing the appropriate thrust in these particular environmental conditions. At these speeds an abort for any malfunction can be accomplished with throttles to idle, wheel brakes (usually below the anti-skid level), and possibly deploying the drag chute if required.

The bigger milestone approaching is usually referred to as "go-no-go speed." Beyond this speed the automatic decision to abort becomes problematic—as the ability to stop prior to the end of the runway is no longer possible, but the ability to fly still hasn't been attained. There are a lot more variables involved at this decision point.

That day, on my kneeboard card was a series of numbers. One, RS (refusal speed), was the velocity that I could accelerate to with two good engines and then decide to abort using only anti-skid wheel braking to slither to a halt on the last foot of the runway. While accomplishing that I would also preemptively transmit "barrier, barrier, barrier" so that tower personnel could ensure that the departure-end BAK-15 arresting barrier was in the raised position. Like a giant spider web of vertical nylon straps attached to ship's anchor chains laid out in the overrun, this thing stops any jet rolling into it up to more than 200 knots. The damage inflicted to the aircraft is going to be severe though—the most recent incident had caused $1.5 million in repair costs.

About 2,000 feet prior to the barrier I could have deployed the tail hook to catch the arresting cable. Two considerations were associated with this course of action. The first was that I had determined that I'd end up in the barrier if I didn't deploy the hook, and, ideally, I would have made that decision a full 1,000 feet prior to the cable (3,000 feet prior to the barrier) to give the hook time to stabilize. The reason I don't simply deploy the hook preemptively during every abort is that the hook lives in the belly of the jet and to deploy it I'd need to explosively shatter the panel that conceals it. To initiate this detonation I'd have to actuate something nicknamed the "$50,000 switch," named after the cost of repairing the aircraft's belly afterward. This wasn't an option to be taken lightly. Deploying the hook is still infinitely cheaper than going into the barrier, but you didn't want to make that $50,000 investment if it turned out that the jet could have been stopped with wheel brakes alone.

Other numbers to be considered are the CEFS and CEFL (critical engine failure speed and critical engine failure length). CEFS is the speed attained before losing an engine and deciding to abort or continue the takeoff, while also stopping or getting airborne in the same amount of distance (that distance being the CEFL). This total distance is then compared to the length of the actual runway and the length of the runway prior to the last cable. Every abort decision has a perfect "everything works" component, a brakes work/drag chute fails component, and a brakes work/chute works/but hook fails component. If the brakes fail, ending up in the cable is the best that can be hoped for.

On the flip side, if I decided to avoid these potential catastrophes by trying to take the jet airborne with the one remaining engine, another series of options would present itself. Assuming that I was faster than CEFS *and* that CEFL was less than the actual runway length, I had the *potential* to make it. If I miscalculated this one and hit the barrier while trying to fly out, it would be the last mistake I'd ever make.

Let's assume that I've had my engine failure, correctly analyzed the malfunction quickly enough to decide to take this airborne, have already achieved the abovementioned speeds, maintained control with exactly 5 degrees of bank away from the dead engine, and missed the departure end barrier as I wallow along. I still haven't made it—in fact, I'm in even more trouble. Here is the problem: The runway is now behind me so I can't stop, but I don't have the speed to climb yet either. Until I accelerate to something called SECS (single engine climb speed), I'm stuck hovering along at an altitude of about thirty feet above the desert floor (in my sixty-four-foot-long jet).

In this scenario, I'm in a zone called "the PLAZ"—the "potential loss of aircraft zone." (Who comes up with these names?) I can't stop, and I can't fly. In this nether region my only hope is to hover along in ground effect until, over the course of four to five miles (I hope there are no trees out there), I slowly accelerate to SECS. Now the jet is capable of climbing away from the ground at a whopping performance of a 1-degree angle. From there I can limp the jet around to an emergency landing. If I get impatient and try to force it early I'll stall and hit the dirt.

Why not just eject? Well, assuming the seat worked properly, which it probably would, the aircraft would still crash only a couple dozen feet below me. The fireball created by nine tons of jet fuel that close to my nylon parachute would likely ruin my entire day. At night this whole evolution has the potential to be exciting.

But today was a good day and everything worked as advertised. Beav had chased me out to the airspace called the Beaks again where we primarily did formation work. As a wingman I found that the rejoin line was easy enough to fly, but it could be difficult to see over the canopy rail if the bank angle was too great. And without speed brakes, the jet didn't stop in position as quickly as did other fighters, so you had to plan ahead a bit more.

Back in the pattern I was feeling pretty cocky. I was hitting the perch point right at the desired 195 knots, holding a solid 45-degree bank through the final turn and controlling my speed and angle of attack well on final. Normally the desired landing zone extends from 150 to 1,000 feet down the runway, with 500 feet being the target. I was aiming, on only my second landing, to land "on the numbers" at the short end of that range for the full stop. But I allowed my aim point to shift as I dealt with a bit of turbulence from some gusty crosswinds, and the jet settled a little sooner than I had planned.

As I crossed, just barely, over the threshold before the main gear hit I commented to myself, *"That was close."* As it turned out, it was a little more than close. While I, in the cockpit, had made it over the line, my main gear about thirty feet behind me had touched down in the over-run by a couple of feet. That is why over-runs are there, so no damage was done, except to my ego. But on that day I also had Beav in his T-38 on my wing to witness the event. I received good comments on the grade sheet for the other parts of the flight and a good overall grade for the sortie, but also a valuable lesson about getting cocky with a new jet so early on.

On Thursday, the following day, we all flew our third transition flights (TR-3). Mine went well and the jet was beginning to give up more of its secrets. The departure was the most interesting part of the flight. Just to the east of the field was a large funnel-shaped valley leading into the Sacramento Mountains. This valley collects the predominate wind from the west and violently lifts it into the colder elevations where whatever moisture is present then condenses. The valley was also a mandatory turn point on the departure procedures headed toward our working airspaces. The point was named Cloud, and the procedures were named, naturally enough, the Cloud Departures.

Of all the many thousands of Federal Aviation Administration–designated points in the country, Cloud is one of the mostly aptly named. There is almost always a cloud at Cloud. And that day there was a big one. In fact, it was on its way to becoming a substantial thunderstorm. The F-117 and heavy rain don't get along well, and while overblown by the press, compared with aluminum aircraft, our external coatings were sensitive to very heavy precipitation and potentially could be damaged. So, on my third sortie, I earned some brownie points for adroitly working my way around this storm without violating any other airspaces or corridors on the way out, getting the mission accomplished efficiently, and doing all of the planned approaches through the gathering weather that had generated by the time we were ready to head back. A successful sortie is always a great way to end a week, especially when there is a party waiting.

After work the annual monsoon party was being hosted at the club for the F-117 squadrons. At first thought the term *monsoon* doesn't seem to apply to the sort of weather conditions you find in a desert. But the weather that we do get is usually in the form of severe thunderstorms. The press has been infamously running stories about how our jet, as well as the B-2, would simply dissolve in the rain. That was nonsense, but a boring truth rarely seems to win out over sensationalism in the fourth estate. No aircraft does well in a thunderstorm. But conventional fighters fly most of their sorties in daylight and usually also have radar to aid in weather avoidance. Neither applied to us so, since we couldn't avoid what we couldn't see, we knocked off flying at night during the summer (the monsoon season). Additionally, with the sun setting as late as 21:30 through the summer months, we'd never get home before 04:00 if we continued operations as we did through the winter. We wouldn't resume training flights at night again until October. Regardless, the transition to a more normal schedule was as good an excuse for a party as any.

The theme of a monsoon party was always vaguely Hawaiian, and the wives all turned out to officially welcome us back to the daylight world. For my family in particular this was a good opportunity for Bets to meet some of the others in the unit. Around the squadron proper names were rarely used and people were usually referred to by their call signs. So there I was, trying to introduce her to all of these people I'd been working with, while none of us were wearing uniforms or name tags. "Guys, this is my wife, Betsy. Betsy, this is Speedy, Tot, Scooby, Draft, Seldom, T-Dub . . ." I slowly trailed off as it occurred to me that I had no earthly idea what half of their real names were.

The program was going fast. Only a few days after our first flights, we were scheduled for our transition check rides the following week, and we would be graduated out to our squadrons for mission qualification training in about three weeks. On the morning of Saturday, July 4, I drove the family down to the airport in El Paso. They would be on vacation in the northeast for about six weeks. I could have used a vacation, too, but this changing of planes every other year, and deploying in between, had kept me busy for the last half decade. I hoped I'd be able to use the time while the family was away to get some heavy work done around the house.

The following Monday, I flew TR-4 with Tripp. It was a standard profile out to the area for some aerobatics, formation work, and an introduction to the autopilot system. Then back to the field for a TACAN (tactical air navigation) approach, a low-circling approach, an ILS (instrument landing system) approach, and three overhead patterns.

The next day we flew about the same profile but introduced autopilot-coupled instrument approaches to the mix. The autopilot system had great potential, but I'd need more practice before its operation became seamless. I decided that after my training was complete, I'd turn off that system most of the time. It does so much that I could see how pilots could get lazy and not hand-fly the jet enough.

I thought the sortie had gone well, but Tripp thought otherwise with respect to my switchology. I really couldn't read these guys. The community had been so small and isolated for such a long time that their standards and expectations had diverged from the rest of the U.S. Air Force. Not in any negative way, just different. In any case, the ride was good enough for me to be passed along for my check ride the following day.

The squadron commander, Smear, with Beav in the back seat of the T-38, chased me through the check ride profile for an average sortie. Nothing great, and nothing awful.

A small but significant percentage of military pilots are very superstitious about evaluations. One guy in the 8th openly tells people that he has never taken a check without wearing his "lucky" T-shirt and that he would be tempted to call in sick if he couldn't find it on check ride day. Most pilots are neutral. Not me. I'm actively anti-superstitious, and if I had ever begun to think of a particular T-shirt as "lucky," I would have made it my next oil rag.

I suppose the truth was that I just couldn't get excited about check rides anymore. Some pilots put incredible amounts of effort into them to get their grade bumped up to the EQ (exceptionally qualified) level. But in the long run, it's all a pass/fail attempt. I'd prefer that they were all no-notice without any special preparations or study occurring beforehand. That would give a more accurate representation of our real skills on a day-to-day basis.

Every USAF check ride is documented on a sheet of paper called the Form-8. The bulk of mine read as follows:

Mission Description. The examinee planned, briefed, and flew this Initial Instrument/Qualification evaluation as Holloman AFB, NM. Mission elements included standard climbout to the Beak-B MOA for aerobatics, pitchouts and rejoins, and formation work. RTB was via fix-to-fix navigation to SMATI for TACAN holding, penetration, and approach, followed by vectors for an ILS approach, and missed approach. VFR pattern work included a simulated single-engine straight-in approach and a closed overhead pattern to a full stop landing. The flight examiner conducted the evaluation from a T-38 chase aircraft. The 7 FS/DO was debriefed.

Recommended Additional Training: NONE

Qualification Level: 1

A generic, no-frills pass. Never documented are the gags or practical jokes that often occur during a mission. The gag played on me this day involved a system called the PAARS, the pilot-activated automatic recovery system. In the early black days of the jet when only night flying was allowed and the pilots were perpetually exhausted, there had been several incidents involving pilots becoming spatially disoriented. They literally became so confused that they didn't know which way was up. A couple of deaths had resulted.

To address this problem, the PAARS system had been added to the jet. A little red button directly under the pilot's index finger on the control stick activated the response. When the button was pushed the jet would automatically engage the autopilot and auto-throttle functions and fly the jet to a 5-degree climbing attitude at 300 knots. The idea was that if a pilot were to recognize his own disorientation he would hit this button and then let go of the controls. After sitting still for a while and trusting the system he would presumably recover enough to fly the jet home. We were required to practice using the system at least once a year.

The response could seem rather violent to someone already disoriented. Depending on the jet's pitch and bank attitude, the jet might command as many as 3.8 positive g's or −0.8 negative g's simultaneously with as much roll rate as was required to get right-side up. The jet was going to immediately maneuver in the shortest direction to that 5-degree climbing attitude. It didn't care in the slightest about the pilot's comfort along the way.

So there I was, happy and comfortable, all of the area work done, my approach book opened to the appropriate page and laid neatly on the side console, all ready to head back for the pattern work. Then Smear called for one last set-up with a request to pull the nose up about 45 degrees and then roll 45 degrees to the right. Once that was accomplished I was told to activate the PAARS. So I did. And the world exploded.

From that pitch and bank attitude, the closest path to a wings' level climb was something resembling an outside negative-g barrel roll to the left. My feet rose up off the rudders and I whacked my shins on the bottom of the instrument panel as I was suspended upside down by the lap belt. All the dirt from the floor came up in a cloud, and what looked like a white seagull flew across my face and over my left shoulder.

After everything had settled down I disengaged the PAARS and looked over at the chase ship with both pilots still shaking with laughter. *Ha, ha, guys, very funny; you got me good that time!*

Now that it was time to head back for the approaches I realized that the "seagull" had been my approach book. I could just barely see it behind my seat way down to the left. It looked out of reach. In pilot training everything is normally strapped to a knee, but in the fighter world that would make for too much clutter, so pubs and guides are tucked aside until needed. Since the weather was good I normally wouldn't have cared and could retrieve the book after landing, but I needed that thing to fly the approaches. My in-flight guide had ended up back there, too, but I could live without that for the rest of the sortie. I considered doing the approaches from memory, but that would have been stupid on a check ride. I could have had the guys in the T-38 read me the appropriate data from the approach plate in their jet, but I wasn't about to give them the satisfaction.

I had to reach that thing.

So I loosened my straps and leaned over to snake my left arm through the maze of wires, struts, and other protrusions toward the book. At full stretch I could just get the ends of two fingers over the corner of a page and began to draw it back toward me slowly. Then my watch band got caught on something and I was stuck.

Just great! My check ride was turning into a Laurel & Hardy skit. In the meantime I couldn't answer the radio calls because the transmit button is on the left side of the cockpit and I needed to keep my right hand on the stick to fly the jet. I didn't want to let go of the book for fear that it would fall farther down under the seat entirely out of reach. I was stuck like a kid with his hand caught in a cookie jar.

It cost me another circle in the area, but I eventually got my act together and did (as far as I'm concerned) a dazzling job of hiding any of these further embarrassments from Smear and Beav. The subsequent approaches and pattern work all went well.

As far as the air force was concerned I was now a qualified F-117 pilot—after just five sorties and a check (compared with 149 sorties and six checks in pilot training). Not combat-ready yet, just able to operate the jet safely without an instructor on my wing. But with that important hurdle securely behind me, I could now begin to concentrate on the weapon systems.

Our class was scheduled to graduate on July 22—just a couple of weeks away. It would be good to be assigned to an operational squadron again. That morning we sat through several hours of weapons academics. After class we spent some time planning for our Bandit party the next night. Normally the party would have been the previous week, the first Friday after our sorties, but we'd been preempted by both the monsoon party and the long Fourth of July holiday.

* * *

Probably because of the secrecy shrouding the early days of the Black Jet, the idea behind Bandit numbers, and the origin of the F-117 designation itself, have never really been explained. While several of the details are still fuzzy, here is my best guess:

For years all of us in the operational squadrons knew that something was going on out in the desert. Pilots would disappear for a few years and then not talk about what they had been doing. An entire wing of A-7s on the ramp was readily visible to anyone visiting Nellis AFB, even though the A-7 had supposedly been retired from the USAF inventory a few years previously. And the A-7s didn't seem to fly very often. The few people who admitted to being in the unit were unusually evasive about what they did and where the vast majority of the people were during normal working hours. Something was going on out there but we didn't know what it was, and we had been taught not to speculate publicly. Naturally we suspected some secret aircraft program without knowing its name. The designation F-117 wasn't mentioned until 1988.

Several years prior to 1988, the air force had announced the Northrop F-20 Tiger Shark, skipping a number in the current series. It was widely assumed that the designation F-19 had been set aside for that secret program out in the desert, but Northrop had simply wanted their new product to be designated as the F-20 to give the impression of belonging to an entirely new generation of aircraft to help with overseas sales. The modern designation F-19 had simply been skipped over and the F-117 wasn't a part of the modern numbering system at all. Under the pre-1962 designation system, the last jet publicly announced had been the F-111.

From 1977 to 1989, the air force ran a brilliant clandestine project at Tonopah code-named Constant Peg. For more than a decade captured, acquired, or purloined Soviet fighters were flown as training aids by a secret squadron of U.S. aggressor pilots. More than fifteen thousand sorties were flown against U.S. Air Force, Navy, and Marine Corps pilots. Real U.S. aircraft and tactics were tested, and U.S. combat aircrew were trained, against actual adversary jets. The variety of MiG-17s, MiG-21s, and MiG-23s were operated by about a dozen or two U.S. pilots at any given time. Instead of call signs, each pilot was assigned a "Bandit" number once he was checked out, eventually reaching Bandit-69.

When it came time to find a home for the clandestine stealth-fighter unit, Tonopah was the natural choice. The two units overlapped for several years and shared many of the same security, record-keeping, and operational procedures. The established MiG unit also allowed the new stealth guys to share in the Bandit number tradition.

To keep the two groups separate, the operational stealth guys started with the number Bandit-150. Pilots trained solely to act in a test capacity at Edwards or Palmdale used the series of Bandit numbers from 100 to 149. For record keeping, the plane was given the cover name F-117A, and later, to avoid having to republish all of the paperwork, the designation was carried over to the real world when the jet's existence was announced to the public in 1988.

Twenty-two years later I'm number 545, which is the 394th in the series. Of the many career paths thought to be exclusive, a bit of an example may be in order. On any given Sunday more NFL players will suit up to compete than the total number of pilots ever allowed to fly the F-117 in two-plus decades. NASA recruits what it considers to be the best-of-the-best test pilots and scientists to fly in space. The number of people selected to become astronauts this year was twenty-five. By comparison, our class had added only the tenth, eleventh, and twelfth members to the F-117 community that year. (Eventually seventeen of the eighteen who started training in 1998 would graduate.)

* * *

The day of the Bandit party, we sat through a few more hours of weapons academics before setting up for the festivities. Tradition within our community requires the individuals getting their numbers to host their own party. Any previously numbered Bandit, no matter where they were stationed at the time, was invited and only Bandits, or other F-117 students, were allowed in.

Part tradition, and part college fraternity, events like Bandit parties are endemic throughout the fighter pilot communities. Many people I've met are genuinely baffled by fighter pilot culture. They expect a rowdy drunkard or knuckle-dragging Cro-Magnon warrior and are surprised to meet a teetotaling church deacon or Ivy League engineer. Conversely, others hold an image of the virtuous silver knight, selflessly putting himself in harm's way to defend liberty across the globe, and are then confronted by a seemingly overgrown fraternity brother.

So, what is a fighter pilot? While no single definition will ever suffice, here are a few generalities. A fighter pilot is almost always aggressive, but with control. He is adaptable and stress-tolerant (and generally intolerant of those who aren't). Considered to be reasonably intelligent without being an intellectual—though often with triple the book collection of the English teacher next door. Usually more intrigued by technical versus artistic pursuits, competitive even if quiet about it, part animal lover and part hunter, and a workaholic who thinks nothing of working ten to twelve hours a day for years on end and who is truly amazed once back in the civilian world that people expect you to leave work after only eight hours regardless of whether the task is finished. Very often meticulously organized and systematic, action-oriented versus contemplative, goal-oriented, and the one in the crowd who makes a decision and starts off toward a solution regardless of whether (and probably not caring if) anyone else is following. He is someone likely to assume responsibility without being asked, sarcastic *and* self-deprecating, a coarse frat boy *and* the defender of liberty, a studious technician *and* a steely-eyed killer who lives to turn bad guys into a cloud of "hair, teeth, and a pink mist."

So, is he the humble born-again church deacon, loudmouthed agnostic, carousing bachelor, unassuming family man, or the father who has trained his three-year-old daughter to respond to the question "How many different kinds of airplanes are there?" with "Two—fighters and targets"? Which one of these characteristics defines a "fighter pilot"? Confusingly, the answer is "All of the above." Our culture doesn't fit into any conventional cubbyhole.

As a fighter pilot I suppose that I should apologize for not shedding much light on the question. But then again, as a fighter pilot I really couldn't care less. We are what we are.

The master of ceremonies for a Bandit party is usually the 7th's Opso, and the script always follows the same outline. The crowd is welcomed to the Goat Sucker Bar and, with a nod toward the old sign salvaged from Tonopah, reminded of the original bar during the black days. Back then it had been known as the TOCACL (pronounced *toe-cackle*), which stood for "Tonopah Officer's Club and Chinese Laundry." I've never picked up the story behind the name.

The Bandit with the lowest number will then be recognized. Unless there are guests in town for a function, that usually turns out to be Klaus, though sometimes it may be Pete. Then there will be a reading from the 7th's history or, more likely, stealth lore. Stealth lore is usually about the early development of the F-117 or some anecdote from the black days at Tonopah.

The reading for our party was the story of one of the earliest attempts to create a stealthy jet: a program code-named Passport Visa. Back in 1958 at Wright-Patterson AFB, sheets of flexible RAM were glued over the entire structure of a Lockheed T-33 trainer, as much as it could carry and still, barely, become airborne. The results were disappointing. The aircraft behaved poorly and was dangerously unstable. More importantly, all of that RAM still wasn't enough to significantly mask the jet's radar signature. So the program was discontinued and the dubious young test pilot, Gus Grissom, happily left the project behind to take part in his next assignment as one of the original seven Mercury Astronauts

The painful part of a Bandit party comes next. Like those before us, the three of us got up in front of the crowd and were presented a glass-bottomed pewter mug of a foul concoction known to every fighter pilot in the Air Force as Jeremiah Weed. Weed is supposedly a cheap, high-octane liqueur. But most of us suspect that it is really the tail-end waste product of kerosene distillation. The only reason why Weed can possibly remain in production is that fighter squadrons keep buying it to abuse their new members. This tooth-enamel-dissolving "stuff" is often kept under lock and key. Not because anyone would dream of stealing any, but to prevent commando-style raids from sneaking in secretly to water it down prior to a naming.

In any case, the three of us were collectively to empty this mug in three swallows. No allowance was made for being a small class of only three versus the usual five or six, and the mug was filled to the brim. If there was any left at the end, if the mug left your lips once you had started to drink, or if any was spilled, there was someone standing by with a fresh bottle for an "in-flight refueling," and we'd get to start all over. Every single person in the audience, other than the new junior class, had already stood their ground on that stage. So our success on the first attempt was worthy of a round of applause.

Our reward was the presentation of our Bandit coins. This was special. Superficially, mine looks like any other challenge coin. It is embossed with images of the F-117 on both sides, and has various slogans around the edges. The unique part is the number 545 stamped on the back. Only one coin in the world is just like this, and it belongs solely to me. We carry these on our person constantly and are prepared to present them whenever challenged by the holder of another coin. Our first challenge was right then as everyone in the crowd presented their own coins before coming up to shake our hands.

CHAPTER 6

The Black Sheep

Pilot's axiom: The only time you have too much
fuel is when your plane is on fire.

THE FOLLOWING DAY, THE THREE of us went back to the
squadron to clean up after our party. That took a while, as it
looked like much of the remaining food had exploded over the walls
at some point during the evening. My share of the leftovers came out
to be about 18 inches of big sandwich, a case of mixed beer brands,
and a couple bags of potato chips.

A few days later, I flew my first surface-attack flight (SA-1).
Before climbing into the jet I had to make a quick dash back to the
squadron after realizing I'd forgotten my photo pack in the briefing
room. A photo pack is a series of black-and-white images printed
out on letter paper with our run-in lines and targets displayed. I
momentarily considered doing the route by memory, but discretion
won out and I made a run for it.

The ride was a ball. I did pretty well and scored simulated "hits" on all but one of the off-range camera targets and got all four BDU-33 practice bombs off during the range work. We normally get to make simulated attacks on twelve to fifteen buildings, towers, or bridges along the route using only the IRADS—infrared acquisition and designation system—and camera. Once on the range we did the same thing, but actually swung the bomb bay doors to release little 25-pound BDU-33s.

BDUs (bomb dummy units) are essentially blue cast-iron bowling pins with fins and smoke spotting charges on the rear. They never really hit particularly close to where they are aimed in this jet. They simply "exercise the system" to ensure that the release signal makes it all the way from the little red button under my thumb on the control stick down through the computers to the weapon pylon in the bomb bay. All in all I had a great time.

This had been the first time I'd dropped even practice bombs since leaving Egypt five years earlier, and the last time I had been allowed to really concentrate on bombing had been in the F-16 at Homestead Air Force Base a decade before. One of my last sorties there had been as No. 4 in a formation representing our wing at TAC's "Long Rifle" Gunnery Meet. I was having a good day and won the 10-degree dive-bomb plaque and came in second place in the overall completion (missing first by one stupid bomb with a bad fin). Bombing had always been one of my strengths in the F-16 and would likely be again in the F-117.

The next day's flight also went well, but the day after that was tough going. We were fighting weather the whole way and barely got a tenth of our planned events done. I suppose that it was a good training experience anyway. The real fun would begin the following Monday. We were each scheduled to drop an inert 500-pound laser-guided bomb—a GBU-12. It would be a full-up device, other than the explosive charge being replaced by an equal weight of cement.

After work, Mauler and I went to the club to unwind over a few beers and trade weather-avoidance stories from the last sortie. While we were there a lieutenant colonel, G-Man, strolled over to introduce himself as our new commander. That was news to us.

We were apparently headed to the 8th Fighter Squadron—the Black Sheep. The three F-117 squadrons on base, the 7th, 8th, and 9th, all traced their lineage to the 49th Fighter Group famed for their World War II combat exploits in the Pacific. Amongst many other notables, the 49th had been home to America's greatest ace, Dick Bong of P-38 fame. Had I been asked, I probably would have picked the 9th for the very trivial reason of liking the way their patch looked, but otherwise I didn't have a preference.

G-Man looked a little perplexed that we didn't already know our squadron assignment. But he shrugged it off with a sort of growl and said, "Well, you're Sheep now. Let me introduce you to the others." He called over a half dozen pilots from around the bar, who scrambled at his beckon.

I'd met him before and had heard some of the stories. G-Man looked like someone who might have been a boxer once. He was stocky with perpetually squinting eyes over a smile that would make the Cheshire Cat proud. The almost universal impression most people get on their first meeting is that the guy might just be a bit full of himself. But that wasn't on the mark.

He was a warrior, fighter pilot, and natural-born character. Talk to anyone in the stealth world long enough and eventually the conversation will get around to "Okay, I've got a G-Man story." After getting to know him for a while you could love him or not, be impressed by his many accomplishments and awards or not—but you were going to notice.

He had his own way of communicating. To cut off a line of argument he may have tired of he might thrust out his arm and turn his head away while barking "Talk to the hand," or, if he were really serious, "Talk to the doggie-doctor." There was no appeal once the "doggie-doctor" had been invoked. So off we'd go, comparing notes as to what we thought he meant when he told us to go fix the "hooter-schloggan." A target was never attacked or engaged, it was "schwacked." And if the result was particularly impressive, then it had been "bodaciously schwacked."

One thing everyone could always agree on was that G-Man was *always, 100 percent,* on the side of his team. And make no mistake, *his* team was the 8th. If he had any hobbies or interests, outside of the squadron and club, I never heard of them. Other than his family, the true love of his life was his command. He seemed to have been created to command the Sheep, and as far as he was concerned, the Sheep had been created for him to command. He told everyone who would listen that his nightmare was that this tour of duty would end before he had an opportunity to lead the 8th into combat.

The following Monday was our heavyweight bomb delivery to the range. We each got a full-scale LGB (laser-guided bomb) to drop. LGBs are our bread and butter and the primary reason for operating a fleet of F-117s in the first place. The Tritonal explosive had been replaced by cement, but otherwise this was a complete GBU-12 weapon with a Paveway-2 laser-guidance kit fitted. The Paveway series dated back to Vietnam and was specifically designed to hit very small targets—such as bridges.

Bridges have been the bane of aerial attacks since the first time a bomb was hand-pitched out of an open cockpit. Bridges are critically important chokepoints for an enemy's mobility and logistics, which makes them prime targets. On the other hand there are relatively few of them and are in fixed locations, easy to find, and desperately important to the enemy, so they are always heavily defended. To top it off, they are damn hard to break since they are narrow, extremely sturdy, and usually surrounded by shock-absorbing bodies of water.

In Vietnam there was a road/railroad bridge in Hanoi called the Paul Doumer Bridge. Over it ran four of the five major rail lines in North Vietnam. More specifically, it was the only rail link to Haiphong Harbor. A mile and half long but only thirty-eight feet wide, the bridge averaged twenty-six freight trains every day and infinitely more trucks. Naturally it was heavily defended. Three hundred AAA positions were fielded by the North Vietnamese with everything from 37mm to 100mm anti-aircraft cannons, about eighty-five SA-2 SAM sites and MiGs to boot.

In 1967, the first raid involved thirty-six F-105s and dozens of supporting aircraft dropping conventional iron bombs to take out just three spans of the bridge. It was back in operation in about seven weeks. Subsequent heroic raids succeeded in closing the bridge for only short periods of time, and the losses were enormous. Eventually, it was left alone for four years. Then in 1972, a single raid by a handful of F-4 Phantoms dropping LGBs with the new Paveway seeker heads put the bridge out of commission for the remainder of the war. Precision-guided bombs have been a mainstay of modern air forces ever since.

The principal of the Paveway guidance system was simplicity itself. The target could be designated by having a laser spot beamed at it by the dropping aircraft, a second aircraft, or even a troop on the ground hidden nearby. The bomb's seeker head was designed to filter out everything in the world except for the specific frequency of that laser. That spot became its universe. Its "eye" was divided into four quadrants—up and down, left and right. As the bomb fell it made simple decisions. If it saw the spot to its left it commanded the guidance fins to turn hard left with a bang until the spot was on the right. Then the fins would be commanded to turn hard right with a bang until the spot was on the left and so on—back and forth all the way. The up and down commands worked the same way. It was called bang-bang guidance. In this manner, the bomb would wiggle its way toward the spot until impact. It wasn't especially sophisticated or efficient, but it worked. The Paveway-2 kits we use now are just refinements of the original system used in Vietnam.

Most of my flight went pretty well other than an occasional tendency to ham-fist the tracking button on the practice targets. Each jet has its own personality and sensitivity. The tracker requires you to be smooth and precise, and I wasn't applying the right "touch" for this jet. The problem popped up again on the heavy pass after I had released the bomb. The laser spot just wouldn't stay still for me. I did some frantic last-minute corrections, and the bomb hit the wing tip of the F-4 target hulk. I had gotten lucky, but my tracking technique still needed work.

The next day was even more eventful. I flew the AR-1 profile. On this ride we'd become qualified for aerial refueling in the F-117. The check-out process was pretty simple. Since we could only fly solo, a pilot could either refuel safely the first time or he couldn't—pass/ fail. This was also the only training ride where we were chased by an instructor in another F-117. A T-38 doesn't have the endurance to chase the entire AAR—air-to-air refueling—profile. The refueling track was east of the Sacramento Mountains over by Roswell.

Compared with F-16s or EF-111s, the jet wasn't especially hard to refuel, but it had its quirks. The power response was a little lacking, pushing through the bow wave of the tanker felt different, and there was just a bit of instability while on the boom. The heavy canopy framing got in the way while looking up at the tanker and was an annoyance. The refueling receptacle was well behind the pilot's head, so judging closure the last ten feet or so was a bit of a trick—nothing terrible though. The old "Wobbly Goblin" reputation was obviously made up by someone who had never flown the jet or, at least, not recently. I plugged, backed off to reset, and then accomplished the entire process all over again three separate times.

The route and bombing afterward went well also. Because of the fuel I'd taken earlier, there was some excess after returning to the pattern, so I decided to practice a few instrument approaches. My next challenge occurred after the second low approach.

I had raised the gear handle and watched the indicator lights for the left main gear and the nose gear indicate "up and locked," but there remained a glaring red light in the gear handle and a little green light on the panel indicating that the right main gear was still down. As I climbed away I asked the control tower what they saw, and they confirmed that my right main gear had not retracted. One lonely little wheel was pointed down into the wind. I was riding a 35,000-pound unicycle at 250 miles per hour.

Not good.

Only one gear handle is in the cockpit, and no way is available to extend or retract any gear in particular without all three legs doing exactly the same thing. It wasn't supposed to be possible, but I feared that the sequencer had somehow become reversed for that one gear so when the handle was repositioned, the two good gear legs would extend and the right would retract. I knew that couldn't be it, but every gear malfunction the checklist referenced, other than the handle just being stuck, involved the gear being stuck in the up position, not the down.

In short order I became the star attraction of the base. Everyone in the pattern was essentially told to land or get out of the way. The OG was interrupted from a meeting (which he hated) with the question, "Do you know that one of your jets is flying around the pattern with only one landing gear?"

While orbiting around the outside downwind pattern I reviewed my options in the checklist. The obvious response, Plan A, was to use the emergency extension system, a one-shot pneumatic bottle,

BEFORE LANDING CONSIDERATIONS
1. FUEL SYSTEM – INERT (IF AVAILABLE)
2. REMOVE OR LAND PAST BARRIER UNLESS OTHERWISE INDICATED
3. USE LOW SINK RATE LANDING
4. DEPLOY DRAG CHUTE AFTER NOSE (GEAR) IS ON THE RUNWAY

 **NOSE GEAR UP OR UNSAFE STUB NOSE GEAR OR BLOWN/ DAMAGED NOSE GEAR TIRE**	**LOWER NOSE GENTLY**
 **NOSE GEAR UP AND ONE MAIN GEAR UP OR UNSAFE**	**IF GEAR CAN BE RETRACTED, RAISE GEAR AND LAND** • **A/R SELECTOR SWITCH – ALL/FUS ONLY** • **ENGINES OFF AT TOUCHDOWN** **IF GEAR CANNOT BE RETRACTED** • **EJECT** **IF EJECTION NOT POSSIBLE, APPROACH END ARRESTMENT** • **HOOK DOWN** • **ENGINES OFF AFTER AIRCRAFT STOPPED**
 **ONE MAIN GEAR UP OR UNSAFE**	**IF APPROACH END ARRESTMENT AVAILABLE** • **HOOK DOWN** • **ENGINES OFF AFTER AIRCRAFT STOPPED** **IF APPROACH END ARRESTMENT NOT POSSIBLE AND GEAR CAN BE RETRACTED, RAISE GEAR AND LAND** • **A/R SELECTOR SWITCH – ALL/FUS ONLY** • **ENGINES OFF AT TOUCHDOWN** **IF APPROACH END ARRESTMENT NOT POSSIBLE AND GEAR CANNOT BE RETRACTED** • **EJECT**
 **BOTH MAIN GEAR UP**	• **A/R SELECTOR SWITCH – ALL/FUS ONLY** • **ENGINES OFF AT TOUCHDOWN**
 **ONE OR BOTH STUB MAINS OR BLOWN/DAMAGED MLG TIRE(S) SCISSORS LINK FAILURE**	**LAND OFF-CENTER ON GEAR DOWN/ GOOD TIRE SIDE** • **ANTI-SKID – OFF**
 **ALL GEAR UP OR UNSAFE**	• **A/R SELECTOR SWITCH – ALL/FUS ONLY** • **ENGINES OFF AT TOUCHDOWN**

Landing Gear System Emergencies Landing Guide

and hope that it worked on the good gear without moving the bad gear. There wasn't any obvious reason why it shouldn't work, but then again there wasn't any obvious reason why I should be in this predicament in the first place. If that didn't work, the checklist went on to provide nice little pictures of the jet in various landing configurations with the recommended course of action.

The generic recommendation to apply to any gear problem is to flood the fuel tanks with an inert gas to suppress any tendency toward fire if the gear were to collapse after landing. Unfortunately, the gas used for the INERT function is regulated by the ozone-protection laws, and though readily available in commercial fire extinguishers, the administration at the time had forbidden us to fill the tanks. We only had permission to pressurize this safety system during wartime, so the tank was empty and that option wasn't available. The instructions went on to say that I should try to touch down as gently as possible *(Well . . . duh!)* and that I should deploy the drag chute after everything that could touch the ground—wheels, wing tips, nose, whatever—was touching the ground.

Those were the instructions that applied to all gear problems, anyway. For the unicycle picture that matched my current configuration in particular, the checklist recommended that if I could retract that one remaining gear I should land on the belly. But the handle was already up, so if that were possible I wouldn't have been reading this page to begin with. The second recommendation was an attention grabber:

IF GEAR CANNOT BE RETRACTED: EJECT

Okay.

Normally I would have an implicit faith in the ACES-II ejection seat. I thought that it was the best one ever fielded by the air force. The parachute is built into the headrest of the seat, and once the ejection handles have been pulled, everything is automatic. The seat knows the altitude and airspeed it is falling at and will initiate seat-man separation and the parachute deployment sequence in the most survivable manner. The nagging doubt in the back of my mind didn't concern the seat, but the jet's history. To this date, including the two Have Blue prototypes, a total of eight of the sixty-one Nighthawks built had crashed. That record for a modern aircraft, frankly, was dismal. The very first crash, HB-1001, had occurred because of a damaged main landing gear—the right main gear coincidentally. The pilot survived the ejection but was so injured during the process that he never flew again. In fact, two of the eight pilots involved in the crashes had been permanently disabled. Three never got out of their jets at all and died upon impact. Only three had walked away relatively uninjured. (In the context of fighter ejections, the term "relatively uninjured" means bruises, lacerations requiring stitches, and an occasional broken arm or leg—as they will eventually heal.) Three in eight uninjured wasn't great odds. That wasn't necessarily the seat's fault. Ejection would still be infinitely preferable to a manual bailout. If that had even been possible, and attempted, the poor schmuck would have been diced into julienne fries by either the intake grilles or the V-tail.

So, bad enough . . . but there was one last recommendation:

IF EJECTION NOT POSSIBLE: APPROACH END ARRESTMENT

Surprisingly, engaging the approach end arrestment cable was considered the worst possible option. Evidently extending the tail hook (hidden away in the belly behind that explosive $50,000 panel) and flying into the approach end cable, which is how navy jets stop every day, was considered even more dangerous than throwing away a limited national asset while trusting my butt to a rocket-propelled ejection seat and a parachute.

This page sucked!

My personal Plan B, assuming I couldn't get three gears down, was to recall the tanker from over Roswell, if it was still airborne, and start taking fuel to slow this whole thing down while we sorted through other options. So it was back to the emergency extension page.

By this time a T-38 that happened to be in the pattern had rejoined on me (dangerously low on fuel himself) to look for other signs of damage. He watched as I held my breath and performed the emergency extension procedures.

Anticlimactically, the other two gear legs extended properly and the right main gear stayed where it was. It still wasn't to be trusted, but it was at least a configuration that was considered "land-able." I set myself up for a long, smooth straight-in approach, touched down as gently as I could, lowered the nose, and deployed the drag chute.

The SOF (supervisor of flying) called down from the tower to remind me not to turn the jet at all while jettisoning the chute to avoid any side loads on the gear. No problem. The book answer was to then sit there in the middle of the runway, with engines running to maintain hydraulic pressure, until maintenance troops could install safety pins into all of the landing gear legs.

Unfortunately, because of the same malfunction that had started this whole incident, maintenance couldn't get the pin into the right gear leg. It turned out that the steel armature that physically moves the leg up and down and locks it in place had broken. So I sat a while longer while they hauled out a huge tripod jack. They jacked up the right wing right there on the runway before letting me shut down the engines. Without being able to pin the gear, there was a chance that the down-side hydraulic pressure was all that was holding the right leg where it was and, consequently, that entire side of the plane up now that I had landed—hence, the jack.

One of the IPs later said that he didn't think that I was experiencing a very serious problem because I had never sounded excited over the radio. I considered that a high compliment. For fighter pilots, it's a personal objective always to sound bored over the radio no matter what is happening around you. Some of the early tapes of test work back in the glory days at Edwards AFB in the 1940s and 1950s captured very calm comments from pilots wrestling their aircraft all the way to ground impact. Maintaining your composure during an emergency and fighting the problem all the way to the end is a much valued characteristic we all strive for.

Once as a young lieutenant, I had been tasked as a first responder to accompany the initial crash recovery team to the site of a CT-39 wreck at Wilkes-Barre/Scranton International Airport in Pennsylvania. The accident and subsequent fire had killed the then current commander of TAC, Gen. Jerome F. O'Malley. A handful of others and I had been assigned the grizzly task of recovering the bodies of the five people on board and gathering the preliminary evidence and tower tapes to be preserved for the full investigation team. The general had been in the left seat of the aircraft acting as the PIC (pilot in command) at the time of impact.

He had fought like a real pilot, with the control yoke still in his hand to the end. How did we know that? Because it was still there! We had to cut off part of the yoke to get him out of what was left of the cockpit. Later on, when I got to that part of the story while talking to the guys in my squadron, they would imperceptibly nod and relax an infinitesimal bit. Somehow that made it a tiny fraction more acceptable, that at least he had died as a true aviator, keeping his cool and fighting to the last moment to save his jet and passengers—and he had never once sounded excited over the radio.

* * *

Thursday, July 23, 1998. That morning saw the final flights of class 98-HTH. It was the SA-5 profile (much modified) through a lot of weather. As was customary in fighter units, we had a bet riding on our performance that day. One of the guys suggested a $10 bet for the TOT (time over target, the precise moment at weapon impact) versus the more traditional quarter-a-bomb/nickel-a-bullet wager.

I was lucky and everything came together for me. I popped every target, and my timing for the money shot was within a second, so I won the bet by an easy margin. After work, I sprung for beer at the club with my winnings.

The next morning, we went in to have our class picture taken for graduation. Norm had presented us with a very odd terracotta sculpture that he had picked up in Mexico. It was some sort of impressionist pottery with three large pink orbs entwined together. Other than looking vaguely obscene, the idea was that it represented the last class to go through the OCIP (offensive capability improvement program) course. The OCIP jets we had been flying used the old B-52 inertial guidance unit with three beryllium spheres spinning as gyroscopes. The new RNIP modification replaced all those moving parts with lasers. So he wanted us to be remembered as the "last class with beryllium balls."

Afterward there was a short ceremony in the 7th where we received F-117 shoulder patches and were presented with our Bandit certificates. These were identical to those given out during the black days before the F-117's existence was acknowledged. Nowhere is any type of aircraft actually identified.

CERTIFICATE OF FLIGHT

> With our enthusiasm and admiration,
> for his exceptional skill in the performance
> of a remarkable aeronautical feat,

We do hereby recognize and commend
Maj William Bradley O'Connor
His command of the aerosphere with special
technical competence and physical fortitude
earns him a lofty and privileged place
in the hierarchy of pilots.
Thus becoming an aviator who has
successfully joined the ranks of the
NIGHTHAWKS

We were then told to gather our flight gear and were unceremoni-ously shuffled out the door to make room for the next incoming class. That afternoon, at the 8th FS, we were formally introduced to the squadron at a "hail and farewell" party in the squadron bar. Most of the guys were pretty easygoing. G-Man was still a force of nature in front of an audience. The operations officer, Woody, seemed the more level-headed. Usually the commander is the calm and quiet personality within a squadron while the Opso plays the part of enforcer. In contrast to G-Man, Woody seemed very reserved for the job.

In any case, the party was fun and the beer was free. One tradition the Sheep have is "the bullet." Like the challenge coin, which all F-117 pilots carry, pilots of the 8th also carry a chromed .30-06 rifle round (blank, of course) with their call signs and Bandit numbers engraved upon them. Like the coin, this was carried at all times and could be subject to a challenge by any other holder of a bullet. Unlike the coin, this thing didn't really fit anywhere and was slick, with a tendency to slip through holes in your pocket.

I was now an official member of the 8th, but I did wish our ancestral brethren hadn't named themselves "Sheep." The name goes back to World War II when the 8th was being forced to accept older P-47s cast off from the 7th and 9th as they converted to new

P-38s. The 8th felt as if they were being treated as the "black sheep" of the group. Unfortunately, a rendering of a sheep doesn't translate onto fabric very well. The 9th calls its representation on our patch the "electric poodle."

Near the end of July, I had my first flight with the 8th. It went pretty well, and I enjoyed being out there on my own without an instructor for the first time. I was supposed to have flown the day before and got as far as last chance before I had to abort for a bad heads-up display (HUD). The thing just died on me as I was entering some data. The weather had been crummy anyway, so it was probably just as well.

The next Monday, I flew a 1.4-hour sortie for my upgrade ride to the RNIP system. It was also my first time flying the squadron's regular training route. The usual arrangement for mission planning at Holloman was that a single pilot in the squadron spent an entire week creating and briefing the week's missions. He created the route on a specialized system called AFMSS (air force mission support system) and loaded it into the EDTM. Helping with this process, and maintaining the equipment, were several experienced civilian contractors. In time of war, a few of these civilians would actually deploy with us.

Then the planner worked with other specialists required to pull the whole thing together. First came the enlisted targeteers. A targeteer is someone specially trained in identifying critical elements and vulnerable points on a target, estimating the probability of collateral damage, and suggesting ways to avoid that and in the preparation of the actual target photos required for the attack.

A weaponeer, usually an officer from the vault, would suggest the best number, type, combination of bombs, and fuze settings required to achieve the desired results. He would also have an input on the final run-in heading required, which in turn feeds the route-planning process. Intel and weather representatives would also get speaking parts at the brief.

The planner is responsible to pick the targets and photos, build in a few glitches and challenges to be overcome, and present the route to the pilots twice each day. Though there is a small cadre of pilots (and a *tiny* cadre of EWOs) who specialize in this work and will be responsible for most of the wartime planning, everyone is expected to take their turns to become more familiar with the process.

The planner didn't fly at all that week, but there were enough of us in the squadron that each pilot usually only had to be the "fish in the barrel" a couple times a year. For the rest of us, this was pure luxury. Unlike any other community I've been involved with, the pilots walk into the briefing cold. We showed up at brief time without having done any preparation at all, and a complete mission was simply handed to us. All we had to do was fly it.

My photo work and targeting was getting better, and the new RNIP system would be a dream to work with *after* I became a little more familiar with it. But at that time, some aspects of its operation still fell in the "black magic" category. With the integrated GPS system, the inertial platform didn't drift at all, and the only flaws to be dealt with were those the planner had deliberately inserted. These might include incorrect target elevations, upside-down photos, wrong coordinates, and look-alike targets. I was on the schedule for another early flight the next day.

Over dinner that night I watched a show portraying the Egyptian desert. That brought back a lot of memories from my year in the Sinai. Back then, armed only with an aerial map and a history book, several of us would head off into the desert for the weekend to find the ruins of old castles left over from the Crusades or the tank hulks, trench lines, and other debris from more recent wars. As time passes I regret not getting out to explore more often while there. In particular I would have liked seeing more of the monasteries in the south with their ancient libraries, and I should have ventured into the Western Desert more often.

Over the next few days, I became more efficient with the RNIP system. I'd also been working to create a personalized condensed checklist. By the liberal use of abbreviations and acronyms, most of the routine checklist procedures could be compressed to two or three 6x9-inch pages that fit neatly on a kneeboard. This allowed me to leave the complete, and heavy, 2-inch-thick checklist off to the side instead of strapped to my leg and only accessed when needed for emergencies or other unusual circumstances. For some unknown reason these condensed versions were known as "Hooterized" checklists.

One afternoon that week we had a violent thunderstorm. Mauler called saying that half the trees on base had blown over. But there was no damage where I was, and when it was over I was treated to the sight of an incredible double rainbow against the mountains. The cliff face itself was illuminated by the setting sun as background. The air was marvelously fresh and cool and the colors were amazing.

The following Wednesday, I briefed to fly a standard sortie, but was delayed an hour in the jet trying to fix a flight control system problem. Eventually maintenance got the jet up to speed and I taxied out for an abbreviated ride. That afternoon we were hit by another wild thunderstorm. This place might not get very many inches of rain each year, but they all seemed to come at once. You would think that a desert would suck up any moisture, but the water just had no place to go. Great torrents went charging off across seemingly flat areas and down every culvert toward no place in particular.

The next morning, I was rescheduled to have my first mission qualification training (MQT) simulator mission instead of flying. The check ride I had flown with the 7th had only qualified me in the jet. Every fighter pilot had to complete MQT with his squadron before being designated mission-ready and available for deployment. In many cases MQT is more involved—and may take longer—than learning to fly the jet to begin with. Normally, I would have rolled right into MQT as soon as I got to the 8th, but since all of the required sorties occurred at night, the training had been delayed for the monsoon season. There would be another check ride waiting for me at the end of the process before the hardest part, the verification.

A verification usually sucks a couple of weeks out of your life as you immerse yourself in the vault for study, plan a real-world mission on an actual target, rehearse for several days, then brief it on stage to the members of all three squadrons and the wing's leadership. At the end of the brief, you get peppered by dozens of "stump the dummy" questions carefully prepared in advance by members of the audience. At the end of the ordeal, you are asked to leave the room while the audience discusses your performance for an hour or so and takes a vote on whether or not you passed. The process is similar to defending an academic thesis.

The simulator ride went well enough, but the sortie I had given up to Mauler wasn't flown. During his preflight inspection he had walked into one of the weapons' bay baffles and was led away bleeding. No stitches, fortunately. Ducking around a dull black aircraft (consisting only of sharp angles) in the shadows of a hangar often led to this result. I'd suggested that we change his call sign to Gash, but there were too many others around who could also claim that title.

I had planned to observe a practice verification brief that would be presented on Friday, August 7. It would have been great to see an example of what I'd be preparing myself for, but I was bounced out of the audience for lack of a high enough security clearance. I actually held the required level of clearance but since I was new, no one there could vouch for me and I couldn't produce a document proving that I'd already been "read in" to the programs that would be discussed. No skin off my nose, but a missed opportunity to learn some useful information. I made sure that the security office posted a copy of my clearance with the squadron the next day.

All that Friday morning was spent in MQT academics. Some of it was very interesting. They had begun to expand the theories of how stealth worked and how our jet in particular took advantage. Many people just assume that stealth is a physical attribute of a plane created by science and engineering. Though partially true, the reality is more along the lines that stealth isn't simply the result of a series of technologies—the least stealthy aircraft in the world is still invisible if it's hidden behind a mountain. Stealth is a result, and there are many ways to help that result along with technology and tactics. The science of it was fascinating.

By that afternoon, I had sorted out the security clearance problems and was allowed to sit in on the verification. The rehearsed part of the presentation went as expected. But the question-and-answer phase that followed seemed rather tough. I couldn't have answered half of the questions right then.

The following week, I had my mobility bag packed and in the back of the Jeep for a threatened recall as part of an upcoming operational readiness exercise (ORE). An operational readiness inspection (ORI) certifies that a unit is deployable for combat on short notice. A wing commander's "grade" for his time in charge is often measured by the results of an ORI administered by headquarters. And for us to do well enough to keep certified, and for the boss to be promoted again, we'd go through several rounds of practice OREs.

These exercises may start as early as a year in advance of the actual inspection. OREs are a pain and are often referred to as "practice bleeding." While inspections are undoubtedly necessary, a time-proven saying asserts that "No combat-ready unit ever does well on inspections, and no inspection-ready unit is fit for combat." But this is the best we can do.

That week I had tactical sims on Tuesday and Wednesday.

Thursday was just academics and vault study. The normal schedule was wiped clean on Friday so that we could spend the entire day preparing for the ORE. Flying was canceled, and we started the day off by updating our water-survival training in the base pool. This usually involved a bunch of overaged kids playing with rafts and parachutes in the water, practicing with signal mirrors, and then getting to fire off a multitude of flares and smoke grenades. I think we all felt much safer about our chances of drowning in the desert after that.

Then we were marched off (under orders) for the first in a series of anthrax vaccinations. Shots are common in the military, but these things were like getting a slug of Elmer's Glue injected into your arm, and they burned like hell. The med techs tracked which arm was getting the shot so that they could alternate shoulders during the series. For some reason, they were concerned that neither shoulder be exposed to two doses within one month. Naturally, rumors floated around about how safe this stuff might be. The women were all closely questioned as to any chance of their being pregnant. Anything even remotely like "I don't think so" or "I'm not sure" got them excused until a pregnancy test could be done. Oh well, we'd probably all been exposed to stuff more likely to kill us in the long run than this.

That afternoon the OG called all the majors together to offer some career counseling on how to get promoted. We were treated to the uncomfortable experience of another pilot telling us that residence at command and staff schools was more important than experience in a cockpit; that creating projects for publicity was more likely to get you the notice to be promoted than channeling that effort into improving your combat capabilities; that desk time at headquarters was more important to the U.S. Air Force hierarchy than air time in fighter squadrons. I hated hearing any of it being spoken out loud—mostly because it was all true. The boss had long since broken the code and was only trying to pass on his advice, no matter how awkward that advice might sound. Not that it mattered to me—I'd already been passed over. That evening we all went to the club for a few beers and to talk about absolutely anything except what had been happening all day.

The following Monday morning, I got as far as the squadron thinking that I'd get to fly, but the ORE recall kicked off just as I arrived. The first part of most exercises is the "generation" where a number of jets are prepared by maintenance for the deployment, so local flying was canceled in the 8th and 9th. Fortunately for me, the 7th was still in business, so I got a training sim and a flight to upgrade to no-chute landings.

Landing the jet without a drag chute used to be considered an emergency procedure. But over the years the brakes and flight control software have improved enough to get away with it under certain conditions. The primary reason for an intentional no-chute landing is the concern that landing with excessive crosswinds may cause the chute to get entangled with the rudders. Another reason to practice is for the not-uncommon occurrence of a chute failure— the thing doesn't always open. Some of the additional restrictions we had to abide by included having less than 6,000 pounds of fuel or stores on board, a dry runway, no tailwind, no trapped fuel, at least 10,000 feet of runway, and a departure-end barrier available.

The next night I drove down to El Paso to pick up the family from their vacation. Everyone looked tanned and great. We were home just before midnight and had the alarms set to get up at 06:00 to start the new school year. On Thursday, I had a practice emergency procedures sim with OB and then did the actual sim check with Handy on Friday. The ORE ended successfully, and my son and I played with his new flight-simulator program on the computer.

I tried to call the research guys at NASA down in Houston, but couldn't get through to anyone in a position to do hiring. I was checking to see if they, Lockheed, Raytheon, or similar organizations were even remotely interested in any additional master's degrees that I might pick up. I was going to need another career in three years, so it couldn't hurt to start planning.

That week my days were almost entirely consumed by AFMSS academics. AFMSS was the U.S. Air Force's most current mission planning system. Like fads, these systems come and go every couple of years until we just get them working correctly—then we spend a half-billion to start all over with a new program. This one was particularly non-user-friendly, and I didn't think it was a good juncture in my training for it to be introduced.

One morning I was updating my logbook. I figured that I would have to average a little over twenty-four hours of flight time per month here to hit the 5,000-hour mark before retirement. There wasn't anything magical about that number other than being big and round. But since I'd been measuring my career by my flying versus my advancement, it would be quietly gratifying since any colonels or generals in my retirement audience would possess on the order of only 2,500 to 3,000 hours total flight time. (A memorable instructor I had in pilot training used to squelch arguments by proclaiming: "Don't argue with me. I have more time in jets than you do at the dinner table.") Unfortunately, twenty-four hours a month didn't seem likely judging by the current sortie rates.

Toward the end of August I finally got through to the chief research pilot at Houston and learned mostly good things. He didn't care one way or another if I finished another degree. Flying time and experience were all that he asked about—*exactly* what I wanted to hear.

On Friday, August 28, the general spoke to us for a while to dispel rumors and grumblings about our anticipated workload in the coming winter and spring, but ended up confirming most of those rumors as fact. I didn't think that the meeting went over well at all. Instead of the broader view of events we had expected, he seemed overly detail oriented. He spent a great deal of time talking about trash cans, for example. We were warned repeatedly of an extended series of exercises coming up. All units have practice exercises before an inspection, but he made these sound different.

The general had been the wing commander since June. I liked the guy, but I only got there at about the same time he took over, so I had no knowledge of what went on before. I got the distinct impression that he was getting off to an uncomfortable start with this group. The extended series of exercises coming up seem designed to prove something to someone.

This was the third wing he had commanded, which was unusual in itself. His first was the NATO pilot training wing at Sheppard Air Force Base, Texas; the second was the AWACS wing at Elmendorf Air Force Base, Alaska. Coincidentally or not, he took over those other positions after notorious accidents and had the reputation of being a "fixer" within the service, which bothered a lot of people since they didn't think that our performance needed "fixing." Morale wasn't in a very good state.

Afterward I did another MQT sim then waited around for the evening's party at Woody's house. It was a "scheduled no-notice roof stomp"—which is a contradiction in terms.

A roof stomp, sometimes called a "no-notice hospitality check," is a fine old tradition where large numbers of people sneak up on someone's house unannounced after dark and pitch several of the younger/drunker members of the group up on the roof to make noise until the owner opens the front door. When the door is opened, the crowd surges through to take over the house and clean out the cabinets and refrigerator of whatever beer/liquor/wine can be found. A host's "hospitality" is often tested after good news such as command notification, promotion, a plum assignment . . . or as a diversion to fight off a slump in morale.

One of the first stomps I had been involved with was in upstate New York during a blizzard. There was about two feet of snow on the ground already and it was really cold, so we decided just to throw a token lieutenant up on the ranch-style roof for the stomp. It took a while, though, as it was icy and he kept sliding off. Eventually we got him up there, and he was creeping toward the peak as the front door opened and we all crowded inside. Ten minutes later it occurred to someone that Torch wasn't around. It turned out that he had slid off the back side of the roof into some bushes and needed rescuing.

I didn't know it at the time, but my involvement in roof stomps, and personal adjustments to morale, were both about to take an upward vector.

CHAPTER 7

Promotion

*It is always better to be lucky than to be good;
after all, you can only be so good, but
luck can get you out of anything.*

O N MONDAY, THE LAST DAY of August, I was at work at
05:00 for a brief and my first flight in two weeks. The sortie had
been modified for MQT, but followed one of the standard squadron
routes that everyone else would be flying. It was good to get back in
the air again and see that my targeting skills were improving. I even
got to slew my sensors over toward Cannon AFB for a while to look
down on our old neighborhood.

My afternoon was spent getting fitted for a new survival vest,
helmet, standard oxygen mask, and a chemical warfare (CW)
oxygen mask. The new CW masks, while still cumbersome, were
infinitely better than the old fireman-style masks we used to have.
Hopefully, everything would be ready and back in locker 19 before

the next day's exercise. Not a bad day at all. But the evening was to hold one of the bigger surprises of my career.

After a leisurely dinner at home, we were settling down for the evening. The kids had had their first day of swimming lessons with the local team that afternoon and had enjoyed it. I was a competitive swimmer even before high school and continued on with the varsity team at Columbia. I never made it to the National championships, but made finals in the Ivy's each year and Eastern's once. Until flying came along I lived for swimming. So, vicariously, I was getting as much pleasure from this as they were.

The familial bliss was interrupted by a tremendous pounding from out front. It sounded like four or five people were trying to break down the door with their fists. My first thought was that a bunch of drunks en route to a party had stopped at the wrong address. It turned out that I was partially correct. Everyone was working at getting drunk, but they had exactly the right address.

When Bets opened the door the floodgates burst as G-Man, Woody, Speedy, Stump, T-Dub, and a dozen others poured in. The only recognizable words being shouted were G-Man's bellow.

"Is this the residence of the *former* Major O'Connor?"

I was slow on the uptake, but Bets figured out the score right away, said "Yesssss!" and did a little dance right there in the entryway. Speedy exploded in laughter at the sight and later proclaimed it "a great air force moment." It really took me a few minutes to understand that they were all here to congratulate me on being promoted to lieutenant colonel. By some bizarre twist of fate, my name had appeared on the promotion roster released that afternoon.

There had to be some mistake.

I didn't believe that they were playing a poor joke on me; they obviously believed the news. Instead, I was trying to explain to them why it had to be an error. For all practical purposes, no one gets promoted above the zone, especially with only a P on the recommendation. Maybe they had misread the name.

But there it was on the printout—William Bradley O'Connor, 8th Fighter Squadron, 49th Fighter Wing, Holloman AFB, NM. Part of my surprise was that I could honestly say that I hadn't even been tracking that promotion cycle and had no idea that a roster was being released. It was only by a quirk that someone in the 8th had bothered to check for my name.

Since the number of officers within any grade is fixed by law, every promotion roster is ordered by seniority. As a number of officers already holding that rank are either promoted or retire, an equal number of people on the roster can move up to take their places. Five years earlier as a major-select, with a date of rank in December within my year group, my line number had been 2,081, and I'd had to wait fourteen months for everyone with a lower number to shuffle up. Now my number was thirty-four. I'd be on the first round of promotions from this roster. In hindsight, coming from the last month of my previous year group to the first month of this one, I'd lost only one month of status. The harder part would be to jump-start my attitude and ambition after having spent a full year thinking that I'd been left behind. When I'd gotten the disappointing news the previous year, while deployed to Al Kharj Air Base in Saudi Arabia, General Rayburn had mentioned that of the ten eligible majors at Al Kharj only one had made the list. Only one-of-ten officers actually flying sorties in the U.S. Air Force's only combat zone had been deemed promotion-worthy. I had joined the service to fly and had done just that, and wouldn't have traded any of my flying assignments for the rank, but I still wanted the recognition and respect I felt I'd earned.

The news was slow to sink in. As an ABZ guy with only a P on the recommendation, my odds had to have been around 2 or 3 percent to have been selected. I seem to remember that twenty-five of more than a thousand or so ABZ eligible had made the cut last year. Only days earlier I had been on the phone trying to nail down a retirement job. Now I was back in the game through at least my twenty-eighth year of service—and the potential for another eleven years of flying.

I wondered what made my record stand out this time when it hadn't last year. Maybe I had been right on the edge and had just squeaked over this time. G-Man didn't have any answers, but just pronounced, "Who cares? A wrong has been righted."

Overly generous no doubt, but I wasn't going to argue. While the chances of being struck by lightning are small, that bolt still has to come down somewhere.

The next morning we were all at work early for the mass brief. Everyone who had one was wearing his sand-colored desert flight suit and playing the game enthusiastically. Of course my mood couldn't have been much better, so the week just flew by. Hodgie called with congratulations from his exchange with the navy at Naval Air Station Whidbey Island. Cootch, in Alaska, got our answering machine. The colonels on base were all quietly cornering me and pumping questions trying to figure out what happened. The rules that they all lived by and had thrived upon had been altered somehow.

"No—just a P on my recommendation. . . . No, I've never done a staff tour . . . No, sir, really, I don't have a sponsor out there." That last bit of information was cause for open disbelief.

The *Air Force Times* that arrived that Wednesday had the most recent promotion increment from last year's list. Several of my old classmates from Officer Training School were on that increment, which meant that my name should be on tap as soon as the following month.

The official numbers were finally released on an AFPC website. My guess of maybe twenty-five out of a thousand being selected was wildly off. Of the 1,219 previously passed-over officers who were being considered with only a P, a whopping total of five were selected. So, not 2 or 3 percent made it, but just four-tenths of

1 percent. I still had absolutely no idea how this had come about and could explain last year's result much more easily.

On Thursday I flew in the third go of the day. A "go" is a wave of sorties within a single scheduling block. Three goes in one day is pretty much unheard of in the F-117 community. My sortie was short but fun. The best part of the day was the mission debrief that evening. Everyone from all of the goes gathered in a small room to watch the tapes to see who had won the bets we'd placed earlier. The beer flowed freely and we had a ball. I don't even remember who took the prize that day.

Since we had used up so much flight time during the exercise, Friday was a down day. We used it to burn a few burgers and show some appreciation to our maintenance troops. In the afternoon, I truly enjoyed spending a fair amount of money buying lieutenant colonel rank insignia for my uniforms. Then, in the evening, Mauler and his wife came by to drop off their kids at our house so that the four of us could attend a party in the neighborhood. We were in our formal mess dress uniforms, which are essentially military tuxedos, and the women were in their best evening gowns.

The F-117 community has maintained two long-standing exchange positions. The 8th perpetually hosts an exchange pilot from the U.S. Navy, and the 9th has an exchange pilot from Great Britain's Royal Air Force (RAF). Both positions date from before the American public ever knew of the jet. That night Reverend, the RAF exchange guy, was hosting his annual "Battle of Britain" party. The weather cooperated beautifully and the full moon made for an amazing evening. We ate, drank, told tall stories, saluted our Spitfire and Hawker-Hurricane pilot brethren from fifty-eight years prior, and howled at the moon. There was an email from Cootch waiting for me in the evening:

> Brad: Unless I'm badly mistaken, I think I saw your name on the O-5 list. Well, it only took them a year to realize their mistake!

That's great. I'm happy for you both. How's the stinkbug?
Cootch

I responded:

Yes, it's time for all of us to buy lottery tickets since the odds of
probability have been suspended. But like they say, while the
odds of being hit by lightning are slim, that bolt has to come
down somewhere. We're still waiting for a call saying "No,
sorry—we meant someone else."

The F-117 is a great jet. I enjoy the flying except that there
isn't that much of it (compared to EFs anyway). Alamogordo is
okay, and it's nice having Cloudcroft a short drive away. Being
in a competitive squadron again is a lot of fun. I talked to Hodgie
a couple of days ago. They are settling in well up in WA. How is
Alaska? I've always wanted a tour up there. It must be amazing
this time of year.
Yukon

Over the next few days, I received calls and email congratulations
from several dozen old friends. The one from Bond was tough to
read. We had both been passed over the last time around and now
only I had managed a reprieve:

Brad, congrats!! How did you manage this minor miracle? Did
you have a P or DP? My Wing King "said" he was going to bat
for me, however. . . . So, I'll continue as a Major until 20 years
and retire in early 2001. At least I'm flying Vipers and having a
blast in Germany for my last assignment. Little K. is doing just
super and T. now has her driver's license and is a senior at that
"wonderful" age of 18. Between the two of them we have our
hands full. Again, big time congrats on "breaking" the code as

my 2 paper-pushing, non-tactical desk assignments sure didn't impress anyone. Take care.

Bond

I wrote back:

> Bond, the mystery has no answer. I wasn't supported by my last Wing at all. The PRF was sent up with just a P. My only theory is that the board-charge said not everyone in our year group has had a chance at good staff jobs (technically not applicable to me as I've always run and hid from desks). But if they had to put a few tokens through to fit this charge there aren't many others with my hours. I'm flying a little but miss the F-16. If you get back this way to see Carlsbad or White Sands give us a call.
>
> Brad

On Thursday, September 10, I got another sortie and had to fight through some significant weather (for the F-117 anyway) on the way back. That Friday we didn't do too much other than get another shot of the anthrax series in the afternoon (which still ached two days later). I also helped with the training of a few of our technical troops. I brought a half dozen of them out to a jet so that they could see what we went through manipulating and loading the EDTM into a jet.

The EDTM weighed around 5 pounds, measured 6x9x5 inches, and had a swing-up handle on top. Nicknamed the "lunchbox," it was the 1970s version of the smallest and most powerful portable hard drive that money could buy. They originally cost the air force around $50,000 each (in 1970s dollars) and held a whopping 40 MB of information. Laughable now, but that was state-of-the-art technology when Jimmy Carter was president. In any case, we had to carefully preserve and make do with these antiques since no one was going to buy us any more—hence, the training session.

Friday evening was our promotion party at the club. As always, parties in the air force are never given to those being honored (below the rank of colonel anyway), but are self-hosted. Eight of us on base being promoted dropped credit cards for the festivities, and everyone had a good time.

Saturday evening we had a visit from Scott and his girlfriend. Scott was a young enlisted troop with the 8th and away from home for the first time. He had the idea that we were somehow related. He was my mother's sister's first husband's sister's grandson, which made us . . . uh . . . pretty much strangers. He was a good kid though, and also a member of the stealth community's most unique band of specialists—he was a Martian.

The RAM coatings on our jets require unique application and repair skills. These people work out of the Material Application and Repair Specialist shop—the MARS shop. Naturally, if you come from MARS, you must be a Martian. On paper they were all designated as F-16 sheet-metal specialists, but only because the air force had to call them something. And there was absolutely no way the U.S. Air Force was going to officially advertise that we had a group of Martians working for us in a state that included the city of Roswell. Imagine the nut-jobs that news would attract. The kooks who sidle up next to us at every airshow are bad enough already

The following week I briefed and flew as No. 3 in a formation. The whole thing was an abomination. Almost nothing went correctly within the formation. Things only settled down after we had split up for our individual target lines, but as soon as we got back together for the recovery everything took a nosedive again. This was also my second no-chute sortie. The jet stopped just fine without the chute and saved a lot of worries about rudder end-cap strikes.

In the afternoon, Woody offered to nominate me for the wing XP (exercises and plans) job. While not very exciting, it would be a better match for my new rank, I supposed, but G-Man seemed inclined to hold me in the squadron for a while. I didn't really have a strong preference either way.

Other than the designated command positions, the 49th was a very rank-inflated community. During World War II, a squadron commander would be a major. By the 1950s, both he and his Opso would be lieutenant colonels. ADOs were majors, flight commanders and shop chiefs were senior captains, and the bulk of the rank and file were junior captains and lieutenants. In contrast, it is rare to find a junior captain in the 49th, and lieutenant F-117 pilots simply don't exist. We have a rather overaged community trying to find useful roles to play, so traditional rank versus position relationships are skewed. T-Dub (a captain), the flight commander for the section I'd been attached to, was actually the youngest member of the flight. Beyond his scheduling function, he had little to do. He couldn't even write our annual OPRs since everyone he supposedly "commanded" outranked him.

My promotion to O-5 seemed to be on hold. Because of the transition to a new fiscal year the Senate hadn't signed off on the promotion roster yet, so there was still no quota for the month of October. Whenever the ceremony occurred, I decided to be true to my nature and do the thing in the squadron bar wearing a flight suit.

Monday and Tuesday were used up in training for the upcoming ORE. Many hours were spent refreshing our chemical warfare skills. One of the more awkward parts of that was the "apple orchard" drill.

An apple orchard is a theoretical location far enough from the flight line to be free of whatever chemical agents have contaminated the base. It would be the place we'd be bused to for decontamination. The process for this decontamination was long and convoluted. The concept involved contaminated individuals going into one end of a long series of tents joined end to end and slowly shedding their protective clothing and gear under controlled conditions until they tripped out the far end in their underwear, but essentially clean. I'd always suspected that it was designed more to give us confidence about going into a contaminated area than actually to get most of us out. In any case, this process was one of the more heavily graded items during an inspection, so it was practiced a lot.

The next day was productive only in that I got to provide some training for the crew chiefs. I did six full jet starts and taxi trips around the canyon in order for a group of a half dozen new crews to become certified in launch and recovery procedures. Normally all USAF maintenance training was consolidated at Sheppard AFB in Texas, but since our fleet was so small we couldn't spare any jets, so all our maintenance training was also done in-house at Holloman.

On Thursday I flew one sortie. It was in an OCIP jet through some thick weather. My shooting was lousy, but at least I was airborne again. On Friday I spent the day wearing short blues with half the squadron. An aviator never wears anything other than a flight suit by choice. The blue uniform, especially with the short-sleeved "office attire" shirt, was only worn when required for formal occasions and ceremonies or when being reprimanded. Our alpha squadron status had just rotated to the 9th, but G-Man had been pushing (too hard evidently) for us to get this next rumored deployment anyway. He wouldn't back off, so he was put in blues for the day. We were showing support for him by volunteering to dress as he was being required to.

On Monday, October 5, I was looking at one of the AFPC websites at work and beginning to suspect that my line number might have been activated on October 1. There hadn't been an official notification in any form though. I flew another OCIP sortie Tuesday and got in some good practice experimenting with a couple of different tracking styles, but hadn't come to any definite conclusions yet. We also had a tanker up there to update our aerial refueling currency.

Wednesday morning I'd slept in as late as I could before going in for my first night sortie. It went extremely well, and I was astounded by how crisp and clear the FLIR—forward-looking infrared—picture was without the interference of sunlight. You could really see how the plane had been optimized for just this one mission. I didn't get home until midnight; this new lifestyle would mean missing out on a lot of time with the kids.

After talking with G-Man, I went into work that week wearing lieutenant colonel rank insignia, feeling very conspicuous sporting silver oak leaves for the first time. I'd arranged to host my promotion ceremony sandwiched between a verification and a naming ceremony. The timing wasn't ideal, but Friday afternoons were the only opportunities to host events after flying operations had terminated, and still before midnight.

Thursday evening I flew a NAAR/NSA (night air-to-air refueling/night surface attack mission). Air-to-air refueling at night is a critical skill within the F-117 community. Rarely will a conflict be prosecuted close enough to a secure airfield not to require tanker support. Fortunately, once a pilot is comfortable with night operations, the NAAR process isn't significantly more difficult than in daylight.

The rejoin can be the trickier part of the operation. Broadly speaking, two techniques effect the rejoin: the "fighter turn-on" and the "point parallel" methods. The major difference between the two is which aircraft, the fighter or the tanker, will do the majority of the maneuvering. This night the latter was in effect.

A standard air refueling track is essentially two long parallel lines with the ends joined by a 180 degree turn. Entry to the track will be via the end of one of these lines—designated as the ARIP (air refueling initial point). Once the tanker was established in the orbit, the fighter (me) approaches the ARIP. This particular night, my speed was 330 knots, while the KC-135 tanker was at 275 knots. As we approached each other on opposite sides of the track, both aircraft had their air-to-air TACAN navigation equipment set to preselected codes, which provided the relative distance between our aircraft.

I called over the radio, "Exxon two two, Hobo four three, A, R, I, P inbound at twenty-one thousand feet, nose cold," which meant my laser was off.

The KC-135 responded, "Exxon two two is at twenty-two thousand feet, cleared down track."

The plan was to fly at each other on these reciprocal headings like jousters until the distance separating our aircraft was exactly twenty-one nautical miles. At that point the tanker would begin a turn toward my leg of the track. Thirty seconds later the tanker would be halfway through the turn. If all were going to plan, the tanker would call "push it up" and accelerate to 300 knots. The fighter had the option to call for an early push if it looked like he was too close and in danger of overrunning the tanker. Conversely, if it looked as if the tanker would finish his turn with the fighter more than about two to three miles aft, the fighter could accelerate himself to either 360 or 390 knots. Increments of 30 knots made it easier for following wingmen to anticipate what the flight lead might do. If everything worked as advertised, the tanker would roll out of his turn a mile or so out front, and the remaining distance could be handled with power alone. To avoid conflicts, approaching fighters would be at least 500 feet below the tanker's altitude until their closure was under control and visual contact had been established. Once the refueling is complete the fighter leaves the track above the tankers altitude.

The tanker rolled out just a little more than a mile in front of me. I called, "Exxon two two in sight," and adjusted the throttles to maintain about 20 knots of closure as I slowly climbed up to the tanker's altitude. A few moments later Exxon 22 called, "You have one chick on the boom, and one on the left." (A "chick" is another fighter from your unit.) Since I'd have to wait my turn, I hung back about a half mile. I also stayed a little to the left, as the inside of the turn made it easier to stay in position, and I knew that the fighter currently on the boom would exit to the right once he was done.

After the fighter on the boom finished his refueling, he slid back until clear of the tanker's tail and then eased off to the right before climbing above the tanker to exit the track. I could see the other fighter sliding over toward the boom as I pushed my throttles up to take his vacated place on the left wing. The observation position on a tanker is much higher than a usual formation position. I flew high enough to see the tanker's right wing tip over the top of his fuselage, and then moved forward until both wing tips were lined up. From this position I was looking down on the entire operation. From here, any fighters that overshoot the tanker during rendezvous would pass safely below me.

I ran my pre-refueling checklist. The refueling door on the spine of the fuselage was rotated open, exposing a series of small lights around the refueling receptacle, called APEX lights. These dim lights are for the benefit of the boomer to help ensure no damage is done to the top of the aircraft—even small scratches or dings to the RAM coatings caused by the boom would require the mission to be aborted. In the cockpit I saw a green "RDY" light and could set either "FUS ONLY" (the fuselage fuel tanks) or "ALL" (both fuselage and wing tanks) on a selector knob that directed which tanks the incoming fuel would flow to. That night I only needed a partial offload so I set "FUS ONLY." Then one last check to make sure the TACAN was off, the IFF emitter was in standby, the laser was off, the autopilot functions had all been disabled, and I was ready to move to the pre-contact position.

The throttle was reduced slightly as I eased the control stick to the right to slide down into a position 50 feet directly behind the boom. I could just barely see the dim pale yellow light at its very end to help guide me into position.

"Hobo four three, pre-contact."

The tanker responded, "Hobo four three, cleared contact."

I gently eased the throttles forward to create a closure that approximated walking speed. My "horizon" was the tanker. My wings were level with the tanker's wings—period. My orientation to the rest of the world was irrelevant. My up/down reference was set by imagining that I was trying to drive my forehead onto the then end of the boom. The aircraft yawed slightly left and right as I walked through the pressure disturbances created by the tanker's wake. With ten feet to go I transitioned my reference to a line of lights along the belly of the tanker, the boom was still coming at my forehead. Five feet out the boomer would gently fly the boom to pass just to the left of my canopy (lots of trust here). I could see it bobble by in my peripheral vision, but I had to ignore that. If a pilot tries to "help" the boomer, the rhythm of the rejoin will collapse. My concentration was focused on maintaining my forward "walk" while trying mentally to visualize where the end of the boom was behind me. There was only a small window of opportunity to make the "plug" happen. Once the connection occurred, an entire series of lights on the belly of the tanker would illuminate so that I could maintain a correct position. These director lights would tell me to move forward and aft, up and down. I'd have to acquire the left/right reference visually by comparing the tanker's wing roots and splitting the distance between the inboard engines.

It was in everyone's interest to get a contact right away so that I could fly off of the director lights. If the boomer couldn't establish the connection immediately he'd have to begin giving verbal directions over the radio. Calls of *"up three," "forward five,"* and *"left two"* would be used to try to "talk" the aircraft together. The total allowance for error can be imagined as box, plus or minus about 6 feet, centered around the end of the approximately 40-foot-long refueling boom bouncing around in the turbulence 10 feet behind my head that was impossible for me to see, while we fly in tight formation at 300 knots and 20,000 feet of altitude. As I said before, *lots* of trust going on.

My first attempt was good though, and I was rewarded with a set of director lights as the green RDY light transitioned to a blue LATCH. The boomer could now talk to me directly through an intercom connection that had been established through the boom.

"Contact. Tail number and request."

I respond, "Hobo four three, tail number eight eight zero eight four two, requesting five thousand pounds."

"Copy, five thousand pounds, you have good flow."

Out of the corner of my eye I noted that my fuel quantity gauge was increasing. Maintaining position was a little harder than other aircraft such as the F-16 or EF-111. The visibility forward and up was worse, while power response was better than the EF and worse than the F-16. Stability and trim were slightly more variable as the jet took on fuel and the center of gravity shifted. Nothing insurmountable.

At 2,300 pounds per minute rate of flow, a little over two minutes passed before the boomer called "offload complete." With the pinky finger of my right hand I tapped the paddle switch once to disconnect us. Like all modern aircraft most switches must perform multiple functions. This same paddle switch was also used to control nose wheel steering while on the ground and the autopilot during flight when that particular system as engaged. The blue LATCH light had now reverted back to a green RDY as I called "Hobo four three, disconnect" and eased off the throttles to slide back. Once I could see the boom ahead of me I banked to right until clear of the tanker's right wing then climbed 1,000 feet before exiting the track. I heard Hobo 44 calling pre-contact as he took my place.

The ride went well, from my standpoint anyway. But the overall plan had pretty much fallen apart in terms of timing when some of the preceding formations were late getting off the tanker. I ended up having to cut almost every corner along the route to get one pass on the range. My tracking had been working well since I'd settled upon the "MASH" technique, and target acquisition at night was a piece of cake.

On Friday, I went in to wear the CW ground ensemble for several hours both to check its fit and to receive more apple orchard training. At 15:00, we all attended a verification that ran a bit long. That worked out well though, since it gave the family time to set up the bar for my reception.

My promotion ceremony in the squadron auditorium was short and to the point. Unlike some others here who did their pin-on wearing full blues, I'd decided that this would be a pilot's ceremony.

G-Man began by calling me up on stage. He started off with the formal tone of voice he reserves for official occasions, though he was obviously ad-libbing and quickly loosened up.

"We are gathered for this emotional event, pinning on the rank of lieutenant colonel. You may have noticed that this day is the ninth of October. Some of us get the *Air Force Times*, and they said that there was no promotion increment to lieutenant colonel for the month of October. Suddenly someone got on the web and noticed that there actually was indeed an increment this month. Three phone calls later, 'What the heck are you guys doing?' and we finally figure out that, yes, indeed, Brad O'Connor has been a lieutenant colonel for eight days and that maybe we should pin him."

"I don't have a full biography, but I can tell you that this man has combat time in the EF-one-eleven, air medals aplenty, aerial achievement medals aplenty. He has landed on boats and has more hours in jets than I have. I have thirty-five hundard, and he has over four thousand. Pretty impressive. I used to have that claim to fame in this wing, and that's just not true anymore." He slowly turned to

me and said, "So you're fired. [laughter] Another impressive creden-
tial for the pilots here: [speaking slowly] he has never been on a staff
tour." There was a short ovation from the crowd, which made the
colonels in front squirm a bit. "So, we're going to move him to the
OSS just to fill that square. Sorry, just another fact of life.

"But we have a different thing to do today. With the threat that is
developing around the world today, and the way things are going in
the country of Serbia, not only do I wish to swear in Brad to the rank
of lieutenant colonel, but I think I'd like to have all of my officers
stand and reaffirm the oath of office. With that please. . . ." A lifting
of palms brought everyone to their feet.

"All, repeat after me, and sing out." And for the first time since
being commissioned a second lieutenant seventeen years earlier, I
raised my hand and formally reaffirmed the oath. In short staccato
phrases, G-Man intoned and we repeated in unison:

"I, state your name, do solemnly swear, that I will support and
defend, the Constitution of the United States, against all enemies
foreign and domestic, and that I will bear true faith and allegiance to
the same, that I take this oath freely, without any mental reservation
or purpose of evasion, and that I will well and faithfully, discharge the
duties of the office upon which I am about to enter, so help me God."

When it was my turn to speak I knew what I was going to do at
the end, but only had a very vague idea of what I'd actually say. So
it was a bit of a ramble.

"This will be short. 'Above the zone' with a P—that doesn't
happen very often. A few months ago I would have been among
the last in the air force to think that I'd be standing here right now.
As the boss said, seventeen years in the cockpit without a staff tour.
That was a conscious choice. I knew the gamble I was taking and
thought that I'd paid the price last year.

"But I got lucky. I have enjoyed every assignment I've had and
have truly enjoyed every jet I've flown. So when I was sitting in a

tent in Saudi last fall and was told that I had been passed over . . . in addition to being pissed for obvious reasons [laughter] . . . one of the first thoughts that went through my mind was that when I hit the twenty-year mark I'd have to stop flying jets." I paused to brush my shiny new silver oak leaves, "So, now thanks to these, I don't.

"I want to thank everyone for being here—my kids for putting up with every move, and my wife, Betsy, especially. I think that she was more annoyed when I was passed over last year than I was. So, last month when she answered the door with G-Man and Woody trying to pound it down . . . well, I'll let those who saw it finish that story in the bar later." I reached into my ankle pocket to take out a softball-sized baggie of my old rank insignia and shoulder boards.

"Chip, where are you?"

Not thinking that he had a part to play in any of this, he was caught off guard. "I understand that you'll be the next guy to pin on major." I casually tossed the baggie to him in the center of the crowd while saying, "I don't need this stuff anymore." To those cheers I added, "There is food and drink next door," and I led the way out of the room. We retired to the squadron bar where the family had laid out a huge spread of food and drink.

The reception was great, and after a while we rolled right into a naming ceremony. Four guys went through the process. It was great fun as the new guys got tagged for the first time and the older guys "bought" their historic call signs back at the expense of many shots of Weed. I was pretty well in the bag by the end of the evening, so I called Bets to give Flounder and me a ride back home. Flounder, an F-14 driver on exchange from the navy, lived right around the corner from us. He was trying to entice me into buying his absolutely gorgeous 1967 metallic-blue Corvette Sting Ray with white leather interior. Tempting, but it would have taken the place of the plane I'd rather buy.

CHAPTER 8

A Rumor of War

War is God's way of teaching Americans geography.

I'M HALFWAY THROUGH *OFFICERS IN Flight Suits*, a book about the guys who flew the first U.S. jets in combat during the Korean War. An excellent book so far. It really captures much of our fighter pilot culture, which the general public almost universally misunderstands. Other than creeping political correctness within the military, and lower standards coming out of pilot training, not too much has really changed in a half century.

On Sunday morning, October 11, I drove the family up to Ruidoso to wander around and have lunch. Back home there was a call from T-Dub waiting for me on the answering machine. We were all to be at a 08:00 briefing the next day for a possible deployment to Italy. The news from Kosovo hadn't sounded much different than it had for months, but evidently someone up the chain thought otherwise.

Most of what used to be Yugoslavia had been killing off various parts of itself for a decade. This most recent phase of carnage had involved the ethnically Serbian part of Kosovo trying to suppress the ethnically Albanian part of Kosovo—greatly incited by Slobodan Milosevic in Belgrade on the one side, and aggravated by Kosovo Liberation Army (KLA) terrorist attacks on the other.

After a half decade of refusing to become involved as the other Bosnian, Croatian, Serbian, Macedonian, Montenegrin, and Slovenian factions each massacred their neighbors to various degrees, perhaps the Clinton administration had finally been embarrassed long enough actually to do something. Though he had originally run on a platform of getting involved in Bosnia six years earlier, that promise never made it past the inauguration. The Dayton Accords only came about after the hostilities in Bosnia had pretty much stalemated after the various parties had killed themselves off in sufficient numbers to grow weary.

The Clinton administration certainly couldn't claim any moral-high-ground motivations. The Rwandan massacres, in terms of their ferocity, had been as barbaric as anything that has occurred in recorded history, and the Clinton administration had very carefully and pointedly looked the other way.

With the exception of Britain's Tony Blair, the Europeans certainly hadn't been interested enough up until that point to get significantly involved in their own backyard. The most famous summary of their long-standing attitude was made in a previous century by Bismarck: "The Balkans are not worth the life of a single Pomeranian Grenadier." Other than a lot of hand wringing, little had changed.

To be honest, I was having some trouble with this one also. The carnage had been horrific at times, but not interfering in a foreign civil war was one the most indelible of lessons from Vietnam that had been pounded into my generation of officers. Sometimes involvement may be inevitable, and sometimes it may be in our best interests, but it was hard to see our interests in this one.

Neither location nor natural resources made the area strategically important. Milosevic was a thug and unworthy of anyone's support, and our own government listed the KLA as a terrorist organization. So which side were we going to support, the oppressors or the terrorists?

Oppression alone couldn't be the discriminator. Half the countries in the world suppress break-away factions within their borders, and terrorism that doesn't spill over a border, rightly or wrongly, has traditionally been dealt with as an internal matter. Even within NATO, no one talked much about our good ally Turkey and its cross-border attacks against the Kurds in Iraq.

The Balkans had always been a mess. The first great upheaval (at least of this past millennium) was due to the region's unfortunate central location during the Great Schism of 1054, when the Eastern Orthodox Church split off from the Western Catholic Church, followed by its partial invasion and occupation by the Ottoman Empire for about five hundred years, followed by the partial invasion by the Habsburg Empire—leaving the region roughly split into three major camps. The Orthodox Serbs were enslaved by the Turks, the Catholic Croats were exploited as mercenaries for the Austrians, and the Bosnians were playing willing host to one of the territorial high-water marks of the Islamic invasion of Europe.

World War I was precipitated by the assassination of the heir to the Austro-Hungarian Empire by a Serbian nationalist. In addition to the impact of the war itself, Russia's early involvement in the Balkans was one of the primary catalysts for the Bolshevik Revolution and all of the political upheavals and superpower frictions that event led to this past century. Europe had always been ambivalent about getting involved in the region. One writer summed it up with the statement that in European eyes, "First and foremost, nothing good ever happens in the Balkans." There never seem to be any clear-cut good guys or good results.

World War II was especially confusing. No scorecard could keep track of who was fighting whom or for what particular reason at any given moment. Alliances and loyalties regularly shifted like the tides. Croatian Fascists, called the Ustashe, fought alongside the Nazis against the Communists and the Serbs. The Communist Partisans, under Tito, fought the Ustashe, the Nazis, and the Italians. The Serbs formed groups called Chetniks, who fought mostly against the Partisans and sometimes the Germans, but especially against the Ustashe. The Bosnian Muslims and Albanians sided with the Nazis, while still hating the Ustashe, and welcomed the Germans as liberators. Tens of thousands of Muslims enlisted to form the Skanderbeg Waffen-SS Division or volunteered to work as guards in the death camps. The only groups left out were the Jews and the Gypsies, who were routinely abused by all factions.

The slaughter, rape, and destruction was so horrific that even Nazi commanders in the area became frustrated enough to turn their backs on them all. By the war's end over a million Slavs were dead—almost all at the hands of their own neighbors. And just over the border to the south the Greek Civil War of 1946–1949 was kicking off, much of it centered around Macedonia, technically a southern region of modern Yugoslavia, but emotionally the birthplace of Alexander the Great, a northern region of historic Greece. Tito—last man standing—held this artificial nation together with an iron hand for a few decades until shortly after his death, when all hell broke loose again.

A more recent accident of history preceding this round of conflict was the United States' misadventure in Somalia during the early Clinton years. After watching GI bodies being dragged through the streets by dancing mobs, what little appetite we may have had for meddling in foreign civil wars diminished. And without the United States to take the lead, Europeans, who should have been dealing with the Balkan mess from the beginning, were hanging back, as they had been for the last half century.

This last flare-up was likely just the most recent chapter in a long and ugly history, since we didn't really intend to actually effect any changes, just to suppress the currently winning side, while fully intending the Serbs to retain sovereignty over Kosovo when it was finally over. In some ways the whole situation reminded me of the firemen who walk through a recently extinguished blaze in the woods, snuffing out isolated pockets of flame in the residue of what used to be a forest. We may have been finally snuffing out one of the last remnants of the Yugoslavian civil wars or perhaps a last remnant of the Cold War. But that was probably too optimistic of a viewpoint— the region had been in flames off and on for a thousand years.

In the meantime I was working on my mobility bags and mentally preparing to leave my family again on another ambiguous military adventure.

The next day, we went in to hear that we would start packing *in anticipation* of a deployment order. No order to deploy had actually been issued. But it all looked pretty solid there for a few hours before we got word that the Serbs and KLA had agreed to another ceasefire. The Serbs had also agreed to allow 1,500 UN observers in on the ground. So now we were just sitting around waiting for additional instructions.

As it turned out, the MQT guys were going to be left behind with the 9th, so a Christmas in Italy was never in my cards anyway. A postponement was welcome on a selfish level, because the only thing worse than going would have been being left behind while everyone else from the 8th went. This short reprieve might allow those of us in MQT enough time to be ready for the next call. Unfortunately, that night's sortie was canceled since all of the tools and equipment necessary to launch the jets had been packed away on pallets for the possible deployment.

In the meantime, my routine continued. On Wednesday night I flew the NSAT-1 sortie, and it went well. I noticed that my tracking skills improved greatly after the first few passes, so I was working on some ground warm-up drills. During the flight I hit 100 percent of the targets to include two "dirt" targets on the range with BDU-33s. A dirt target is considered anything without real vertical development or material that holds heat well, making it tougher to pick out with IR from the background.

Our deployment to Italy had been delayed another two weeks awaiting developments on the ground in Kosovo. So there was a slim chance I'd actually be able to finish my training and become deployable since I was scheduled for three MQT sorties the following week. To be honest though, no one really believed the deployment was going to happen. We reacted to false-start notifications like this all the time.

I did as much studying as I could with the bulk of our gear and publications still packed away on pallets. One afternoon we were introduced to our most recent squadron mascot, "Emmitt," a new black sheep (number two or three—recently, anyway) to replace the last one. The previous sheep had been kept by one of our guys (call sign Shepherd, naturally) tied up behind his house near Cloudcroft. Shepherd thought this one was about the forty-third in the series before it had been eaten by a mountain lion. I suppose that's what you get when you have a sheep for a mascot instead of something that isn't considered prey in the animal kingdom. Emmitt, a skittish and twitchy little animal, baptized the squadron by defecating in front of the commander's chair.

Later on there was a short burger burn in a hangar, followed by a Bandit party for the new guys in the 7th. There were five in this class, though one was headed to Palmdale as a test pilot. We had a good time, and it renewed my desire to get into that unit in a year or so—not only for the flying hours, but also to be dual-qualified to fly both the F-117 and T-38 at the same time.

* * *

Over the next few days, I realized that my lifestyle was making for some very late nights and an unusual family life. My kids had begun saying "good-bye" instead of "see you later" to me before they headed off to school on Mondays. It seemed odd the first time I heard that until I realized that though we all lived in the same house each and every day, we were rarely awake at the same time.

After seeing the kids off to school on Monday, I'd do some chores around the house and yard for a few hours before heading in for lunch at noon. The first flight briefing would begin around 13:00 or 14:00 for the afternoon sorties. The second briefing wouldn't happen until 17:00 or 18:00 for the night sorties. Those of us who weren't flying were either helping with the brief, up in the tower as the supervisor of flying, working on the schedule, or doing the dozens of other tasks each squadron required in order to function. The night flyers would usually be done by 23:00, and the squadron members would often be finished and home an hour or so after midnight.

By the time I got home the family had long since been asleep. I'd still be up another hour or two reading the mail and unwinding enough to go to sleep myself. They would all be up again for their morning routine only three to four hours after I'd hit the sack. When I woke up the next morning it would be 10:00 or 11:00 and everyone would be gone. It only took the kids a few weeks of this routine for them to figure out the score and to begin saying, "Good-bye, have a good week, see you again on Friday," each Monday morning.

Around Halloween, I received an odd notification: I was being sent TDY (temporary duty) to Tucson, Arizona. For two weeks I was going to act as the F-117 expert in a war-game exercise. *F-117 expert?* That title was more than a little farfetched at this stage of the game, considering that I hadn't even finished MQT yet.

During the first week of November, I was scheduled to fly three sorties and was hoping to get a fourth. The first two went extremely well and set the stage for my mission check ride. I presented my computerized brief to G-Man, who pronounced it "most excellent." Then I flew a great off-range sortie shooting at all eight of the camera targets.

I was required to shoot only at two, but elected to show off and shot them all, hanging it out unnecessarily. My goal was to come back ten for ten. Unfortunately, a low cloud deck hid the ground on my first range pass so I had called "no-drop" into my tape. But toward the last few seconds of the run I caught a few glimpses of the target through the clouds and believed that my second pass on a target a little further south might be possible. I was fired up to do this because I was carrying an inert GBU-12 again and didn't want to bring it home.

On my second, and last, pass on the range I got sight of an OAP (offset aim-point, an easily recognized geographical reference point used to find the target), took a quick squirt of laser ranging to validate the drop, and let the bomb go. But then the clouds thickened, and I lost the target area for a WX-Void. I distinctly saw the bomb silhouetted against the cloud deck as it fell away, futilely searching for the laser. Both OAPs were visible throughout the fall, but I never got a good laser spot on the target.

Fortunately, I had all the required tasks on tape, so it was decided that I'd done enough to complete the ride. I was now officially considered to be combat deployable. Mauler was five minutes behind me on the route and elected to bring his GBU home after I'd told him my story over the radio. So he had to fly his check ride again to finish up.

I ended up flying a fourth sortie on Thursday afternoon of that week. The transition from several night sorties back to a day sortie really emphasized how optimized the F-117 was for the dark. The IRADS picture was comparatively dismal in daylight.

Friday morning I made some calls to Davis-Monthan AFB to figure out the plan for this upcoming temporary duty. I went to fly again that afternoon, but had to abort for a variety of reasons. That would have been five sorties in one week. Way too lucky.

A couple of days later I packed a bag before heading off to Tucson. The trip was about 350 miles total, but a relatively easy straight shot across Route 10 with barely a curve or two in the road along the way.

There were no billeting rooms available on base so I was sent off to a local hotel. After in-processing to the exercise, I found that I had been assigned to the plans group. We would be working the 18:00–06:00 shift straight through the weekend and Veterans Day holiday.

The planning system that we were being trained to use was called CTAPS. It was designed to generate the overall air tasking order (ATO), which is essentially the battle plan for each day of an air war. The CTAPS program wasn't very user-friendly—specialty programs rarely are.

The outline for this exercise was a fictitious scenario set five years in the future. The nation of Panama had been invaded and occupied by a "regional hostile power" (we never actually said Cuba), which was barring our access to the canal. War had broken out in Europe and we needed to reopen the canal immediately to get our navy and merchant marine traffic from the Pacific to the Atlantic. We had air force, navy, airborne, and marine resources at our disposal to retake the canal and liberate Panama. But we only had them for one week.

Our role in this exercise was to come up with a game plan and generate the battle orders in real time that would be required to prosecute the whole venture. My role in particular was to help either destroy or suppress the anti-aircraft forces in Panama long enough for the marines to take the coastal areas at each entrance to the canal while army airborne forces dropped in to secure the locks along the length of the canal. We had six days to make all of this happen as the first hypothetical convoy was already en route and was scheduled to enter the canal from the Pacific side in seven days. The exercise was labeled "Fuertus Defensus."

Wednesday was Armistice Day. World War I had ended exactly eighty years earlier, on the eleventh hour, of the eleventh day, of the eleventh month. I drove to the Pima Air & Space Museum. It is one of the largest aviation museums in the world and has a great collection of hardware, though most of it is outdoors. Almost three hundred different aircraft are on display. The museum has two tremendous advantages. One is that it is right next door to the military's aircraft boneyard, AMARC, and has easy access to examples of whatever is being retired. The second advantage is the huge military retiree population in Tucson, hundreds of whom volunteer their time and expertise as technicians and docents throughout the organization.

Talking to a few of these volunteers was probably the most rewarding part of my visit. An entire group of B-24 combat veterans were there just to chat to people wandering through their particular exhibit. Amongst countless other planes there was a gorgeous Ryan PT-22 trainer hanging from the ceiling. I've always liked the Ryan's lines, but it looked to be a small plane. I wondered if it would fit me.

That afternoon I caught a CNN report implying that we were about to deploy a dozen Black Jets to Kuwait to spank Saddam again. I drove right on base trying to find out which squadron had been tasked, but I couldn't get anyone from Holloman on the phone before the exercise kicked off.

At work we spent our first full night building an ATO. The target allocation process bothered me a lot. There was little or no thought given to applicability of weapons, threat rings, or deconfliction. As intel presented targets that needed to be struck, representatives from the various communities just sort of shouted out, "We can take that one if no one else wants it."

I was casting about for the overall plan to use as a template before it occurred to me that our little group *was* that plan. The allocation most closely resembled a militaristic Wheel of Fortune—"Vanna, I'd like to buy a weapons bunker for two GBU-10s." Expensive CALCMs (conventional air launched cruise missiles) were being thrown at undefended targets while flesh-and-blood pilots were pitching iron bombs at targets right beside SAM emplacements. Targets were being snapped up as if the various communities worried that the targets would run out before they got into the game.

Then we were off to the planning floor to enter those targets, and tanker, weapons, and timing requirements into the CTAPS system to generate the unit orders required for the following day's strikes. The ATO was the compilation of these plans for the next day. The fragmentary portion of an ATO that applied to an individual unit, which might be only a half page in a document the size of a phone book, is called "the frag." Finding and understanding that half page within a squadron is known as "breaking out the frag."

By the next day, CNN had film of the armada in flight toward Kuwait. I finally got a call through to our scheduling shop to learn that the 9th has been assigned the deployment. I made them promise to call me if the 8th were also notified. I figured that I'd only need about seven hours notice to abandon this excercise and be back in time to deploy with the squadron. He said they'd call, but was convinced that we'd missed the boat on this one already. So while I'd been left behind again, at least it wasn't my own squadron doing it. G-Man must have been crying in his beer.

Before the exercise began again, I was surprised to meet several of my former Marine T-2 students from when I had been an exchange instructor at Meridian NAS in Mississippi. They were all F/A-18 drivers then, on a TDY in support of the A-10 schoolhouse.

I distinctly remembered having flown with at least three of them, and two others claimed we had flown together also.

Back at work the target allocation went much more slowly than the previous night, but also more efficiently. The "feeding frenzy" atmosphere of the first night was gone and aircraft capability, weapons availability, and logic began to prevail as we assigned the targets sets. Making up for the slower target allocation, we were much quicker on the CTAPS computers and were still done by 03:00. The size of our group was much smaller. Several of our original number had been recalled by their units overnight and had disappeared for the deployment to Kuwait.

The next day, we got good feedback on our simulated strike. I then got to start double-tasking most of my jets—assigning each F-117 two separate targets per sortie. I was still done by 03:00. I called Bets later on to hear the local news about the 9th deploying. CNN had stated that we were about thirty minutes from launching cruise missiles before Baghdad backed down. This seemed to be shaping up as another winter stalemate. One plan was for the 9th to remain in Kuwait for about 120 days before we replaced them in rotation.

We continued on with the exercise planning sessions. We'd seen the target list shrink down to just a few hours of work. Once the high-priority air-defense targets, and a smattering of bridges, had been taken care of on the first few days, the remaining targets began to fall mostly into the "close air support" category. That was a job for A-10s, F-16s, and F/A-18s—not F-117s and B-2s. The hard part for my subgroup was pretty much over, and now we were just coasting toward the finish.

On Tuesday, November 17, we had a three-hour "hot wash" (debriefing) of the enitre exercise. Evidently, we had followed the usual path from the impending chaos of the first few confused days toward some semblance of competence by the end. The training team deemed that we'd developed the skill sets they had set out to teach us. I checked out of the hotel and hit the road for Alamogordo. After stopping by the squadron for a few minutes to check the schedule, I continued on home to reunite with Bets and the kids.

The 9th guys who had deployed only got as far as Rota, Spain, before being turned around. One item of interest in my email inbox was the announcement of another astronaut selection board. I could put in an application package in March for the indulgence of hoping and dreaming before it was rejected.

Thanksgiving Day turned out to be gorgeous, and on Friday I took my son to the municipal airport for the Turkey Festival of Gliders. Every year on the day after Thanksgiving sailplanes from all over the region gather for this event. The strong and consistent westerly winds blowing up against the slopes of the Sacramento Mountains make this area a mecca for record attempts. People from all over the country come here to train for, and accomplish, amazingly long unpowered flights. I counted dozens of sailplanes lined up before the flying began, and they had three powered aircraft in constant use giving tows to altitude.

Back home we began to drag the Christmas decorations down from the attic. Winter was making its presence felt. I saw a car coming down from the mountains with about 6 inches of snow still on the roof. The night air was crisp and still, lacking only the smell of wood smoke to complete the moment.

On the evening of Tuesday, December 1, we were presented a great briefing from the F-117 test detachment on a new LGB fuse that was being developed. The video of the test drop was impressive with angles from both at impact and from inside the underground room where the weapon actually tunneled through before detonating.

Several years earlier the air force had developed a series of penetrating bombs designed to dig out underground bunkers. The most common was the well-known BLU-109 2,000-pound bomb. These weapons were designed so that the case wouldn't break up on impact, but would retain its shape and structure long enough for the bomb to get through to whatever was being struck. The trick then became to delay the fusing function of the weapon the correct amount of time so that the bomb would go off within, or adjacent to, the actual underground target. Previously this had been accomplished with a simple timing delay. But not knowing the exact composition of the soil and thickness of the bunker ceilings made that an inexact science.

This new concept being developed was to fit the fuse with accelerometers sensitive enough to determine how many layers of soil, concrete, and steel had been passed through before detonating and robust enough to survive the trip of course.

Soon we'd have the ability literally to dial in which floor of a multistory building we wanted the bomb to detonate on or drop a weapon over a buried bunker and know that the thing wouldn't detonate until it actually entered the structure's void. The nickname being used was the "floor-counter fuse." This would be a great tool once perfected.

The next day was a mad thrash of paperwork and scrambling about in preparation for an upcoming inspection. Then the weather closed in and my evening sortie was canceled. Before heading home I stopped by the club at G-Man's insistence. He told me that I'd been chosen to pick up another job, as the ORM guy, tracking the squadron's training status and combat readiness. While it was nice that I was being offered positions, this wasn't a welcome assignment. Picking up a new job just prior to an inspection usually isn't advisable. Unless the last person had left it perfect, you're the one who takes the hits, and if they had been running a perfect shop in the first place then they probably wouldn't be leaving the job before being able to take credit. But I didn't have a valid reason to say no.

Thursday was another long day of nothing but paperwork, but we made some real progress. I had some fun with Mauler at one point when he mentioned that he would pay a substantial reward for the recovery of a gray pen he'd owned for a long time and had been missing for several weeks. I asked how much of a reward he was willing to fork over before casually picking it up from the floor right in front of his desk and tossing it to him—which says something about how often our offices are cleaned.

That morning I got a pickup sortie from the 9th. Our scheduler was wandering around looking for a volunteer to go down the hallway to fly with the other squadron. This didn't happen very often, but enough 9th guys were out sick that they couldn't fill the schedule with their own people. Surprisingly, there was enough of a rivalry between the squadrons that Draft was having trouble finding someone to go. I didn't understand that at all. So when he got to me my response solved his problem.

"You're asking me if I want to fly someone else's jet, burning someone else's fuel, without it counting against my own quota in this squadron? Absolutely!"

Draft said that we were going to get along fine.

It was good to fly again, but my shooting was lousy. The 9th hadn't fully converted to the RNIP configuration yet, and I'd been assigned a rather beat-up OCIP jet. The navigation system of the jet I'd been given was drifting badly, and my OCIP skills were out of practice.

After I landed I finished some of the end-of-month training reports I'd inherited as part of the ORM job. That took a few hours, but I got it done in time to attend the last part of a Bandit party.

The following Sunday night, Bets and I went up to Cloudcroft for the squadron Christmas party. The event had been catered in one of the area's nicer resorts, the Lodge. It was a good gathering but rather low-key. Everyone was just tired I supposed.

At the party, G-Man presented several of us with a unique gift. In the early black days of the program there had been no way to identify oneself as an F-117 pilot while away from Tonopah. So a quantity of small lapel pins had been procured. They depicted a nighthawk, with talons outstretched, swooping down on some unsuspecting prey. The eye of the nighthawk was a small red ruby, symbolizing the laser, I suppose. For many years these ruby-eyed nighthawks were the only way that previous and current F-117 pilots could identify each other in a nonsecure setting.

Perhaps because of that early secrecy, we still didn't have a great handle on identifying ourselves. Pilot communities are often very particular about how they are referred to: Viper driver, Eagle driver, test pilot, Buff driver . . . each community usually has a well-defined label. We really didn't. "F-117 pilot" wasn't used much, and real F-117 pilots never used the term "Nighthawk" when referring to the plane. "Stealth pilot" probably came closest and was on some of our patches. But it didn't specify either our aircraft or mission or even separate us from the B-2 guys for that matter. "F-117 Nighthawk Stealth Fighter pilot" was way too long and presumptuous to roll off the tongue in casual conversation. I guess everything just sounded a little too over the top. When someone asked, they usually didn't get a title but an explanation.

For entertainment several of the guys who had formed a singing group performed for us. Tripp had been the group's founder before moving on to the 7th but Shepherd, Flounder, and Draft were still with us. Harkening back to the founding of the first fighter squadrons during World War I (overly represented by Ivy League gentlemen) they ended their show with Yale's famous "Whiffenpoof Song."

The song is familiar to anyone who has ever seen the World War II B-17 movie *Twelve O'Clock High*, or the TV series *loosely* based on Pappy Boyington's Marine Corsair squadron, *Baa Baa Black Sheep*. Since we had also been christened as Black Sheep during World War II in the Pacific, we lay claim to the song as part of our heritage, primarily for the last few verses:

> We are little black sheep
> Who have gone astray.
> Gentlemen songsters off on a spree
> Damned from here to eternity
> God have mercy on such as we.
> Baa! Baa! Baa!

The next week I flew a sortie on Monday afternoon and another on Tuesday. Both went reasonably well, and once again I'd improved my tracking skills. Tuesday evening I was tagged to be one of the guinea pigs for Doc Brown's "eye-tracker" experiment.

Doc was a part-time F-117 pilot and a full-time flight surgeon at Wright-Patterson Air Force Base in Ohio. He was one of only eight or nine "physician pilots" floating around the U.S. Air Force at any given time. Most of these guys had previously been fighter pilots who had departed the service to attend medical school before returning to the cockpit. A few start out as doctors before taking several years away from their practice to attend pilot training and complete an operational tour. Either way, they bring a unique perspective to the man-machine interface and are given a lot of free reign in their research.

The technology for this project was interesting. Before getting started, the Doc and his two assistants fitted me with a very awkward piece of headgear. This thing had IR reflector plates in front of my eyes and was linked to a tracker and a video camera. Hot dry energy was beamed at my eyeballs to be reflected back through the plates to be analyzed. Then I was put into the sim to fly an ordinary profile.

After the process was complete there was a video showing precisely where my eyes were focused. If I were to look at a page of print from several feet away they could see which letter of a word I was dwelling on at any given moment. This was displayed as a small red cross darting around the video screen.

The objective of the experiment was to track where a pilot actually focuses his attention while performing normal tasks and where and for how long he focuses his attention during emergencies. The eventual goal was to design cockpits that display the most relevant information where the guy is going to look anyway and in a manner that can be absorbed most quickly. In the short term, guys having trouble with their instrument cross-checks in the 7th were being helped now that the IP's could tell exactly where their scan was breaking down.

I loved the science, and I had been forewarned about one of the more embarrassing pitfalls that a few of the earlier subjects had stumbled into. The Doc's two female assistants were attractive, and a complete video record of *exactly* what the pilot's eyes were focusing on was recorded at the end of the exercise. Far from being offended, the assistants thought that it was hilarious and had already put together a "greatest hits" tape of the first guys stealing inappropriate glances. They should have set it to music. But like I said, I'd already been warned so my video recorded a lot of time of me casually staring at a wall when I wasn't focused in the cockpit and only, carefully, coming down to eye level during conversations.

On Wednesday, I swam and biked before work and was trying to clean up some ORM paperwork when I was tapped to pick up a sortie. It was to be in an aircraft designated as a spare for the primary flyers, so I had to lag behind in case someone else had needed the jet. Once in the cockpit I had some intercom problems while still in the shelter, then I had both radio and intercom problems while taxiing out. I had decided to quit by the time I got to EOR. That turned out to be a good call because I began having brake problems while trying to get back to the shelters and had to abandon the jet on a taxiway to be towed the rest of the way. The history of aviation is full of stories about gremlins—imaginary creatures responsible for an aircraft's ills. If real, then this jet was certainly infested with them. Not a good day for the home team. And I never did finish my paperwork.

That evening we flew the Nighthawk competition route through some very marginal weather. The pre-eminent award within the F-117 community is the Nighthawk Trophy. Competition between the squadrons for the right to display this trophy for the coming year is ferocious, and the routes are infamous for their difficulty. Every single attack is misplotted, the photos are wrong, look-alike targets are side by side . . . and so on. In general, the best shooters in the wing average about 98 percent on local training sorties while the newest, or just bad, pilots still shoot in the low 80s. But a successful Nighthawk sortie may yield up fewer than half of its targets to the eventual winner, even when the weather cooperates.

I encountered actual icing just once, but also saw only two of the targets through the weather well enough to attack. The same two targets everyone else saw, so the competition was pretty much a fizzle and would be re-staged. But it was flying.

Other than those two holes through the clouds the night was *black*: moonless, with a high overcast blocking the stars and a thick, low undercast blocking the ground lights. The F-117 community is familiar with the concept of darkness, but this was something else. The usual words didn't do it justice. Pitch black, inky, black as coal, Stygian darkness—none of those were adequate. Ordinary nighttime is when there are lights off in the distance. Being able to see them out on the horizon is what makes it just "night." Nights have depth and distance and empty space in between. Black is something else. Black isn't empty, and it doesn't have depth; it has substance and a surface, and that surface is just on the other side of the canopy glass. When I put my hand against the glass I could feel a slight vibration as uncounted tortured little air molecules were battered aside and silently screamed their way around the sharp corners of the canopy just centimeters from my glove, while I sat in my comfortable and quiet little bubble inside, staring at that black wall just a foot or so away. We lived a surreal life at times.

CHAPTER 9

Final Preparations

How do you know if there is a fighter
pilot in the room? He'll tell you.

WEDNESDAY, DECEMBER 16, 1998. BECAUSE of the
exercise I didn't have to be on base until 19:00. It seemed odd
to have dinner at home before heading off to work. My first stop was
a parking lot near the logistics group (our simulated apple orchard).
We were processed into the war before suiting up in ground-
ensemble CW gear, with gas masks and helmets, to be bused to the
squadron. The operations building was in blackout conditions, and
we had to show our ID cards through a little window to be admitted,
which was tough to do wearing all of our CW gear. The door guard
actually went through the charade of looking at the pictures on the
ID cards and comparing those to our "faces" under our gas masks and
Kevlar helmets before letting us in. The mass briefing was presented
at 20:30.

While waiting around for our flights, there were several simulated "alarm reds" and "alarm blacks." An alarm red is an attack in progress. The drill was for all of us to duck under the nearest table or desk or huddle in a corner as we donned our masks and helmets, if they weren't already on. To add a sense of realism the alarm sirens were occasionally accompanied by the concussion of explosions being set off around the base. The inspectors expected to see "a sense of urgency" while all of this was going on.

An alarm black often follows the alarm red. This means that the presence of chemical agents is either suspected or has been confirmed. In either case we could move around again and continue whatever it was we had been doing while still wearing our masks and helmets indoors. Hopefully after fifteen to thirty minutes an all clear would sound and we could remove the masks. But if the presence of chemical agents had been confirmed, then the alarm black might last for hours, or days, and we would have to go through decontamination lines before reentering any building.

For ground personnel this was bad enough, but their gear was the same stuff the army has developed for soldiers in the field. And as long as it isn't too hot out, you could function reasonably well for extended periods. For the aircrew, the gear was more of a hodge-podge of required flight gear and improvised means to protect that gear.

As I headed out the door to fly, I was wearing a layer of long underwear covered by a charcoal (and other stuff) impregnated flight-suit-like garment to stop any chemicals from getting through to my skin. Over that I had a rubber-lined anti-exposure suit that we normally used for long overwater flights. This suit stopped most of the chemicals from getting through to the charcoal suit in the first place so that it would last longer and could be reused—we didn't have an unlimited supply after all. Unfortunately none of this stuff was flame resistant so we wore a regular Nomex flight suit over all of that. Everyone kept a couple of oversized flight suits in their closets for just this reason. The normal g-suit and parachute harness topped it all off. Then cotton gloves, covered by rubber gloves, covered by Nomex flight gloves (again, very oversized in order to fit). Each foot got a little plastic bootie over the leather boot. Then we pulled on our regular flight helmets, but with a chemical mask fitted. The visor of the mask was sealed to a large green hood that covered the helmet down to below our shoulders. The oxygen hose to the mask went through a large filter pack hanging from a lanyard around our necks.

To be able to communicate, breathe a little easier, and most importantly keep from fogging up in all of this stuff, there was also a battery-powered blower unit. This helped pressurize the filter and send a stream of "cool-ish" air across the inside of our visors, and it connected a little speaker to the helmet's intercom system. This last bit of gear was a nice intention, but most attempts to speak through it sounded like the adults in a Charlie Brown cartoon. Shouting didn't make it better. Many conversations ended up in notes being written.

All "Michelin-Man'ed" up, you then picked up your helmet bag containing checklists, pubs, and whatever flight gear you weren't already wearing in one hand and the EDTM lunchbox in your other. To supply one last line of protection before you were shuffled out the door, someone would pull a full-length clear plastic bag over your head down to your ankles. This was called the body condom. Body condoms aren't very wide at the bottom, so it can be awkward to walk. You have to take short little steps to keep from tripping.

If things were going according to plan, a van would be waiting for us on the other side of the door as we waddled out like penguins. Once there, hopefully someone would be waiting to help us up into the vehicle. In case this part sounds a little silly, the next time you climb into a pickup truck try holding your arms pressed to your sides and climb in without using your hands, elbows, or shoulders at all. By the way, all of this is going on in almost complete darkness.

Once I got inside the aircraft shelter I could pull off the body condom at least. But my jet wasn't ready, and I couldn't use the phone through all of my gear to call for a spare. So I waited through another couple of simulated attacks out there while the jet was being worked on.

That got old pretty quickly. There I was, hunkered down under a maintenance table, wrapped in layers of fabric and rubber, sweating and shivering simultaneously. In no time at all I had come to the conclusion that I was really getting too old for this shit.

Eventually the jet was ready and I got airborne, but so late that I had missed the tanker window. It was a dark, dry night, and since there were only two targets on the route (paralleling the fact that in combat I would only have two bombs), there was time to look outside and enjoy the flight.

After landing we got to do the whole CW thing in reverse. The slick plastic booties and body condoms went back on as we ventured outside the shelters.

But since the jets tend to drift in one at a time after their flights, the transportation part of the plan had sort of collapsed. And because the canyon area was still in blackout conditions it was tough to wave down a ride. Eventually three of us (I have absolutely no idea who the other two were under all of their gear) huddled together and started walking—waddling actually. A safety technique we had been advised to try was to turn on a flashlight inside the body condom if you had to cross any open areas of the ramp. This didn't help you see where you were going at all, quite the opposite actually, but it illuminated the inside of the bag so that the drivers of the pickups, fuel trucks, and other vehicles running around the flight line might see you in the dark through all of their CW gear.

So there we were, three plastic-wrapped, Chinese-lantern, human-sized burritos trying to waddle quickly across the ramp without getting run over. This is how baby ducks trying to cross a busy street must feel. But the best was yet to come.

On the other side of the ramp we had slowed down for our quarter-mile walk to the operations building. A large six-pack pickup pulled alongside and the driver began to shout something that sounded like *wahnh, wa, wahn, wahhh, wa.*

Huh? Then he waved his arm to climb in. Okay, I got that. I tried climbing in the passenger-side door but couldn't lift my foot enough under the body condom to make it, couldn't hop up high enough, and of course I had no arms or hands. After a couple of attempts I gave up. The other two guys must have already anticipated this and had headed right for the bed of the truck. Fortunately the tailgate was already down. If we turned backwards to the truck we could just jump up enough to get our butts onto the tailgate. Then, lying down, we did a spastic little inchworm wriggle to work our way forward.

One last indignity awaited us. The bed of the pickup had one of those vinyl corrugated liners. So, wrapped in plastic, having no free arms, and wearing plastic booties, it was impossible to get enough traction to sit up. A ride to the squadron lying there like three logs was going to be as good as it got.

But as the truck accelerated away, the lack of traction once again made its presence felt. Just like a magician pulling a tablecloth out from under a set of dishes, the truck scooted out from under us leaving us momentarily suspended in midair as we slid out the back. It was a good thing that we were so thickly padded and still wearing helmets. The driver hadn't seen us slide out and never stopped. We waddled our separate ways as I again confirmed the thought that I had truly, truly, truly gotten too old for this shit.

The next day I was called in a little earlier so that I could fly twice. We weren't in alarm black yet so I got out to the shelter easily and launched right at sunset for an excellent sortie. By the time I had returned to land after what should have been my first sortie, all of the airfield lights had been turned back on. A series of cruise-missile attacks on Baghdad had precipitated an order for the wing to launch twelve jets back toward Kuwait. The exercise had been canceled.

Again, the 8th wasn't chosen to go. So, as the bravo squadron, we did the preparation and planning for the deployment while pilots from the 9th went into crew rest and packed to depart.

To ensure that twelve jets would arrive in Kuwait, the plan was to launch sixteen. Once at least fourteen had gotten airborne and had successfully refueled from a tanker, the extra two jets would return to Holloman. The remaining fourteen would continue nonstop to Rota Airbase in Spain. The next day all fourteen would launch. When at least twelve had gotten airborne and had successfully refueled, the extra two would return to Spain before making their way home over the next few days. I volunteered to fly one of the spares to Spain but was disqualified as they only wanted guys with at least a hundred hours in the jet. The irony was that not too many others wanted the trip and I would have logged my hundredth hour before we got as far as Rota.

Even if all went as planned, and I didn't end up in Kuwait, getting stuck in Spain and missing Christmas was still going to be a possibility. It looked as though they might actually be allowed to do something this time, and I'd missed out again.

On Saturday, I was dressed to help inspect the deploying jets when the squadron called. The deployment to Kuwait had been canceled. The short bombing campaign had been halted. Clinton was being impeached for committing perjury about the Monica Lewinsky affair while testifying under oath to a grand jury during the Paula Jones sexual harassment trial. The Speaker of the House, Bob Livingston, had voluntarily resigned for an extramarital affair of his own (though without the perjury) and had called upon Clinton to follow his example. A hell of a busy day in the news.

Locally, G-Man would be leaving for AWC (Air Warfare College) that coming July. In fact, all three squadron commanders on base would be leaving in the summer, which would make for lousy continuity. The ORE/ORI process would continue unabated, which offered very little other than a lot of work for the squadrons, and a scorecard for the wing commander.

I was scheduled for a CW sim Monday evening, but no IP showed up to run the console. So I was home a little early to meet the in-laws who had just flown in through El Paso. My father-in-law's new hobby was detecting radio beacons on a directional scanner. With all of the base and NASA activities, he would find all sorts of interesting things to hunt down around here. I was scheduled to fly twice that day, then we had five days off for the holiday.

I called AFPC for an astronaut selection package to be mailed to the house. My odds of being selected were nonexistent, but it couldn't hurt to try.

A couple of days before Christmas Eve, I went in for two sorties and actually got to fly both. That was the first time that had happened for me in this jet. The first was a 1.7-hour day flight that was a little tough, then a great 1.8-hour night sortie where I nailed all the targets.

We had a great Christmas morning. Everyone enjoyed themselves, and the kids immediately set off on their new bicycles to explore. That weekend I drove the family out to the White Sands Missile Range to take a guided tour of Lake Lucero, source of the gypsum that makes up the White Sands' dunes. We saw the interesting gypsum crystals that form as the lake evaporates. They vary from an amber color to almost clear. Some were very large, and they littered the shore everywhere. There was a little water in the lake and it created a picturesque reflection of the snow-covered mountains to the east.

At work, we started the first week of the new year with several contingency deployment meetings. My training shop reorganization was coming along well, and Woody dropped the news that the OG asked about me specifically in reference to future command opportunities within the wing. It was nice to know my name was at least considered for a moment or two.

In my spare time, I made a call to a museum in Kissimmee, Florida, to talk about a 1941 Ryan PT-22 advertised for sale in Trade-a-Plane. They didn't sound as if they were willing to come down on the advertised price. I could have had a ball, and it would have been an investment, but that was a lot of money for an antique.

The following week I flew both Monday and Tuesday and was likely to get another flight the next day. The flying was always great, but I hadn't been satisfied with my shooting recently. Whenever I had good laser ranging I did fine, but my manual tracking was poor without it. That would never be a factor in combat, as I wouldn't be allowed to drop without laser ranging anyway, but I still thought that I could do better. Practice would be the cure, no doubt.

There were large body shuffles being planned for the near future, and Woody had been asking me about my plans. Evidently there was a list of guys who had already identified themselves as non-players for the higher positions—Mauler and Sugar-D amongst them, surprisingly. Their plan was just to finish out this tour before retirement without fighting for the higher-profile jobs. I told Woody that I would like to stay in the game and compete for the next round of jobs. He mentioned that there was a commander's selection board (called a Hawk board) for training command in a few months and asked if I wanted to be considered. I surprised myself when I said that I was actually interested.

Becoming a commander had never been one of my primary goals, but the thought of getting back to Training Command was appealing, and it would keep me in the cockpit for another tour after this one *(my eighth jet!)*. Playing at OREs and ORIs indefinitely held little appeal if there wasn't a good chance to deploy and put those skills into practice.

The drawbacks would be having to move again after only a year or so in one place and being completely out of the combat loop—probably for good this time. Bets didn't care; she really hadn't warmed up to the place yet. On the other hand, the house was comfortable, in a good neighborhood, and the schools were okay—until high school anyway.

On Thursday, I did a CW sim wearing the full ensemble as the controllers threw emergencies at me while, I suspect, they had the heat cranked up to ninety. That was a tough ride.

On Friday, I finished working on my slides, then ran a tactics review board. I was primarily just a facilitator, but I thought we got some good ideas down on paper. That afternoon was the naming ceremony. Since I was one of the guys up to be (re)named with a call sign I came prepared.

A pilot's call sign is traditionally derived from one of three main sources. The first would be variations, or abuses, of his actual name. Most people named Campbell will be called Soups. A last name of Waters will become Muddy, Hawn will get tagged as Goldie, Sharp becomes Not-So, Wright becomes Seldom, Hooker might be Two-Bit or Happy. Rogers will end up as Buck, naturally.

Another source of names would be related to some humorous story. A friend of mine who accidentally fired off a flare pistol in a vehicle became Smoky. Blow your tires on landing and you'll be known as Skids or Boom Boom. Say something stupid in public and it's likely to follow you for a long time.

The third category was a bit fuzzier—variations on an appearance or personality trait. A quiet person becomes Mauler or Nordo, a redhead may be Torch or Ginger, the navy guy will almost always be Squid or Flounder. Talk too much and you'll become Spam. The big guy will become Moose, Bull, or Tiny, and a not-so-skinny guy might be named Shamu, Whale, or Slim. Sometimes a series of letters like SDA or VBF will stand in for a phrase that is publicly unrepeatable, or just won't fit on a name tag.

Not all names are acknowledged by the actual individual. The OG was known by, but didn't go by, the POD, which stood for the Prince of Darkness—which I thought was a cool name, but he evidently thought otherwise and preferred Pitbull. A long name may just become abbreviated to J-11 or D+11. And sometimes we just can't come up with anything better. There are often a lot of duplicates. In fact, there are so many Bucks out there that they often have to be differentiated a bit more. At one point we had a Big Buck, Little Buck, Good Buck, Bad Buck, and Buck the Insignificant all at the same time—though the last two were actually the same guy, depending on who was talking.

Each squadron has its own tradition for a naming. In some squadrons the already named pilots have secret discussions that usually come up with absolutely horrendous, obscene, or otherwise physiologically-impossible-to-duplicate suggestions. Sphincter Boy, Pond Scum, and Anus Wrinkle aren't uncommon. Once the new call sign is proposed, the horrified recipient will attempt to influence the judge's final decision with frequent bribes of a variety of beverages. Eventually the bribes win out and some more acceptable name will be approved—usually the same one the guy has had for years, though I've met at least two Pond Scum's out there.

In the 8th, every naming was officiated by an individual known as "The Coat." The holder of the Coat is periodically selected for his ability to be funny and to remain sober(ish) until the end of the ceremony, and *he* has to fit into the Coat. There is only one Coat—mustard yellow with a fuzzy black silhouette of a sheep on the breast pocket, passed down since sometime around the Korea/Vietnam eras. It isn't a pretty thing.

The 8th's naming tradition is that The Coat will bring the victim up front and call for nominations. Everyone who has a call sign to suggest will get up in front of the crowd to make their presentation, usually with some sort of story as to why that call sign should be adopted. The rule is that while embellishment is expected and to be encouraged, the story has to be at least 10 percent true. Though I suspect that for several of the stories the only "true" part was pronouncing the guy's name correctly. Then, to share the pain, the person making the nomination will take a shot of Weed.

Toward the end, the guy being named may need to have a friend propose the call sign he actually wants. After eight to twelve new call signs have been proposed and marked up on the board, a series of votes by applause will winnow out the list a little. If the proposals are still too bad, the person being named can help the process along by "drinking away" a few of the more objectionable suggestions. Toward the end The Coat will usually try to steer the process toward something that can at least be repeated in public. The entire process has the potential to become raucous, especially if more than two or three people are being named on a single night. You *don't* want to be last.

The only inroad I made was to donate a bottle of my choosing to the event in order to limit the amount of Weed consumed. I'd bought a bottle of Yukon Jack and had modified the label to read "Yukon Brad." Yukon was the name I'd be shooting for anyway, and this particular brand of poison described itself as the Black Sheep of liquors, so G-Man had to approve. It didn't hurt that I'd had it in the freezer for a week so that it would go down with a minimum of burning. The bottle didn't make it to the end of the evening, but it still went down a lot more smoothly than Weed while it lasted.

After the three of us eventually "won" back our traditional names, we were escorted to the club. Pete (who never got a call sign that stuck) was there and we talked a while. Bets picked me up later on.

The next week started off chaotically, with tons of paperwork and other chores that needed to be done immediately. Before stepping out the door to fly on Tuesday evening I was told that I'd have to do my verification the following week. The three of us verifying would be Shepherd, Draft, and me. We began right away with a few briefings on how the whole process was structured and what the intel scenario would be.

The next day I flew two good sorties. On Thursday we worked on our verification training before I had to break away to sit through a training-curriculum conference (which was of no value to me at the moment). Friday included a full-blown aircrew CW training session in the morning before more academics. I was feeling a little burnt out and would be glad when this verification was over. Of course then there were the OREs and ORI coming up, in addition to whatever else popped up along the way. I guess what I was really looking toward was the summer when the inspections would all be behind us.

We spent the entire week after that in preparation for the verification, which was on Friday. The scenario was to strike several targets in Baghdad in concert with a limited contingency operation. As part of the process we created a complete attack plan, selected and studied the appropriate target photos, and created some charts and a Powerpoint briefing with which to present the thing. The rest of our time was spent studying a variety of subjects, as the hardest part of this evolution wasn't the planning and presentation but the question-and-answer session that followed.

A representative from every specialty within the wing such as intel, planning, weapons, ops and so on had a set of questions for each guy. Then each of the leadership in attendance would pitch in with their pet questions. Naturally they'd all had days to research obscure bits of subject matter while we had to deal with them on our feet. The OG in particular was infamous for posing questions that were notoriously hard to answer. Almost every subject involved was classified well beyond anything you'll ever see written down outside of a vault.

We gave the presentation Friday morning, and the entire thing was done in about three hours. The vote went in our favor. Having to do it all over would have been discouraging, to say the least.

While all this was going on, I also worked on my Hawk Board application. I'd decided to request command of VT-3 at Whiting Field, Florida. Getting back to Training Command, and closer to the beach, made the idea of an early move more acceptable. I finished my part of the package and passed it along to G-Man for his endorsement. As we ground through meetings in preparation for the next ORE, the thought of getting a command in Florida became more and more distracting.

The ORE ended up being short. I briefed and stepped to a jet but had to ground abort for maintenance. There was a spare jet available, but I was running very late. There was no slip time available for my TOT, so I was told to launch and cut as many corners as required to get to the range on time.

I took off fifty-eight minutes late and skipped every leg of the planned route. I just charged straight north up the basin between the mountains and the eastern edge of the Red Rio bombing range. Once on the northern border of the range I did a little hook turn around the top corner, and it looked like I was actually going to pull off the attack. But then, with just two minutes to go before release, I got a DLIR cooling warning light.

Several critical pieces of avionics in this jet had built-in self-protection systems. This one in particular was telling me that the DLIR wasn't getting enough cooling air from the jet's pressurization system to maintain its internal temperature within limits. On a long mission I would have shutdown the DLIR entirely and allowed it to cool off before turning it on again just before the target. But there wasn't enough time for that; I was already on my run. The machine was going to take care of itself when it eventually got too hot, and there was no way for me to override the impending shutdown, so it became a race. I thought I was going to make it, then the picture went black just twenty seconds before bomb release—frustrating!

Another little bit of frustration awaited me that flight. Because I had taken a jet that had been intended for a full route, but had only been airborne for about fifteen minutes, I was too heavy to land. Most jets have a maximum weight for landing, and I was well over this one's max. So I had to go to the holding pattern for a half hour to burn off enough fuel to get the jet's weight within limits.

On Wednesday, January 27, I drove on base for a 16:20 bus ride from the apple orchard to the squadron. I flew two sorties and both went well. The first was a 2.1-hour flight followed much later by a 2.0-hour sortie, hitting all of my targets. During recovery from the second sortie the field went alarm red, quickly followed by alarm black, so I again got to spend time in the holding pattern before landing. Once on the ground, I spent a full hour going through the entire CW decontamination process before getting off base. That sortie put me over 4,200 hours of total jet time, and over 100 in the F-117. I wasn't home until 04:15—a long day.

I could tell that morale was beginning to slip among us. We were looking forward to this being over. Maybe there were areas of our performance that could still be improved. But, from our perspective anyway, it was easy to see how the first couple of OREs were productive, then the following OREs perhaps made us just a little sharper. But we were well past that point, and now we were just grinding the troops and jets down. Everyone was tired and cranky, and the jets were breaking at a greater rate than was comfortable.

April promised to be a good month. The formal inspection would be done. A new OG and an entire complement of new squadron commanders would begin shuffling in. For better or worse it would be a big change of pace.

On Thursday, the bus rolled into the squadron area in the middle of an alarm black, and it stayed that way through the first launch. The weather wasn't very good, but I saw the ground to the west well enough to hit one off-range target. The weather over Red Rio was bad. I half expected that the second go would be canceled altogether, but the brass wanted the sortie count.

I was the first to take off on that second wave and led the conga line of fourteen jets through a sucker hole in the storm front up toward Denver. The weather cleared out pretty well north of Santa Fe, and I hit both of my targets. The return was a lot trickier though. I had to penetrate a solid overcast deck with imbedded snow and icing all the way down. After I broke out of the clouds to get sight of the runway, there were snow showers on final approach. Fortunately I had been managing my fuel-burn carefully and had a comfortable reserve for the approach. Several of the guys behind me were very tight on gas. We pushed too hard to accomplish the mission and were lucky we didn't ding any jets.

Early in February I was assigned to conduct a short investigation of an airspace violation. One of our guys had received a violation notice from the FAA (Federal Aviation Administration), and the wing was required to make a response. A violation notice isn't terribly uncommon, but we always went to pains to keep the FAA happy and our pilots anonymous. The audiotape for Munk's event arrived midweek, and I had my first chance to listen to it that night. He was at fault—plain as day. He mistook an altitude assignment and climbed before he should have. Everyone makes mistakes. His was caught. But I had to put it all together into some sort of report and wasn't able to find any previous examples to use as a template, so I had to invent a format. I spent several hours finishing up the transcription and violation report then hunted down the OG that Thursday evening to present it formally.

On Friday, I got a flight in the morning and then spent the rest of the day chasing a letter around the offices. We were trying to get a revalidation for Doc Brown to keep flying with us as an attached pilot, but the OG wanted some other information before he'd sign the letter.

The following Monday, I went in early to fix the Doc Brown problem by calling directly to a couple of offices at Langley to make sure that I was forwarding the correct forms. The OG wasn't available so I got the deputy OG to sign before sending the package off. We were following the format provided by Langley, but he still wasn't very comfortable for some reason. In the afternoon, I flew a sortie that went well. Then three of us rejoined for some much-needed formation practice before the recovery.

The next day I went to work a little early to get some paperwork done. I reformatted the LOX to make it more efficient and to better match the 9th's version for continuity within the wing. An LOX is a legal document signed by the commander certifying each pilot's level of qualification at any given time. Then I began reformatting a few of the squadron's grade books. I hadn't originally planned to them all, but I got into a rhythm and just continued until I was done. It turned out to be a long but productive day. Just looking at my shelves of perfect grade books—all exactly alike and aligned—was gratifying. I wanted to lock a glass door over the case so that no one could mess with them.

My Hawk package had been forwarded through the wing for approval. Then Woody passed on a compliment that wasn't entirely welcome. At the weekly staff meeting the OG had proclaimed that the violation report I had written on Munk's incident was now "the standard." While I appreciated the recognition, I hoped that didn't mean that I'd get stuck with them all from then on.

I'd expanded my plane search. An aircraft with four seats seemed a lot more practical for traveling. I saw a Mooney advertised nearby, but I'd sat in one before and had found that the cockpit was rather cramped. There was a classic 1958 Cessna-182 for sale in Phoenix for about the same money. Much roomier and simpler to maintain and operate, but a little slower. Neither choice was terribly exciting compared to an antique.

Tuesday of that week was rough. One of the more staff-weenie-inclined members of the squadron faulted me. Evidently, I hadn't followed proper staff protocols while talking to Langley concerning the Doc Brown issue. Never having been a staff officer, my first instinct when I saw a problem I couldn't fix was to pick up a phone and talk to whoever I thought was most likely to help. Evidently that was not the staff way, and I had offended someone's sensibilities.

Later on I was clued in that the root cause of the Doc Brown problem had been that the group hadn't wanted the waiver to be approved in the first place. It had wanted the revalidation to die a natural death at the staff level, done in by the hand of an anonymous bureaucrat. I'd been oblivious and had stepped on toes by success-fully pushing it through. If I was supposed to have taken a dive, someone should have said something.

After that, I had to scramble around to find my temporarily misplaced Hawk Board package. It had been lost in the shuffle coming out of group. Maybe that was supposed to have died a natural death also.

Wednesday morning we were informed that the squadron was on tap for a possible deployment to cover unfolding events in Kosovo. We would be staging out of Aviano Air Base in the northeast corner of Italy. Iraq was still simmering also. I wasn't sure how much credibility this latest notification warranted. Between Iraq and Kosovo, we'd been getting false warnings every other week since I'd arrived at Holloman. And I wasn't sure that there was much substance in this particular rumor since we still stepped to fly the evening sortie. Other than my jet's computers dumping several times along the way, the flight went well. In the dark dry night, I shot an easy 100 percent.

I was home by midnight and was unwinding a bit before going to bed. The phone rang at 01:00, and I was told to come in with my mobility bags packed to deploy. All I had to ask was "greens or tans?" Green flight suits were worn in Europe and the Pacific theaters. Tan flight suits were for desert climates. After a moment's pause the response was, "Greens this time."

So we were going to Italy.

CHAPTER 10

Pasta Express

Three things a pilot has no use for:
runway behind him, altitude above him, and
a tenth of a second ago.

A S THE SUN ROSE SATURDAY morning I found myself somewhere over the Atlantic. The previous Thursday I'd said goodbye to everyone. I'd had to be careful with my son, as he was sick again, and I didn't want to be dealing with a stomach bug while cooped up on transport planes. I had been carrying a single A-3 duffel bag stuffed with my best guess of the clothes and gear I'd need for northern Italy.

In the squadron, we packed out our offices in a ruthless manner. That usually involved pulling out every desk drawer that might hold something of use and then just dumping the contents into a cardboard box. Any sorting functions would have to wait. Then the boxes were collected until they formed a complete pallet load. Each pallet was then wrapped in plastic and strapped down with a cargo net. After the morning's sprint we suddenly ran out of things to do, so we sat around waiting for something to happen. The old saw about "hurry up and wait" is gospel.

Toward evening we made quick trips to the simulator building to practice the instrument approaches at our destination, Aviano Air Base, and also Istrana Air Base (our primary divert field). Becoming familiar with the approaches was mostly a precaution for the pilots who would actually ferry the jets over. This wasn't a trivial consideration, since the first time anyone would actually see them they'd be exhausted after having been awake for maybe twenty hours and having been airborne for twelve to fifteen hours. I was supposed to go over with the bulk of the pilots on C-17 transports, but everyone was preparing to step in at a moment's notice. Unfortunately, the transports weren't ready for the deployment, so we were all sent home to go back into crew rest and await a recall.

Our squadron had been allocated a half dozen C-17s from Air Mobility Command (AMC). In AMC any grouping of designated troops, equipment, and/or general cargo that constitutes a complete aircraft load is called a "Chalk." I was to join Chalk-4 and had to be in place to begin processing at 15:00. Since I had several hours to kill, and mostly to burn up some excess energy, I decided to go to the pool at 11:00 for a last swim.

As I was approaching the lobby, an attendant was waiting for me at the door with a message. Bets had gotten a call saying that events were accelerating and that I was to report to the staging area immediately. Naturally, thoughts of missing the boat were going through my head as I raced home to throw on a flight suit and head in to the squadron. Bets had had enough time to pick up our daughter from school early to say goodbye once more.

Once on base, the story turned out to be that some of our equipment pallets had been packed improperly and would take a while to be redone. So it was decided that ten of us from Chalk-4 were to shuffle forward to Chalk-3 to occupy the weight/volume capacity not taken by those pallets. Since the ten of us were running late compared with the rest of the people who had already been processed, the lines were much shorter for us. Most of this processing involved being issued our real-world mobility bags—"mo-bags," for short.

There are a minimum of three separate mo-bags required for each individual and a fourth for aircrew—in addition to the personal bag I had already been dragging around for two days. Each combat wing maintains a warehouse with shelves to the rafters stocked with these generic A-, B-, and C-bags.

The A-bag contains the usual go-anywhere stuff, such as a Kevlar helmet, pistol belt, knife, canteen and cup, sleeping bag, flashlight and spare batteries, mess kit, first aid kit, sunscreen, pairs of leather and neoprene gloves, mosquito netting, cord, poncho, and other miscellanea.

The B-bag expands that inventory with winter-specific items, such as a parka, lined field caps, mittens, mukluks with felt inserts, wool socks and sweater, and long underwear. Everything you'd need to camp out with (minus food).

The third, the C-bag, was the one that reminded you that this wasn't going to be a camping trip. It held our real-world chemical defense gear to include several sets of the over-garment, which looked like a pair of heavy arctic coat and pants (only impregnated with charcoal powder and other stuff), a gas mask with several spare filter canisters, lots of special hoods, gloves, boots, cotton long johns to wear under all of this mess, an assortment of chemical detection papers and tapes that we could affix to the outside of our bodies, and a small decontamination kit.

For aircrew, there is an additional D-bag, which contains the flight-gear equivalent of the chemical defense stuff in the C-bag.

So after going through all of the lines to drag this stuff around, have our shot records checked, ensure that our life insurance was paid up and that we had a last will on file with the legal office (there's a pleasant touch), we had a relatively short wait of a couple of hours before boarding the transport.

Throughout all of these preparations I was still trying to understand our involvement in this expedition. None of the traditional criteria applied. This wasn't like keeping Saddam or North Korea in check. The civil war hadn't shown any signs of spilling its borders or sponsoring outside terrorism. Unfortunately the most noble reason, simply fighting for the democracy of others, had long since fallen out of fashion.

Were we going to be just another foreign power interfering in another obscure civil war in a corner of Europe where civil war has been a hobby for the better part of the last millennium? The Serbs were already accusing Clinton of staging this as a distraction from his impeachment for committing perjury during the Lewinsky scandal—which coincidentally matched the premise of a movie at the time called *Wag the Dog* pretty well. Well, at least we'd be living in a civilized place as we asked these questions and contemplated our role.

Because Mauler and I were the ranking members of our group, we took on the troop commander role and got to ride in the cockpit during takeoff. The C-17 has a nice comfortable office, so it was much easier to travel in than the old C-141s. There were about forty of us on cargo seats along the sides of the plane with dozens of pallets and two trucks chained down along the center. The plan was to swap C-17 crews in Charleston, South Carolina, before pressing east. The lucky, and fast-thinking, troops quickly staked spots on the floor to sleep. The thought of stretching out on the cold aluminum deck became an inviting prospect after a while.

"Operation Pasta Express" (our unofficial reference for this as yet unnamed deployment) was soon rechristened "Operation

Ham and Cheese," as that was all we had to eat in every single boxed-lunch meal, morning, noon, and night for the next couple of days. Two slices of somewhat squished white bread, a slice of American cheese, and a slice of pink luncheon meat all hermetically Saran-wrapped to a waterproof state. Yummy!

By Saturday evening, February 20, we had arrived at Aviano AB, Italy. Large employments of multiple transports rarely went exactly as planned, and this one was no exception. During the layover in Charleston, we passed Chalk-1. Their jet was having all sorts of maintenance difficulties, and they were contemplating unloading their cargo to transfer to another aircraft. Chalk-2 had already gotten off and was a couple of hours ahead of us.

A few of the guys from Chalk-1 were lounging around taking turns being handcuffed to small rolling suitcases. They were escorting some of the more critical equipment we were transporting, such as the classified documents and hard drives for the AFMSS computers we would plan our missions on. Most of that was transferred to guys in our Chalk as soon as it became clear that we would get airborne before them. Our next stop was Lajes Field, Azores, Portugal.

Lajes was one of our regular stops when ferrying EF-111s back and forth between Cannon and Saudi. I'd visited the island several times and had once been stuck there for two weeks after an engine had come apart during what should have been a takeoff roll. The island was cool and green, but we were only there for a couple of hours before having to press on. Chalk-1 had finally gotten airborne and was trying to catch up with us. They broke again as soon as they hit the ground at Lajes and were going to stay there overnight. I would have gladly traded places with them. I could have gotten a real night's sleep and probably would have been able to get off base for dinner at one of the best seafood restaurants in the universe,

Pescadores, in the small village of Praia da Vitória, just a couple of miles outside the gate.

We had arrived at Aviano shortly after sunset and were met by the ADVON (advance echelon) team. An ADVON team is a small group of people who will immediately scramble to the deployment site by whatever military or civilian means is quickest. They are responsible for the initial legwork of organizing the in-processing, transportation, and lodging arrangements so that the entire squadron can be absorbed as smoothly as possible by the host base.

As I looked around at my squadron mates disembarking, I was struck by their searching looks as they tried to take in the scene. I suppose this is the universal reaction of a unit being introduced to a combat zone—trying to absorb the sights, smells, sounds, and feel of the air as quickly as possible, all the while trying to feign a casual attitude as their squinting eyes quickly scan the area.

This being a military operation, we couldn't escape the inevitable paperwork. There was no electricity in the hangar where we had been sequestered for some reason, so we endured a very cold and dark in-processing to our new unit, the 31st Expeditionary Wing. This was my second association with the 31st. The wing had been resident in Aviano since being blown from Miami, Florida, into the Everglades by Hurricane Andrew in 1990. I'd been flying F-16s with the 31st, but had been lucky enough to have transferred to Texas just prior to the storm.

The only glitch for me during all of this was being denied a local driver's license. My U.S. license had expired a few weeks earlier, as it turned out—embarrassing. After the required bureaucracy, we were then bused to a rather far-away hotel in the town of Azzano Decimo, south of Pordenone. We thought we were employing all sorts of great operations security, but we quickly found out that everyone else seemed to know our business. Before getting on the shuttle that was to take us to our hotel, some civilian had been bouncing around and insistently pestering everyone in our group for their patches.

Patch collecting is a near fanatical hobby for some, but this guy's timing was inappropriate, so we sloughed him off so as not to call attention to our presence in Italy. Forty minutes later we got off of the bus at our destination to be greeted by that very same guy and a couple of his friends he had phoned in. They had known exactly where we were going to be billeted before we did and had driven there before us. We bought him and his friends off with a few donations so that we could check in without them following us inside. So much for security.

We were starving by then, so several of us walked to a local pizzeria that was still open for some excellent food. The next day we checked out of the hotel and drove directly to Aviano to begin the work of rebuilding our squadron. We had been assigned an abandoned and (we later learned) condemned vehicle maintenance shed near the flight line to work out of.

On Sunday, February 21, the weather was foggy with low clouds and drizzle throughout the day. That afternoon, we caught the deploying F-117s. They came in amid crowds of international press and CNN coverage. I suppose politically that was half the point of our being there. "They've sent the Stealth, they must be serious." The guys were zombies after their nearly fourteen-hour flight. We'd been allocated a half-dozen large concrete aircraft shelters, adequate to stuff all twelve jets inside with a little twisting.

After getting the guys settled into their quarters (we had all moved on base by then), we trekked off to the bowling alley in search of food. Then a half dozen of us went to Haiji's room to have a few beers while watching *Gettysburg*. The movie devoted a lot of time to the slaughter and carnage of Pickett's Charge—perhaps not the best entertainment selection under the circumstances.

Afterward, we talked a lot, trying to determine the United States' role here at this juncture in history. In my generation, Yugoslavia had always been viewed as an extension of the Soviet Union. We never had to think about it much in singular terms. With the exception of the civil war in Bosnia, it had always been a small part of a larger scenario.

I was reading everything I could find, but trying to sort out the players in that region was tough. The fighting in and around Bosnia had received the most attention over the last few years, but that was only the most publicized part of the story. During the Cold War, Yugoslavia was described as a country with six republics, five nationalities, four languages, three religions, two alphabets, and one political party (and that one political party was actually just one politician named Tito).

While Israel had been the crossroads of civilizations and religions in the ancient world, what eventually became Yugoslavia after World War I had become a crossroads of cultures and empires this past millennia. What is left of its borders encompass the high-water boundaries of the Roman Catholic Church to the west, the Eastern Orthodox Church to the north and east, and Islam to the south. Like continental tectonic plates these geopolitical forces had been grinding against each other since at least 1389—June 28, 1389, to be precise. The historical focal point around which all Balkan events seem to revolve was a medieval battle on the plains of Kosovo Polje on that date. Though an ancient dispute, the battle at Kosovo Polje was still inflaming emotions in the area as if it had happened the day before.

Back in those feudal times, the expansionist power in ascendancy was the Ottoman Empire, and Kosovo was next on their list. The timing for the Serbs had been bad. Back then, Serbia was controlled by several feudal princes, more inclined to fight with each other than to unite. The Ottomans under Sultan Murad, on the other hand, were battle-hardened and competently led under a strong central authority. But with rapid expansion, the empire was also getting stretched a bit thin. So the outcome of the battle wasn't necessarily a foregone conclusion.

The leader of the Serbs, Prince Lazar, had managed to form a shaky alliance with two of his neighbors, Tvrtko and Vuk Brankovic. Vuk was also Lazar's son-in-law. Lazar's greatest supporter and warrior was a nobleman named Milos. But Vuk and Milos had hated each other ever since their wives had gotten into a face-slapping contest at a banquet over who had the tougher husband (you can't make this stuff up).

Vuk had been running a smear campaign against Milos ever since. As the battle approached, Milos, to prove his loyalty to Lazar and guarantee victory for the Serbs, decided to martyr himself. He pretended to defect to the forces of Murad. The Sultan, impressed by Milos bowing and scraping, allowed the nobleman to approach too closely, whereupon Milos drew a hidden dagger and killed Murad. Milos was put to death immediately, of course, and never knew that his sacrifice had been in vain.

Knowing that the Ottoman forces might be disheartened and flee if news of the sultan's death got out, his bodyguards kept the assassination secret long enough to contact one of his sons, Bayazid, to say that he was now the new sultan. This may have been a mistake, as Bayazid's brother was actually the older of the two. In any case, Bayazid lost no time abandoning his troops in the field on the Ottoman right wing as the forces began to clash. He rushed to his brother's side, in command of the left wing, not to tell him of their father's death, but to kill him before there could be any questions raised about the succession to the throne. Bayazid then returned to fight on the right wing.

With all of this confusion going on within the Ottoman command structure, the Serbs had a real chance. But they never learned that Murad had been killed until after the battle. And Vuk, who faced the now leaderless Ottoman left wing and could have dealt a crippling blow, inexplicably left the field at the moment of truth, taking his twelve thousand soldiers with him. The Serbs under Lazar and Tvrtko who stayed to fight were slaughtered, their bodies left in the summer sun to rot and be scavenged by an enormous flock of blackbirds swarming for days—*"thick as a velvet sea."* Lazar was captured and beheaded without ever learning of Murad's death, Vuk's betrayal, or Milos' sacrifice.

Technically, the Ottomans controlled the field and had won the battle, but they never capitalized upon their victory by pushing further north, and Bayazid's attention was quickly drawn to other areas within his empire. Technically, the Serbs had been defeated, but the circumstances of the defeat had defined their national identity. Centuries later, the Ottomans are long since gone, but the Serbs are still here and commemorating each June 28.

But why are they obsessed by a defeat? That's easy. Ask any American if they've heard of the Battle of Bunker Hill (which we lost) and everyone will respond, "Of course. Don't shoot until you see the whites of their eyes, and all that." Now ask those same people about the Battle of Monmouth, one of Washington's more inspired displays of leadership, and you'll probably get only a blank stare in return. Similarly, the Alamo and Pearl Harbor will live in our psyches far longer than and the battles of San Jacinto or Leyte Gulf.

The population occupied by the Ottomans quickly changed their religion to Islam and pledged their loyalty to the new sultan—an act of betrayal in the eyes of both the Catholic Croats and Orthodox Serbs. Just to add a little insult to injury, the Hungarians shortly thereafter took advantage of the situation by attacking and taking some Serbian land in the north, beginning their long expansion into what eventually became the Austro-Hungarian Empire.

So it isn't especially surprising that the themes of betrayal and backstabbing reverberate through the Serbian mentality. The Field of Blackbirds (Kosovo Polje) has become a cultural icon, and both sides have been fighting to maintain control of the region ever since. Serbian suppression of Kosovar autonomy is only the most current expression of this age-old struggle.

On the other side of this conflict you have the Kosovo Liberation Army, the KLA. Until recently the U.S. State Department had listed them as a terrorist organization. Unlike the Bosnian Muslims, who were mostly the victims of ethnic cleansing, the KLA had actively provoked this showdown, and they were doing it in a brilliant way. Their only recognizable figurehead, Ibrahim Rugova, was a pacifist poet, and every brutal attack they instigated upon their neighbors, the local Kosovar Serbs, was designed to invite a brutal overreaction by the government—which the Serbs invariably provided. If the KLA won, they won. If they lost, they looked like victims. There didn't appear to be a good side involved here, just two bad sides, with a lot of innocent farmers caught in the middle.

On the surface, it could be argued that this was the only armed conflict within Yugoslavia that we *shouldn't* become involved in. The big difference being that the others were primarily internal events. This time thousands of people were beginning to stream over the borders into Albania and Macedonia. And when that occurs, when a government can't keep its dirty laundry within its own borders, it becomes an international affair. So there we were.

Fighting for the displaced farmers would be a noble cause at least.

CHAPTER 11

Aviano

What's one difference between God and a fighter pilot? God never gets drunk and stumbles into the bar on Friday expecting to be treated like a fighter pilot.

MONDAY, FEBRUARY 22, WAS ANOTHER long day of scrambling at a frantic pace. The target set and attack plan were late in coming. At least that gave us time to finish setting up our temporary squadron spaces and to get the planning equipment up and running. Eventually we were divided into Gold and Black teams for the two planned waves. The Gold team would fly the first wave of sorties. The Black team would maintain crew rest to fly the second wave after maintenance had a chance to turn and rearm the jets. There wouldn't be enough hours of darkness for a third wave.

I was on the Black team, but had been in danger of not flying any of the first night's sorties at all. Fortunately, during the planning process I was redesignated as the spare pilot for the second go. Then another shuffle moved me up to be a primary player. The weather seemed to be the only limiting factor now.

By 04:00 the next day, the planning was essentially done, as much as I could help with anyway. The fine-tuning required the touch of AFMSS specialists, of which I was decidedly not one. I made myself useful by coordinating with the weapons troops to ensure a correct mix of bombs was being built for us. Specialized equipment such as laser-guidance kits and fuses may be deployed with a squadron, but the bulky stuff such as the actual bomb bodies are already stockpiled in place. All of the components of a bomb are stored in separate bunkers for safety and wouldn't be assembled until a unit requests a specific weapon configuration to be built for them.

Once requested, the actual explosive is rolled out of its bunker. The tail kit with fins and the guidance kit (if required) are installed. The fuses, arming wires, and initiators are added after the weapon has been transported to the jet.

My job became acting as the liaison between the squadron planners and the bomb-builders to ensure that the right number and configuration of weapons we might need over the next forty-eight hours were being assembled. Our initial mix of weapons included GBU-10 Paveway-II and GBU-27 Paveway-III guided 2,000-pounders and a smaller number of GBU-12 500-pounders for targets where limiting the potential for collateral damage was a consideration.

At one of the coordination sessions I ran into Cookie, a marine who had been our operations officer with VT-7 during my exchange tour with the navy. He was now the executive officer (XO) of VMAQ-2. They were the marine EA-6B Prowler squadron we'd be relying upon to provide electronic jamming for us, highlighting once again the fact that the air force's jamming capability disappeared with the forced retirement of the EF-111.

While the Prowler wasn't a bad plane, it was hardly state-of-the-art. When the air force had first begun contemplating the development of a new electronic warfare platform in the mid 1970s, the EA-6B had been considered since it was already in production. It didn't take long to discard that idea. The Prowler, which had first flown in 1968, was based upon an even older airframe from 1960 and was considered to be relatively obsolete even then.

A loaded-up Prowler can carry from four to six jammers all in external pods versus the EF-111's ten jammers carried internally. The plane is also subsonic, cannot be refueled by a standard "hard-boom" U.S. Air Force tanker, requires external fuel tanks, and, due to a lack of automation, needs three dedicated electronics officers to navigate and manually steer those four to six jammers versus the EF-111's single EWO operating ten jammers by himself.

The Prowler does have the ability to carry a single HARM missile, but there are no shortages of other HARM shooters, and the Prowler would have to sacrifice two jammers to carry that missile. It also has some comm-jamming capability. But there are entire squadrons of EC-130s in the theater providing far more extensive capabilities in that field.

To be fair, many upgrades have been installed over the years, giving the Prowler some enhanced capabilities, but the simple fact is that the plane is range-, speed-, and jammer-limited compared with what it replaced. Most of this could probably have been overcome if we'd had enough of them. But again, we'd stood down thirty-six EF-111s and replaced them with only sixteen additional EA-6Bs pulled from the boneyard. (Twenty were actually removed from the boneyard to be refurbished for joint use, but the navy kept four of those for themselves.)

I heard a rumor that the air force had frantically investigated whether or not it could reactivate a few of the EF-111s that we had delivered to the boneyard the previous summer, but it turned out that none had been fully preserved. The stored Ravens had already been stripped for parts to help stand up the additional EA-6Bs and were no longer flyable on short notice.

I still hadn't been able to get a call through to Bets because of the phone lines being saturated. Tomorrow would be the start of the war—if there was one—and I'd wanted to talk to her before launching.

February 23 dawned clear and blue for the first time since we'd arrived. There was an incredible view of the snow-covered Dolomite Alps just to our north. The housing area where we were billeted, a few miles north of the main base, was enveloped by the town of Aviano. The town itself was very clean and neat and reminded me of southern Germany. I had finally gotten almost eight hours of uninterrupted sleep and a decent lunch, so I was feeling pretty good. At work, a few small tweaks were being made to the plan and the weather was holding steady for the time being. All we were waiting for was the order to execute. We expected to have been in combat before the sun rose again.

But then we got word through our representatives at the CAOC that the night's mission had been postponed. A little later we were told that the postponement had been extended back to at least the middle of March.

The peace talks in Rambouillet didn't seem to be producing anything, so this was puzzling. The very poor explanation of the situation we were given went something along the lines of this: We were going to start a war to enforce a peace, but there was still no peace to go to war to enforce, so we couldn't go to war for peace. *Huh???* Too many non-sequiturs to wrap my little brain around! None of it ever made much sense.

We had been officially stood-down early enough to go to the club en masse for some real food. Then we took over an entire bar and kicked everyone else out. The pent-up tensions of the last few days had to go somewhere, so the stories and songs were uproarious. I've read that elite units have an almost tangible *esprit de corps*, that their warriors exude confidence the way a lamp gives off light. If so, then we certainly had it that night. We were supermen surrounded by our own kind *(in our own minds anyway, since we hadn't actually done anything yet)*.

The gathering quickly became an impromptu naming ceremony for both Haiji and another guy. It was absolutely tremendous. Haiji was hilarious and eventually kept his call sign at the cost of too much alcohol, almost entirely self-inflicted since he just wouldn't stop talking. The other guy didn't give as good a performance as Haiji, which would have been a tough act to follow anyway, and was rechristened. Not being able to win your old call sign back is unusual, but the crowd was pretty much out of control by that point in the evening.

I'd left more messages on the answering machine back home. That was four failures to get through so far. I gave up on the phones and finally got access to a computer long enough to send an email instead. I got a reply a few hours later:

Hi, Sorry to miss you yet again. I haven't talked to anyone from the base since Monday night. M. has gone out for the track team. I have to pick her up every day at 4:30. I think she will still swim but not all the time. We had the Blue and Gold dinner for the scouts tonight. S. got his last Cub Scout pin. He will have his Arrow of Light ceremony in a week or two. I am at the thrift shop on Tuesday all day and at the Jr. High Fridays. We have the Klondike games out at White Sands on Saturday. Maybe we can talk on Sunday. My mom is coming on the 30th of March for a week. Your sister is expecting her baby Tuesday. Take care babe. Fly carefully.

Life in a military family always goes on.

At least we were missing the OREs and ORI back home by being here. Rumor had it that the OG might be headed back to Holloman for the inspection. Meanwhile, I did a little studying of our potential target sets and a few other odd jobs. The tension level had almost entirely disappeared, and much of the day was spent creating a plan for local training sorties to begin the following day. Due to the limited number of jets we had there, I probably wouldn't get a sortie until that Friday. But since we didn't intend to fly weekends, a potential day trip down to Venice was also being planned.

By the weekend, the news coming out of Rambouillet and Kosovo didn't seem entirely to rule out action, but it wasn't a sure bet. Just to the north of our location there had been a series of avalanches up in the Tyrol. The news was full of the ongoing rescue efforts.

On Friday, we'd started with the usual 14:00 mass brief and then did some leisurely studying before stepping out to fly. The ground operations went smoothly except for getting flight clearances out of the Italian controllers. Evidently, we weren't doing something right in the filing process. Eventually I got airborne on Fu's wing, and we flew down the eastern Adriatic. After almost a decade of civil war, the coast of Croatia looked about as well lit and peaceful as Italy. We continued south to hit a tanker for a short while to update our refueling currency before heading back toward Aviano. I locked up a ship with the DLIR on the way back to practice my tracking, but its gyros gimbaled before TTG so I didn't get much out of it.

Our return timing was poor, and just about everyone airborne was trying to recover into Aviano at the same time. We had to orbit over the holding fix, called Penny, with aircraft stacked up to 23,000 feet. After a quick conversation over the radio I stayed in fingertip formation on Fu's wing (illicitly—we usually don't fly fingertip at night) versus asking for an altitude of my own, which I wasn't likely to get anyway, to keep the confusion level down a tiny bit. It turned out to be a two-hour flight, and I learned a lot about operations in this airspace.

We had a beer blast in tent city afterward. Unlike the pilots, the vast majority of our troops were being billeted in a canvas city consisting of hundreds of ten-man tents. They called the compound the Caserma Barbarisi, which translates to something along the lines of barbarian barracks. The troops racked out on sleeping bags and fold-up cots. The tents were heated by extremely scary-looking kerosene furnaces that looked too old to have been used as props on an episode of *M*A*S*H*. This wasn't even up to the standards we had in the Saudi desert. The bulk of the equipment that could make life more bearable was still stored away in the local depot, being held in reserve in case it was needed for a "contingency." (So what was this?) The troops were improvising and adapting, as they always do. Midnight chow in tent city was good anyway.

Originally, we were congratulating ourselves for snapping up the few on-base billeting rooms for our aircrew, but it turned out that the units that followed us in had taken over entire resort hotels up in the mountains and were living like kings. We jumped the gun in that respect.

On Saturday several of us took two vans on a trek up some very icy roads into the Alps to look at some incredible scenery. We went through the "tunnel of death," bored through almost two miles of granite and nicknamed after the large number of workers done in by its construction. Our van was running more poorly the higher we ascended. It was barely turning over as we climbed an isolated snow-covered one-lane road that was becoming more and more narrow. Eventually we were stuck. The snow was too deep to continue (even if the engine would stay running), and the road too narrow to turn around on. As the engine sputtered to a halt for the last time, Shepherd admitted that he had accidentally put unleaded fuel into the diesel tank.

With the help of everyone from both vans, we slid and pushed the vehicle around enough so that we could roll downhill. With more pushes around a few of the flat corners we eventually got to a low enough altitude for a chugging re-start and limped to the motor pool. It turns out that Shep was actually the second guy to put unleaded fuel in the tank so the workers were ready for him. They helpfully provided a hand-cranked pump to suction the tank dry before refilling with diesel. It seemed to run reasonably well after that, though I still chose to ride in a different vehicle that night.

That evening we went back into the mountains to a restaurant that appeared to be an old hunting lodge. The place was called The Bornass, and our dinner was fantastic. Red wines and bottled waters, breads, pasta with red sauce and mushrooms, tortellini with sausage gravy, chicken cacciatore, new potatoes, mounds of sautéed mushrooms, wild boar stew in brown gravy, blueberry and blackberry tarts . . . course after course kept appearing. It was one of the most fabulous meals I've ever sat down to, and all for about 40,000 Lira, or $25.

On Sunday, February 28, I took a walk down to the BX and bookstore. I bought a few postcards to mail to the kids and two books for myself. Munk was leading the way on local purchases by ordering a Harley-Davidson Fat Boy motorcycle to be delivered home. He thought he'd save enough on taxes and import fees versus just buying the same thing back in New Mexico to make it worth his while.

It was a slow day. If I'd brought my laptop I could have done some serious writing, which is about all that old computer was good for anymore. In the meantime, events in Kosovo seemed to be quiet on the surface, but troops and equipment were still moving toward the borders. The Serbs were gathering on the northern and eastern borders while NATO was working mostly through Macedonia.

In deference to the Greeks, we were supposed to be referring to Macedonia as the FYROM (Former Yugoslav Republic of

Macedonia). Evidently there was a dispute between the two countries over the right to use the name. But since the Greeks were generally opposing us, and the FYROM government was falling all over itself to be helpful, we usually called it Macedonia.

The next day the weather was slowly folding, but we launched eight jets anyway. Shortly thereafter the visibility began to plummet. A weather recall was initiated, but the decision was too late. We got back two of the eight jets before the fog pushed the ceiling and visibility down to zero-zero, and the following six guys began going missed approach. Those six jets, and dozens of the aluminums, were diverted to Grosetto AB on the western coast. The rest of that night and all of the next day was spent in arranging their recovery. Since there was no U.S. security presence at Grossetto, the poor guys had been up all night guarding the jets. Our leadership was frantic that we had jets off station.

The OG had returned to Holloman until at least the fourteenth, so if he was confident enough to leave the theater, life should be fairly calm for a while. I was scheduled to fly, but the weather stayed foggy with a constant light rain, so we canceled early. G-Man was probably a little gun-shy about launching into the weather after the other night's adventures.

In any case, Fozzy and I used the free time to calculate just how many training sorties we'd need to generate to maintain everyone's flight currency. The squadron would be hurting very soon from a training/currency perspective. One plan was to rotate guys on and off probation monthly to stretch out what few sorties we had available. A far from ideal situation, but with the masses of aircraft that had been deployed, the Italians were only allowing us one go per day, and the weather was taking out most of those.

The first week of March was predictable. On Thursday, the weather was poor, and the Italians canceled us for airspace reasons anyway.

I worked some training issues before heading back to finish reading my book.

One bit of news was that Draft's departure for home (his wife was about to deliver) had moved me up to the Gold team. So if even only one strike was launched I should be in on it—but he'd probably be back in a few weeks. Back in the States the marine Prowler pilot who was involved in that ski resort gondola accident the previous year had been acquitted. A few dozen people had died after the Prowler had impacted the supporting cable while on a low-level training mission. The jet had been flying out of Aviano so we were locked down in case there were any anti-American protests from the locals.

After lots of rain all day, the weather broke up enough toward evening for us to launch. I got airborne to do little else but look down on a lot of clouds before coming home to some large thunderstorms in the area. Speedy and I walked to the bowling alley for a burger afterward. He's a great guy, always smiling. His call sign is also very apt. The guy is so energized he makes coffee nervous. Speculation about the body shuffles that would occur in summer was a subject of conversation. Before leaving for Holloman, the OG had said that he had picked out my next job, but that I didn't need to know what it was yet.

That Saturday was cold and miserable. At various times it drizzled, rained, and hailed. Both the heat and hot water were out all day. Sunday was another drizzly day. All of the dead time was annoying. I appreciated time off, but I thought of the lost hours I could have used writing and getting other work done on a laptop. On Tuesday, I used one of the work computers to send an email to Bets asking for the old machine.

That evening I flew again and even saw the ground for three camera attacks. They were all along the western islands off the coast of Croatia. The sorties were short, but still productive in acclimating us to the area and weather patterns.

The next week we ended up canceling flying due to weather for two days in a row—prematurely each time it turned out. G-Man, probably rightly so, wouldn't back away from his conservative stance since the diverts. I helped out in the planning cell for a while before heading back to billeting. During that time, my only other interest was talking to some of the more serious marksmen in the squadron. I was getting talked into buying a good semi-automatic rifle. A classic M1 Garand would probably be the way to go.

The following Saturday was absolutely superb. A dozen of us spent the day in Venice. We drove to Sacile to take a train down south. The train was very clean and modern, putting every U.S. train I've ever ridden to shame. Once we got to Venice, four of us split off to wander through the narrow and winding alleyway-like streets.

Mostly just to rest, we stopped at a little piazza with an outdoor café called the Taverna Capitan Uncino. Figuring that we ought to be polite while sitting there it seemed appropriate to have a little lunch. Buster seemed to know what he was doing and did most of the ordering. Just a "little" red wine, breads, lasagnas, sausages, veal, and grilled vegetables took us two hours to enjoy properly. Everything was excellent. Back home, it would be my sad duty to inform all Americans who think they know what great lasagna is that they have absolutely no idea what they are talking about.

Toward the end of the meal it occurred to Woody that even as we were enjoying ourselves, the 9th was suffering through the ORI. So we raised our glasses in salute to the Knights that warm spring day because, as Woody stated, "Somewhere in the world at this very moment it is alarm black." We could have easily sat away the afternoon in that piazza, but there was too much to see.

From there we wandered over the Rialto Bridge to the Piazza San Marco (St. Mark's square). The Basilica was as spectacular as expected, very ornate in the Byzantine/Gothic tradition. The tiled mosaic floors were amazingly impressive, as were the multitude of differently styled and colored marbles used throughout. The gilded ceilings and arches were dazzling. Then we walked along the waterfront to look at the palaces and gondolas. You could spot the locals easily because they seemed to dress exclusively in blacks and dark grays. The tourists stood out by their bright colors and their obsession with feeding the pigeons. There were countless jewelry shops, glass stores, and shops selling the unique Venetian Mardi Gras masks. There was a thick, gauzy haze that lent grandeur to the views. It was a great but exhausting day.

The next day we went in to watch Fozzy and Mauler present their verification in the afternoon. They briefed two lines in Yugoslavia that had actually been planned by the cell. There really weren't any questions. Other than missing the trip to Venice, they got off pretty easy.

Afterward we had a discussion as to why there wasn't a "lessons learned" report available from the Gulf War. Sugar-D had been there and remembered having worked on parts of the report. But over the years it had been classified and tucked away long enough so that no one knew where it was hidden anymore. Secrecy certainly has its place, but you had to question why the report was important enough to create in the first place if it wasn't going to be available for future F-117 pilots to study and prepare with.

The OG had returned from HMN with news of the ORI results—all good. Another bit of news he brought back was that if things remained calm, we might rotate back to the States in three to four weeks to be replaced by the 9th.

The news from Rambouillet was ambiguous. The Kosovars were saying that they would sign the agreement, although no such "agreement" with the Serbs existed to be signed. What we thought Secretary Madeleine Albright and General Wesley Clark, the SACEUR (Supreme Allied Commander Europe), were actually doing was creating a framework that would provide an excuse to drop some token bombs on Milosevic for a day or two to push through a treaty, similar to what happened before the Dayton Accords. Supposedly the Albanian rebels, the KLA, were as bad as the Serbs when it comes to atrocities. Of course, it's always the uninvolved masses that suffer most. But, when all was said and done, we'd hit our targets when called upon.

I was scheduled to fly with G-Man on Tuesday evening, March 16, and got as far as the shelter before we were canceled for thunderstorms over the Adriatic. The news from New Mexico was that no one from Holloman was selected for colonel on the most recent promotion board, so we held a "hospitality check" at G-Man's for a few hours on Wednesday night. He was a full two years below the zone for promotion, so I don't think he was especially disappointed. He'd be off to National War College that summer anyway and would likely be picked up on the next board.

The news from the peace talks was still poor. It was looking more and more likely that we'd fly a few strike missions soon. The race for us would likely become trying to get something accomplished before we were replaced by the 9th the following month.

On Thursday, I flew a 1.2-hour sortie over the Croatian islands. It was good to get airborne again, but my jet was limping. After landing I gave it four write-ups that would all have to be fixed before it could fly again, including a very strange donut-shaped hole cut into the right main tire—almost as if I had taxiied over an industrial-strength cookie cutter. The electricity had been out for most of the afternoon and evening, so it was cold both inside and out. We finally had to choose between preserving our residual heat or light, so we propped open a bay door to shine a Coleman spotlight flooding into the building.

In the evening, we had a farewell party for one of the support lieutenants in tent city. She was headed back for a new assignment. The marines had created a damn good bar in one of their tents.

While there, I ran into another one of my old students from Naval Air Station Meridian. He was now an EA-6B pilot with VMAQ-2. I remembered him mostly for an incident when we had been flying a training mission. He had screwed up while maneuvering for a formation rejoin and was jammed right behind the guy ahead of him. I took control of the jet and performed a lag roll to create some better spacing. Evidently that wasn't in their books, so I spent the next couple of days demonstrating the technique to others.

We were going to be locked down again that weekend. It was beginning to appear that we might get to play a part in this episode of history. There had been a lot of protests and demonstrations outside the gates against any form of NATO action. In Rambouillet, the Kosovars had signed the agreement, though the Serbs still wanted no part of it—begging the question as to why the word "agreement" was being used in the first place.

On Saturday, I went in at 15:00 for a few hours. I checked my email and then escorted a group of B-2 pilots from the Vicenza planning cell out for a tour of an F-117. The buzz around base was that events were about to unfold. In the background there was also ethnic warfare breaking out in Indonesia, India, and southern Russia. It didn't appear that this would be a quiet summer.

The next day, G-Man called us all together at 23:30 to announce the latest lineup. I was back to the Black team again, but only as Fu's shadow in case he didn't have enough notice to make it from Vicenza in time to fly. If he did, which was likely, then I wouldn't get a line until the second night at the earliest. And if this was a one-night war as we were being told to expect, I'd end up missing my chance at combat altogether. *Damn!* I knew that after only a few months out of training I was one of the more inexperienced F-117 pilots there, but I didn't want to miss out on the action.

Serbian forces, both the VJ and MUP, had pushed the border and were moving openly against the Kosovars. The final diplomatic efforts in Belgrade were being expended. In the meantime we were going to our wartime schedule. My team wasn't supposed to even show our faces in the squadron until 21:00 each night.

It rained all day the following Monday—cold, drizzly, and miserable. The laptop finally showed up in the mail. Bets had packed some of the loose spaces with little bags of peanut M&Ms, some of which had broken open and the package had become infested with ants along the way. So I had to spend time literally "de-bugging" my computer.

After dinner those of us on the Black team went in at 21:00 for a brief on the combat search and rescue (CSAR) procedures that had been implemented. Another aspect of our CSAR preparations was to review our ISOPREPS (isolated personnel reports) yet again. This page contained fingerprints, photo, personal data such as our weight, appearance, and identifying marks and scars—all of which could be used by rescue forces to ensure that they were picking up the right person.

The more valuable section of this page has a series of easily remembered sentences we'd created from personal experience. They were each crafted to hold several specific bits of information that could be picked out for challenge and response inquiries over a radio. One of my sentences was "The first car I owned was a used, two-door, blue Chevy Citation, which I bought before pilot training." So if a rescue helicopter wanted to challenge my identity before landing (to ensure that he wasn't flying into a trap) he might ask:

"What was the color of your first car?"

"Blue."

"What was the model?"

"Citation."

By being selective, you could get four or five questions out of each sentence, and there were six or seven sentences available. Once any part of a sentence had been used, it could easily be replaced on the next ISOPREP by something like "When I was six years old we adopted a brown-and-white Springer Spaniel puppy named Frisky."

We were also given a brief by the intel troops on their best guess about the Serb's latest SAM and AAA deployments. The rest of the night was spent studying the strike packages. I had intended to find Fu's folder to review my anticipated role as his understudy, but evidently there had been one last body shuffle. While digging through the pile of first-night attack folders, an electric shock ran through me. There it was. A strike folder with my name on it! I was to fly the No. 2 line in the second wave of attacks and have two separate target runs.

My first target was the SIGINT (electronic signals and intelligence gathering) site at the Zemun Air Defense Headquarters. The spot was just north of Belgrade and only a mile or so off the south end of the runway at their main air defense fighter base at Batajnica. My second target was another SIGINT site on Sombor airfield in the northwest corner of the country. Both were very distinctly shaped buildings, which should make them easy to find and hit—weather permitting.

G-Man would lead the first wave, of course. He had commented on numerous occasions how he could never fathom why a previous squadron commander had allowed a relatively junior member of the squadron, Major Beast Feest, the honor of dropping the first bombs in both Panama and the Gulf War. There had never been any question that G-Man would be out front on the first night and that one of his bombs would hit the ground first. Standard air force policy didn't allow for both the commander and the operations officer to fly at the same time, so Woody would have to wait a few hours to get his chance.

As package commander for the second wave, Woody decided to force our team's schedule around by ordering us to stay awake until 09:00 the following morning. Living in a windowless world with little regard for the time of day can lead to some abrupt transitions. When we finally stepped out of the planning building we were dazzled by a perfectly clear morning with the sun casting a brilliant glare on the newly snow-covered mountain range to the north. But watching the sunrise before you've been asleep is bad for us vampires, and everyone was completely beat by the time we got back to billeting. I pulled shut the curtains and closed the Rolladen shutters on the window, which made it as black as night inside. I slept like a log until 15:00, but my sleep-cycle rhythms hadn't been consistent enough to allow me to stay out any longer, no matter how tired I might be.

The news from Belgrade was bleak. Holbrooke left Yugoslavia after having failed to get an agreement from the Serbs. Milosevic flat out said that he expected NATO to begin bombing soon. Perhaps our limited scope of operations had allowed him to decide that he could ride out a few days of strikes. Recent history certainly hadn't given him cause to think otherwise. We really hadn't carried through on a threat since 1991.

Other than tweaking a few details here and there, we were ready and just waiting for the word go. While I was satisfied that I'd be a participant on the first night, I was still having trouble grasping the fact that this was really going to happen. My generation of officers was indoctrinated with the belief that the lesson of Vietnam, reinforced by the Beirut bombing and the Mogadishu street-battles of 1993, was to not become involved in foreign civil wars. It was hard to believe that we had a lot to profit from in this conflict. But NATO had put its reputation on the line, so it looked as if we were going to see this one through.

* * *

Wednesday, March 24, was to be Day 1 of the strikes. (For planning purposes a "Day" runs from sunrise to the following sunrise. Calendar dates/midnight are irrelevant). The night before we attended another 21:00 gathering for a package brief with all the players. I was still in the game as No. 2 on Woody's wing with the second wave. Afterward, five of us walked the line, with our previously seldom-used Dash-34 weapons checklists in hand. Our task was to preflight every single bomb out there.

It was heady stuff to see all of that armament prepped, loaded, wired, and ready to go. The bombs looked subtly different from what we were used to with their yellow color-coded bands painted around the nose signifying a live weapon versus the blue-colored bands that identified practice bombs. Each jet was carrying its weapons on extended pylons looking like a bird of prey clutching bombs in its talons. Like the poster said, *Ready to Provide Kinetic Solutions to a Troubled World.*

The mood wasn't exactly one of tension, but more like a reserved focus. If someone went off to the side to study an attack folder, he was left alone, as in a library, face intent, but otherwise betraying no emotion. Our preparations were complete, so studying became a way to kill time—to be doing something useful, even if redundant, in order not to be thinking about other things. An infantry soldier might check an already clean weapon over and over to occupy his mind while he waited for battle. We had folder study.

Everyone seemed to be feigning a casual optimism and attempting to keep up the illusion that nothing extraordinary was about to occur. The unspoken reality of course was that some people, somewhere, were going to die soon. The only literary phrase I can think of to describe the atmosphere is cribbed from Beowulf: ". . . fate hovered near, unknowable but certain."

The time for questions had ended, and everyone seemed quietly prepared to do their jobs without regard to how unfolding events might harm them. The intel troops pored over reports and maps they already knew by heart, the maintainers were fine-tuning every jet, the armorers checked, rechecked, and checked again each and every bomb. Every pilot could find his targets by memory alone. It was all quietly magnificent. I was proud to be counted among such people.

I finally left the squadron with enough crew rest to be legal for the following night's action and was in bed by 09:00. I slept until 16:30. After a 17:00 breakfast/dinner I took a short walk under the setting sun saying good morning to the people I met. Our circadian rhythms were completely out of sync with the real world now and "morning" had become whenever we woke up.

On TV, CNN was carrying all the press conferences and announcing Russia's (very negative) reaction. The slim possibility that we might be helping to start World War III hadn't escaped anyone.

One of the bigger questions left unanswered was, "What's next?" This conflict was widely seen as containing aspects of a personal vendetta on the part of General Clark and Secretary Albright. General Clark had been involved in the region for a long time and had a widely publicized personal grudge against Milosevic. This dated back to a vehicle accident in Bosnia some four years before when three of Clark's people had died. General Clark had always blamed Milosevic personally for not arranging a safer trip.

Secretary Albright, whom I met briefly and gave a short EF-111 capabilities briefing to while in Saudi Arabia previously, was cut from a different bolt of cloth. Her attitude more closely paralleled that of the post–World War II thinking—the "noble crusade" mentality that had prevailed until Korea, Vietnam, and Lebanon took the shine off it. There had been a brief post–Cold War resurgence of the attitude, but that only lasted until Somalia. She had made comments to the effect of "What is the point of having this superb military you're always talking about if we can't use it?"

Tony Blair had also been a hawk during this buildup, but that was certainly more appropriate as this was, after all, Europe's backyard. Clinton hadn't really been out there making a case at all. Very uncharacteristically, he was avoiding the media and letting Holbrooke, Albright, and Blair do it for him—preserving deniability if it went wrong, perhaps.

In any case, all the leaders were absolutely convinced that this would be a one- to two-day war at most. The word being forwarded from the planning cells at Vicenza was that General Clark's only worry was that we wouldn't have time to hit a significant number of targets before Milosevic threw in the towel. There was no exit strategy prepared, and the only resolution being contemplated or planned for relied upon the cooperation of our enemy. We'd see what happened if Milosevic didn't choose to oblige us.

Sometimes civilized people don't understand that in large tracts of the world, power doesn't come from dialogue and the consent of peoples and never has. Mark Bowden in *Black Hawk Down*, though speaking specifically of Somalia, summarized the disconnect:

> Civilized states had nonviolent ways of resolving disputes, but that depended on the willingness of everyone involved to back down. Here in the third world, people haven't learned to back down, at least not until after a lot of blood flowed. . . . Intellectuals could theorize until they sucked their thumbs right off their hands, but in the real world, power still flows from the barrel of a gun.

Unfortunately this limited-strike belief had also been driving us toward political versus wartime targeting. Everything we had done up to that point was predicated on this only lasting a couple of days. We had been specifically ordered not to plan for a long war and had altered our targeting strategy accordingly. If this thing didn't end in a day or so we'd have missed our only opportunity to properly suppress the Serbian air defenses in accordance with USAF doctrine. In two days the threat systems would have been dispersed, and we'd end up fighting a war in the midst of SAMs and AAA that we should have taken out up front but didn't.

Ever since the air force separated from the army in 1947, it had been assumed that we'd get to run our own business. The Goldwater-Nichols Act screwed that up. The act's original intent, to force the services to act more jointly, was a noble one. But its implementation left a gaping loophole. As long as the overall theater commander was willing to follow the advice of his service-component peers, the potential for great efficiency existed—as had happened with Gen. Norman Schwarzkopf during the Gulf War. Schwarzkopf had had the confidence in his people to hand over operational responsibility for the air war to the person on his staff best trained to accomplish the mission, his air-component commander Gen. Charles Horner, and then didn't interfere. But if a commander chose not to do this (as was his prerogative), then you got airmen playing sailor, sailors playing soldier, and soldiers playing airmen. The net result in our particular case left the air force subject to the sometimes misguided ideas about airpower held by an army general and lacking the autonomy to do what we considered best within our own field of expertise.

This wasn't the army's doing. When the Chairman of the Joint Chiefs had asked for nominations to fill the role of SACEUR, General Clark's name had not been on the list. The army hadn't wanted him. In fact, his previous position, as commander of SOUTHCOM (Commander in Chief Allied Forces in South America), had also come about as an imposition from outside, not nomination from within. The Chairman of the Joint Chiefs had appointed General Clark anyway, instead of officers nominated by the army. Just to register his disapproval, the Chief of Staff of the army at the time, General Reimer, had pointedly refused to sign off on the posting.

General Clark was reputed to be brilliant, ambitious, driven, connected, self-promoting, and *very* political. What he was not perceived as was one of the team—he was thought to be more courtier than warrior. The most cutting description was the Perfumed Prince of Europe. Having said that, I'd never met the man. He was valedictorian of his class at West Point and a Rhodes Scholar. By all accounts, in Vietnam he led his men well in combat for several weeks before being wounded and sent home. Maybe he was the right person for the job, but that wasn't the vibe we were feeling right then. The general feeling in the USAF units at Aviano, and at the Vicenza CAOC in particular, was extremely uncomfortable as to how this was about to unfold.

So there we were, the prime actors, though certainly not the directors, in what was perhaps the early phase of a drift toward a wider war. And we weren't even allowed to refer to it as a "war." The White House had specifically ordered all agencies to avoid the words "war" or "combat," but to refer to it only as "strikes." Shades of Harry Truman—who thought that the Korean War was only a "police action"! General Clark referred to it as "diplomacy by force."

Later on that evening, the news services were reporting that airstrikes had begun over Serbia and Kosovo. The tension in the air reminded me of the Gulf War start. The difference this time was that I was dressing to go in to work, and my first real combat, within the hour, instead of watching it on TV.

I would do my best, and just hoped that I wouldn't let anyone in my squadron down. T-Dub and a few others had written letters to their wives and children to be delivered if they didn't come back. I gave that a lot of thought before deciding against it. How could I possibly say enough?

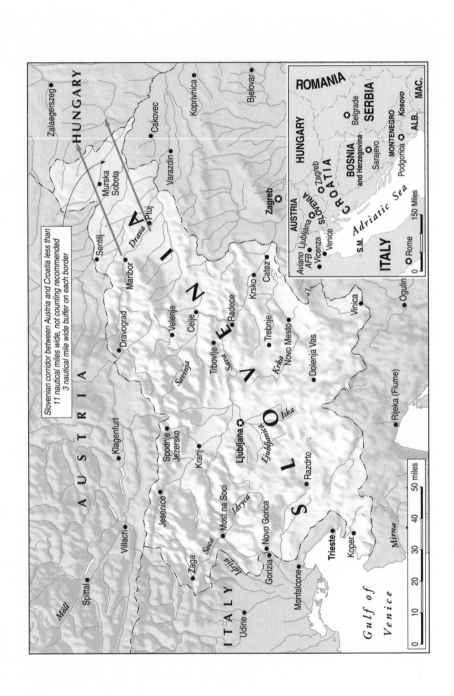

Slovenian corridor between Austria and Croatia less than
11 nautical miles wide, not counting recommended
3 nautical mile wide buffer on each border

CHAPTER 12

First Strike

Always remember that every weapon and each piece of equipment you will rely upon to survive your first combat was provided to the government by the lowest bidder.

O N WEDNESDAY, MARCH 24, THE Black team gathered at 21:00 in front of billeting before being driven to the squadron. Along the way we had to run a gauntlet of crowds outside the gate. Occasionally I'd catch and hold the eye of someone on the other side of the van's window. That thin sheet of glass separated two very different worlds. The media's camera vans were positioned so that our aircraft would have to fly directly over them on takeoff. One thing this war wouldn't have much of was security.

After a last trip through the life-support area to check our flight gear (every available pocket now stuffed with survival food, evasion maps, and other last-minute odds and ends), we briefed the plan one last time. The first-wave guys were beginning to filter in by then. Most were reporting good results, but also some misses for several bombs not guiding. The OG's bombs missed both of his targets through no apparent fault of his own. He had also flown through the middle of a dogfight and had watched an F-15 shoot down a Serbian MiG-29.

At 00:30 we stepped to fly. Before getting out the door intel had a last parting gift for us—a piece of surgical tape for the back of our left hand. On this thin bit of tape was written the *very* classified bits of information we would need during an escape and evasion situation in the event of being shot down. A few code words, a location, and several numbers were printed out. The reason for using tape was that it could be stuck to the back of our hands under our gloves— making it likely to remain with us during an ejection—and because it was small it could easily be balled up and discarded, or swallowed, if it looked as if we might be captured.

Out at the shelter I did the preflight inspection of my jet and bombs in a thorough and almost leisurely fashion before strapping in and linking up for the start. We had deliberately stepped unusually early to avoid any hurry that could lead to foolish errors. A few guys were doing the old World War II thing of writing messages on the sides of their bombs. My crew chief offered me a piece of chalk, but I passed and let them have their fun. There was a light mist falling on the jet but I didn't think it was anything too serious. The start went smoothly.

Things were looking good until just a few minutes before taxi when my jet began to rapidly shed computers. The water must have gotten to them. All three were gone before I could even reach for the power switches. Fixing the problem quickly wasn't in the cards, so my only option was to shut down and make a run for the spare.

The singular thought going through my mind was that if I missed this night I would probably miss the entire war. The Libya and Panama raids were one-nighters, and all of our leadership above the CAOC level seemed convinced that Milosevic would cave in at the first show of force. It had already been a couple of hours since the first strikes—so the phone could already be ringing to cancel this wave.

Our rules of engagement (ROE) dictated that we had to be within sixty seconds of a designated time over every preplanned turn point once we crossed the border. If not, then we'd turn back for deconfliction. Taking off on time was critical to the plan. Just before climbing out of my first jet, Woody called for a radio check. This check normally occurred just a minute or so prior to taxiing. I quickly relayed my problems and told him that I was going to try for the spare.

In peacetime, where you have all the time in the world to sort through delays like this, he might have elected to wait for me so that we could launch as a formation, but that wasn't the case tonight. His response over the squadron frequency was a clipped, "Good luck, see ya!" And off he went.

I swore a bit, but would have done exactly the same as thing if our places had been reversed.

I was now convinced that I was missing the show as I ran toward the spare jet. With my gear flapping and oxygen hose swinging around I huffed over to tail number 840-828. As I got closer I noticed the red tail flash that marked this as a 9th FS–assigned jet. I couldn't have cared less. It was available.

After having previously done one of the more thorough preflights of my career on that first jet this one was a bit more abbreviated. And whether I actually said it out loud or not (and I'm pretty sure that I did) I was certainly thinking, "Two wings and three tires, we're going—*NOW!*" to the waiting ground crew.

They all looked a bit startled as I blew by them skipping our normal preflight routine. I just circled the bomb bay in a breathless trot to make at least a cursory check of the armament wiring. Mostly I needed to see that there were two GBU-10s loaded, and that I knew the laser codes for each seeker head. Then I scrambled up the ladder into the cockpit. By then the crew had gotten into the spirit of the moment and my crew chief was right behind me to help me strap in and secure all of the connections.

To help the GPS platform align itself before taxi, the jets had been towed so that their front halves were hanging out of the shelters. That allowed the antennas an unobstructed view of the sky to catch satellite signals better, but also allowed the weather access to the jets. The light rain and mist that had also been falling on this jet was a little disconcerting now. The F-117 wasn't especially known for its "all-weather" characteristics, and I'd already lost one jet tonight.

In the F-117, perhaps because we usually fly alone, we always follow a procedure of taping every takeoff, attack, landing, and any other remotely significant event. Hitting the "record" button on the upfront control (UFC) as you title your tape, line up on a runway, or approach a target had long since become automatic. Also, as a single-seat fighter pilot, like most of my brethren, I had gotten into the habit of talking to myself throughout a flight—usually in the second person. The busier I am, and the more frustrated I get, the faster, and more, I talk.

Since tapes are usually recycled after every training flight, a pilot will "title" each tape when he first gets power on the jet to make it easier to sort them out later on. This tape title generally follows a standard eight-point format and should always include the following: 1) the security clearance for that particular mission (pretty much always "secret" until after it's over); 2) your name; 3) date; 4) call sign and mission number; 5) the aircraft's tail number; 6) weapons load and associated laser codes; 7) TOT; and 8) any other extraneous remarks.

The combination of having to speak through a small microphone embedded in a rubber oxygen mask that is sealed over your face and the not-so-great quality of our 1980s-vintage recorders absolutely required that you speak slowly and clearly in order for your words to be understood at all later on. But all you heard from my tape was the sound of an intake of breath then the exhalation of this:

SECRET,oconnor,twentyfivemarch,vegaonetwo,missionnumber XXXX,tailnumbereighttwoeight,leftrightbaysgbutensbothsides, lasercodeXXXX,lookingatleftbombXXXXXzemunsigint,right bombXXXXXXsomborsigint,totzerotwothirtyfivespottwoseven whichiszemunsigint,insparejeteighttwoeight.

All in one breath. And it wasn't a long breath either. Clarity had obviously suffered, but no one was going to fault me for brevity.

After cranking the engines and aligning the INS, I got the last chance inspection from the armorers right where I was. Usually that was done after taxi, but I didn't have that sort of time. The team was on a dead run under my plane as they dashed between their tasks trying to get me airborne. I couldn't have been prouder of those guys and how they rose to the challenge.

While waiting those last few moments for the armorers to finish, I was trying to have a casual conversation with my crew chief over the intercom, but our feigned nonchalance was a little too forced, and we both gave up after a few lines. With two fists raised I jerked my thumbs outward to signal for the chocks to be pulled from under my wheels. To the sharpest salute I'd been offered in years I taxied out—as fast as I dared. I was already out on the parallel taxiway and halfway to the end of the runway before it occurred to me that I should have requested a taxi clearance. So, sounding as casual on the radio as I could, I did. It was granted with tower being none the wiser to my actual location. Being painted black on a dark night has its advantages.

As I approached the EOR, I noted that several Strike Eagles had gotten there first and were marshaled in the hammerhead. No time for niceties. I transmitted a bogus priority request to tower and received the go-ahead to cut to the front of the line. In fact, from initially pulling out of my parking spot until I was airborne, the wheels stopped rolling only once—just long enough to run up the engines. Sometimes this "We're Special, We're Stealth" crap comes in handy.

I was going to launch an hour and twenty minutes before my first TOT, but I still had to fly across three countries, find a tanker to refuel, cross the border into Yugoslavia within sixty seconds of my assigned push time, and navigate through unfriendly skies for another twenty minutes before getting there. I was already twenty-one minutes behind schedule. But at least now I had a chance.

The jet was overweight with its load of more than 4,000 pounds of ordnance and a full 18,000 pounds of fuel, so my takeoff roll was going to be extreme. I had never taken off an F-117 with more than 500 pounds of ordnance before, let alone two tons of it. I had never taken off with a full load of fuel before either. In terms of weight, more than a third of the plane wasn't intended to return that night.

The jet practically groaned as we rolled along, making all sorts of little noises that I couldn't remember having heard before. At 01:15Z (to account for vast distances, and differing time zones, all military planning is done reference to Greenwich mean time—also referred to as "Zulu" time, hence the Z), I pulled onto the runway and jabbed my toe brakes three times in quick succession to pump up the pressure. The sensor display between my knees was set to terrain mode, which means that the FLIR seeker heads are trying to look in the direction the jet is going, but because of the way the jet sits on its gear the best it can do is a slight angle downward. All I got to see was the center line of the runway as it passed beneath me. The airspeed readout was about the only useful data on the sensor display being presented at that point. I was really flying off of the HUD. This was significant in the F-117 because takeoffs and landings were about the only times we ever looked through the HUD.

Another interesting feature built into the jet is an audible annunciator system of beeps telling you what the angle of attack of the jet is when the gear is down. At low angles of attack (faster than you need to be) it sounds like a slow and deep *boop, boop, boop*. When on the proper speed the sounds merge to one long steady *booooop*. That's what you want to hear on landing. But, when you are slow the tone becomes a short and high-pitched *beep, beep, beep*. If you are dangerously slow the beeps become positively strident as they increase in both frequency and pitch.

In peacetime, it is strictly prohibited to carry a load that would require a takeoff run before liftoff that exceeds 80 percent of the available runway. In peacetime, you would also never plan a takeoff run that went past the last arresting cable (usually about 2,000 feet from the end of the runway) in case that cable might be required to engage the tail hook during an emergency abort. But this obviously wasn't peacetime.

With full power indicated on my engine gauges, I released the brakes and began to roll. I commented in a rapid-fire staccato, to no one in particular obviously:

"Off we go, way f'ing late, it's zero one fifteen hours, I'm running twenty-one minutes late, but I've got thirteen minutes of void time, I think I can make up the rest if I can get on the tanker pretty quick . . . and maybe cut a few corners."

Fifteen seconds later the sensor display showed that I was still only going 87 knots.

"Looking for one hundred ninety knots."

Not to fly, mind you—I needed 190 knots just to rotate the nose gear off the runway. This plane wouldn't actually fly until well over 200. Twenty seconds after brake release I stated the painfully obvious.

"Man, this thing just doesn't want to go tonight."

Thirty seconds after brake release I was going 179 knots and commented, "There goes the two-board."

The last arresting cable, and my last hope of an abort, was now behind me. And with less than 2,000 feet of runway remaining (while going about 200 miles per hour), all three wheels were still firmly attached to the ground. Up ahead all that was left was a little bit of runway and then a chain-link fence at the perimeter of the field. Running parallel to that fence was a public road. After the announcement of the first wave of strikes, our activities had become a media event, and the fence was thoroughly lined with camera vans and their improbably bright white lights trying to illuminate the historic "action"—which happened to be me at that particular moment.

While I'm not especially shy and might have appreciated the attention at another time, I've got to say that being blinded by a face full of arc lights as I was about to crash on takeoff didn't seem like such a great idea at the moment. I tried to check my speed again but my night vision was shot and I couldn't see a thing in the cockpit.

Screw the numbers.

I reverted to instinct; this had become pure seat-of-the-pants flying. I rotated the plane's nose up, not at any precomputed tech-order speed, but simply in an attempt to miss the fence. The plane broke ground a touch over 200 knots (slower than planned), and the speed annunciator I mentioned earlier immediately sounded off with a higher pitched squealing of *beep-beep-beep-beep-beep-beep-beep-beep* than I had ever heard before or have ever heard since.

I was holding my breath as the plane drunkenly wallowed over the fence before slowly attaining some useable airspeed. The *beeps* slowed, became *boops*, and then blissfully faded away.

I'm pretty sure that I didn't hit the top of the fence with my wheels as I went by, and I don't have any conscious memory of raising the landing gear. I was just consumed with cursing the morons in the vans behind me. Those idiots didn't have a clue the mess I would have made if an engine had so much as coughed during that takeoff roll. The footage would have been spectacular though as 50,000 pounds of shattered metal, burning jet fuel, and the two tons of Tritonal in my bombs came tumbling through their party at more than 200 knots. The chain-link fence between me and them would have only added some extra shrapnel to the event.

Ah well. That was all in the past as I settled down to business and my night vision slowly returned.

"Departure, vega one two with you passing through one thousand."

"Vega, departure, roger, roger."

And I was on my way. Time was still most definitely an issue. In the short term I helped myself by flying at the maximum airspeed the jet would give me. Normally that would cut into my fuel plan but, due to my late takeoff, I was already carrying another third of an hour of excess fuel than I'd anticipated. So I was going to try to trade some of that excess for a few precious minutes. I also, very carefully, began cutting a few corners en route to the tanker tracks situated over Hungary.

The flight-planned route took hundreds of coalition aircraft through a ridiculously narrow corridor directly over Slovenia that night. Though not "officially" part of the coalition they also "officially" chose not to notice the airspace incursions. They, the Croats, and Bosnians had far more reason to hate Milosevic than we did. Regardless, from north to south the Slovenian corridor was only about a dozen miles wide. To the north was neutral Austria. To the south was Croatia and Bosnia. Even though Bosnia was being patrolled by NATO aircraft 24/7, those forces were artificially being kept segregated from NATO aircraft participating in the airstrikes. General Clark wasn't allowing our strike aircraft to use any Bosnian airspace for ingress, egress, or tactical maneuvering. The northern border of Serbia fronting Hungary that we were allowed to transit was only about fifty to sixty miles wide. There were no surprises about where we would be coming from. This was very cramped airspace—and all the more annoying because all of the restrictions were political and artificial. So much for deception or tactics!

Hungary had been a Warsaw Pact nation throughout most of my military career. Now, just a few weeks after joining NATO, they were getting the opportunity to fight for the West. I had to wonder what their officers of my age thought about that turn of events. As I crossed into the zone of action I checked in with the AWACS that controlled operations in our area—call sign Magic.

"Magic, vega one two, up on freq."

Most of the AWACS crews working our area were from the United Kingdom, and I have to say that a British accent sounds good over the radio. Quite proper.

"Vega one two, Magic copies."

Then he immediately transmitted, "Magic, time check, time check, time check."

I instinctively replied "Vega one two" before realizing with a little embarrassment that they were broadcasting that time check call to the world, not just me.

The time check reminder was so that we altered one of the codes in our transponders to a preselected value that changed every thirty minutes, the idea being that if an adversary were to capture a downed aircraft or somehow figured out the code on his own, then that information would quickly expire before he was able to make much use it.

While heading east toward Hungary, I also had the opportunity to fine-tune my INS by selectively taking updates on some turn points along the route. Several easily identifiable points had been built into the flight plan just for this purpose. Once acquired and tracked, a quick "squirt" of the laser on these precalculated points also updated the altitude function of the INS.

Lacking a radar, one of the challenges in the F-117 was completing a tanker rendezvous at night. All we had was the A/A function of the TACAN navigation system. By dialing in a pre-arranged frequency, we could get a readout of the distance between our aircraft and the tanker, but there were no bearings involved. The respective directions the two aircraft were heading relative to each other was also a matter of speculation. A pilot would only know where he was relative to the refueling track, his speed, and his own altitude.

You couldn't simply get on the track and go fast to run down the tanker. That might take an hour. What you did was analyze the rate that the distance between you and the tanker was changing, build a mental image of where everything was, and plan to cut across the circle at the appropriate time so that once you rolled out of your turn, the tanker would be less than a mile in front of you. This short distance could be dealt with by power alone without consuming more than a few minutes. Pilots who could take this raw data and build a mental picture of what was going could effect a rendezvous with a minimum of fuss. Unfortunately, this was a skill that didn't come naturally to some, and no matter how good you were individually, a train can run only as fast as its slowest car. When you had to cycle a lot of time-critical aircraft across a tanker in a timely manner the potential for even a little confusion or delay could be significant.

To get around this particular problem, someone with a little common sense had come up with a brilliant plan. It was brilliant because it was so simple. Everything would be based upon precise timing. Each tanker was normally assigned to a track at a specific altitude. Shaped just like a running track with two long legs capped by the curved turn at each end, the legs could be anywhere from just a few miles to twenty to thirty miles in length. The turn circle at each end was usually around five miles in diameter. The end of each straight leg had a set of coordinates associated with it and one point in particular would be designated as the anchor point. Tonight the sole requirement for the tanker pilot was to cross that anchor point, on speed, on altitude, wings level, and heading in the proper direction exactly every ten minutes of the hour. Our goal then became to fly across a few countries to be at that same point, on speed, on altitude (minus a few hundred feet), wings level, and on the proper heading exactly ten seconds after that ten-minute mark. Piece of cake!

And it would have been a piece of cake—had I been on time. Unfortunately, my carefully choreographed arrival time had long since lapsed. Even after cutting corners and flying at my maximum speed, I was still going to arrive at the anchor not ten seconds after my mark, but twelve minutes late. The tanker would have crossed the point a full two minutes before I got there. That doesn't sound too bad except that it translated to more than a dozen miles at the speeds we were flying. That was too far away to run down the tanker just with speed, and I couldn't afford to waste another eight minutes by holding at the anchor point while waiting for the tanker to come back to me. So, I got to do the rendezvous the old-fashioned way. As skill/luck would have it, this worked out great and in a few minutes I was safely trolling up behind the tanker at 21,700 feet (the tanker altitude was 22,000 that night) and a few thousand feet back. Unfortunately, as luck would also have it, I wasn't alone.

The tanker I had been scheduled for was a KC-135 going by the call sign Dollar-02. From a distance I could see that Dollar-02 already had two other jets hanging on (and in my way), but Dollar-02 also had the fuel I'd need to finish this mission. I was working on another bogus priority story like the one I'd used to steal the runway earlier, but that plan faded as I saw that both of the other jets were also F-117s from my squadron. I wasn't going to bluff them. I still considered asking for priority, but it wasn't the others' fault that I was running late, so I held my tongue, all the while cursing to myself and calculating the impact of every minute's delay. I'd just have to wait my turn (which, technically, had expired some fifteen minutes ago by then).

As soon as I punched in the tanker frequency I heard Fozzy (Vega-81) transmit "Dollar zero two, if you could do gentler turns this time that would help us."

Uh, oh! Not a good sign. I knew what the problem was as soon as I heard that call. Of the many fine attributes the F-117 processes, the ability to fly at higher altitudes (for us), heavy-weight, and at slow tanker speeds isn't one of them. The shape of our wing was wonderful for stealth purposes, and allowed reasonably high speeds, but it was a drag-creating barn door, hovering on the edge of a stall, at these slower speeds. The simple act of the tanker turning at each end of the refueling track was causing our jets to lose enough lift to fall off the boom. Our relatively weak engines couldn't compensate for the extra drag created by high angle of attack in the turn. Fozzy was asking the tanker for help. The "this time" part of the transmission meant that more than one attempt had already been made. Not good for my timing!

By now I'm stacked about 300 feet below the tanker, about 500 feet back, and slightly to the left side as I wait my turn. Vega-82 is on the tanker's left wing as he watches Fozzy getting his fuel.

F-117 night-refueling protocol dictates that the first jet to arrive goes directly to the pre-contact position behind the tanker. The next jet will fly to the tanker's left wing (the inside of the turn). Then everyone else will stack up in trail as we wait our turn to move forward. Jets coming off of the boom will cycle off to the right (the outside of the turn).

I could see by the nose-up angle of Fozzy's jet compared with the tanker's that he was just barely hanging on. It was going to take a while to get my fuel. There were thirteen minutes of holding time (called "void time" in the flight plan) built into our routes so that everyone could be fully fueled and ready to push simultaneously from our assigned locations. My thirteen minutes of void time had long since been used up on the ramp at Aviano. I had made up some of that en route to Hungary, but it was still going to be tight. Any more delays or random glitches were going to do me in.

Two minutes later I'm still watching Fozzy and figuring that I've got about five minutes, maybe a little more, to make this work. The tanker interrupts that thought with a check-in. "Vega one two, understand that you're in trail now."

I reply, "Vega one two, that's affirm."

"Copy."

After a few deep breaths it occurred to me that in all of my rushing forward I'd never been given "the words."

"Dollar zero two, Vega one two, understand that we are 'Rock and Roll'—I never got the words." "Rock and Roll" were the code words for this wave to execute the mission.

"Affirmative, Rock and Roll."

I had no idea if the tanker was actually carrying a code sheet, but I figured Fozzy or Vega-82 would have interrupted by then if I was setting off to do something stupid. After all, they were on time and should have been more composed than me. Even though most of our actions were comm-out to preserve some semblance of security (in spite of the media's real-time broadcasting of our takeoffs), it still seemed unnaturally calm and businesslike on the radio, and I didn't want to be the screw-up who went off on an international killing spree if this wave had been recalled.

And I waited. Mentally I was urging, *Come on, Fozzy, take your gas and get off.*

Other than some background chatter amongst other flights, the dominant sound was that of my own breathing into the oxygen mask. What seemed like an eternity later, Fozzy's jet faded back slightly and glided off to the right. As I watched him disappear into the southern night his lights went out and I felt a glimmer of hope. He was stealthing-up his jet and must have been getting ready to push the border. Vega-82 slid over to take his place as I moved up to the tanker's left wing.

"Vega eight two, stabilized pre-contact." Pre-contact is a stationary point about 50 feet directly behind the refueling boom.

A few moments later the boomer called, "Contact." They had made the connection.

"Vega eight two, one two, how much more time?" I ask.

No answer. He was probably communicating with the boomer through the intercom system now, so I radioed up to the tanker pilot. "Dollar zero two, Vega one two."

"Go ahead."

"How much longer is this guy going to need? I'm getting real short on time." Only eight to ten seconds elapse as my question is relayed through the tanker's intercom system back to the boomer. The boomer repeats it through the intercom link built into the boom to Vega-82. The answer goes back forward through the boomer to the pilot who responds.

"He thinks about two more minutes."

So I waited some more.

The five or six minutes I had thought might be usable when I had first rendezvoused had elapsed. Eventually I saw a puff of fuel spray from Vega-82's receptacle telling me his tanks had been topped off. I was practically pushing him aside as he glided off to the right.

The tanker was in a turn as I moved forward through the pre-contact position. Both throttles were full forward just to create any closure at all. My problem was going to be that as I took on weight I'd need even more power to hold myself in position, and I only had a small margin of power left between 100 percent and what was required to hold my fore/aft position on the boom. Any of the small throttle movements I'd need to adjust my position were going to be very close to exceeding that margin.

The total fore/aft refueling envelope of a KC-135 is about six feet in either direction. Too far aft or down, and you fall off the boom. Too far forward, and some serious damage is going to occur to both aircraft. The EF-111 used to have this problem at heavy weights also, so I decided to try a trick that worked in that plane. Instead of flying the plane with both engines, I set the left engine to 100 percent, took my hand off that throttle entirely and only adjusted my fore/aft position with the right engine. That allowed a little more "throw" to make small corrections in my position. Maybe everyone uses this technique, but as far as I was concerned at that moment I had just invented it. And it worked!

I blew off the "stabilized pre-contact" call since I had no intention of stopping there anyway. The jet wallowed slightly as it moved through the bow wave created by the tanker as I got closer. My refueling receptacle door rotated open and presented me with a welcome blue light reading RDY (ready) as I slid into position. The boom reached out for me.

I felt a small "clunk" as the blue RDY light went out and was replaced by a green LATCH light. A new voice called "Contact interphone." The boomer was talking to me directly through our now-linked intercoms so no radio transmissions were required. Out of the corner of my eye I saw the fuel quantity display increasing.

The author posing in front of a 7th Fighter Squadron "Screaming Demons" F-117 after graduating from the basic qualification course. Consisting of only twelve sorties in the jet, the basic course is only offered to experienced fighter and bomber pilots who have completed tours on other combat systems. *Author's collection*

A Northrop T-38 Talon climbing away from Holloman AFB. Universally known as the "38," the jet has been the U.S. Air Force's advanced trainer since the early 1960s. This supersonic glossy black stiletto of a jet is used as a companion trainer and chase aircraft to F-117 for the instructors to fly—helping minimize flight time on the vastly more expensive F-117. *Photo courtesy of Lonnie Pickett*

An F-117A on initial takeoff from Holloman AFB, New Mexico—caught in mid gear retraction. Note that the gear retracts forward via 3,000 psi hydraulic pressure. This forward-retracting design feature allows the slipstream to aid the gear's rearward extension if hydraulic pressure were to be lost during an emergency. *Photo courtesy of Lonnie Pickett*

An F-117 receiving the "last chance" inspection immediately prior to takeoff. Masters of their specialized domain, each member of this ground crew has unquestioned veto power over any flight for any maintenance or safety of flight issue. The pilot may be consulted—but the last-chance crew has the final vote. *Photo by Master Sgt. Val Gempis, courtesy of Lockheed Martin*

No one ever accused the F-117 of being conventional. Here a pair of maintenance troops conducts a post-flight inspection. Since the intakes are covered by radar-reflecting grilles, access to the engine bay is via doors normally designed as alternate air intakes that open at slow speeds. *Photo by TSgt. Kevin J. Gruenwald, courtesy of Lockheed Martin*

It was said that if you saw an F-117 being built on the factory floor that you would recognize it as some sort of vehicle. But that it was an aircraft, or of what possible use it could be, was not immediately clear. *Photo courtesy of Lockheed Martin*

Though apparently cluttered, the cockpit of the F-117 was reasonably well-suited to its mission requirements. Once familiarized with its layout, it became a comfortable "office" in which to work. *Photo courtesy of Lockheed Martin*

Day and night in the cockpit. Although the night shot is wildly over-illuminated for this photo, the normal ambient lighting made it almost impossible to see outside during a mission without dimming down the attack displays significantly. *Photo courtesy of Lockheed Martin*

An F-117 flies over the northern portion of the "canyon" at Holloman Air Force Base. Each F-117 is allocated an individual climate controlled flow-through hangar. *Photo courtesy of Lockheed Martin*

An F-117 on the boom during a refueling operation. In addition to the poor visibility out the front of the jet, the total allowable envelope of motion is approximately six feet in any direction from center. The wingspan of the jet is a little over forty-three feet. *Photo courtesy of Lockheed Martin*

Just a cool shot of four jets queued up behind a tanker. *Photo courtesy of Lockheed Martin*

The bulk of the stealth characteristics of the jet were created by its shape, but a significant percentage was achieved by its coatings. The RAM (radar-absorbent material) was glued in sheets over most of the exterior of the jet with the exception of the engine exhausts and the cockpit transparencies. In this picture, you can clearly see how individual sheets have been fitted together. *Photo courtesy of Lockheed Martin*

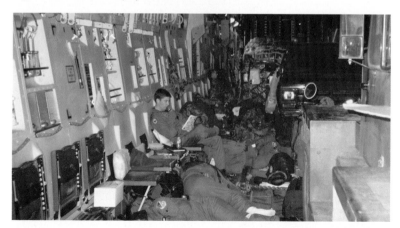

Somewhere over the Atlantic en route to Aviano AB, Italy. Though severely lacking in creature comforts, the cavernous hold of this C-17 transport easily swallowed several medium-sized vehicles, dozens of equipment pallets, and scores of personnel. *Author's collection*

With its braking chute fully deployed, G-Man's F-117 rolls to a halt in Italy after a fourteen-hour nonstop flight from New Mexico. After three days of hush-hush operations, hoards of international reporters were invited to document our arrival. *Photo by Senior Airman Mitch Fuqua, courtesy of the U.S. Air Force*

One small sub-division of tent city. With well-practiced efficiency, the entire tent city was created in a day to bed down thousands of deploying troops. *Photo courtesy of Holloman AFB public affairs office*

During the six weeks leading up to hostilities, there were several impromptu naming ceremonies. The Coat (the title) is periodically chosen to preside over namings based upon his humor and the ability to remain standing until the end, and he has to fit into The Coat. The Coat (the garment) is a mustard yellow thing with a fuzzy silhouette on the pocket—handed down within the squadron for some unknown decades. *Author's collection*

Prior to hostilities, the squadron made one mass outing for dinner. The meal was fabulous, and the camaraderie was tangible. We were forced to wonder if this was going to be one of those "remember before the war happened . . ." moments. *Author's collection*

After a sucessful mission, six pilots—myself, the POD, Mauler, Shep, Speedy, and OB—decompress with four of our maintianers outside the MX-debrief station. *Author's collection*

The Marine Bar became a great refuge (being about the only place that had 03:00–08:00 hours). During many a rousing dice game of "4-5-6," small(ish) fortunes regularly traded hands (author excepted—I suck at gambling). *Author's collection*

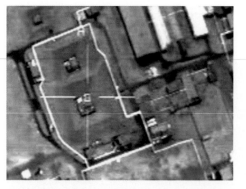

An infrared image of the Baric Munitions plant west of Belgrade approximately thirteen seconds before impact. The bomb has already been in ballistic free fall for fifteen seconds. The tiny white rectangle at the center of the crosshairs is what I am using to track the target manually as the aircraft flies over at 381 knots of ground speed. In five seconds (eight seconds until impact) the laser will automatically transition to auto-fire mode and illuminate the target for the bomb's Paveway-2 seeker head. *Author's collection*

A fraction of a second before impact, the GBU-10 2,000-pound bomb (circled) is a black streak clearing the protective berm of earth surrounding the target. The impact angle will be approximately 30 degrees off the vertical. *Author's collection*

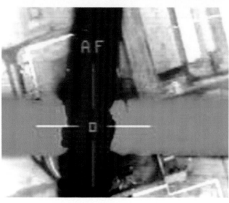

A direct hit. The weapon is in full detonation and the attack display is flooded with energy—obscuring the view of the target area. Within the community, this is called "blooming." *Author's collection*

Author with a pair of GBU-27 bombs—after the fusing problems had been solved—unfortunately, these bombs were destined to make a round trip due to our many weather "no-drops." Landing an unstable jet at night with two tons of armor-piercing explosives a couple of feet under your seat makes for a surreal moment. *Author's collection*

During a series of photos for the historical archives (virtually all of which were destroyed a few years later), we were all posed in our natural work environments. None of the classified material (which was everything) could be photographed, so the machines had to be turned off and all paperwork and charts hidden away. In this shot, one of our targeteers, Kat, completely fails to keep a straight face while pretending to study a blank screen. *Photo courtesy of Holloman AFB public affairs office*

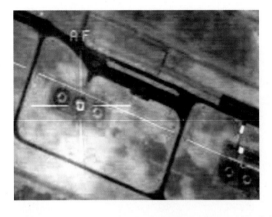

I am in a storm of anti-aircraft fire attempting to attack a gas-storage sphere at the Novi Sad Petroleum plant through intermittent clouds. Five seconds from impact, a momentary gap in the clouds affords me a (mostly) clear view of the target. The "AF" above the crosshairs indicates that I have selected the auto-fire mode of the laser, and that it is active. *Author's collection*

Two seconds to impact, a narrow band of clouds obscures the target. The "bang-bang" guidance of the Paveway-2 LGB system pitches the bomb off on a false direction while the target is obscured, and there won't be enough time to fully correct. *Author's collection*

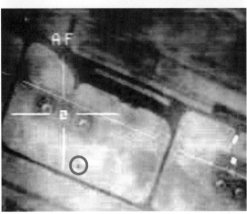

Moments before impact, the bomb (circled) is just clearing the access road. The bomb impacts forty-four meters short and right of the target. Intel surmises that the spheres were probably ruptured or destroyed by the concussion—but it is still frustrating. *Author's collection*

After F-117 combat sorties had ended at Aviano, and just prior to consolidating the squadron at Spangdahlem, Germany, Speedy flew one last sortie before his early return to the States. Front row: Diesel, Draft, Speedy, Opie, Haiji, OB, Yukon, and G-Man. Back row: Bronco, Earp, Mauler, Munk, Stump, Weather-boy, Fozzy, Woody, and Fu. *Author's collection*

The legendary Brig. General (ret.) Robin Olds had twelve confirmed kills flying the P-38 and P-51 in World War II and very nearly became the first ace of the war in Vietnam with an additional four MiG kills. This shot was behind the author's 1943 Stearman after a sunset flight along the Sacramento Mountains in New Mexico. *Author's collection*

Making a pass-in-review down the canyon on our return to Holloman at the end of the deployment. I am tail-end Charlie on Buck's wing, landing last to become the longest deployed. *Photo courtesy of Holloman AFB public affairs office*

"Okay, can you hear me up there?"

"Roger, sir, I can hear you loud and clear."

"Sounds good. Understand we're Rock and Roll?"

"That's a-firm, sir, can I get your tail number real quick?"

"Uh, yeah—eight two eight . . . sorry, that's eight four zero eight two eight." The requirement to do a little accounting paperwork at 22,000 feet, just north of a combat zone, threw me off for a moment (this was a government operation after all, and *someone* had to pay for this gas).

"Yeah, it's been a busy night and I'm running about a half hour late, sooo. . . ." I left them with that motivating thought, but I could already tell that this guy knew his stuff. My plane was settling slightly as it got heavier.

"We'll try and make this easy. Up three."

He reminded me to recheck my vertical position and to move up a few feet. I already knew that I was hanging low on the boom, but there wasn't a whole lot that I could do about it. I pushed the right throttle up against the stop and a gentle nudge back on the control stick did the trick vertically, but I slid back a few feet. There wasn't any more power left. And the post-strike refueling was supposed to be a lot higher.

"Understand you're going up to two-niner-zero [29,000 feet] later on?"

"Yeah, that's a Charlie, sir."

"Same track?"

"That's a Charlie, sir. Up three."

Damn!

Well, first things first. I would deal with the post-strike refueling (if I even needed it) when the time came. But if I hadn't unloaded those bombs by then I wouldn't be able to work at that altitude. I was already sliding off of this boom and had no power to stop it.

"We show no-flow."

I was full. Just in time.

I tapped the disconnect switch once to release myself from the boom, gently slid back to make sure that I was clear of the tanker's tail, parked the throttles up at full, and peeled off to the right for the border. By pure blind luck, my refueling had terminated close to the far southern point of the refueling track. By the slimmest of margins, it looked as though I was going to make it.

As I left the tanker behind, I ran through the "stealth checklist" one last time to deal with everything I hadn't done before refueling. The stealth checklist was utilized to ensure that any piece of avionics that could betray my position had been turned off, all exterior lights were extinguished, and most significantly for our radar signature, all antennas had been retracted.

This last item was a double-edged sword. By retracting the antennas, our radar signature was greatly reduced, denying the outside world the ability to detect us easily, thus enhancing our survivability—but our ability to communicate with the outside world went down correspondingly. We retained a weak residual ability to transmit, and we could still receive reasonably well, but the guarantee that we'd hear a recall, or be able to transmit a mayday if we were in trouble was now a bit questionable.

The IFF/SIF had been powered down also. This piece of equipment is usually the main source of information for the F-15C fighter caps, and their AWACS controllers, used to separate friend from foe ("friends" transmit a secret code in response to properly coded electronic interrogations; "foes" don't know the code and therefore can't respond correctly). So, electronically at least, all the F-117s now fell into the "foe" category. Our best defense against being "fratricided" by friendly fighters was to be just as invisible to them as we hoped we were to the enemy.

"Interior lights—dim. Exterior lights—off, off, off, off, off, and the APEX light is off," as I cycled through the toggle switches.

"Radar altimeter is off. IFF/SIF is in standby."

I skipped the holding legs and ran as fast as the plane would go straight to the border crossing point. Improbable as it may seem, just like a cheap movie thriller, I made it with five whole seconds to spare. I had crossed the border into my first real combat with enough time to comply with the ROE and prosecute my attacks. I actually sighed into the tape as I relaxed. I had made it.

Once settled down, I glanced at the target photos draped over my left knee (creased down the center to keep from sliding off my leg). Every target has three pages dedicated to it. The photo on top is labeled OVERALL. This shows the entire town/area surrounding the target and has a slender white line running up the middle to a white triangle that pinpoints the DMPI (desired munitions point of impact, or more simply, where you want the bombs to hit; pronounced *dimpy*). This photo shows huge features, such as the course of rivers, coastlines, and mountains, to assure the pilot that he is generally pointed toward the correct area.

It also contains OAPs (offset aim points), marked by white crosses. OAPs (useful ones anyway) consist of large, easily recognizable features such as distinct highway intersections, river bends, unusually large or oddly shaped buildings, and so on. By cycling a switch on the throttle quadrant the image seen in the sensor display will cycle from pointing at the target to pointing at the desired OAP. Switch up for OAP-1 and down for OAP-2. The center position of this switch moves the sensor display image back to the target. Using this technique the pilot can assure himself that he is in the correct area and perform his rough slewing even if the actual target isn't in view yet.

Next comes the medium photo that zooms in enough to cover about a mile either side of the DMPI. In the medium, you can begin to discern the shapes of normally sized buildings and distinct road patterns easily. This photo is used to make the final refinements to the attack run-in before releasing the weapon(s). Most pilots can slew the cursors of the DLIR directly over the target by this time.

The third page is the close-up photo. The detail of this photo allows the pilot to pick out the exact spot the weaponeers and mission planners want him to hit. The accuracy of modern laser-guided weapons can allow a pilot to pinpoint, and hit, not merely a particular building or wing of a building, but a particular corner of a particular room. This accuracy also allows the pilot to pitch his weapons down elevator shafts, through skylights, or even through the hole created by a previous bomb. This last option is particularly useful for "digging out" underground bunkers, tunnels, petrol storage tanks, etc. Ultimately, the limiting factor in which enemy targets can be destroyed has become a function of knowing where they are.

During a normal training mission back home, these were the most important bits of information we carried to the cockpit. Now they were almost entirely redundant. These eight pages, representing my two targets, a route map, and a glaring red-bordered cover sheet labeled SECRET had been in my hands for a while now. Nothing could have held my attention more. Fifty years from now I'll be able to recreate more of this mission from memory than I could have recited from my wedding vows the following week.

The Serbian countryside was still well lit, and I can't say that I saw any significant AAA or SAM launches. The only visible indications that a war was in progress were several fires on the horizon from the previous attacks. Though localized, the fires looked huge. The red and orange of the flames roiling through the black smoke at night looked surreal. More like a movie special effect than the result of our little planes. The bigger fires were mostly off in the direction of the Pancevo aircraft factory east of Belgrade (a first wave target). The first wave guys had also seen two MiG-29s being shot down by our F-15s, but their quick disposal seemed to be keeping the other MiGs tucked away in their shelters.

I certainly wasn't disappointed to see nothing being shot at me, but it was puzzling. I was expecting something along the lines of the CNN footage from the Gulf War. But then again, visibility is so poor from an F-117 that I would have missed most of anything that was actually out there. Other than the fires, and occasional warnings from Magic, things seemed unnaturally quiet.

I was busy monitoring my timing and flight path as the jet weaved left and right, up and down, fast and slow. No two legs were ever in the same direction, altitude, or airspeed. This was deliberately done to confuse any radar that might make a momentary contact. By constantly changing our parameters, a few radar hits couldn't be extrapolated to predict our flight path because that path was constantly changing.

I weaved my way over the suburbs of Belgrade and just south of the main Serbian Air Defense Base at Batajnica as I attacked my target from the southwest. This was planned so that the first leg after the bomb went off would find me over relatively uninhabited, and hopefully undefended, territory. Before takeoff I knew what my route would be of course, but was still surprised to find myself flying over the enemy capitol that first night.

I didn't have much free time to look outside for threats. In the F-117 taking care of the mission is almost exclusively an inside-the-cockpit affair. But after being brought up on old World War II movies, the one image that was astounding to me were the lights of Belgrade. The city was lit up like New York—not even an attempt at a blackout. The lights from apartment windows and store fronts, car headlights navigating the well-lit streets, and traffic lights changing from red to green were all clearly visible. To be honest though, whether the city was lit up or not had no bearing on how we navigated, identified, or attacked our targets. The Serbs probably knew this. But still, it seemed surreal.

AWACS broke in with, "All stations be advised Firefly-three, Firefly-three at Novi Sad, Novi Sad."

Someone in our Recon/Intel chain has detected an active

surface-to-air missile (SAM) site, an SA-3 in particular, at or near the city of Novi Sad, northwest of Belgrade. I was further away than the missile's known range so I wasn't especially concerned, but it made me look in that direction anyway.

The target imagery and coordinates I'd been given were right on the mark, and I never had to select an OAP throughout the flight. My first target had been described to me as the Zemun SIGINT building at Air Defense Headquarters, right on the Danube River. The building was large, distinctly shaped, and easy to pick out as I tracked it spot on. Compared with the tiny little targets we practiced on back home, the place was *huge*. This was so much easier than training.

About two minutes from drop I began my mantra, "Ready, level attack, record, narrow, cued, MPT," as I checked each mode of my attack displays. It was looking good.

Another call from AWACS: "All stations, Firefly-six, Firefly-six, Novi Sad, Novi Sad, Firefly-six." The mobile SA-6 batteries were becoming active.

A minute out, the display automatically switched from the forward-looking IR system to the downward-looking system. This was critical if I was going to be able to illuminate my target with the laser in order for the bombs to guide.

"Auto-fire, laser ranging is good, time to go [TTG—until bomb release] forty seconds, armed, armed, armed."

"Magic, Firefly-six, Novi Sad."

In my peripheral vision I saw a large fire just to my right. I pushed it out of my mind. This was not a convenient time to become distracted.

An F-15C guy called "[static] . . . [garbled] . . . six . . . bearing one sixty." No time to think about that now—even if I'd understood his call.

At TTG-5: "On the pickle button, laser ranging is good," and then the TTG display counted down to zero.

"Bombs away, I felt it go." The act of suddenly releasing a ton of weight from a plane would have been hard to miss anyway, but this was the first time for me with anything this large, so it caught me by surprise.

I confirmed that the bomb bay doors had closed, and I turned off the master arm switch. Both actions ensured that the doors were closed. If they were to stay open, my radar signature would blossom to the size of any other aircraft. My TTG display now read TTI (time to impact). It would take the bomb more than a half minute to fall to the target. I kept giving myself a running commentary of what was going on.

"TTI-twenty, looking for nine." At nine seconds before impact, I'd ensure that the guidance laser was firing.

"Twelve seconds, looking for nine." Things were coming quicker and becoming more exciting.

During the last few seconds the F-15Cs were calling, "Hedge one [an F-15C flight-lead] has a single group [possible hostile aircraft] over bull's-eye [just behind me], six thousand feet, moving fast." Maybe he saw my bomb as it was falling, or maybe a MiG had launched from Batajnica, just two miles off my left wing.

I forced myself to tune that out as I was at the most critical point in the attack. Talking over that last call, I said to myself, "Auto-fire, good laser ranging, three, two, one. . . ." All my concentration was focused on manually tracking the DMPI with the cursor.

At the bottom of my attack display, I could clearly see the bomb zip up to the target and smack into the roof exactly where the laser was pointed. The impact caught me by surprise as the flash of the explosion and the shock wave flooded my display. This is called "blooming." I had read about it, but the real thing is different. My spontaneous outburst, caught on tape, was on the order of *"Holy shit!"* and then lots of unrecognizable hooting and hollering. I tried to look over my shoulder, but couldn't see anything. Fighter pilots are taught never to look over their shoulders to spot their own bomb impacts—but we always do.

That lack of discipline lasted all of a few seconds before my training kicked back in and I ran through the post-strike checks and began preparing for the second target. The target photos were laid out and I got a few moments of relative calm for some of the radio chatter to begin registering.

"All stations, Firefly-six at Baker, active Firefly-six at Baker."

I had no idea where Baker was, and didn't care to bury my head in the paperwork to find out at that moment. But since I had just attacked something associated with air defense, it wasn't too hard to make an educated guess.

"Hedge, clean, mud, launch, south." Translated into English, this meant that the F-15C flight lead (Hedge) had announced he had no aircraft contacts, but saw a SAM being launched from someplace to his south. Hedge was north of me, so he was looking in my general direction as he was describing all of this. I saw nothing in front of me, so the SAM must have been right behind me (about where my target just was).

"Hedge one's going out." He was turning away from the threat.

"Launch faded, blow north." He'd lost sight of the missile and was telling his flight to continue running north.

"Hedge, blow north."

For the millionth time, I proved that it was physically impossible to twist around hard enough to see squat behind an F-117, but I was trying anyway. When the aircraft made its next turn I got a better angle and picked up a fire in the general vicinity of my first target, but after so many turns in the dark, I couldn't be sure that it was mine.

The AWACS was having trouble with its system and had momentarily lost the ability to identify airborne targets, so he called out the three separate groups he saw as raw data. All were directly in front of me. Fortunately, three separate sets of F-15Cs called in with their positions, which matched well enough with the AWACS' calls. They all appeared to be friendly.

My second target was another SIGINT control building—this one on the Sombor airfield in the northwest corner of the country. While everything was easy to find in general, I had some issues with my infrared display. The airfield had already been targeted by CALCMs, and the heat from the fires and smoke was obscuring my IR visibility. It was hard to pick out the fine details for exact targeting.

The building I was after in particular had already been hit by a CALCM, and one wing of the T-shaped structure was collapsed and burning. That altered what I thought I would see, but the coordinates were so good that the DMPI finally became visible right under my cursors. I threw my weapon directly into the front of the building. It might have gone in the front door.

My response to this hit was a simple "All right, let's go home." Quiet and blasé. Could this be becoming old hat so quickly?

Moments later my flight path carried me over the Hungarian border, and I turned toward the Slovenian corridor. It turned out that I didn't need to refuel again, and the return to base (RTB) was mostly uneventful. The only real glitch was the comm plan being profoundly screwed up. The check-in procedures in our instructions didn't mesh with what AWACS thought we were supposed to be doing. So for about twenty minutes a few others and I were officially "missing."

As I was egressing, I got to reflect upon my first "real" combat sortie. I had flown seventy-nine missions over Iraq, but this was the first time ordnance had been expended. The GBU-10 makes a hell of an impression, and I wondered how many, if any, people I had just killed.

After landing, one last surprise awaited me. As the engines

wound down and I was unstrapping myself, it became apparent that the canopy handle wouldn't unlock. It was stuck in the closed position. I'd never heard of such a thing, and the checklist wasn't of any help. I was trapped in the cockpit, which was quickly becoming very warm despite the cool temperatures outside. Eventually, the ground crew broke through a small access panel to get at the locking rods (which had bent somehow) and was able to pry me out. Since the seat won't eject if the canopy is in place, I had just flown my first real combat mission without a functioning ejection seat. I also had to wonder how long I would have been trapped if I'd been forced to divert to a field without the expertise to get me out.

After finally getting free, the ground crew and I carefully looked the plane over for any signs of damage, thinking that I may have taken a small hit that had somehow damaged the canopy mechanism, but we didn't find anything.

The crew inspecting the now empty bomb bays presented me with two foot-long lengths of white Kevlar cord, each with a clip attached at one end—the arming lanyards for each of my bombs. I also retrieved my security line badge from the aircraft forms where I'd left it for safekeeping while I had been flying. Then the van showed up. Tradition has it that whoever's turn it is to drive the crew van is responsible for keeping the cooler in back well stocked, and I've got to say that first beer went down very smoothly.

Maintenance got a chance to question me as to the state of the jet, and then intel got its turn. Watching my tape during debrief was interesting. People were called over to laugh at my outburst after the first target. I didn't care. I was two-for-two, which was a lot better than most. The majority of the GBU-10 attacks had been successful, but there had been a lot of problems with the GBU-27s. One of the more gratifying moments came after debrief when I had a chance to look at some of the others' tapes. Stump's, in particular, was good. He had flown over both of my target areas about ten minutes after I had and recorded the results of what I had done. The Sombor target was just a large IR smudge by the time he had arrived.

As far as I was concerned, the war could end right then. I would've preferred that very much actually, but it appeared that the Serbs were going to stand and fight for a while. They hadn't asked for more negotiations, but instead had broken off diplomatic relations with the United States, France, Germany, and the United Kingdom. The population seemed to be rallying around Milosevic. So much for our leadership's expectation of a quick surrender!

More ominously, the Russian ambassador to the UN had demanded an "immediate cessation of this illegal military action." The Russian prime minister scuttled his trip to Washington. Yeltsin was standing with the Serbs, but hadn't announced that he'd provide them with advanced double-digit SAMs yet (SA-10s or SA-12s), which would change the nature of the threat immensely.

Our leadership still seemed convinced that this thing wasn't going to take long. Hamstringing any pressure we might be applying to Milosevic, Washington kept assuring the world that this was going to be a limited endeavor. NATO's Secretary General Javier Solana actually said that the operation "could" continue for "a few days."

Clinton gave a good speech justifying the strikes, then dropped a bombshell of his own when he specifically ruled out any threat of a ground war or the introduction of U.S. combat forces. He flatly stated that he didn't "intend to put our troops in Kosovo to fight a war." (I guess we didn't count.) What a horrendous message to send to Milosevic. Now all he had to do was wait us out—if he could.

However it turned out, at least I'd been there, proving that I could do it properly and survive without letting my squadron down. Churchill once said that the most exhilarating thing in the world was to be shot at to no effect. While I wasn't entirely sure that I had been shot at, I could now better understand the sentiment.

After a tent city breakfast of scrambled eggs and potatoes (it's a good thing I like them because that's all we seemed to eat), I helped in the MPC for a few hours. Pete was there as a contractor with the planning cell and congratulated me on my first mission. It occurred to me that there was a wonderful symmetry at work. Pete, my first flight commander and mentor in TAC, was helping plan the front end of my sorties, while my old T-2 students in the EA-6B's were out there covering my back.

I got back to my room at noon. My schedule was completely shot now. Letting the sun hit me before sleeping threw everything off. I'd gone from vampire-mode straight to zombie-mode in a single day/ night/whatever. Either way, I slept as if I were dead.

Later on, I did a little research to discover that the jet I had flown, 840-828, had also been on its first combat mission. It had first flown in May 1987 and had been delivered to Tonopah the next month, but had been in depot at the wrong time and missed being deployed for the Gulf War. We were both blooded together. There wasn't a name on the canopy rail yet, so as soon as I returned to Holloman, I planned to lobby for mine to be painted there—though the fact that it was a 9th-assigned jet might present a few problems.

CHAPTER 13

Vega 31

If the enemy is in range, so are you.

THURSDAY EVENING, MARCH 25, I woke up at 20:00 to the sounds of more strikes launching. There wouldn't be a second wave because we'd already used up all of the preapproved targets. Evidently, Milosevic had been scheduled to surrender the night before, but someone forgot to tell him.

One aspect of our organization that was overstretched was the planning process. The procedures and technologies were bizarrely cumbersome. It took far too long from the ATO drop until someone actually walked out the door, so the planning couldn't be done by the same aircrew that was expected to fly. We probably needed teams of WSO/EWOs and dedicated planners whose sole function was to crank out these packages. I wasn't sure that we were capable of going at this rate of operations indefinitely, and contrary to what the politicians were still saying, the news didn't suggest there was a quick end in sight.

By the way, the official name of this gaggle was now Operation Allied Force, though the U.S.-only part (read F-117, B-2, and cruise missile) was still being referred to as Operation Noble Anvil. Having an operation within an operation was a coordination nightmare, but it seemed to be required. Intelligence and strike planning being released to our NATO "allies" was ending up in Serbian hands faster than it could be distributed to us via normal channels. The probability that there was a mole somewhere in the CAOC was being investigated. The fact that information was being compromised to the enemy was a given, but with the vast number of organizations, militaries, and countries involved, the leak(s) could be coming from anywhere. Though all nineteen NATO nations were officially equal partners, it was no secret that several were adamantly opposed to the strikes.

The French military has traditionally had close relations with the Serbs. Only a few months earlier France had arrested and imprisoned one of their own officers for spying against us on Serbia's behalf. The French major was found guilty of treason and received a sentence of two years. He had been assigned to NATO headquarters in Brussels and was caught providing the Serbs details of the military sites and actual target points being cataloged for potential strikes. Supposedly, this was being done out of his sympathy for the Serbian cause versus purely for the money. If true, then that sympathy might be acted upon by others. During his trial, he claimed that he had actually been acting under orders from French intelligence (which they denied).

The Greeks were even more vigorous in their opposition. In spite of this being right in their backyard (or maybe because of that) the Hellenic Air Force was refusing to provide any forces for the campaign at all. Public opinion there was running around 95 percent against us, and there were public demonstrations daily. President Stephanopoulos went out of his way to express his country's "sympathy for the entire Serbian people, which is fighting for its rights," as if the Serbs and NATO were the only players in this conflict. The Kosovar Albanians didn't get mentioned at all. Perhaps it was because of the Greek's kinship with their fellow Orthodox Christians or perhaps because of their general antipathy toward Albanians/Muslims.

The leader of the Greek Orthodox Church went even further and had labeled NATO forces the "Pawns of Satan." There was no ambiguity as to where his sympathies lie. It was disconcerting to see how comfortable religious people could be with the concepts of ethnic cleansing and genocide. In any case, NATO solidarity didn't last long.

Though billed as a unified NATO operation, the truth was that only eleven of the nineteen NATO member nations were providing even token forces for the strikes. The contribution from several of the nations could be counted on the fingers of one hand—with digits left over.

To add to the leaks coming directly out of NATO, there were Russian reconnaissance ships trolling up and down the Adriatic. Whether or not they were sharing information with the Serbs, or what sort of information that could be, was another subject of conjecture. Even if our act was tight (which it wasn't), we had become so enamored of electronic communication that vast amounts of information were just floating all around us. And for an even more readily available source of information in terms of aircraft types being launched, numbers, and takeoff times, all the Serbs needed to do was turn on their TVs.

The next day, I was wide awake at 10:30 after only about three hours of sleep—not nearly enough rest. A few of us went in at 23:00 with crew rest to fly in case we would be needed. Since we'd used up the limited set of preapproved targets, the first-wave guys were shooting at misses and leftovers from the first night. I was actually scheduled to fly in a tentatively planned second wave for a short while before the proposed target set shrank away and every single line was canceled. The guys down at the CAOC were scrambling to put together a new list.

Those of us not flying were redirected into the planning cell to help as best we could. Most of our planning efforts were toward a list of "proposed" targets in the hope that some might be approved before launch time. Later on, Woody called a meeting where he presented his plan to sort out some of the planning and scheduling inefficiencies we'd been experiencing. All that really got set in concrete was to assign titles and specify the tasks to the people already doing those jobs. We still had the same number of people with access to the same resources cranking out the same products.

The inconsistent performance of a few of our bombs was also a subject of concern. One notable loss was one of Speedy's bombs going stupid. The next day Serbian TV broadcast a segment from a cemetery, which we thought might have been long of his target. It had a fresh crater near it. If that was his bomb, then this was our first evidence of causing collateral damage.

My most useful accomplishment of the day was to create a bomb tracker spreadsheet. During what I thought was a casual conversation with the OG about our spotty success with the GBU-27, to that point, I mentioned the possibility of creating a product to catalog our bomb guidance results to look for trends. He liked that idea, so now I had another job.

I broke the categories down by aircraft tail numbers, dates flown, the type of weapon dropped, whether it came from the left or right bay, and the laser codes employed. Our success rate, for the relatively few bombs we'd dropped so far, was hovering around 69 percent for all reasons combined. My mandate was to update the product with any bit of information I could think of and to brief the boss regularly.

There was no real trend evident other than that the vast majority of the problems were related to the GBU-27, not the GBU-10.

The highlight for the evening was seeing the first round of official BDAs (bomb damage assessments) from the first night. Stump and I rifled through the pages until we came to our mutual first targets at Zemun and Sombor. The verdicts were a simple: confirmed destroyed/roofs collapsed. You can't say more than that. We shared a silent high-five.

I got out at around 06:30 to catch a few hours of a nap before going in for another twelve-hour shift. There was now a regular bus service running an hourly circle around the bases. That brought me to the tents for lunch around noon. While sitting there with some of the guys, a couple of young public affairs officers circulated the news that a group of CNN camera crews would be coming through. The camera people were exercising commendable discretion though, and none of the pilots were photographed.

It's sad to think how poor the relationship between the military and the media has become. There was a time when the U.S. media openly sympathized with the causes for which the United States was fighting. No longer! The Serbs were unlikely to knock me down, but an unguarded comment to a reporter, or any comment to one with an agenda, would get me sent back to the States before the day was out.

I did talk briefly to one reporter from the *Washington Post*. He had been called up from his regular post in Nairobi after Arkan, one of Milosevic's warlords, had kicked his reporter brethren out of Belgrade. He seemed like a regular guy, and he appeared to accept our standard preprogrammed "Happy to be here, proud to serve" line.

It was mostly a light conversation until he slipped in a very technically pointed question about the specific tactics we planned to use against a SAM system known to be in the Serbian inventory. After a nanosecond's hesitation I chose to treat it as a joke instead of getting into an argument and laughed it off as I walked away. I was surprised mostly because I couldn't believe that this *Washington Post* reporter had even asked it and, worse yet, would have printed the answer if I'd given one. Imagine Edward R. Murrow broadcasting to Hitler the numbers and types of British aircraft being launched during the Battle of Britain or the tactics they planned to use.

Standing right behind the reporter was Ghost, an EWO from the planning cell. One of his primary jobs was to plan around threats like the one the reporter had just asked about. I saw him stiffen up until I laughed. As we were walking away, he offhandedly mentioned that he'd been poised to strangle me if I'd even tried to open my mouth.

I spent the rest of that day and night working in the MPC. It felt good to be productive, even if it wasn't for my own flight. We were still tossing a few no-guide bombs out there, so those negative results were included in the bomb tracker. The rain had been constant, and it didn't look too likely that the weather would allow many more sorties for a while. Our lieutenant weather officer had taken on a much more significant role than he would ever have rated back home. He got the first speaking part at every brief or planning session.

We spent most of our free time watching the strike videos. Their analysis allowed me an odd use of my Ivy League education. My old professors would be aghast at how I was now utilizing my engineering training. Everything was in reverse as we figured out how to break, versus build, things. Now gravity wasn't a force to be overcome but an ally to harness. Foundations weren't what held up objects, but the weak points that could be kicked *just so* to topple them. In any case, I was out early enough to have crew rest for a likely mission on Day 4.

Sunday, March 28, 1999, Day 5—what a wild night! The weather was unexpectedly holding, and I was looking forward to getting my turn in the saddle again. The day leading up to that evening seemed ordinary enough. The flyers for the first go had been driven in that afternoon, and we were expecting to be picked up at 21:00 for the second-wave briefing.

The first indication that something was wrong was not having a van waiting for us at billeting. Thinking that a lieutenant had just screwed up, we tried calling the squadron, but the phones were dead. Time was being wasted, and we were starting to look for a vehicle to commandeer when a van finally squealed up. The driver wouldn't answer any questions, but said that we'd understand after we got in.

We hustled into the squadron building intending to ask what the hell was going on before Grinch bluntly cut us off with the announcement: "Sugar-D was shot down tonight."

All anyone at our level really knew at that point was that he had been hit and had ejected somewhere over Serbia. To control information from leaking out, leadership had ordered all phones to be unplugged and email access cut off. The squadron was still in a communications blackout.

We hustled over to the secure planning area where we expected to receive our now late flight briefing. None of us harbored the thought that we'd be canceled. This was a war after all, and shoot-downs happen during a war. Unbeknownst to us, having a stealth fighter get knocked down had changed the rules. The guys in Desert Storm had flown for almost two months without a serious hit, and now we'd lost a jet on our fourth night out. Some of our earlier concerns about going up against the shooting skills of "university-educated Europeans" for the first time versus the mostly third-world villains we had been facing for the previous fifty or so years began to reemerge.

The last time we had faced such shooters, fifty-five years earlier, a bomber crew in the 8th Air Force had only a one in five chance of completing twenty-five missions. More than three-fourths of all aviators who flew over Germany before D-Day ended up as casualties or prisoners, and bomber crews in the "Mighty Eighth" alone counted more fatalities in World War II than the entire United States Marine Corps.

The scene in the planning area was more confused than I care to remember. We got a quick rundown on what little was known to that point. Vega-31 had gone down for causes still unknown, over a location still unknown, but within Serbia. He had actually gotten off the first distress calls with a handheld survival radio while hanging in his parachute. A few of the tapes had caught it.

"Mayday, mayday, mayday, Vega three one . . ."

After a quiet spell where others on frequency began calling out for him and passing on that first call, he radioed again.

"Roger, roger, out of the aircraft! . . . Vega three one is out!" You could hear the wind whistling by as he spoke.

We had copies of his route, and Sugar-D himself had transmitted that he had been near the first point after his target, but we didn't know if he had been forced off his line or exactly how far he may have drifted in the chute after getting into trouble. The rumors had been rampant. He was in downtown Belgrade and basically screwed, or he was off in a remote corner near the northwestern border and the helicopters could be there in minutes. Essentially we just didn't know. But it really wasn't our job to know. The CSAR people were working the rescue effort. Our job was to prepare for the second wave, and honestly, we weren't doing that very well.

The second wave was initially canceled outright. G-man had told the planners in the cell to stop. That surprised most of us. To be fair to our leadership, they were thrashing through some unfamiliar territory. We were supposed to have been invisible, right? There seemed to be an undercurrent of thought that maybe the whole stealth advantage had somehow been compromised.

But this was war (even if we weren't allowed to say the word). These things happen in war. There was a vague feeling that we were treating it like a peacetime training accident by grounding the fleet. We knew that wasn't the case, but that's what it felt like as we sat around for the rest of the night waiting for developments— developments that we were not a part of.

On further reflection, the second wave was reinstated and then canceled again. I was getting worried, not about flying the mission, but that we'd thrash around so much that none of the required preparations would get done in time if it were actually to get launched.

Then G-Man did something that has been interpreted differently by various people ever since. He suggested that maybe we could still launch the second wave, but first he wanted a show of hands for volunteers to fly it. He later said that it had been one of the prouder moments in his life when every single hand in the room immediately shot up.

While I completely agreed with his sentiment, I also believe that he was misinterpreting the gesture a little. I don't think that most of the rank and file in the room ever thought that the mission should have been canceled in the first place. And in particular, several of us were concerned that he was asking for volunteers to fly sorties that we were already scheduled for. That was *our* wave, and we weren't asking to be replaced.

Plan A was to go out and bomb the wreckage of Vega-31 as quickly as possible. But the truth of the matter was that we simply didn't know where it was. Intel sources that did know the exact location never got that information to us quickly enough to be useful. For some sources, that was okay—their efforts were being channeled toward the rescue effort. But other sources just hadn't learned how to share yet. It was a glitch that we couldn't overcome when needed.

Plan B was to launch the already created missions. For the lines that coincided with, or crossed, Vega-31's line, the idea was just to look for smoke and hope that the wreckage would show as a target of opportunity. This idea actually stood a small chance of working. Because General Clark had cramped our ingress and egress routing so severely and had forbidden overflight of Bosnia entirely, we weren't really covering any new ground each night and had been operating in some very tight corners—and we did have that call from Sugar-D about the "point after the target." Unfortunately, while all of these discussions were going on, our tanker plan was collapsing.

The second wave was again reinstated with the original players, paused once more due to a lack of tankers (most were being redirected to the rescue effort), then pared down to just four lines—of which mine wasn't included. With all of these changes, our carefully arranged timelines had been run out and the last bits of briefings were given to the guys on the run as they were gearing up in life support. They got as far as cranking the engines before the final cancellation came through after the last of our tankers had been redirected.

The stand-down allowed us to pore over the tapes from the other guys in the first wave, trying to break out clues as to what had happened to Vega-31. After the earlier confusion had faded, we learned that he had gone down in a somewhat inconvenient location just west of Belgrade. The details of his ordeal on the ground belong to Sugar-D, and he can tell it better in his own words. But essentially, he had holed up in a drainage ditch by a plowed field. As Serbian forces were closing in on his location, a couple of CSAR helicopters, flying out of places unnamed, pulled off an amazing snatch. By around 04:00, we had gotten the word that he had been scooped up and was on his way to a base near Tuzla, Bosnia.

Our hopes to bomb the wreckage evaporated when CNN began broadcasting footage of tail number -806 lying on its back and still smoldering as civilians climbed all over it. We weren't going to blow up hundreds of civilians on live TV.

After his trip over the border, an MC-130 brought Sugar-D back home to Aviano, and he was on our ramp by 07:00. More than a hundred of us were out there to greet him. The sun had just risen and was amazingly bright as he stepped off the Hercules transport. Another crewman followed, with what looked like a trash bag of what was left of Sugar-D's gear slung over his shoulder.

A few of the enlisted troops were his first attention. The crew chief of -806 was reassured that nothing he had done had caused the jet to go down. The intel briefer and targeteer each came up to give a welcome-back salute. It was then that we witnessed a "Norman Rockwell moment." All of us had been carrying souvenirs for various personnel on missions the previous few days. On this mission, Sugar-D had been carrying an American flag for Kat, our favorite targeteer.

Even from my distance away I could see what an emotional event it was. After the salute, as Kat was about to turn away, he stopped her. No words were spoken

He pulled out the flag that he had been carrying tucked inside his flight suit. Through a bit of premonition he had purposefully placed it there before he strapped in, instead of off to the side of the cockpit where we would normally store souvenirs. So instead of going down with the plane, when he ejected it went with him. In the future, people would never believe that was real, that we hadn't made it up for the media. They'd say that it was just too corny to be true. But we were all there and saw it happen.

That would have been a great, and upbeat, ending for the war. But the reality was different. The myth of our invincibility had been shattered, even though we always knew that it contained as many elements of myth as reality. And in any case, I had to leave the ramp for crew rest. I was scheduled to fly the first mission after the Serbs had proven to themselves that we could be hit.

After a slow breakfast and few hours of sleep I spent the afternoon in front of the TV watching developments. CNN was showing the news from Belgrade and Kosovo. The refugee situation was becoming reminiscent of World War II footage—hundreds of thousands of displaced peasants fleeing ancestral farms, taking only what they could carry on their backs or pile on top of tractors. The part of our prewar strategy that was going to halt the ethnic cleansing had failed. This half-assed gradualist targeting we had been limited to was only encouraging the Serbs. They seemed to be scrambling to take advantage of our timidity and indecision. The Serbs called it Operation Horseshoe—the mass expulsion of all Kosovar Albanians from the country.

In Belgrade, the lights were still on, and they were holding outdoor concerts. All of the children had been fitted with little paper targets pinned to their clothes. People were holding up signs with crude silhouettes of the F-117 and the caption in English, "Sorry, we didn't know it was invisible." *Ouch!* Round one went to the Serbs.

Earp and I had a long talk on the subject. It would be interesting to see how the rules of engagement would change after the shoot-down. And to think that all of this had started only a few days earlier! It seemed like ages now.

I got through to Bets on the phone eventually. She had been camping up in the mountains with the kids and hadn't heard the news of -806 being lost. When they pulled into the driveway, E.T. was waiting for them. E.T. hadn't deployed yet and was one of the guys sent around town to notify the families that everything had turned out alright and that the person on the ground hadn't been their husband/father. He was also smart enough to be driving his personal car and wearing a flight suit as opposed to a blue uniform.

Every military wife knows what it means when a staff car pulls up to the house and commanders and chaplains climb out wearing their service dress uniforms—looking as uncomfortable and out of place in that suburban environment as penguins in the desert. There is always an order to "stay off the phones until we can get there in person," but it often doesn't work out that way.

Usually the word has already leaked out to everyone *except* the wife involved. Some guy would clandestinely call his wife and say something like "If you hear something—it wasn't me, I'll explain later. By the way, don't tell anyone I called." But they always did, and by comparing notes as to who had talked to whom, and who else hadn't been accounted for, the search quickly narrowed down to the unlucky individual. By the time the staff car pulled into the driveway, there was often a host of wives discretely off to the side waiting to help once the official part of the notification was over. The wives' network can often distribute information faster than any other communication system known to mankind.

E.T. stopped them in the driveway. "It wasn't him, and in any case it's all over."

To which Bets responded, "What are you talking about?" No one had contacted her before then.

There are no Nervous Nellies on that home front. Inside the house, she counted thirty-one messages from friends and family waiting for her on the answering machine before it had run out of tape.

Sugar-D's wife turned out to be easy to find. She was an active duty officer, and happened to be on-call as the acting commander for her section that weekend. She was recalled to work on some pretense where she could be notified without the entire neighborhood looking over her shoulder. As she approached the general's office suite, the PA officer was just leaving and, recognizing her as they passed, betrayed a momentary flash of horror as he hurried away. By then she pretty much knew what was waiting for her on the other side of those doors.

One of the small ironies of Sugar-D being the one to go down was that if you had to pick out the one individual from the squadron most likely to pull this off, it probably would have been him. As one of the few F-117 Gulf War veterans deployed, he had been dismayed by the poorly thought-out evasion plans initially offered us (one plan had advised us to pretend we were lost UN inspectors). He had worked to create something more realistic to our situation, and only a few days before the strikes had begun, he had given a brief on these revised procedures. He was a fitness fanatic and an unusually focused individual when it came to things like nutrition and hydration.

Every pilot is required to go through survival school, and I distinctly remember my weeks in the camps. The training had been divided in two. The first week was in the field, learning evasion and survival techniques, improvising shelters from scraps of parachute fabric, trying to catch fish and squirrels (we were sent into the woods for a week with a one-meal supply of food) and learning to navigate and hide in the forest. The second week had been devoted to how to act if captured. The time spent in the mock POW camp and interrogation facilities was ingrained in every aircrew member's memory. On the whole, what it mostly taught us was to make damned sure not to get shot down in the first place.

In any case, the U.S. Air Force had now paid the first round of wages for neglecting the SEAD (suppression of enemy air defenses) and the electronic warfare lessons that had been developed during these past three decades since Vietnam. We'd simply given up too much capability in the drive to cut budgets. In hindsight, what would the military have paid for a squadron of EF-111s Ravens and F-4G Wild Weasels to have been airborne the night before?

It was easy to see how this could have been avoided, but the simple truth was that we were stretched thin. Not in strike aircraft: we already had far more than could be justified by the approved target sets. As early as Day 2 our second wave had been canceled altogether due to a complete lack of approved targets. The shortage was in support assets. The EA-6Bs were doing the best they could, but due to their numbers and limitations, they needed to be rationed toward communities more in need of their services than we were. And pretty much the whole world's fleet of Block-50s was already tied up in the Balkans and Middle East to the point that stateside training was grinding to a halt. (Within a month, the navy would be forced to move the USS *Kitty Hawk*, the first carrier I had qualified on during my exchange tour, to the Persian Gulf—leaving the western Pacific without even a single carrier for the very first time since Pearl Harbor).

One good thing did come out of this. Almost immediately we were informed that General Clark's prohibition from flying over Bosnia had been rescinded. Now we could get out of the "phone booth" and begin employing more realistic tactics at least.

It looked like we'd be in this one for a while now. This couldn't be another phony "three-day strike then quit" campaign like Operation Desert Fox or some of the other limited punitive actions these past few years. Churchill never said, "We'll fight them on the beaches, we'll fight them on the cliffs . . . but we'll give up if they shoot back." Maybe it was no longer entirely a case of "We Own the Night," like our patches read, but more simply, "We're Just Painted Black." But as far as we were concerned, this was going to be played out to a conclusion.

CHAPTER 14

An Unwelcome Routine

It is generally inadvisable to eject directly over the area you just bombed.

BY DAY 7, I'D COMPLETELY lost track of the real date. Sometimes it was dark out, sometimes light. We ate when we were hungry and slept when we could. Distinctions beyond which day of the ATO cycle was being either planned or executed seemed rather superficial. At the end of a long "day," perhaps 08:00, we ate dinner, which everyone else in the world called breakfast. Then we blacked out our rooms as best we could, hung a "Do Not Disturb" sign on the door, and slept until maybe 17:00. We got up, did a few chores, then wandered off in search of breakfast as the sun went down before putting on a flight suit to go in to work to start the new "day." We might take a break around midnight for "lunch," which was also a breakfast, and it all occurred on the same calendar date.

A funny story came to us from Holloman. As soon as the Serbs had broadcast pictures of the canopy from -806, with the name of a pilot, Wiz, painted on the canopy rail, the media had immediately stormed the guy's house back in Alamogordo. Not understanding that a name on a canopy rail is just a courtesy accorded by time on station in the wing and doesn't have any bearing on who flies it any given day, the reporters thought they had a scoop on their hands. Expecting to inflict some shock journalism by cornering a tearful wife ("How do you feel now that your husband has been shot down?"), they were instead surprised when Wiz himself answered the door. He played it up by feigning surprise.

"What? I was shot down over Serbia last night? That's news to me! I could have sworn that I was home watching TV with the kids." When the reporters explained that his name had been clearly seen on the canopy, he came right back with, "Oh, so that's where it is. I reported that plane stolen months ago," and went back into his house. The confused and disappointed reporters wandered off scratching their heads.

As soon as we had our crew rest after welcoming Sugar-D's return, we got right back to work. I was in that first lineup and flew on Stump's wing through a lot of nasty weather to a tanker in the south Adriatic. I was going by the call sign Merc-62, in aircraft -803, loaded with a single GBU-27 in my left bomb bay. My right bay was empty. That bothered me more than a little, as we had only been shooting around 50 percent with the GBU-27s so far—and what was the point of going into combat with only half a weapon load anyway? The sad answer was that after only four days, almost all of the approved targets had been used up, and we'd been reduced to picking at leftovers and previous misses.

Our route was long enough to require two refuelings—one pre-strike, and one post-strike. Our first tanker was where it was supposed to be, and we rejoined easily. Stump cycled through first before peeling off alone toward his holding point. The last I heard from him he was getting his clearance over to Magic's frequency as I was pulling up to the boom for my own fuel. Our formation to this point was just a convenience, and I wouldn't see him again until after landing. After Vega-31's adventure last night, we were minimizing our radio calls and had been working almost exclusively comm-out. I didn't make any transmissions to the tanker at all.

The next words I heard were from the boomer as he talked to me through our now connected intercoms.

"Contact."

After my vast F-117 combat experience of a single sortie, this one was running much more smoothly, and the patter was professionally bland.

"Hey, sounds good," I replied.

"Aaaand you're taking fuel."

"Thank you much, my number is eight two eight zero three. You guys got any words for us?"

"Ah, negative, sir."

"Okay. So as far as we know everyone is still pressing?"

"Yeah, I guess so."

The conversation lagged as there didn't seem to be much else to talk about. I didn't know the boomer, I couldn't talk about my mission, and he was smart enough not to ask anyway. The gas continued to flow from the KC-135 into my tanks for several more minutes. Hanging on the tanker was a lot easier this time around since, with only one bomb loaded and the long fuel-burning trip down the Adriatic to get there, I was several tons lighter than I had been the first night. We had also requested, and been granted, refueling altitudes several thousand feet lower than those we'd been assigned previously.

A few minutes later, I tapped the paddle switch on my control stick to ensure a disconnect from the boom. Simultaneously, I banked off to the right to clear the refueling track. Once clear, I dropped down 5,000 feet and proceeded to my holding pattern while checking in with Magic.

"Magic, Merc six two, checking in."

"Merc six two, you are loud and clear, push three, three, x-ray."

In another attempt to preserve security, we were not given the combat frequency before taking off—just a long list of hundreds of potential frequencies. The actual frequency, in this case the thirty-third in the "X" column, was the one we were using that night.

"Copy, three, three, x-ray—understand that's where the other Mercs went?" I was just confirming that I wouldn't be accidentally shunted to a frequency for another sector.

"A-firm."

After check-in on 33X, I settled down to listen to the admin calls being made, mostly for the F-15C's benefit, and methodically ran through my stealth checklist. My target was in the heart of Pristina, the capitol of Kosovo Province. I was fragged against the MUP Headquarters.

What a great target! A *worthy* target, symbolic of everything we were supposed to be doing there. I was sure that the building was probably deserted and no longer held real military value, but it would be satisfying to pop it anyway—just because.

The Serbian Ministry of Internal Affairs (Ministarstvo Unutrasnjih Poslova, or MUP) was the local version of the national police, a paramilitary organization loyal only to Milosevic. In coordination with the national army (the VJ), the MUP had been the prime players in the ethnic cleansing of Kosovo.

A "reported" tactic (though possibly exaggerated or KLA propaganda) was to swarm into a small farming village at dawn, summarily execute the first male they came upon to cement their control, arrest the military age males, then send the women, children, and elderly off on foot. Some of the younger females would be held back for the rape camps. Identification papers were confiscated to eliminate the potential for future claims to the land. Then, after being looted, the entire place was burned to the ground, so that there was truly no home to return to. Any resistance resulted in more deaths and a trench mass grave on the outskirts of the village. After a few of these assaults, just the rumor that the MUP was in the area causes a spontaneous evacuation. We'll never know exactly, but the number of displaced Kosovars was at that time widely reported to be on the order of eight hundred thousand.

As I was preparing to whack this worthy target, I realized that there was a huge discrepancy developing between where my INS thought it was and where the GPS knew it was. A drifting INS is never a good thing (that is what points the FLIR and DLIR toward the target) and therefore required some attention. The eastern end of my holding pattern was near some islands for which I had coordinates and where I could use the DLIR and laser to update the system. But because of the spotty low clouds, I never got a clear shot and could only guess that I was within a mile or so of my intended track. If the weather was clear headed toward the target, I might be able to get an update later. Then things became a bit worse.

The small half-inch-diameter tracking button on the front of my throttle popped off as I removed my hand. It landed on the side console. That turned out to be a mixed blessing. If it had fallen on the floor it would have been gone for the rest of the flight, and I probably would have wasted a lot of contortions and flailing about trying to get it back. As it was, I didn't have to go through that, but quickly discovered the plastic had cracked and the thing wouldn't stay on its mounting post no matter how I held it. The button was useless for controlling the sensors, so I put it in my sleeve pocket. As far as I knew this had never happened before or since—and on only my second combat sortie!

The sharp threaded post now held my attention. If I could manipulate that directly perhaps I could pull off the attack. My fate was quickly presented to me. While I could indeed manipulate the DLIR, I did it at the expense of a fair amount of discomfort. In order to apply enough pressure on the post to get anything to work, the sharp point on the end went through the thin leather of my glove. Folding over the glove in order to make a thicker pad took away the control needed to point the DLIR. In short order my middle and ring fingers were perforated. I was saving my index finger for the attack. To add to my frustration, the weather to the east didn't look any better as I pushed off toward my target.

I had gotten into the habit of constantly updating the direction of the nearest friendly border so that if hit I wouldn't waste even a second deciding which way to turn. Tonight I crossed the borders of Bosnia, Montenegro, Albania, Macedonia, and Kosovo during my run. Bosnia was occupied so didn't much count. Montenegro was mostly staying out of the fight—except that there was a Serbian early warning radar on the coast that General Clark wouldn't let us take out. Albania was on our side, as was Macedonia, but both lacked facilities to handle an F-117. Bulgaria, just off to the east, supposedly had some valid divert bases by recent agreement. If I had to, I wouldn't hesitate to go in that direction—we could always sort out the details later—but they were very much an unknown. Obviously, the Serbs occupying Kosovo were definitely not an unknown. All this just illustrates how tight the airspace was where we were working.

Another change in our tactics driven by the shoot-down became the more liberal use of PET shots. A PET shot is the preemptive firing of an AGM-88 HARM. A HARM is a behemoth of a missile, almost fourteen feet long and ten inches in diameter, designed to home in on the emissions of any SAM radar within a radius of around eighty miles.

But even at supersonic speeds, it takes a while for a missile to travel upwards of eighty miles. The trick for the SAM operator then becomes a high-stakes game of chicken. Can he turn on his radar, acquire and track a target long enough for a kill, before the HARM arrives? If he can turn off the radar soon enough, the HARM will lose its guidance and impact somewhere else—but he will also lose the ability to guide the SAM he has fired.

What a PET shot did for me was to put a missile in the air well before I arrived over a critical area. That way it had the time to fly up to the ionosphere and was racing toward the general vicinity of a suspected SAM as I was entering the engagement zone. If a SAM's radar was emitting while I was vulnerable, then the HARM, already arcing down at supersonic speeds, was just seconds away from delivering 150 pounds of high explosive.

The pitfall for our side was that the timing was critical. If I arrived a minute early the missile wouldn't be able to get there in time. If I showed up a minute late then the missile would not only have impacted harmlessly in the area, leaving me defenseless, but would also have highlighted the fact that something was about to happen. At around $280,000 a pop, we couldn't just sprinkle these things around like confetti.

In any case, I saw "my" shot fired from well off to my left and watched it pitching up, spitting orange fire, to what looked to be straight upwards until it wasn't visible, knowing that it would be arcing back down toward the target area when/if I'd need it. But even then I knew that it was probably all in vain. I was still going to overfly the target area, and I'd be glad that thing was out there to pop any SAM trying to kill me, but I wasn't likely to drop as the weather wasn't improving. The HARM shooter called out, "Club two one, Magnum," over the frequency just so that we'd all know there were HARMs in the air.

From two minutes out I could see the ground through some gaps in the clouds. Things began to get busy as the F-16 guys started actively engaging SAMs as they came up. Among the other chatter I picked out:

"Club, Magnum, SA-three." He was shooting at an active missile site now, not just a suspected location.

"Club two four, Magnum, SA-six, Pristina," which I was over at the moment.

With thirty seconds to go I was in the heart of a bad place, between HARMs raining down toward active SAM radars and SAMs arcing up in search of targets. There were intermittent gaps in the clouds large enough to orient myself, even with my bad system—but I wasn't going to drop. Because my target was in the very center of Pristina it was designated as an NCD target (no collateral damage allowed). Since there was a chance that I could lose the bomb as it fell due to a cloud coming between the target and my laser, I couldn't release the weapon. The bomb could end up in a civilian neighborhood, so I'd do the civilized thing and not chance it. We'd risk our lives again in a few days to accomplish this mission when the risks were only to ourselves and the targets. Of course, that didn't stop *them* from shooting at *me*.

I slapped the master arm switch off to close the weapons bay door, thus spoiling their aim a little, and slammed the throttles full forward to go home. As quick as that, it was over. I exited the SAM zones and everything became quiet again, except for one more little thing.

I was still deep in enemy territory when I could see the glow from the sun beginning to rise in the east. What the hell? The F-117 is a black, unmaneuverable, damn near defenseless airplane to anyone who can see it. That's why we only fly at night. Fighting in daylight goes against everything in our doctrine. Something had gone seriously wrong during planning. The only thing we had going for us at that moment was that the same cloud cover that had hidden our targets now hid us from ground observers looking up.

It was a lot easier finding the tanker in the morning light. That was a good thing because my jet was acting up very badly by then. Maybe it was because of the constant drizzle over the Adriatic. In any case the DLIR had frozen pointed off to the far high-right corner of its range. Then time stopped—or at least the computer generated clock stopped. It didn't break, it just stopped. How did a computer without a sense of time function? What an odd night!

After landing, all of us who had flown vented our frustrations about the rising sun. An impromptu investigation afterward taught us the very real differences between civil, nautical, and astronomical twilights.

Traditional civil twilight is defined as beginning when the center of the sun is 6 degrees below the horizon. For roughly thirty minutes, terrestrial objects are easily visible. Nautical twilight—used (obviously enough) at sea where there are no surrounding objects to block the light—is defined as when the sun is between 6 and 12 degrees below the horizon. The dim outline of objects are visible at close range. Both of these assume that you are at ground level. The effects are magnified correspondingly when the objects being viewed (us) are several degrees *above* the horizon. This is where astronomical twilight kicks in (the sun is between 12 and 18 degrees below the horizon), where the outline of objects can be seen while looking up. The difference between civil and astronomical twilight is about an hour. We had been using the correct times, just from the wrong tables.

How come this was all news to us? We (were supposed to) own the night!

After that I was nabbed to work in the MPC straight through until 15:00 that afternoon. I grabbed about three hours of sleep before coming back in at 20:00 to update my bomb tracker spreadsheet. I hadn't found a single cause that linked the GBU-27 failures yet. I was hoping for something simple like common tail numbers or laser-guidance codes, but no such luck.

One odd little rumor was circulating. Since the Serbs had been thumbing their noses at us by holding large outdoor rock concerts every night, some bright boy got the idea of sending a message. The idea was to take a GBU-27, filled with cement instead of explosives, paint it bright NATO blue, and drop one right into the middle of a public square. Telling them, in effect, that they were able to hold these concerts only because we allowed them to. Fortunately, that idea was dying a well-deserved death by being ignored.

The number of targets was still limited, so we only launched one go that night. After our string of weather problems, we had finally put a better recall system in place. The F-15Cs usually pushed partway toward our targets before we did in order to sweep the approach corridors and throw off the early warning net. Weather doesn't affect their mission, but sometimes they get close enough to see whether or not there are any clear areas further on. There weren't any, so our guys never had to cross the border, and for the third night nothing hit the ground.

On Day 8 I was scheduled to fly again and dressed for combat with a black T-shirt (always cotton), fire-retardant Nomex long-john pants, a black cotton turtleneck over my dog tags (keeping tags between the T-shirt and turtleneck meant no metal against the skin in case of fire), a one-piece sage green fireproof Nomex flight suit, our brightly colored peacetime patches replaced by a single green/black subdued cloth name tag, and subdued rank. Then a winter-weight Nomex flight jacket on top of that. Everything else that might identify me, or my unit, was sanitized except for my wedding band, which I carried in my sleeve pocket when flying (all pilots take off their rings before approaching an airplane for safety) and my official military ID card (required by the Geneva Convention). I also carried a fair amount of both U.S. and Italian cash in case I had to divert.

On top of this ensemble came the g-suit. The ankle pockets of the g-suit held my gloves, helmet liner, and glasses (clear or dark depending on the anticipated environment). Then a green mesh survival vest. Our parachute harness was worn over the vest, so most guys gave some attention to distributing the vest load around a bit to make it a little more comfortable. The vest was loaded with all sorts of goodies, such as a survival radio, spare batteries, a handheld GPS, signal mirror, pin gun flares, day/night smoke flares, a couple of folding knives, and a tiny first aid kit about the size of a credit card. The contents of this first aid kit consisted of something along the lines of a couple of bandages, a pack of Chicklets gum, and a condom (for carrying water). The vest also carried several flashlights, a strobe light, and few other odds and ends—like a pistol.

The personal weapon we carried was the M9 pistol, which is essentially just the military designation for a stock 9mm Beretta-92. I own one myself, and I like them. There had been some bad press during their procurement for chambering a 9mm round versus the .45-caliber round it was replacing in the army, which was a valid argument, but I thought that they were well built and fell into my hand comfortably. They were infinitely better than the old .38-caliber revolvers pilots were issued previously. For one thing, each magazine contained about triple the rounds that fit in the revolver, and we even got a spare magazine. With the revolver, extra rounds (if you were given any) were carried loose in a plastic baggy, where they rattled around and had to be loaded one at a time. The holster for the M9 was permanently sewn onto the side of the survival vests we wore each sortie. The only question was where to carry the extra magazine. I found a bit of room in the pocket with the survival radio.

During the Gulf War, there weren't enough M9s to go around, so many pilots were allowed to carry their privately owned weapons. Of course they had to be cleared first to be deemed allowable by the "rules of war." All rounds had to be FMJ (full metal jacket). By international agreement no hollow points were allowed in combat; those were just for civilians to shoot each other with. I would have liked to carry more magazines, but there wouldn't have been a lot of extra room to carry them. By the time we were fully geared up to fly, we were olive drab Pillsbury Doughboys.

The arguments, for and against, carrying a weapon at all had been going on since at least Vietnam. One of my instructors from when I had been a student pilot had flown A-1 Skyraiders over Vietnam. CSAR was his business. He once explained that in Vietnam there had been three distinct schools of thought concerning pistols. Some guys had their survival vests modified in order to carry hundreds of extra rounds of ammo evenly distributed to keep the weight balanced. The thought was that if shot down over enemy territory they were going to "John Wayne" their way out or at least make their captors work for it.

Others would carry only the absolute minimum required by their squadron. They fully intended to throw away the pistol as they were swinging in the parachute so as not to invite violence after landing, but instead to rely upon the mercy of their captors. This wasn't necessarily defeatist; instead, they carried lots of spare batteries and perhaps a spare survival radio (or two), figuring that was the bit of equipment more likely to get them home. The third group either decided that a mix of both strategies was best or, more likely, chose not to think about it all and just took what was issued.

The only two stories I had direct knowledge of didn't help much. Years earlier, during pilot training, I met an officer who had been a POW during Vietnam. He was serving as an F-4 GIB (guy in back—a pilot working the radar before WSOs and EWOs had been invented). Their jet had been hit and was burning, so the pilot up front called for an ejection. Just as the GIB punched out, the pilot thought better of the situation, regained control of the jet, got the fire extinguished, and flew home. None of which did our GIB any good.

During the ejection, he had broken his right arm (he was right handed). As he was gathering himself up from the jungle floor, a solitary and overexcited NVA soldier came charging through the woods at him wildly spraying shots from an SKS rifle. Our guy drew his .38 and killed him with a single, left-handed shot. That freed him to hightail it through the jungle for a while in an attempt to escape. Chock one up for the John Wayne camp so far. He never made it out though. Shortly thereafter he discovered that the pocket that should have held his survival radio had torn away during the ejection. The radio, and any chance of calling in a rescue helicopter, was gone. The next day he was captured while trying to walk his way out. He ended up spending several years in the Hanoi Hilton. The mixed lessons to be taken from this instance were that while a weapon had probably saved his life initially, lack of a radio had doomed him to capture in the long run.

Closer to home was the recent downing of our guy, Vega-31. He had kept his weapon until about halfway through the ordeal when he had decided that he wasn't going to shoot his way out anyway. He decided that if captured he didn't want to hand over a souvenir to some Serbian soldier, so he buried his M9 in the mud of the drainage ditch he was hiding in at the time. In the long run, his radio did get him home, but the M9 was found and became a souvenir anyway.

Another change to our procedures as a result of the shoot-down had been the issuing of a new combination GPS/survival radio called the PRC-112A, nicknamed "The Hook." This thing has been around a while, but hadn't been issued because it was a complicated mess. It was easier to plan a combat mission than to operate this thing. There wasn't a chance in hell of fully utilizing this piece of equipment in the dark, or even in the daylight, without an operator's manual. Eventually, most of us settled for learning how to use the comm, bull's-eye, and position reporting functions. Everything else was just deadweight.

Later that night I flew my third sortie. It was another high-risk, no-result weather check. Another scary takeoff roll where I just set the engines to mil power then rotated to miss the fence, more or less regardless of speed. The thought that any momentary mechanical problem would have put me through the fence and into the fields in a spectacular fireball still haunts me a little. But, past that hurdle, I wallowed along just above stall speed until some semblance of usable aerodynamics became evident. At least the police were keeping the media and spectators away from the fence now.

I was Club-27 on Woody's wing headed toward the northern tanker tracks over Hungary. The rendezvous was a challenge; the AWACS kept giving us vectors to the wrong tanker. Time was getting a little tight, but since the crowd had been getting smaller, we had a little more latitude to work with. Woody and I eventually blew off the AWACS calls and just "bootlegged" a conveniently close KC-135 to get our fuel. There was a low undercast cloud deck stretching off to the south as far as we could see. It didn't look promising, but since we hadn't been officially canceled, we were obligated to fly the black line over our targets to at least take a look.

Once again, I had only one bomb loaded that night—a single GBU-10. Given the trouble we'd been having with the GBU-27s so far, I was glad that it was a GBU-10, but annoyed that there was only one of them. Granted, I only had one target, the operations building for the Batajnica MiG-21 squadron, but I thought that two bombs would have added both a degree of destruction to ensure a kill and a degree of redundancy if one bomb went bad.

Another option, which in hindsight would have been appropriate, would have been to load an ordinary unguided Mk-84 into the empty bay. While we are famous for our PGM capability, we also had exceptional accuracy with dumb bombs. With a good GPS system, I could have easily hit a target as big as that building without ever seeing it. This must have been discussed and decided against previously, because my suggestion during the brief was cut off in midsentence. The OG wouldn't even entertain the idea of carrying

M-84s for weather drops. For mostly political reasons, our leadership didn't want us to be thought of as dumb-bomb droppers.

Still, the thought of sending out multiple aircraft with only half weapon loads so early in the campaign said a lot about how this war was going to be run. Nonetheless, I was glad to be involved at all and flew my assigned route through the heart of Serbia, directly over their national air defense fighter base, just to look at the tops of clouds. AWACS kept warning us of SAM activity in the area, but we didn't see much.

There was an incredibly bright full moon overhead. That, combined with the solid white clouds beneath us, negated any advantage to our being painted black to anyone looking down. We were, in Shep's words, "standing out like roaches on a sheet." I used to like flying with a moon. Not anymore. Fortunately, both for them and for us, their MiGs chose not to come up and play. Our F-15C guys were already starting to sound itchy.

In a way we were just airborne chaff, something for the SAMs to look for so that maybe they'd expose themselves long enough for our HARM shooters to get off a shot and something for the MiGs to come up and chase so that maybe the Eagles could get a chance to pop them. Human bait.

The clouds finally broke up before the Romanian border, where I wished they wouldn't. There was nothing below me that I needed to see over there, and no one over there I wanted to see me while looking up. In any case, I logged three hours of combat time and one night refueling and landed gingerly once more so that the armorers could defuse the live bomb still loaded in the belly of my jet.

My last two sorties had carried all of the risks with none of the results. We knew when we stepped out that the weather might shut us down, and for a long while I was convinced that I was the only idiot who had pushed the border that night. Later, when I quietly admitted that after the sortie, most of the other guys exclaimed something similar. "Yeah, me too! I thought *I* was the only one, but didn't want to say anything."

This was a lonely way to fight a war.

After everything had quieted down, I had a chance to look at the little "pocket rosary/crucifix" that Kat had given to each of us before stepping out to fly. Her folks' church had sent out an entire box of the things at the suggestion of one of their older parishioners. It was silver, just a bit over an inch in diameter with the ten beads encircling it, and a half-inch crucifix on top—the story being that during World War I, the crucifix neck chains would hang out of a soldier's shirt as he crawled along and would get caught up in the wire and debris of the battlefield. So they were redesigned as a solid metal beaded ring instead of the chain, sized so that they could only be carried in a pocket, not on a finger. I didn't know if there was any real history to that story, but I still carried the thing. It was an interesting souvenir and appropriate for the part of the world we were fighting in. Maybe it would earn me some brownie points if I were captured by an Orthodox Serb.

The news was filled with pictures of long lines of Kosovars walking or driving their tractors toward camps along the Albanian and Macedonian borders. The refugee situation was becoming overwhelming. Something like half of the population had been displaced. Milosevic's Operation Horseshoe had, at least temporarily, made that aspect of this war so much worse than it was.

Closer to home, we had been cut off from contact with our families. There was a new computer virus out there called "Melissa" that had shut down most of our Internet access and wiped clean our email files. A week into a war, some so-called American had let this loose, an act that in my mind was tantamount to treason.

The crowd of protesters outside the gate was becoming significant. The press and the protestors were in a self-perpetuating cycle. The more press there was, the more protestors showed up to be seen, and the more protestors who showed up, the bigger the story for the press to cover. However, the Italian police didn't fool around and were keeping everything under control for the time being.

The next night we only stepped three guys to fly. There just weren't enough approved targets left to justify more sorties. The list hadn't been significantly expanded since we began, and if the weather hadn't been so poor we would have run out of stuff to hit days before. Javier Solana, General Clark, and the rest of the NATO leadership seemed to be hunkered down waiting for the phone call from Milosevic they had talked themselves into expecting on Day 1.

Before this had all kicked off, there had been several articles written to the effect that never in modern history had the commanding general of one side known and understood his opponent more thoroughly than General Clark did Milosevic. Evidently that didn't really matter. There was no plan for dealing with an enemy who chose not to cooperate, and even as we scrambled to create a war plan from the ground up, the politicians were beginning to interfere with the target sets just like the old Vietnam days of the Johnson luncheons. An army general was running what was exclusively an air war, and our president (who had slickly avoided service during Vietnam) was personally approving, or disapproving, every target and target category from a couch in the Oval Office. Then, just to top off all of these happy thoughts, some idiot in the Rivet Joint community compromised the night's target set over an open telephone line. So the mission had to be scrubbed, and our three guys walked back in.

I was scheduled to try another mission again the following night, with a trip to the Vicenza CAOC the next day. I didn't even know how I was supposed to get there, but thought maybe I could use a little of what I'd learned at the Fuertus Defensus exercise the previous November.

The news from the war was that three U.S. Army troops had been captured along the Macedonian border. There were all sorts of rumors as to how this happened. One embarrassing version was that they got separated from their convoy, then left their weapons behind in the vehicle while looking to buy some soft drinks. I hoped that wasn't true.

The refugee exodus was becoming enormous, and no quick end seemed to be in sight. On the plus side, the weather was getting at least marginally better, and the OG loved my bomb tracker. After mentioning that fact once in public, Woody came over to touch my shoulder, hoping that something good would rub off—he'd been having a tougher time than me.

Another rumor had it that the 9th, with another twelve jets, was deploying from Holloman to Spangdahlem, Germany, to stage from there. While that might have been useful the first two nights of the war, now we had virtually *no* approved targets left at all. We were only going after the one or two new targets approved each day, or chasing after old targets that had been spared by the weather or still had a wall or two standing. What were we going to do with twelve more jets?

Not unexpectedly, we were told that Sugar-D would be sent home in a few days. He had decided to maintain his anonymity for the time being. I think that's just the way he was, but also that he wanted to avoid having his reputation sullied by association or his life becoming the media circus that surrounded Capt. Scott O'Grady, the F-16 pilot who'd been shot down over Bosnia in 1995 and evaded capture for six days before being rescued by the Marines. Sugar-D earned enormous respect for preserving his reputation and remaining anonymous by not cashing in.

Locally, children still played in the gym, kindergarteners still snuck across the parking lot to get fries from Burger King during recess, school buses gathered kids up for field trips to museums, and families wandered through the stores on weekends. Superficially, life appeared to be normal. It was very hard to reconcile these sights of daytime normalcy with our nightly war. It was all very surreal.

* * *

The next night, as soon as I walked into the squadron, I was greeted by two of our life support troops. One, Big Red, was holding a large shoebox with a hole cut in the end. With a mischievous smile, she said, "Stick your hand in here and tell me what you feel."

"Yeah, right," I replied. "What sort of gag is this?"

"No, no, this is serious."

I played along. "It feels like the strobe light from a survival vest," I said.

"Exactly. Now turn it on with one hand without looking."

After losing Vega-31 and some of the problems he had had operating his equipment in the dark, the troops had come up with this game to train us to identify and operate the survival gear one-handed by touch alone. *Damn clever!* They planned to put a different piece of equipment in the box each night.

Unfortunately for the missions though, as was becoming all too standard, our ten-line go was whittled away as call after call from the CAOC canceled bits and pieces of the plan. We briefed ten pilots, dressed five, stepped three out to the jets, then canceled altogether as the previously approved targets were slowly pulled from the lineup. All ten missions were canceled. You had to wonder how important they had been in the first place.

The MPC guys were about ready to mutiny. Because of the lead time required to plan a mission, their work wasn't reduced in the slightest by mission day cancellations. I spent the remainder of the night updating my bomb tracker and setting up a couple of color printers. Back at Holloman there was always a scarcity of computer printers. Not so in war. All you had to do was make an idle suggestion that something might be useful, and it miraculously showed up a few hours later.

CHAPTER 15

The CAOC

*If you ever find yourself in a fair fight—
then you didn't plan it properly.*

O N FRIDAY, APRIL 2, GENERAL Leaf, the OG, and I drove down to Vicenza. The general had to go there on business anyway, so the OG scrounged a couple of seats for us. The general's chauffeur was an interesting old guy—very dapper, precise, and rail thin. He had been a professional bicycle racer from Belgium in his youth who ended up in this corner of Europe by some vagary of fortune. We talked about the increasing anti-U.S. protests and flag burnings going on across Europe, the ones in Russia being the more ominous.

Once signed in at Vicenza, I took over Grinch's slot in the U.S.-only (Noble Anvil) planning cell and spent what was left of the day trying to get a feel for the operation. The whole organization struck me as rather chaotic all the way around. The targeting process was more hand-to-mouth than an actual process. There didn't seem to be a plan, just moment-to-moment reactions—a heck of a way to run a war. My twelve-hour shift was supposed to run from 15:00 to 03:00.

There was no billeting available on the base, so around midnight someone showed me the way to the hotel. I got some real food in the hotel lobby before getting called in early to work some ATO and coordination issues. My first impression of the entire process being very haphazard was borne out. It reminded me greatly of the first few days of the exercise in Tucson, except that this had been going on for a long time. Not that it mattered much, since the entire mission turned out to be just another border cancel due to weather.

The highlight of my day was running into Bergy. We had flown T-33s together at Griffiss AFB with the old Air Defense Command during the Cold War—about a million years earlier. He had been stationed to the CAOC here before the war as permanent party and had been with the operation from the beginning. He clued me in on how the system *really* worked, who to talk to, and how to get things done.

The CAOC was an "in-place" organization composed of pilots and WSOs from various systems performing a staff tour. Though greatly augmented in time of war, the core of the planning cells were all permanent party. They were specially trained in the organizational nuances of creating a target folder set (both proposed and approved) and monitoring the approval status of those targets. Tanker availability, support assets, and airspace coordination issues had to be factored into the process. They worked as the liaison between intel and command leadership to create missions that achieved specific tactical results and strategic objectives (if we had any, that is). Finally, the work of dozens of people had to be translated and distilled into usable instructions for the tasked units.

This product was called the air tasking order, or ATO, for short. More commonly, it was referred to as "the frag." "Breaking out the frag" was the first step every unit had to accomplish before beginning to plan its individual missions. The frag dictated the number of aircraft a unit launched, the targets to be hit, the weapons to be used, and the times those targets would be hit along with any special instructions (called SPINS) that were applicable. There was also purely administrative data, such as which call signs would be used and tanker track assignments. A unit's page or so of instructions would be embedded in a document as thick as a phone book, and an entirely new and unique ATO had to be produced and distributed each and every day of the war.

Everything that flies must be accounted for and coordinated via the ATO process, whether air force, navy, or NATO, manned or unmanned. One of the small bits of progress made following the Gulf War was to standardize the communications systems used by the U.S. Air Force and U.S. Navy. During the Gulf War, navy helicopters actually had to ferry paper copies of the ATO onto a ship where the information could then be manually retyped into the U.S. Navy system. Fortunately, we'd overcome some of that older parochialism and had begun to act more like one team.

The presence of augmentees, like myself, within the planning cell provided the interface between the professional planners and the units actually flying the missions. We ensured that the targeting conformed to our unit's capabilities and complied with the most current tactics and doctrines being practiced. Knowing how the MPC at Aviano functioned also gave the squadron input as to how targets were allocated. Sometimes this allowed the targets to be grouped in sets and patterns that permitted a more logical application of force—Fuertus Defensus writ large.

That was the theory anyway. In practice, chaos was always threatening, deadlines loomed, and a constant stream of changes kept throwing the entire process awry. Some changes were important, like a lack of required assets, weather patterns, or updated SAM locations provided by intel. Some changes were just frustrating, like some politico up the chain "changing his mind" about the target sequencing at the last moment.

"Destroy the electrical distribution yards at AA, then take out the TV transmitters at BB the next day." Plan, plan, plan.

"No, wait, we just realized that if the electricity is already out they won't know the TV is off the next day—do the TV first." Re-plan, re-plan, re-plan.

"Umm, I accidentally told my boss that we were going to hit AA first; tell you what, just hit both the same night." Issue change-1 to the already published ATO if there was still time.

"Sorry guys, the French just changed their minds again about BB." Too late to re-plan—call the unit to cancel lines 2, 4, 5, and 9.

"Umm, sorry to bother you again, but the Swiss ambassador is having a party at CC tonight, which is sort of close to AA—let's not bother him." Takeoff is in thirty minutes! Quick, call the unit to cancel the mission before they launch.

"Sooooo, since you aren't doing anything else tonight why not just hit DD? What? You can't?" Followed by a faintly heard mutter, *"Uncooperative prima donnas. Don't they know there's a war going on?"*

Fog and friction, CAOC style.

One of the guys in our planning cell became so frustrated with the many cancellations of the manned attacks while the cruise missile attacks continued unabated, that he wrote a poem en titled "Ode to a TLAM." One line went something like this: "So at the end of Day 11 the last thing from the 49th Fighter Wing to hit the ground was an F-117 on Day 4." *Ouch!*

My initial idea to work the 15:00–03:00 shift fell apart early, and I instead had to cover the time frame of midnight to noon. The first night I went in early, at 20:00, just to be able to find the place in daylight. The directions were the easy part. It was the driving that was a challenge. Don't get me wrong, I'm not an especially timid person behind a wheel. I'd learned to drive around Boston and was confident that there wasn't a traffic situation I couldn't deal with. It turned out that I was wrong.

Italian roads have a preponderance of rotaries, and for some unknown reason the right-of-way rules are exactly backwards from the rest of the world. Entering vehicles have the right of way. Traffic already in the rotary is supposed to yield to the inside. The obvious problem with that is traffic already established can't get out of the circle if it has to keep yielding to the incoming traffic. Saturation soon follows. I felt like Chevy Chase in a *National Lampoon* movie as I had to make four loops before being able to escape the first rotary. And since there was a war on, the police were out in force. Traffic police in Italy are organized on a paramilitary model and always work in pairs. The one up front fulfills the traditional role while his partner is about twenty-five yards down the road with a submachine gun, ready to enforce the first guy's orders. It was into this mix that I had plunged myself, half lost, unable to speak the language, in a car that had been loaned to me by a stranger, for which I had no earthly idea who was responsible, and without a driver's license.

Sunday was Easter. Our activities weren't different in any way, but because it was an occasion, at least to the outside world, someone had laid out a real dinner by the snack bar where we would normally buy junk food. There was baked ham, scalloped potatoes, and green beans. We were all happy to throw donations in the can for what was undoubtedly the healthiest meal I'd had in ages. Here I was, planning combat missions and deciding which targets were going to be attacked in a couple of days and the most memorable part of my day was to hold a plate of real dinner. Napoleon had it wired when he stated that an army travels on its stomach.

The shift I covered allowed me to work the floor as the "combat ops" guy for our wing. Since the F-117 normally never makes radio transmissions, has its transponder turned off during a sortie, and doesn't reflect much radar, they aren't displayed on the big situation board that the leadership was running the war from. My role was to hover off to the side with paper printouts of the routes, times, and targets, mentally to track the position and progress of my people— then to pass that information to others on the floor when they needed to know. It turned out to be almost more stressful watching the missions from a distance than actually flying them, especially as threat systems came up near locations I could guess my people were at.

The weather was cooperating for a change that evening, so we got in some good work. There was one emergency, a hydraulic failure on the return to base, but it didn't affect the mission.

After the mission was complete (the part I cared about anyway), I helped the MAAP (master air attack plan) cell with their cleanup details for the next day's plan. At 09:30, I sat through my first video teleconference (VTC). The purpose of these daily teleconferences was to allow all of the geographically separated leadership agencies to electronically "huddle" to coordinate the next day's activities. It was fascinating to see how things were being run. The three local generals, every available colonel and lieutenant colonel, and everyone else who could squeeze in packed the tiny room. The camera was set up so that only General Short and a couple of others were visible. I had to assume that the several other sites represented had similar crowds just out of view.

General Clark, as SACEUR, was working from his headquarters in Brussels. He looked and acted like the chairman of the board at a large corporation and was wearing staff office attire. *Warrior* wasn't a word that sprang to mind, though he reportedly had notable combat experience in Vietnam. He fit the image of a Rhodes Scholar, but I couldn't picture him in combat gear. Admiral Ellis, from his headquarters in Naples, at least looked like he was deployed and was wearing a khaki work uniform. General Short wore a flight suit and just looked frustrated as hell.

Admiral Ellis was in charge of NATO's Southern Command (CINCSOUTH), where all of this war was occurring, and was in reality the legal joint task force (JTF) commander by NATO rules. General Short was the air component commander for the region and should have been in charge of all operations in this "air only" war. For reasons of his own, General Clark had decided to bypass both and run the war himself, which technically was entirely his prerogative. This was more than a little unusual though, since General Clark had openly stated that his primary role was political as opposed to operational.

Not only had Admiral Ellis and General Short been bypassed almost entirely on the strategic level, but General Clark spent a lot of time delving into tactical details better handled by a captain or sometimes a sergeant. While I had no idea what sort of pressures the general was under, this micromanagement wasn't being welcomed.

I was impressed by the VTC's technology, but not at all by the process or the results. After we had packed ourselves in and the roll call had been completed to ensure that everyone was online, the camera panned to General Clark. I had to admit that I was excited. Here it came, the strategic vision we were going to follow in the conduct of this war against genocide and ethnic cleansing.

General Clark cleared his throat then stated right out loud that his number-one priority for the day was . . . to obtain camera footage of an A-10 shooting a tank in Kosovo before the evening news was broadcast on the East Coast. Some of the other new guys' jaws dropped. I thought it was a pretty good joke. Then I saw the resigned look of the old hands. He was serious. How could that be a priority, and why hadn't someone explained to him that it was pretty much impossible anyway? The A-10s (everyone except the F-117s actually) were still restricted from descending below a safety altitude of 15,000 feet. The problem of finding and identifying a tank at that altitude are tough enough (A-10 pilots were actually carrying nine-power image-stabilized binoculars in the cockpit to help identify targets all the way down at ground level). To fire a burst from a 30mm Gatling cannon from that height and hit the target was much tougher.

The real joke was the thought of getting any of that on video from a slant range of maybe four or five miles. The A-10 pilot would have to fire from some tremendous altitude, then keep diving at the ground long enough to follow his cannon rounds visually all the way down until they impacted so that he could film them hitting while still being able to then pull out of his dive at least three miles above the ground. Assuming he could accomplish all of that and still pull up before descending below the minimum altitude of 15,000 feet, the tank was only going to be a tiny speck, if even that, in the grainy black-and-white video the plane carried. Or was the safety altitude going to be waived for the sake of publicity? Attacks against tanks from those altitudes are usually made with Maverick missiles. Fortunately, A-10 operations were none of my business.

As the meeting went on, various developments were discussed and General Clark passed on a few more targets that had been cleared by all the politicians and NATO members—not the hundreds of targets that we needed, but three or four, as I remember. It was disconcerting to see how excitedly the MAAP guys scrambled to write down these scraps that had been tossed to them. It gave them a little something to work with for another half day.

By doctrine, we should have been working from the JIPTL, the joint integrated and prioritized target list. By every rule the U.S. military has, this should have been the master plan that all strategy and tactics were derived from during this engagement. A JIPTL is nothing less than the blueprint for running an air war. Staggeringly, no such document existed. We were literally making this war up as we went.

There had been such a plan once, fine-tuned and ready to go. Code-named Operation Allied Talon, this was a true phased air campaign designed to achieve actual wartime effects and military objectives. Supposedly neither Admiral Ellis, General Jumper (senior USAF officer in Europe), nor General Short could convince General Clark to adopt it. Instead, for reasons of his own and against seemingly everyone's advice, he had cut-and-pasted together this ad hoc endeavor and labeled it Allied Force. The U.S. Air Force's plans to conduct operations according to doctrine had been thwarted at every turn. Perhaps General Clark was being compelled to act this way—but that wasn't the way anyone saw it at the operational level.

Despite Clinton's statement from the very beginning that U.S. troops would not be employed, the planning for a ground war was quietly progressing at the backroom level in at least a theoretical manner. There really wasn't another choice if we weren't going to be allowed to fight a proper air war. The last ingredient required was the task of slowly getting the public and the politicians to accept the idea of a ground assault and the resultant casualties.

For the most part the VJ and MUP had already accomplished their goals on the ground. The Serbs had at least 40,000 troops massed on the borders of Kosovo (in addition to those already in-country) ready to push off before the first bombs fell, and they were now dispersed throughout the countryside. The Serb's Operation Horseshoe consisted of two sweeping pincers to expel the ethnic Albanians. Macedonia alone was reporting refugees on the order of four hundred thousand. How many more were in Albania or hiding in the hills and forests along the borders was anyone's guess. The Serbs claimed to be hunting only for small bands of KLA terrorists, but the reality on the ground screamed otherwise.

Since our politically approved target list had pretty much run out again, we spent a lot of time looking for something to do by picking through old BDA results for DMPIs within target sets that might have been missed or only partially damaged. We heard that some of the NATO countries were checking in on the AWACS frequency and going right to their "dump" targets without even bothering to ask for a mission. While new targets weren't being approved, the previously hit ones were still on the list, so they'd become a place to unload ordnance while still pretending that combat objectives were being accomplished. The term most often used for this practice was "rearranging the rubble."

Day 14 was a Tuesday. I woke up at 20:00 to return to work. The air package went smoothly again except for hung bombs on Speedy's jet. The danger of bringing a hung bomb home is that you never really know how far the release sequence had progressed. So you don't want to fly over friendly territory until the issue has been resolved. After running the checklists, he elected to jettison his de-armed bombs in a clear area of the Adriatic. Naturally, we had to keep detailed records on the exact locations, types, and serial numbers of each jettisoned weapon.

When jettisoning bombs, we can drop them with de-armed fuses while still retaining the ability to guide them to ensure they go where intended. (Weeks later an Italian fisherman would start to net up dud bombs and began demanding exorbitant compensation. The fished-up bombs turned out to be old stuff left over from World War II, which pissed off the Italian to no end since he wasn't going to see any money and had to go back to fishing for fish.)

My major problem throughout the night was battling attempts from someone at the 8th trying to bypass the normal coordination channels within the CAOC. It took a lot of calls back and forth, and smoothing of feathers, to sort it out. Fortunately our three-star,

General Short, was an old F-117 commander and on the side of reason.

The tougher long-term question for the stealth community was figuring out what to do with the 9th up at Spangdahlem. There just weren't enough targets to make a two-squadron operation worthwhile. In truth, there weren't enough targets to employ even one squadron fully, not to mention the tanker and overflight issues that would have to be coordinated due to staging combat operations from over half of continental Europe. Unless the target list opened up significantly, we'd probably have to start alternating nights for each squadron to have a little something to do.

The 9th's inaugural night went reasonably well. Operating out of the vacated squadron facilities of a recently deactivated F-15C unit at Spangdahlem, they launched four jets. The launch came only thirty-three hours after their initial departure from Holloman. Along with their F-16CJ escorts, this constituted the first combat operation to stage from Germany since the end of World War II.

There were some growing pains, of course. They had launched without forwarding their routes down to us at the CAOC. For just a minute, one of the guys up there got a bit puffed up with himself and claimed that, for security reasons, we didn't "*need* to know" what their routes and altitudes over Serbia were going to be. General Short's response went something like, "Then they don't *need* to cross the border and can turn around right now." The 9th just hadn't been in theater long enough to have gotten anyone into the CAOC yet to learn the ropes.

In any case, they did well, except for No. 2, who logged two misses because of a switch error. He had inadvertently left his selector switch in the OAP position and had slewed that cursor over the target, so his bombs went to the reciprocal of wherever that OAP should have been (mistakenly treating the target as the OAP and adjusting to where the target should have been in relation to the correct OAP).

Earp showed up later that night to relieve one of the other guys, so I spent a few hours showing him around and introducing him to the VTC. We'd begun collecting "quotes of the day" from the VTCs. Scrawled on a small whiteboard tucked in the far back corner of our planning area, they were both illuminating and disturbingly funny. A small sampling of these quotes illustrates our whole strategic war-making process and philosophy in action. All are sworn to be quotes by the guys who heard them—though no one ever signed his name:

General Clark, Day 14 of the war: "I have no idea where this air campaign is going."

A local brigadier as he was reaming out some major from a different planning cell: "It is *not* the purpose of airpower to go into a hostile area to attack ground targets." I caught that one myself halfway through the conversation before discretely backing out. To this day I can't imagine what the first part of that conversation had been or a context for that statement.

General Short, rocking back in his chair as he spotted a contractor walking by: "If I could be wearing civilian clothes right now, I sure as shit wouldn't be sitting here."

General Clark again: "This doesn't look anything like Desert Storm. Perhaps we need two hundred more aircraft." Admiral Ellis, knowing that we didn't have a target set for the jets we already had in theater, quietly responded: "Increasing the force flow shouldn't be a substitute for strategy."

A question to Lt. Col. B., a permanent-party expert in charge of the Noble Anvil planning cell: "So, what overall strategy are you guys working under?" Looking up from the contents of a target folder he had been studying, Lt. Col. B. paused to frame a response, began to answer, paused again as he thought better of that response, then stated: "None. We're just blowing shit up," and resignedly went back to his folder.

There you have it.

CHAPTER 16

Settling In?

Whoever said that the pen is mightier than the sword obviously had never been shot at by automatic weapons.

ON MY LAST DAY/NIGHT, WEDNESDAY/THURSDAY, I worked the floor for two separate missions, and they both went smoothly. When we had some targets to work with, the MAAP process was pretty well oiled by then. We were still having to contend with an excessive number of changes coming out of Aviano. At times it seemed that the F-117 community was responsible for more changes to the existing ATO than everyone else combined. Shepherd was on the phone to the 8th once trying to sort out a mess with four sets of conflicting instructions coming from the MAAP cell, the planners at Aviano, G-Man, and the OG. He was just stomped mercilessly.

I was getting awfully tired of being at the CAOC. Bronco, my replacement, couldn't arrive soon enough as far as I was concerned.

The ground war option was being more openly prepped for. Keeping the Russians out would likely be the bigger trick. A hallway phrase used after any discussion of Russian involvement went along the lines of this: "So what did you do in the Great War, Grandpa? Heck, I was there to help start it, Sonny."

The Serbs were beginning to make some noises about a ceasefire again. Maybe they were running out of Kosovars to expel. Bronco got in around noon, and I helped him in-process and get situated. Then I grabbed his car keys and started the two-hour drive back to Aviano (still without a driver's license or even a map). Fortunately, the highway was very good, and I only got turned around for a short while in a few of the smaller villages toward the end.

I unpacked before driving to the squadron to get rid of the little Punto. The Punto is a tiny little car—big enough for about two and a half adults or nine clowns. The night's flying had already been canceled for weather, and I saw that I had been officially scheduled for a down day the next day. That was a bit of a surprise—that we were actually scheduling days off for individuals. I suppose that was an acknowledgment that we were going to be there for a while and/or that we didn't have enough legitimate work to occupy our time.

The bad weather didn't bother me much. A natural delay in our campaign might even allow some breathing room for a diplomatic conclusion, I supposed. Bringing those happy thoughts back to earth, the news was carrying excerpts from a couple of speeches Boris Yeltsin had made. He pointedly used the words "world war": "I told NATO, the Americans, the Germans, don't push us toward military action, otherwise there will be a European war for sure, and possibly a world war."

Later that same day, he was more explicit. "They want to use ground troops, take over Yugoslavia, make it their protectorate. We cannot allow this. Russia and access to the Mediterranean Sea are nearby, so we can by no means give Yugoslavia away."

The thought that Russia still saw Yugoslavia as theirs to be "given away," or not, was disturbing.

A couple of days later, I was ready to go in just to sit through the mass brief when I got a call. I had been assigned to ride in a British AWACS as the F-117 liaison. This was another change that had come about as a result of losing Vega-31 and the security leaks coming out of either the CAOC, Brussels, or . . .

Noble Anvil, which had begun as simply a way of differentiating the planning process of the stealth and cruise missile assets from the conventional assets, had now become the mechanism for segregating all the operational details of the U.S.-only efforts. To that end, Noble Anvil plans were no longer being distributed to the NATO partners in the same manner as the plans for our conventional aircraft. This tightening of security across the board was already reaping benefits, but in order to be integrated with the larger effort, some sharing of information still had to occur.

This was where the AWACS came in. Our flight paths and targets were kept unpublished to the larger NATO audience until they were actually being executed. An F-117 pilot would ride along with a copy of the plan rolled up in his flight suit pocket and only share it with the controllers as the jets were crossing the border. Without being told why, the conventional assets were all planned to be elsewhere at the appropriate times, and only AWACS that were crewed by either U.S. or British personnel were to be involved. For reasons never explicitly stated (though universally understood), French-crewed AWACS were specifically and pointedly excluded from controlling airspace where F-117s or B-2s were to fly. In any case, I caught a ride to the Brit squadron to sit in on their flight brief. Our routing packages hadn't been completed yet, but I still had a couple of hours before takeoff—I thought.

It turned out that we had mistaken their boarding time with brief time. I was already running two hours late, and the crew was boarding. A frantic call to Buster in the planning cell got the ball rolling as I was climbing aboard. But the engines were already running and I'd resigned myself to just being a passenger on this thing when I was told to head down to the wheelwell. The Brit who had led me down into the well tried to shout over the noise before giving up and just pointed toward a small cutout in the bulkhead. A disembodied arm reached up through the small hatch to thrust a package containing our plan toward me. A few minutes later the plane began to move. Score one for Buster.

I had never been in an AWACS before and had to admit that it was a very comfortable way to fly. I got to sit in the jump seat behind the pilot for the takeoff. What really caught my attention was the sudden realization that I could actually see outside. This was the first time I'd been airborne over Italy during daylight and good weather. The view of the many small islands along the east side of the Adriatic was beautiful—looking more like a resort area than a war zone.

We settled down into our assigned orbit at sunset and relaxed for a while. The crew was roughly divided into three functions: the flight crew, the radar controllers, and the technicians. Each segment took its turn either being the center of attention or supporting the group that was. The techs and controllers started off in support mode while the flight crew was engaged getting the AWACS airborne and to the assigned orbit point. After a few hours the emphasis shifted to the controllers as the war picked up. They were essentially chained to their stations and talking nonstop, so the free flight crew and techs shifted to taking care of them. As electronic or mechanical issues arose the techs would then become the center of attention until the issue had been resolved.

In the fighter world, we pay lip service to the concepts of crew coordination and cockpit resource management, but I had never believed that they were especially important. That misconception was permanently put to rest. I had never seen those concepts applied to this degree. That team was truly a well-oiled machine.

Parts of the flight were slow, others were impressively busy. About halfway through the mission the crew was notified that their mission would be extended until the following morning. That meant refueling from a KC-10. I was called away from a conversation I was having with a couple of the controllers to watch. I thought, "Sure. Why not?" I couldn't figure out why everyone was so on edge. It was dark and beginning to get a little turbulent, but refueling was just a fact of life. We did it all the time.

Of course, I'd never refueled a heavy in any circumstances, let alone these. It turned out to be one wild, uncomfortable, and impressive ride. The pilot was going to do it all. The co-pilot was a recent transfer from a Jaguar squadron and wasn't qualified to refuel yet, so he was of little help except with the lookout during the tanker rendezvous. I didn't know it at the time, but the KC-10 is the least compatible tanker for an AWACS. It turns out that the center engine mounted halfway up the KC-10's tail is just about level with the radome disk of the AWACS.

The first attempt to get into position was like driving too fast over a bumpy road. As we got close enough to see the boom, I became aware of the dynamics involved. The AWACS was yawing side to side, but the center of that rotation seemed to be about 25 yards behind the cockpit. The lateral motion of the front of the jet was greatly exceeding any limits of the boom—assuming we could even get plugged, that is. When a fighter approaches a tanker, it has to push through the bow wave created by the larger plane, but because an AWACS is so large parts of the plane are always in the wave—leading to more turbulence and instability.

We fell off and backed up to reposition for another try. This one wasn't much better, and we backed off again before attempting a third time. By now I was just watching the pilot on the controls and listening to the constant encouragement from the co-pilot and flight engineer. The pilot had both hands on the yoke and was throwing it side to side, and forward and aft, seemingly from stop to stop. It looked as if he were wrestling a pissed-off bear.

This time we achieved a viable position and got our plug. The engineer called out a congratulations with the news "we have good flow" as the pilot continued his wrestling match unabated. Then the engineer made a comment that really gave me pause.

"Hang on, just twenty-two more minutes."

Twenty-two minutes! He was going to have to do this for better than a third of an hour. I carefully kept very still and quiet so as not to distract anyone as I witnessed a very impressive feat of airmanship.

Eventually we had our fuel and backed off. As soon as we were clear of the boom, the pilot just let go of everything and flopped back in his seat. The co-pilot had been anticipating this and jumped on the controls to take us back to our orbit so the controllers could go back to work.

My role during the flight was minimal. As the time approached for the F-117s to get involved, I passed along the routing, targets, and times to the appropriate controllers so they could react if anything were to become a factor. The 9th had the northern war but had to weather abort at the border. The 8th pushed through the southern borders to take a look, but only got to drop on two targets—and I was done. Of course there were other flights that the AWACS was responsible for and needed controlling, so I had several more hours to kill before we would be returning.

The sun rose as we were still on station, and for only the second day I got to see the ground from the air during daylight, and both times during the same flight. It turned out to be an 11.5-hour sortie.

* * *

The next day I slept until 19:00 and got up just in time to brief for the evening go. My mission that night was in the south trying to hit two railroad bridges that linked Kosovo with Serbia. Intel believed that the MUP was using those lines to resupply their forces in western Kosovo. My call sign was Vega-08, my jet was -788, and I was loaded with a pair of GBU-10s.

The target study was fairly straightforward. Finding the targets, though small, wouldn't be especially difficult, but the direction of the attacks had to be carefully aligned so that the surrounding cliff faces of the gorges that the bridges were located in wouldn't obscure the laser's view of the target. The only real trick left then would be my carefully hitting the abutments for the bridges. I couldn't aim directly for the spans for fear that the laser, or bomb, might pass through a gap in the rails, and if I aimed too far from the abutment I wouldn't drop the bridge.

I was supposed to have been on G-Man's wing, but he was delayed on the ground with some maintenance issue and radioed for me to launch without him. He'd try to catch up later. The tanker rendezvous plan was pretty well screwed up, and though I'd taken off a little earlier than required, everyone was running late by the time I got behind Ruble-02 in the refueling track.

A new guy had gotten there ahead of me and was having trouble getting plugged and staying on the boom. He should have been long gone before I'd arrived. I believe this was his first combat mission after having just finished training at Holloman a couple of weeks earlier. In any case, precious time was being chewed up. While still waiting for him to get out of the way, G-Man had caught up to us. His place was ahead of me, but after talking it over with him on the boom frequency we determined that he wasn't going to make his push time anyway, so he let me go first.

He hung off to the side while I took my fuel before making a run to the push point. The timing was tight, and I didn't have the opportunity to take on a full load of fuel, but I had enough to do the mission and make it back out over the Adriatic. As I was running toward the border I methodically ran through my stealth checklist, while listening to the boss move onto the boom to take enough fuel to fly home.

The weather along the coast of Montenegro where I had pushed in didn't look too bad initially, but it got thicker further inland. As I swung up over Serbia, the cloud deck thickened to an almost solid undercast. The AWACS sounded bored as it repeatedly broadcast, "Picture Clara."

An oddity as I was pushing in was an attempt on the part of the Serbs to jam our communications frequency. Occasional bits of what sounded like marching music would burst through the static—nothing that was going to be more than a nuisance though.

About ten minutes after the push, I crossed my first target, located just over the border from the Montenegrin town of Biserka. I had the laser in manual mode to see if I could take a quick shot at any sliver of ground that might present itself. Since this wasn't an NCD target, all I would have needed would have been a good-sized gap in the clouds. I didn't need much to justify an attempt out here in the boonies. There were a few small gaps that teased me to think I might get to do some work, but I never saw anything useful.

Into my tape I called, "Weather no-drop, master arm is safe," then a tired, "Son of a bitch." Getting the master arm switch off was necessary to ensure that the bomb bay door wouldn't automatically swing open as I flew over the target. It still sounded quiet, but there wasn't any point in giving the Serbs a better radar picture of me.

The second bridge was further inland near the town of Kursumlija. The only advantage to having not dropped on the first bridge was that now I had two bombs for the second. That would add a little better guarantee that at least one might hit the small target. So I set about resetting the switches for what we called a "dual-door" delivery—releasing both weapons simultaneously. Well, not exactly simultaneously. If both actually fell out side by side, with only a few feet between them, the odds of their colliding were pretty high. So we set a tiny release delay between them. Realistically, there were only milliseconds between each release, but now each could maneuver free of interference from the other. Ironically, due to the geometry of the drop, the second weapon released from the jet would actually hit the ground first.

The weather appeared to be breaking up just a little, so I was hopeful this might work. I even got a quick peek through to the ground over an en route turn point, but it wasn't to be. I had been poised to drop until the last moment but never had a clear shot.

"Damn it! No-drop, no-drop, no-drop."

The Kursumlija Bridge was safe from me that night. While the last few inconsequential seconds to TTI ticked away, I listened to some other guy on our freq maneuvering to avoid the attention of an SA-3.

So there we were, acting as human bait again and without the satisfaction of even shooting back. I saw some AAA well off to the east, but nothing in my immediate area. They didn't seem to bother shooting much when the weather was bad, maybe because they didn't want to highlight their own positions when they knew we weren't going to drop anyway—or perhaps because they were relying on the use of NVGs for targeting more than our intel would admit. In any case, my fourth combat sortie ended the same way as the second and third, with live weapons still securely attached to my plane and a frustrated pilot hauling them back.

I continued my route and pushed out feet-wet over the Adriatic very short on gas. By then it was either get on a tanker quickly or divert to Gioia Del Colle Airbase, just north of Taranto. Getting home with the remaining fuel on board wasn't possible. Diverting to Gioia was a highly discouraged option, especially with two tons of live bombs on board, unless necessary to save the jet.

In a repeat of the pre-strike refueling, I was jerked around by Coastline Control unnecessarily. CC had been off their game a while. They generally set us up for head-to-head passes and assumed we had radar to sort out the intercept in the closing stages—not at all the case in an F-117. A head-on pass at night or in the haze (both of which applied at the moment) usually meant starting all over again after watching the tanker go zorching over your head in the opposite direction. Toward the end of the last attempt, I just began inputting my own offsets so that I'd have at least a chance of making the turn. Had the tanker been unable to pass fuel immediately I would have been desperately screwed. That was my last pass before I'd have to commit to an emergency divert. But fortune smiled a little, and I hit my tanker to take on fuel.

After it had all worked out, I settled down for the long drone back up the Adriatic. I reflected on just how strange an occupation we had. We were risking our lives for often inconsequential targets, over bad weather, for a war that had minimal tactics, zero strategy, or even a hint of an exit plan that didn't require the cooperation of our enemy. That night I crawled into bed and slept, if not well, at least long, for eleven hours.

I got an email from Bets updating me on family matters. She had also read some of the reports that information was flowing through NATO channels to the enemy. We already knew about that single French officer in prison for spying on Serbia's behalf, but it was hard to pinpoint all of the leaks. Though the French were widely believed responsible, agencies within Greece were also suspected. The short answer was that we just didn't know for sure.

On Monday evening, April 12, I was bumped from the schedule at the last minute when my target was pulled off the authorized list again, so I worked on my bomb tracker program for a while. We were finally starting to break out a clearly definable trend with the no-guides related to one specific year group of a production lot of seeker heads. That particular production lot seemed to be accounting for the vast majority of our bad bombs. It was neither the oldest nor newest lot we were using, but at least now we had some real information to concentrate on.

The next night about half of the targets were hit, through some very marginal weather. The OG in particular scored a very nice dual-door hit on a large bridge. A large chunk of either the structure or a guard rail was seen slowly flipping end over end out of the fireball as the tape ended.

CNN was carrying the news that one of our Strike Eagles had hit a passenger train with an AGM-130 earlier that day, killing several civilians. The train had been passing over what looked like it might have been the Kuršumlija railroad bridge. Assuming that bridge in particular was to have been one of my targets the other night, and had the weather been better, I could have dropped that bridge before the train ever got there, and no one would have ever heard of the place. What had been good luck for the Serbs a night before had led to tragedy.

There were lots of interviews with Serbs on the news services. They absolutely didn't believe the refugee stories coming out of Kosovo. They assumed that the columns of thousands of people fleeing their homes were somehow all actors, being paid $5.50/ day by NATO to walk in circles and instead were furious over our "unprovoked aggression." Serbian TV claimed that we were engaged in genocide, that we were using chemical weapons, that the only Kosovar Albanians that had been displaced were actually fleeing NATO, and that the only fighting the Serbs were engaged in was against small bands of terrorists. One woman interviewed even said that it was "perfectly obvious" that it was the Arabs, paying American mercenaries, who were causing all of this. Amazing!

For years, one of the foundations of Western thought has been the assumption that free access to information and news would allow educated people to rid themselves of the misperceptions put forward by propaganda—the idea that conflict resulted from a lack of education. We were seeing definitive proof that this isn't even remotely true. Television and radio service were widely available throughout the region. There wasn't anyone in Belgrade who couldn't watch CNN, BBC, or anything I couldn't see myself. Yet the conclusions derived from those sources differed vastly, proving yet again that reason wasn't absolute, but depended upon perspective and prejudices—you can't "educate" conflict away, which is why militaries have been necessary through all of recorded history, I suppose.

I was scheduled to fly again though the weather in the target area was supposed to get even worse. There was a short-lived rumor that because of the limited target set being approved by the nineteen NATO nations, General Clark, and the other politicians (each with a veto no one seemed shy of using), that we would be sent home, and then set up a rotation out of Spangdahlem with the 9th in a month or so. That rumor didn't survive a day.

Another program that fell solidly into the "silly riendeer games" category had also been implemented. To keep any terrorists or commandos off balance, we were trying to disguise our appearance while traveling to and from base. When we drive off base we would wear civilian shirts over our flight suits to deflect any unfriendly attention. So, picture a large dark blue fifteen-passenger vehicle full of short-haired guys in their thirties wearing an odd assortment of ski jackets and flannel shirts pulled on over military flight suits while en route to an airbase during a war. Yeah, that should fool the Commies!

Tuesday morning was embarrassing. I initially woke up and looked across the room at the alarm clock to see "7:32" displayed in big red numerals. *"Oh, shit!"* The flight brief started at 7:45. There was absolutely no way I'd be able to get to the squadron in time. Sorties were hard enough to come by lately, and now I was going to lose mine to someone else because I overslept, and I would probably get chewed out by G-Man to boot. I scrambled around in a panic, quickly dressing in yesterday's clothes from a pile on the floor. In far less than a minute, I'd burst out of my room into the parking lot planning to commandeer the first available car—only to be blinded by the rising sun.

Only then did I finally realize that the clock was saying 7:32 *a.m.* and that I had only been asleep for about an hour. The brief was still twelve hours away. A sheepish scan of the immediate area revealed that no one had witnessed this little clown act. I slunk back into my room with more adrenaline pumping than would allow any sleep for a while. I did some chores before crawling back into bed after lunch for a few hours of uneasy sleep. I was up again at 17:00 to prepare for my flight.

At work, we were jerked around for a while before being canceled yet again for weather. It made for an easy night, except for a long discussion on how to change the way we mannned the CAOC. Lack of continuity was causing more problems than could be easily smoothed over anymore. The first suggestion was that a small number of people who already had some experience there (like me, unfortunately) would pick up most of the burden by pulling longer rotations. By 03:30, we were seriously considering the creation of a permanent position down there. My name, amongst a few others, was being bandied about on the short list.

That was a depressing thought. No more flying, perpetual CAOC duty, being cut off from the squadron, and generally just getting lost in the shuffle. Sleep was difficult again. I got up at 09:00 to do laundry and a few small chores before going back to sleep at 13:00 for a couple of hours.

The next night I awoke early enough for a real dinner before going in with the evening push. It quickly turned out that Mace was going to be the permanent CAOC guy we'd been talking about the previous night. That was good news. For most of us anyway. The bad news was that two other people, both from the 8th, would assist Mace by pulling twelve-day (versus the previous seven-day) shifts in the effort to improve continuity. I hoped the war would be over before my name came up on the rotation list again. I also suspected, on further consideration, that the railroad bridge on which the passenger train had been hit the other day hadn't been one of my previous targets, but had been further down the line. But my old target folder had already been recycled, so I couldn't confirm that.

Anyway, I briefed against a single target pretty much in the dead center of Serbia, and the weather looked good enough to launch. Perhaps because I hadn't dropped anything that had hit the ground in three weeks, I wasn't too confident. My tape title sounded perfunctory, like I was just going through the motions. My jet was -788 again, and I had a single GBU-27 loaded in the left bay.

The GBU-27 was a weapon specifically modified for the F-117. It was still a 2,000-pound class bomb like the GBU-10, but had a shaped and hardened casing that gave much better penetration before breaking up than the older bomb. The fin kit was modified to fit in our weapons bay, and the guidance system was much improved also. Instead of the old Vietnam-era "bang-bang" guidance of the early Paveway-1 and the current Paveway-2 system we were using on the GBU-10, the Paveway-3 employed proportional guidance. If there were only a small course correction to be made, only a small input would be applied. This way there was very little maneuvering being done during the last few seconds before impact. If the laser spot was lost at the last moment, the bomb was still going to hit close to the target, unlike the Paveway-1, which might be pitching off in any direction. Because of this proportional guidance, the bomb's stability, kinetic energy, and impact angle were also going to be greater—all of which aided the bomb's penetration enormously.

During our preflight planning we calculated that the bomb on this particular drop would be impacting the target about 15 degrees off vertical. From initial impact until detonation, we had programmed the FMU-143 fuse for a 60-millisecond delay. So, in order for the bomb to be in the very center of the building after crashing through a couple of stories en route to the ground floor before detonation, I had to aim just a little short of dead center on the roof to compensate for the impact angle. To that end, I had carefully picked out a corner on the roof formed by the intersection of two roof lines as my aiming point and adjusted the run-in heading slightly.

I was Vega-02 and followed Shepherd, Vega-01, down the coast to our tanker. It was an uneventful night up to that point except that the Serbs were attempting a bit of comm-jamming on several frequencies again. Not the first time certainly, but what caught our attention this time was the content—polka music, of all things. It was odd, but didn't really interfere with the mission.

The coordination and timing were working out well and there was a comfortable pad of almost fifteen minutes of void time spent in holding before pushing the border. The weather off the Bosnian coast didn't look very promising. The clouds covered well over 50 percent of the ground, and I'd need a lot better than that for my target. I was fragged against an army headquarters building in the very center of the city of Kragujevac. Because of its location, the target had been designated NCD, of course.

There were two targets there actually. Both appeared to be identical E-shaped buildings set end to end with their backs toward an athletic field. I was to hit the southern building as Shepherd simultaneously hit the northern building. Our flight paths had been planned so that we would each fly over our targets on almost a head-on course. His altitude for that leg was planned to be 1,000 feet below mine for deconfliction. If things worked out perfectly, we would be able to see each other's hits and I might even pick up his jet in my display as he went by.

Shepherd is a gambler by nature and rarely passes up the opportunity for a wager, so we had a twelve-pack of beer riding on the attacks—not to hit the things, that was a given, but as to how close to being on time the bombs would impact. A TOT bet. The allowable impact window for planning purposes was plus or minus a full minute, but just two or three seconds off would probably lose the contest.

There had been no cancellation while we were holding, so at push time I turned inland to take a look. The weather seemed to be slowly improving as I flew east. Because of the semi-neutral territory I had to fly over before getting to the actual Serbian border, I elected to delay arming the weapon for a while.

The F-15Cs were not having a shining moment that night. Their comm discipline was dismal. One flight was having trouble with our frequency, 57A, and was ordering Magic to have everyone push over to the 58B frequency. Maybe the polka music was getting on their nerves. Another flight was telling Magic not to do that, as 58B wasn't on their list. Magic generally didn't take orders on how to run their business anyway. One of our Vegas quickly clarified the situation by simply stating that all of the F-117s were going to stay on 57A—period. And since we were the primary strikers, and the F-15Cs were there to support us, that ended the argument. We ignored the rest of the chatter.

There was some snow on the hills approaching my target area, which made for an interesting IR picture. I suppose that it had always been there, but this was the first time I'd been able to see through to the ground in this area. Magic kept up their calm patter as the attack developed. "Magic, Picture Clean." This marked them as a U.S. crew, as the Brits were fond of saying, "Picture Clara." The discipline was only interrupted as various individual and groups of F-15Cs found their way back and reported on frequency, inevitably asking if the rest of their flights were also on that frequency. The F-15C chatter was getting thicker than the comm-jamming. One very annoyed Magic controller actually had to broadcast, "Magic, everyone stay this freq, and *minimize*!" To which I silently added a heartfelt "*No shit!*" In the world of tactical communications, "minimize" is a spanking word. It is the verbal equivalent of a kindergarten teacher making an undisciplined child stand in a corner. Everyone dutifully shut up and listened to the polka music. We weren't going to surprise the Serbs tonight anyway.

Ten minutes out I spotted what looked like a pair of SA-6s being launched far off to the north. Straight ahead still looked good, and I was getting good views of the ground through my attack display at each turn point. I could also see the city lights of Kragujevac for miles. As always, I mentally kept up a running update to as to which direction I would turn if I got into trouble, so that in an emergency I'd immediately know which way was the nearest friendly border.

As I got closer to the target I could see some AAA activity dead ahead. Fortunately my jet had been programmed for a significant climb about three minutes out. That would take me over the tops of all but the 57mm stuff. Unfortunately, higher altitudes got me above the small AAA, but also up into a good killing zone for the SAMs, and they all seemed to be active. Two minutes out, I began to pick out a picture of the target area, so I needed to focus my attention back inside the cockpit and ignore the stuff being shot at us.

"Level Attack, Record, Ready, Narrow, Cued, MPT—everything's good."

I moved a switch on my throttle to look at the first offset point, OAP-1. There was haze and a jumble of woods and fields. I couldn't tell where the point was, but I didn't care because, with another flip of that switch, the OAP-2 cursor fell right on the corner of the huge Zastava automobile/firearms factory (source of the ever-popular

"Yugo" compact cars). Unmistakable, but also irrelevant—the target complex was clear.

The picture in my attack display was the clearest I'd ever seen, and the crosshairs were exactly on top of the DMPI. I muttered a quiet, "Good job, Kat." Kat was one of our more competent and colorful targeteers. She was a practical joker and was known for throwing hilarious hillbilly tirades. All of our people were exceptional but when she set up a series of target photos and coordinates you could be doubly confident they would be perfect. She never let us down. I clearly saw the two E-shaped buildings with the soccer field right behind them. Surrounding the area were several tall apartment buildings on my right between the target and the auto factory, suburbia was both short and to the left, and the bulk of the taller buildings of the city were long of my target. This bomb was going to hit *something*, and it was solely my responsibility to make sure that it was the *right* thing.

There was some urgent chatter in the background about SAM activity, but I tuned it out. All of my concentration was focused on tracking the exact spot on the roof that I had chosen before the flight. The only point in my universe was the intersection of those two roof lines. I felt the doors open. I felt the bomb fall away. I interrupted my concentration just long enough to reach over and slap the master arm switch to off. The bomb fell for almost ten seconds before it was time for the laser to fire. The "auto-fire" symbol appeared right on cue, and then, even more so than before, my universe was that spot on the roof. In unison with the computer, I counted down the seconds until impact. "Three, two, one, zero," and then . . . nothing.

Oh, God. For a terrible moment I thought I had a no-guide bomb—and in the middle of an NCD city! "Come on, come on, come on, do your thing," I shouted at the GBU. Then I saw the dot of my bomb zip straight and true right up the middle of the display *exactly* to where it had been aimed (perhaps the adrenaline had made me count too fast). There was a tiny puff of shattered shingles at the inter-section of the roof lines where the bomb entered the building. Then, in seemingly slow motion, a shock wave ran down both wings of the structure as the building was consumed from the center outward. *Yes!*

The jet began a hard programmed turn to the left, and the throttles shot forward to the stops. Over my shoulder I could see the fire I had created. I had just one thought—*what happened to Shep?* There was no sign of him. It also looked as if I'd kicked over a hive of incandescent bees, and they were pissed off and coming up for battle. It turned out that an athletic field is a great place to mount AAA cannons. Too bad for them, I was already in the process of turning invisible again and melting away into the night.

During the planning process, the computers provide a warning whenever a flight might be particularly vulnerable to the expected SAMs. Depending on the severity and length of that exposure, a flight plan will be modified to minimize that risk as much as possible. If this "red time," counted in seconds, becomes excessive (say forty-five to sixty seconds), a supervisor might ask the pilot if he is willing to take that line or if he wants someone else to fly it; no one ever declines. Not one but two supervisors had asked me that question before I had stepped. "Sure, no problem," I'd replied.

My "seconds" of vulnerability on this run had added up to 273.

Now that I was off target, there were only twenty to thirty of those seconds to go, and I had the luxury of being able to look outside for the threat again.

I flew the rest of the route looking at the HARM shots, the lights of Belgrade lit up like New York City, some large fires way off in the direction of Novi Sad, and other seemingly far away events, thinking that I had gotten off relatively easy.

After landing, both Fu and Munk (flying other lines further to my south) hunted me down to ask how it went. I thought that was out of character for both of them until they explained what they had seen, and which I mostly hadn't, because of the angles. The AAA had come in barrage a full ten seconds before the bomb's impact, then followed me away through the turn. Perhaps the Serbs were shooting at sound or had night-vision goggles, or perhaps all of those "seconds" had given me away. Four or five (in the heat of the moment they disagreed on the count) SA-6s had been shot toward me. Of course, the severely limited view down, and absolutely none to the rear, kept me blissfully ignorant of much of that. Maybe their view of the fire from the side was more intense than mine when looking down through it. Not that there was much I could have done about it anyway. My target had still been burning when they departed the area.

Several of the guys kept the white lights turned up in the cockpit so that they couldn't see out at all and thus avoided viewing things that they couldn't do anything about anyway. Not me. As soon as I was off target, the sensor display got dimmed down severely and the cockpit lighting went even lower so that I could see out. I could justify part of that as helping to thwart NVG's, but mostly I just liked being able to see outside. But who can say? Maybe sometimes it's best just not to know what's going on.

Looking at his tape afterward, Shepherd's bomb had looked good at drop, but it never guided. I'd had a tailwind helping me, and he had been fighting a strong headwind, so I would have won the bet even if his bomb had impacted, as he was running a little late. I wasn't going to hold him to the bet, but Shep always pays off.

Intel tried to do some analysis of where Shepherd's errant bomb might have gone, but couldn't find a spot that had unintended damage. Maybe it was a dud. (About a month later, Intel called Shep aside and explained that they had found his bomb. The fin kit had failed to deploy and the bomb had flown off like a spear for about ten miles before landing in a farm field.)

I was giddy for the rest of the night. I had been exposed to more threats than ever before. I had been shot at, but had gotten away clean. I had given fire as well as received it, and the video was glorious. I was content. For the first time in too many weeks, I slept like an absolute log.

Thursday night I went in to cover the brief as a spare flyer. No one fell out though, so I ended up acting as the duty driver through the long and rainy evening. Our takeoffs were getting earlier each night, so everyone was down by a reasonable hour.

Afterward, some of the guys finally broke down and told G-Man that he had been the target of a multiweek practical joke. It had centered on his very first target back on Day 1. The target had been a high-priority radar that covered almost all of northern Serbia and was housed in a small dome. G-Man had to take that out with his first shot so that the following conventional aircraft wouldn't be tracked.

Unfortunately, it was surrounded by several presumably civilian houses. That made it an NCD target. In addition to applying NCD criteria, only the smaller 500-pound GBU-12 bomb was allowed. To ensure that this thing was going to be hit, maintenance had configured one of the spare jets (which he eventually needed) with just this load-out to make sure G-Man would get a shot at it. His tape showed a direct hit—which made him enormously proud, of course—before he continued on to strike an aircraft factory in Pancevo with a 2,000-pounder.

Maybe he was acting just a little too proud—so Speedy, Shepherd, and a few others cooked up a gag. Others were brought in over time to keep up the pretense.

A couple of days into the war the first BDA assessments began to come out. The best photos were posted on our "wall of fame." Naturally, we all flocked around whenever anything new was posted to see how we had done and to brag about our more spectacular hits. G-Man's first target assessment was missing. No big deal; they didn't all arrive at once, and his second target results were there.

A few days later the rest of the post-strike photos from Night 1 became available and were posted. But again, there was nothing for G-Man's first target. The boss instructed the target shop to look into it for him. This is where it began to get fun. A mock post-strike photo was cooked up. It was simple enough to use the pre-strike imagery and just overlay a different date on top (I suspected Kat's fingerprints may have been on that one). The photo was posted on the "wall of fame" with the target looking completely intact and undamaged—a nice round dome set in suburbia.

The boss would occasionally be seen quietly scrutinizing the photo from different angles and trying to account for its unscathed appearance. "Maybe they reconstituted the site because it was so important. Or maybe it's an inflatable dome they threw up to spoof us."

I wasn't there to see it, but one of the guys mentioned during one of these episodes that after Day 1, the Serbs had accused us of attacking a dome housing a university's telescope observatory near there. I can just imagine G-Man's eyes getting big as he thought through the implications of that possibility.

So now, finally convinced that he must have missed the dome on the first night, he decided to request another strike line through the CAOC to attack it again. That's when Speedy broke down and told him. Too bad, he might have kept that going for a long time and only revealed the joke at our tenth anniversary reunion.

My bomb tracker now had several people making data inputs and was being continuously updated and expanded. One of the more recent additions was to include the serial numbers of each and every component dropped so far. I can't take credit for that particular idea, but it singled out the production year group of the bad GBU-27 guidance units. A couple of Raytheon contractors I was escorting at the time pointed out that the only real difference between the bad lot and the other lots that were working just fine was a different model of thermal battery. Perhaps we'd discovered a shelf life issue.

The strikes went well that night. Everyone, except Flounder (he had some inconveniently located clouds), got to take advantage of what was perhaps the last good day of weather and raged over northern Serbia. The Serbs must have been running a little short of petrol and bridges. The more significant event for us was that a trend that had begun the previous night had evidently become Serbian policy—the AAA was being shot in abundance.

Aimed fire being shot at specific aircraft was no longer the rule, and now barrage fires from large AAA pieces were just filling the skies. G-Man made the old Hollywood comment about the flak being so thick that you could get out and walk on it. He wasn't the only one inspired to that sort of hyperbole by the volume of fire. (During the last two European wars, AAA had always been called "Flak," which is a contraction for the word Fliegerabwehrkanonen. Perhaps because the Germans are on our side now, the term has gone out of fashion.)

I was scheduled to fly for two nights in a row, but the weather wasn't forecast to allow much. After the second sortie, I had to return to the CAOC for a twelve-day shift. I wasn't looking forward to that at all. Bronco, who replaced me when I left the first time, had a bad time of it. He was jokingly threatening suicide, after a prolonged murder spree, if he was sent back. At least I was off the list of those being considered for another permanent slot down there.

In the early morning on April 17, we held a quorum in G-Man's room to share the gossip and events of the day. He relayed why the F-117 was getting so much support, allowed so much leeway in our planning, and indulged to suggest so many changes to the Frag. The word was out that we were smacking more strategic targets with our little group of twelve jets than the other several hundreds of aircraft combined. The F-117s and B-2s were still the only aircraft being allowed to fly directly over Belgrade. Compared with the conventional units, we were being allowed a degree of freedom unheard of. Of course, the price we paid was that we were expected to go where others couldn't and that we went alone. To a degree, that has always been the case with aviators. We succeed and live, or we fall. There is no halfway, and in fighters, there are no comrades beside us when we fall.

Our results with the F-117 weren't too much of a surprise, I suppose. History has shown that man for man, the sniper eventually tallies more kills than the machine gunner. He gets to run his own show, just at a slower pace. In Vietnam, the U.S. Army averaged over fifty thousand rounds fired in combat for each enemy casualty. With snipers, the average was 1.3 rounds per kill. Never as fast or spectacular, but as the saying goes, "slow and steady wins the race." Or, as Wyatt Earp once said (the original, not our guy), "Fast is fine, but accurate is final."

In honor of our newfound status, we began wearing small rectangular patches on the bit of Velcro that normally secured the pencil pocket cover on our sleeves. Measuring perhaps a half inch tall by an inch and a half wide, it proclaimed "HMA" in bright gold letters—standing for "high maintenance assholes."

What the hell! If you've got it, flaunt it.

On Friday, April 16, we briefed and stepped. I got as far as taxiing the nose of my jet out of the shelter to get the GPS on line. Then the expeditor drove up to tell me that we had all been canceled for weather in the tanker track area. What a pain.

Back in the squadron I did some more work on the bomb tracker spreadsheet. The seeker problem had been solved by the simple expedient of no longer using guidance units from that suspect year group anymore. But the OG seemed to love the tracker so he wanted to keep it current. I guess it was a useful briefing aid when he was in conference with leadership. I ended up printing updated sheets and taping them together into a roll-up chart each day. I also worked with the Raytheon reps some more as they were trying to figure out the actual failure mechanism with the production lot that caused our GBU-27 problems—they didn't want to blame everything on the thermal batteries just yet.

I was home by 01:00 hours for the first time in ages and watched most of *Schindler's List* on the tube. I hadn't seen the movie before. Very powerful! It helped our motivation to watch that while also seeing the daily lines of refugees coming out of Kosovo. Perhaps we were participating in a noble crusade after all—just doing it poorly. I slept pretty well and got up just in time to catch a late lunch.

The next day, the weather was holding, and it looked like we were going to get some real work done. Most of my pre-mission study had been concentrated on the first target. It was the Baric munitions plant, situated just a few miles west of Belgrade on the banks of the Sava River. The DMPI was a mixing tower surrounded on all four sides by a large berm of earth. My problem wouldn't be finding the target but getting the bomb in through the top of the surrounding berm. I huddled with Chip, who, as chief of the weapons shop, had become one of our more experienced weaponeers, to explain the problem and my plan.

The problem was as follows: First, think of a target as a tin can at the bottom of a cardboard box. You want to drop a golf ball into that can. The walls of the box are analogous to the berm surrounding the target. If you could hover directly over the can, it would be an easy task to drop the ball in. The walls of the box wouldn't be a factor. But now move back 20 feet. The target is no longer visible. The front wall of the box is between you and the can. You can't toss the ball directly at your target without hitting the wall, so an up-and-over toss will be required.

Next, there are three distinct factors that affect the fall of a laser-guided bomb. To begin with, the bomb is released on a ballistic trajectory so that, even without laser guidance, it will impact close to the target. Depending on the aircraft's altitude and speed at the time of the drop, that release point may be as far as five to ten miles short of the target. The bomb then follows a curving arc downward, becoming ever steeper, before impacting the ground. Depending on how high the bomb was released, the impact angle may be nearly horizontal for a low-altitude drop or approaching vertical if dropped from extreme altitudes. For this attack, some mathematics told us that the impact angle was going to be steep enough to clear the berm in front of the target.

The second factor affecting a GBU attack is the laser-guidance phase. The GBUs we employed have a small set of movable fins mounted in front of the bomb case to "fly" the bomb toward the laser spot. These fins receive their commands from a small seeker head. Each seeker head can be programmed to "see" only the laser energy of a spot that is reflecting a specific code. Many thousands of different laser codes can be programmed into a seeker head. In this way, the bomb won't be confused by laser spots from other aircraft that may also have targets in the area or laser decoys distributed randomly about by the enemy, but will only guide toward the specific laser spot generated by the aircraft that released that particular bomb.

Several seconds before a ballistic impact, the pilot will illuminate the exact DMPI with the laser spot. The GBU seeker head will see the spot and begin sending course correction commands to the fins until impact. Unfortunately, all of these small fin corrections create drag on the streamlined bomb body, and cause a small "sag" in the ballistic flight path. Normally this isn't much of an issue, but in the case of a berm-protected target, you have to ensure that the sag isn't so great that the bomb doesn't make it over the wall.

The technique Chip and I had agreed upon to deal with this problem was to release the bomb deliberately as if the target were significantly further away than its actual location (called aiming long)—not so long that the laser spot would be out of view of the seeker head, but long enough so that when the laser came on, the bomb would have to significantly bunt over toward the vertical. Therefore, the bomb would be high enough to "clear the wall" throughout the first part of its fall before nosing over in the last few seconds to hit the target from above.

The third and final factor I had to deal with is called the podium effect, which is something peculiar to the F-117. Suppose that the plane is flying directly over the target while the bomb is falling. Since the aircraft is powered through the air by its engines while the bomb is simply falling, and therefore slowing due to air drag, the plane will not be directly over the bomb as it falls, but will pull ahead of it. The plane will cross over the target and be significantly past it several seconds before the bomb impacts. So, during those final few seconds, the bomb will be looking forward toward the target while the aircraft mounted laser is looking backward. If there is a tall obstacle near the target, such as a wall, the laser will be illuminating the back side of the wall while the falling bomb sees nothing because there is no laser energy hitting the front side of the wall.

Just another little bit of geometry to contend with.

After our earliest brief to date, we stepped out to fly. Again, I was Vega-02 in aircraft -788. Lief was in the lead tonight and had a target at the Baric plant also. It was raining a bit, but nothing too extreme. A few months earlier, we probably would have canceled a training sortie because of that rain. But the jet didn't really seem to mind as long as you didn't let it soak outside for too long, and we were now willing to accept the additional wear and tear on the surfaces.

I had a problem with the tracking system right after engine start, but maintenance promised me a five-minute fix, and I held them to it. A well-choreographed team swarmed around my jet, cut through a section of RAM to access a panel, fixed the problem, closed the panel, and buttered every fastener opening and the edge of the cut RAM section quick enough for me to get airborne on time. ("Butter" is the term used for the quick-drying putty-like stuff used to seal gaps or voids between sheets of RAM.) It was another heroic performance by a team of guys who never got enough credit.

We taxied and launched as the last visible daylight faded.

"Two's airborne."

"Copy, Vega zero one flight go button-four."

"Two."

Our refueling tracks were over the western part of Bosnia. The tankers were wandering off their planned tracks trying to avoid weather, so the rendezvous was a bit of a mess. Lief refueled first as I waited my turn on the tanker's left wing. After he had disconnected, he slid back and over to my left instead of leaving the track. That seemed a little odd. Also, my system altitude was reading just under 22,000 feet, which was several thousand feet higher than I'd expected. After all of the last-minute work on my jet before takeoff, I wanted to ensure that the thing was reading correctly.

Once behind the tanker, I opened the refueling door on the spine of my jet, ensured I had a good RDY light, and slid forward as the boom reached out toward me. A moment later the boomer spoke to me through the intercom system.

"Contact."

I double-checked the lights and responded, "Looks good, I'm eight zero seven eight eight and need a top-off," as casually as if I'd been talking to a gas-station attendant through the window of my car.

"So how are you doing up there?" I asked after the fuel began to flow.

He drawled back with, "Pretty good. How 'bout you?"

"Oh pretty good. Running just a little bit late, but about normal, I guess. Why didn't the last guy leave? Has there been a change to the words?"

"No, he just wanted to try to get a little extra gas after you had gotten your planned off-load. He'll come back for the rest of it after you get done."

"Okay, I didn't think that he had that much time." Next issue. "What altitude are you showing us at right now?"

After a short pause he came back with, "Two, two, zero."

"Okay, we were planned for lower, but I guess we just took the whole cell up here to get above the clouds."

"Ahh, I'm not sure, let me check."

"Never mind, as long as my system is reading the same as yours, it's okay."

A few minutes later, my jet was full. I disconnected, slid back, and then eased off to the right as I heard Vega-01 taking my place behind the tanker.

There were quite a few clouds during the early part of the route, but it cleared out nicely as I got closer in. My approach to the first target was from the southwest over a relatively quiet area. There was some attempt at comm-jamming again, but this time it was being suppressed more efficiently. Mostly it came across as bursts of static, with only occasionally recognizable bits of music.

There was also more chatter on the radio than usual. Calls of "Firefly" and "Triple-A" were being made frequently. Magic had a short conversation with one of the more northerly Vegas about which bull's-eye was being referenced. The calls up until that point had been off a point called "Derringer." Unfortunately, that wasn't the point we already had loaded in our system. We had loaded a point called "Bat." It was an easy switch for the AWACS and F-15Cs to reload a point, less so for us, so everyone on frequency switched to using "Bat."

"Bull's-eye" is important. To call out a location quickly to

friendlies, without simultaneously calling out the same information to the enemy, the location would be referenced as a bearing
and a distance from a known point. So, just like a dart board being
laid over a map, you could describe your position reference to that
bull's-eye as a function of direction and distance from the center
of the dartboard—for example, a threat might be called out as
Firefly-6, Boat, 090, 25—a point due east (090 degrees) for twenty-
five miles from the designated bull's-eye called Boat. If my position
was Boat, 270, 30 at the time (thirty miles west of the bull's-eye),
I'd know that I was fifty-five miles away from that threat. And if
I'd had to call out my own location that night, I could have said
something like "Vega zero two is at Boat, two four zero, one five"
without broadcasting to the enemy where I was. Our comm card
always had a list of planned and alternate bull's-eyes (Derringer,
Bat, Mauser, etc.) in the event that one might be overused
or compromised.

As I approached the Serbian border, I finished my stealth check
by turning on the INERT switch. This switch pressurized the empty
volume of my fuel tanks with an inflammable gas, which would
help suppress any fire if I were to be hit. The inert gas supply wasn't
unlimited, so we always tried to wait until the last moment before
engaging it.

During my turn onto the target run, I heard "Triple-A, Bat, one
four six, three six, low." Someone was calling out anti-aircraft fire
thirty-six miles southeast of "Bat" and was also reporting that it was
being fired into the lower altitude bands.

A quick glance at my bull's-eye display elicited a comment to
myself: "That's where I am." And then, since I was the only one
there: "They're shooting at me."

It was all much too specific. Perhaps they'd picked up a
momentary radar return off my jet while I was in that big turn (it
happens sometimes). Maybe they heard me or, more likely, someone

down there with a $200 pair of night-vision goggles had seen me. It didn't matter at that point. I had less than a minute to get the bomb on its way.

I cycled through the nicely visible OAPs. OAP-1 was a large building to the left of my course. OAP-2 was the western tip of a long thin island out in the Sava River. *Piece of cake!* From thirty seconds out I could clearly see into the bulk of what looked like a factory complex—pipes, towers, and tanks everywhere. My target was on the west side of this complex, and I slewed my cursors over until the bottom edge of the aiming cross was just over the berm wall. The center of my cursor was pointed toward the edge of the river.

"Okay, I've got a good long aim, and there she goes," as I felt the bomb fall away.

Magic and other aircraft were excitedly calling "spikes" (enemy radar signals) and AAA—all very superfluous as even with my face buried in the bright green SD, I could see my own little Fourth of July display going on all around in my peripheral vision. I slowly mumbled to myself, "Don't look, don't look, don't look."

Now that the bomb was on its way, I brought the center of the cursor down onto the top of the mixing tower. All I had to do now was manually to track the spot and ensure that the laser fired automatically at the appropriate time. My right index finger hovered over the trigger in case I had to fire the laser manually. Everything worked exactly as advertised as I watched the bomb zip up the center of the display to obliterate the target.

Kaboom!

I'm getting good at this! I was shooting better in combat than I had in training back at Holloman. As I watched the detonation, an F-16 guy excitedly called out, "Heavy Triple-A west of the city at medium altitude." *Duh . . . tell me something I don't know, it's all around me!*

My jet went into a programmed hard turn to the east—directly toward Belgrade. Other than the fire that was now behind me, the largest concentrations of AAA were off to my north in the direction of Batajnica and Novi Sad. Right in front of me was the capitol. Not for the first time, I marveled at how brightly lit up the city was. There never seemed to be any AAA being fired at me while I was directly over Belgrade. I suppose the Serbs were smart enough to know that what goes up has to come down somewhere and didn't want to inflict damage upon themselves with their own spent shells. Missiles were another matter though, and I kept an eye out without seeing anything (while remembering my last mission that proved that you don't see the stuff being fired directly at you from below).

Another turn brought me up the east side of Batajnica where I began to attract some sporadic AAA fire again. The real attention magnet was still off to the northwest. The AAA fire in that direction was constant. Streams of silvery white fire from the smaller-caliber automatic weapons (possibly 23mm cannons) were swinging back and forth like the spray from a garden hose, each shell ending its flight in a spectacular shower of self-destruction as sparkles and strobe-light flashes went off like popcorn. The scarier stuff was a deep reddish color with a tinge of yellow. Each of these shells was obviously larger, and they were coming up in short bursts of four as if they were coming from heavy clip-fed cannon versus lighter belt-fed weapons. The red stuff was also being fired at greater angles and was reaching much higher altitudes, including above my own at that point. If the red was 57mm, which it seemed to be, then it easily had the range to dig into our planned working altitudes that night.

I had been watching the AAA off to the side of my flight path for a while. I was pitying the poor schmucks over in that zone, before realizing that my next programmed turn was taking me directly into the thick of it. As I approached my second target, a large gas sphere on the edge of the Novi Sad Oil Refinery, the AAA was everywhere.

Sometimes it came up in a random barrage, and then suddenly all of the individual streams would coalesce to form an inverted cone focused on one direction or altitude for a while before going back to sweeping the sky.

It was wild, and it was everywhere. There was no getting around it. My route home lay between the cannon rounds through the middle of that fire.

The target area had a thin solid shelf of clouds just to the east, and at first glance I thought that it might cheat me out of a hit. That certainly didn't stop the barrage fire from my left coming up through the clouds into my altitude though. More AAA on the right was illuminating the inside of the cloud shelf like lightning in a rapid-fire flickering way. It looked like something from a *Star Wars* movie and, beyond its obviously deadly intent, was stunningly beautiful in a surreal way.

I was really hitting my stride now. The adrenaline was pumping. The checklists were being run through as quickly as I could verbalize them. The bomb had been armed and checked several times and was ready to go. I was calling out a running dialogue of what I saw in every direction and even tossed in an update on my evasion plan—"If I'm hit now, I'll turn one hundred twenty degrees to the right for the nearest friendly border in Romania." With a few minutes to go, I noted that most (though not all) of the AAA was below my altitude.

Then suddenly the world was on fire. Dark red clusters of four were arcing around both sides and up past my jet. Little families of hellish golf balls were trying to kill me.

Surprisingly, for the first time on this mission, my mind flashed back to the delay I had on the ground. An entire panel had been dug out of the RAM coating on my belly then replaced and buttered over in about five minutes. If the edges hadn't seated properly, or if the butter hadn't cured enough before flight, I could be attracting more fire than usual because I wasn't so stealthy anymore. As quickly as I had that thought, I discarded it. Our Martians were too good. And I was here to inflict some damage anyway, not just hide.

The weather was still going to be a factor. I disabled the automatic function of the laser to fire it manually between gaps in the clouds. A minute out, my cursor was still pointed right on top of the cloud shelf. "Come on, don't do this to me."

Then the clouds began to break a little, and thirty-three seconds out, I got my first glimpse of the target area. I squeezed off a quick burst of laser energy through the gap to update the ranging. The target wasn't NCD, and there weren't any immediate residential areas either short or long of the target. I expanded the field of view from narrow to wide momentarily so that I could see beyond the target for any other clouds that might interfere. At the fourteen-second point I made the decision that I would drop.

And there they were—three clusters of three spheres each, huge round silver things. My aim point was the center sphere of the cluster on the far left. The clouds were wispy all the way, but I could still just barely make out the shape of the target. With the bomb in the air, I switched the laser back to the auto-fire mode. As the last few seconds ticked away, I noted how shiny the tanks appeared and wondered if my laser might be reflecting off the surface. No time to change plans, though. It was looking good, then with literally two seconds to go, one of the cloud wisps became momentarily opaque. At TTI-0 I saw the target again as the bomb detonated just in front of the three spheres.

"Aw, short. . . . Damn! . . . Close though."

The jet turned hard left as I looked out the window. Lots of red stuff, and tons of silver stuff, surged up in a vertical wave. It slowly fell behind me. All I needed now was to make a quick dash for the border, I thought.

Magic interrupted that thought.

"All stations, all stations, Firefly-six, Bat three two zero for three eight, Firefly-six, three two zero, three eight."

I immediately began to do the fix-to-fix calculations in my head.

"Let's see, from my position that's about seven degrees off my bearing from the bull's-eye . . . and my range is . . . so it's maybe five miles behind me." That range was *not* a good place to have an active SA-6.

An entirely different voice broke in on the radio. "All players, all players, Firefly-six at Bat three two zero, three eight." People were getting excited.

As I craned my neck around a bit further than it was designed to go, I picked up some large flashes at ground level behind me. A few moments later, the jet made a programmed left turn that allowed me a good view to rear for a few seconds.

"Oh Shit! Missile in the air, missile in the air!"

The sight that turn had afforded me was the reddish-orange fire trail of a missile slowly arcing up in my direction. It wasn't moving left or right through the canopy at all. Its line was directly toward me. I was the only one in the area, so it wasn't hard to figure out who they were shooting at. The throttles were already full up, so there wasn't anything to do—except to push harder on them anyway, of course. I caught myself gently touching the top of the ejection handle with my right hand to remind myself where it was if I were to be hit.

But evidently the missile had been fired from out of range. It peaked out at my altitude a little ways back before beginning to fall away as it ran out of energy.

"Okay, it's gone." Then a big sigh before the observation, "What a way to make a living," followed by a long, drawn-out laugh.

I never felt more alive.

The return was uneventful other than a few thunderstorms. Thunderstorms within five miles of the field? We wouldn't have dared fly anywhere near them a month before, but compared to the fire and steel being deliberately shot at us over Serbia, what were a few stray lightning bolts? During the approach my glide-slope indicator malfunctioned (maybe because of the storm), so I just sort of eyeballed the angle.

During my debrief with Intel, they did some triangulation magic with my tape and determined that the second bomb had fallen 44 meters short of the central sphere. Close enough that I had probably ruptured them all with the shockwave and fragmentation. I was given credit for all three.

There was a phrase that came out of Vietnam from the pilots who had been "downtown" in a big way. And after years of reading others' adventures, I was now entitled to say that I'd "been downtown and seen the elephant." Though I'd never understood the derivation of "seeing the elephant" (supposedly it dates back to the Civil War when a soldier was first shot at in combat), I was pretty sure that I was in the club.

Later on, I finally got a good clear BDA picture posted on the "wall of fame." It was of the Kragujevac headquarters building—cleanly missing its middle third.

CHAPTER 17

The Lone Ranger

If your attack plan is stupid, but it works, then it isn't stupid.

AFTER THAT MISSION, FOUR OF us drove down to Vicenza to check into the CAOC. G-Man and another were only along for a meeting and wouldn't be staying. Mace was there for the long haul. That night I got my handoff briefing from Fozzy. Even after my last experience down there, his obvious pleasure at being able to leave gave me pause. Mace was a nice guy, but looked like he'd be tough to work for—everything needed his personal stamp. He seemed to be enjoying the process though, so I thought we might get some good work done.

That first night I worked in the MAAP cell before setting out for the hotel in search of a little sleep. While I was gone, Mace had rearranged our schedules again. I now worked the day shift, and the only way to make the transition was to work from 20:00 that evening all the way to 16:00 the next afternoon—a 20-hour "day."

During the VTC we received guidance to start targeting TV stations, then the power grid—specifically in that order so that they'd know that the TV was gone before they lost their electricity. Silly, but at least now we had something new to shoot at. A few more bridges were added to the list also. It had only been a month, but this war just seemed to be dragging along. People were already discussing how this endeavor would be used as an example of how *not* to run an opening air-campaign.

One of the primary reasons the air force became an independent service back in 1947 was to get out from under the army's idea of air-campaigning and put a firewall between the services so that they couldn't interfere in arenas outside of their expertise. The Goldwater-Nichols reorganization act screwed that one up royally.

After the Gulf War everyone gushed over how great the reorganization had worked. The overlooked reality is that the Gulf War worked because the army CINC, General Norman Schwarzkopf, was astute enough to delegate his power over the air war to General Horner and keep his hands off. But this time, with no tanks or infantry to employ, General Clark preempted Admiral Ellis' and General Short's area of expertise, and played the role of airman— right down to the level of questioning photo interpretations and bomb placements (a sergeant's job). That was bad enough, but General Clark readily admitted that his position was primarily political, as the job of SACEUR was intended. Maybe all of this wasn't General Clark's fault, but he was actively interfering on the fly, so it was hard to see anyone else to blame.

General Clark, as a natural politician, was probably the right guy to help hold the coalition together, while being the wrong guy to be running the details of the air war. While it was certainly within his prerogative as SACEUR to do whatever he wanted, the NATO command structure is designed to keep headquarters staff out of operational minutia. NATO has separate JTF commanders within each region for a reason. By prewar policy, operational control of the air war within the overall southern region should have been delegated through Admiral Ellis to General Short.

Ten days to go. I was getting rundown already and had a cough, stuffed-up head, and a sore throat from some virus. The permanent party there called it the the CAOC crud, and it had been floating around for a couple of weeks by then. They'd all worked through it, now it was my turn. It was miserable!

After a fitful twelve hours of sleep, I still felt like crap but went in to work anyway. There weren't any replacement personnel, and I couldn't infect the group since they'd already had the crud. I'd transitioned to the day schedule, but the cough was really wearing me down.

At least the MAAP cell was running smoothly—even without any strategy or sound guidance. The God's-honest truth is that when people first arrived there someone had to pull them aside to say, "You aren't going to believe this but there isn't a plan—no, really!—we're making this up as we go." There still wasn't a JIPTL to work from. So, this was in essence an ad hoc exercise in gradualism and target practice—with people getting killed.

One of our current tactical problems was dropping one of the larger bridges near Belgrade. It was a classic over-engineered arched structure that just wouldn't fall down. It had been nicknamed the "Paul Doumer Bridge" after the one near Hanoi that had been the nemesis of so many fighter pilots during Vietnam. Our attacks were so predictable that media outlets in Belgrade had positioned video cameras pointed at the bridge, running twenty-four-hours a day, in the full knowledge that they would eventually capture some good footage.

* * *

Friday was reasonably quiet with a mere four changes to the 8th's plan called down from Aviano. The OG and 49th Wing Commander (visiting from Holloman) came down for a short while in the afternoon. Mace kept all the visitor and vehicle passes in his possession to "maintain control of the situation," but had fallen asleep after he took the passes back to the hotel. After a call from the front gate that the bosses were waiting to get in, I had to hustle out there to escort them. I brought General Lake onto the operations floor to meet General Short. Introductions weren't necessary, as General Lake had served as a squadron commander under General Short years before.

One of the ironies of the USAF command structure at that time was that wing commanders didn't actually command wings. They commanded bases. The OG, the operations group commander, accompanied and commanded the flying wing when it was deployed. As a consequence, wing commanders were only *occasionally*, after being granted specific permission, allowed to visit their wings in the field. And even then they were expressly forbidden from flying in combat. The only time a wing commander got to function in his titled roll was when the base he commanded was the one playing host to the deployed units, in this case General Leaf up at Aviano. With both of his combat squadrons deployed for action in Europe, General Lake's role, as Commander of the 49th Fighter Wing, was to run Holloman AFB in New Mexico. It was a short visit.

Haiji was coming down that day, so I'd reached the halfway mark. I'd also been able to watch some English-language news for the first time in a while. There was a lot of coverage of the NATO summit and the results of our most recent bombing—the TV station in downtown Belgrade being one of the more visible examples. The 9th got that one. I hadn't been involved, but was told about how hard it had been to plan the run-in angles for the attack. There were several other structures in the area that needed to be protected, and other than personnel actually in the building, there had remarkably been no other collateral damage.

There was roundabout talk in the CAOC concerning some new type of weapon being sent over from the States to be used against the electrical grid. Evidently the only way the United States got parts of the grid on the approved list at all was by promising to limit the damage to something that could be easily repaired after the war was over.

Of a more immediate concern was watching the unfolding drama of Task Force Hawk. This was the deployment of Apache helicopters to a bare base in Albania. The idea was to use these aircraft for interdiction missions—which they were not designed for. One of the army majors in the planning cell here was pretty much beside himself with frustration as he clued me in. Since this had by default become an air war only, and was being managed by an army commander, there was a lot of political pressure to get some army forces "in the game."

During the Gulf War this wasn't an issue, as the eventual use of tanks, artillery, and infantry were a certainty. But given the Clinton administration's reservations about this war (excuse me—these "strikes"), the official planning for the use of ground forces was verboten. So, if this was to be solely an air war, General Clark wanted to bring in army attack aircraft. That meant Apache helicopters.

The army itself was fighting General Clark tooth and nail to avoid this. His initial request for forty-eight helicopters, when it couldn't be shut off entirely, was pared down to twenty-four. But, in addition to those two dozen helicopters, the army bogged down the deployment by also sending multiple rocket launcher system (MLRS) platoons, dozens of Bradley armored vehicles and Abrams tanks, 155mm howitzer batteries, Stingers, and five thousand infantry troops to protect the whole endeavor. Those extra forces did nothing for the Apaches—other than to slow everything down.

Even with the use of over *five hundred* C-17 transport flights, the units involved looked as though they were being deployed via the proverbial slow boat to China. It was taking literally weeks for the task force to move a few hundred miles from Germany to Albania versus the approximately seventy-two hours it took air force, navy, and marine units to move half way around the world and be ready for action. In particular, the marines moved exactly twenty-four F/A-18 Hornets to a bare base in Hungary, set up shop from scratch, and were engaged in combat three days later. The cases weren't entirely similar, but it illustrates just how little the army believed in the endeavor. A brief teleconference exchange illustrated the differences in air versus army mentality.

After a marine F-18 squadron had shown up the day before, General Clark casually asked General Short how long it would be until they could fly, assuming it would be a couple of weeks. Short told him that the squadron would be ready that night and that they were already on the ATO. Clark questioned how could that be; didn't they need to do rehearsals, mock drills, or planning? Short simply said, "They are airmen, sir."

The base, adjacent to the airport at Tirana, Albania, was little more than a mud pit and essentially had to be built from scratch. Worst of all, the army people there at the CAOC were telling everyone who would listen that if the Apaches ever pushed the border, it would be a disaster.

The problem was that current helicopter doctrine and training assumed that the Apaches would fly in direct support of friendly ground units and that the enemy forces would be fixed in place by those engaging U.S. forces—none of which applied in Kosovo. There was a photocopy of a passage from an army field manual pinned up outside of the army's CAOC cell. The bright yellow highlighted lines read, "An AH-64 battalion never fights alone. . . . Attacks may be conducted out of physical contact with friendly forces, but only when synchronized with their scheme of maneuver." In other words, you only leave airspace near friendly forces when you know those forces will soon be overrunning the area where you are going.

The CAOC army planners were asking in a roundabout manner if the A-10s could act like spotters to find targets for the Apaches (normally army ground troops acted as spotters). The irony was that they were asking our guys to find targets for them, from above 15,000 feet of altitude, that the helicopters wouldn't be able to find from 100 feet. In any case, when an A-10 pilot does spot a target, which is what they were doing already, he rolls in immediately to kill it at 350 miles per hour with a Maverick missile and its 300-pound warhead. He's not going to wait around for an Apache to troll up at 90 miles per hour to shoot a Hellfire missile with its 20-pound warhead.

The threat to the Apache pilots was going to be severe. If our jets were taking hits above 15,000 feet of altitude while flying at multiple hundreds of knots, how beat up would the helicopters get while down at rock-throwing altitudes and automobile speeds? To top it all off, none of the deployed helicopter pilots were qualified to fly missions requiring night-vision goggles.

The army guys at the CAOC were predicting anywhere from five to fifteen shoot-downs per hundred sorties. That was orders of magnitude more than a USAF unit would consider acceptable even for planning purposes. And these wouldn't be the type of shoot-downs a jet pilot might encounter where he might parachute down into a relatively uninhabited area to be rescued (helicopter pilots don't wear parachutes anyway). An Apache crew was going to fall directly into the hands of the enemy unit that just shot them down. If the Apaches were flying according to their own doctrine, in support of ground troops, then U.S. forces would be nearby to assist, but that wasn't how they were being ordered to employ. In Kosovo we'd have to launch real ground incursions for any hope of a rescue.

None of this made any sense, and to be fair to the army planners there with me, they all knew this. Helicopters just weren't optimized for deep interdiction missions away from the front line of a battle. The Apache was an absolutely superb weapon for close air support and urban warfare, but it was being asked to be something it was not. And before anyone accuses me of USAF parochialism on this subject, everything I've just related came from the mouths of army planners at the CAOC.

We had a few relatively calm days. The squadrons were canceling for weather, or lesser reasons, on a regular basis, so a lot of the plan just got recycled. But because of the cancellations, the 49th's reputation as a go-getting unit had faded. I have to say that it was a little more the 8th's fault, though both squadrons shared the blame. An example was having one squadron turn back a target to the CAOC as "impossible" to hit with their resources, then having the other squadron pick it up just for something to do. After its initially fitful start, the 9th was a little easier to work with. Since they were late to the game, they'd been trying harder to get sorties over the border.

The target sets had shrunk to incredibly small proportions. We were beginning to talk again about sending a squadron back to Holloman to begin rotations. But sending back a squadron was purely a political versus a military call at that stage. Regardless of military necessity (or lack thereof), the image and "message" that would send weren't desirable. The problem at our level was that there just wasn't enough for us to do in this half-assed war. It had been structurally screwed up from Day 1, and there didn't seem to be an end in sight barring a ground war (forbidden by Clinton), an unfettered air war (unlikely with the current target approval process and General Clark in charge), or something forced upon the Serbs by the Russians (who remained their last allies).

Planning for a ground war had been progressing at least at the backroom level for a while by then. Of course, that would've also required the logistics of a substantial occupation afterward. The only real progress being indirectly made to that end was the site preparation being done down at TF Hawk, which could be used as a jumping off point—except that the terrain seemed to indicate jumping off from Macedonia. There weren't any real roads between Tirana and the Kosovo border, just a lot of mountains. The Macedonian border wasn't much better except that there were far fewer mountains.

The frustration directed at General Clark seemed near universal. The General saw the center of gravity as the fielded forces in Kosovo, while everyone else saw the decision makers, Milosevic and his cronies, as the targets that would end the war. Supposedly, General Short had threatened to resign in order to force the issue, but was talked out of it by his staff. But at the same time, no one believed that anyone in the Clinton administration (with the possible exception of Secretary Cohen) had the *stuff* to fire General Clark until it could be done quietly. I had no doubt that there might be other dynamics involved, and General Clark might not be responsible for *everything* wrong at the strategic level—but that was certainly the way it looked at the war-fighting level.

We were directed to fly the unmanned Predator drones at low altitudes over Kosovo in broad daylight. A drone in this situation had about the same chance of surviving as a Cessna, or maybe a little worse. General Short, in utter resignation, just turned to the Predator representative at that VTC to say, "We have our orders; send a few out to be shot down." (Eventually, thirty-two of these multimillion dollar drones from the various nations were lost.)

General Clark kept hammering away at the subject of finding "the staging areas," unwilling to consider that there really weren't any. Kosovo was still a part of Yugoslavia. The Serbs didn't have to invade, many of them lived there. And with no real ground threat to oppose them, there were no fixed defensive lines. Trucks, tanks, and other vehicles were dispersed seemingly at random. The extra forty thousand or so troops that were on the border just prior to the conflict had long since walked in and were now scattered throughout the villages. Any chance to hit them effectively while still on the border disappeared a few days before we began strikes.

Dispersed and hiding troops certainly weren't going to be dug out by aircraft (without laying waste to the countryside). That's what tanks and infantry were for, and we weren't allowed to use any. The way to get the Serbs out, barring a ground invasion, was to make it painful enough for Milosevic and his cronies up in Belgrade to call it quits—and none of the targets that would make that happen were in Kosovo, they were all up north.

Toward the end of the VTC you could see General Short just burning. When it was over and the cameras were turned off, he held everyone there for a moment to talk to us.

"Did you all see that? The divide-and-conquer tactics. Trying to play us off against each other. Promise me that if you ever get to a position of power that you won't do that. Don't ever try to pit your own people against each other like that." Then he stormed off.

The rest of us were all mostly just pissed off that we were hanging it out on a regular basis without being allowed to be effective. We could be achieving so much more with the assets we already had in theater. Life was comfortable back home so it was hard to get excited about a ground war in the Balkans. Well, if this dragged on into late summer that luxury would soon change. But so long as GI-stuffed body bags weren't being unloaded at Dover Air Force Base, no one cared.

One of the few amusing aspects of the campaign at that point was a plan to turn the B-52 into a food delivery platform. There were uncounted tens of thousands, or perhaps hundreds of thousands, of refugees scattered through the woods and hills ringing the southern borders of Kosovo. The natural choice of using C-130s to drop pallets of rations to them wouldn't work because of the threat from man-portable SAMs wielded by the Serbs, so some misguided planner had turned to the next best heavy hauler. Evidently, there already was such a thing as a "food-bomb." It consisted of hundreds of packets of concentrated and dehydrated food stuffed into CBU canisters. Each little packet was aerodynamically shaped so that it fluttered down without (hopefully) clobbering whoever might be beneath it.

Naturally, this had led to no end of jokes about what we had christened Operation Biscuit-Bomber. Our poor B-52 representative was huddled in a quiet corner trying to work out the math of how many sorties might be needed realistically to make any sort of humanitarian difference. He had to factor into account the effects of sortie rate, the number of food-bombs that could be loaded on a jet, the percentage of packets that would never be found, dispersal patterns, the adverse affect of training the locals to pick up strange-looking objects (there were lots of unexploded munitions out there), and the drop ballistics of a dehydrated packet of tuna-casserole tumbling along at 450 knots into the woods of the Macedonian border region.

The math wasn't adding up. There were just too many people out there and too few Buffs to make a difference. In terms of the numbers of people needing to be fed, this would be the equivalent of a small Berlin Airlift without the benefit of using airports and cargo aircraft. So, we got to make fun of the poor guy—all the while quietly thanking the gods we prayed to that we weren't him.

Our set of approved targets hadn't increased, so we were looking at about two or three days of good weather putting us out of worthwhile business again. General Clark had recently called for more aircraft in theater, while not having even a third of the targets required to justify the strike assets already there. In frustration that the initial few days of bombings didn't cause Milosevic to surrender, General Clark also ordered the creation of a list of five thousand potential targets to present to NATO for mass approval versus the paltry fifty-one or so that had been allowed us before the first strikes. It smelled a little of, while not panic, certainly not understanding the process. It took his staff in Brussels a while to convince him that in a country the size of Ohio, with an economy maybe the size of only one or two of Ohio's counties, five thousand legitimate targets just didn't exist.

So the new "holy grail" became a list of two thousand targets. The "T2K Plan"—I just loved that they nicknamed it after the Y2K hoax being used to pump up the tech-market bubble. In any case, there probably weren't two thousand targets out there either. And who really cared? We couldn't get even a fraction of the few hundred real targets already on prewar lists approved by Clinton, General Clark, and all of the veto-wielding nations anyway. God, this was frustrating.

Of more immediate concern to us was the perception that the stealth community was beginning to wear out its welcome among factions of the CAOC planners. The F-117 was just too much of an asset-hog. That was acceptable when we were cranking out two full goes each night with a single squadron. But now we had twice the aircraft, operating in two separate countries, and were only flying maybe two or three partial goes per week. The support assets we required per mission hadn't gone down at all, just the damage to the enemy that we were being allowed to inflict.

The 9th got in a few good hits though, including the Socialist Party headquarters. I knew that G-Man would be jealous. He'd been wanting that one himself for some time. The "Paul Doumer" bridge was also put into the water. It was done in by a B-2 dropping a cluster of eight JDAMs, of all things. Overkill to be sure, but we were finally done with the thing, and each end of what used to be a bridge was now officially a boat dock.

Thursday, April 29, began with the assessment from intel, passed on by Mace, that the Serbians were actively targeting pilots in the Aviano area to be kidnapped or killed—not an appealing development. To prove the point that their agents might already be active in the area, an unacknowledged collection asset reported intercepting Serbian messages describing our preparations and takeoffs in a very timely manner. We heard how many jets were airborne through this asset before our own units had reported in. No F-117s were involved though, so it was a quiet night for me.

One small semblance of sanity finally crept into our existence: We were officially notified that Operation Biscuit-Bomber had been shelved—at least for the time being. In addition, new, more spacious, accommodations for the MAAP cell (a very large metal shed) had been completed, and we used the downtime to move our furniture and equipment over. The permanent party guys there, anticipating a long summer, were funding the purchase of a gas-grill through a word-fine game. Each utterance of a curse or a "forbidden" word would result in a penalty. Even at just a quarter a shot, they raised over $200 in three days. We'd been swearing a lot evidently.

The dearth of approved targets had caused us to cut down to not even planning for more than one squadron per day over Serbia. Even then, most of the targets we were forwarding to the squadrons for planning purposes were only "proposed" versus "approved" in the hope some might actually be approved before launch—otherwise everyone would be sitting on their hands. In all likelihood, two-thirds of those attempts would never fly, and that was excluding weather cancellations. The squadrons were preparing to begin training sorties again just to keep up our proficiency and landing currency.

That night I worked the battle staff floor. The northern strike included the 8th. As usual I had my package of maps and timing cards in hand while hovering off to the side of General Short's station. It was a perfect position for someone fulfilling my function. It was far enough out of the traffic flow to be unobtrusive, but close enough to answer questions if required. As a strike was about to push a border, there were usually a few inquiries about the approximate routing of the strikers and what target set they were going after that night. Usually the boss didn't ask for anything specific. His concern was for the overall flow of the war—the big picture. We were responsible for the details.

Covering one entire wall was a series of electronic maps and displays showing the progress of that night's action. Dr. Stangelove's "Big Board" had nothing on this setup. When someone on the floor responsible for monitoring radar or SAM activity in Serbia would locate a threat system that had become active, they would call it out and shine a laser pointer to its location on the overall display. If it was relevant to my guys, the package materials I carried allowed me to provide accurate locations of where the F-117s were supposed to be at that moment. This information would be used to move HARM shooters and EA-6Bs around to better support the strike.

On this particular evening some of the support aircraft had ground aborted, leaving us short of the predetermined minimum deemed appropriate to prosecute the strike. The General huddled all of the unit representatives on the floor to see if the strike could be reasonably salvaged. The consensus was that it certainly could, but since this was a political war, and none of the targets that night were particularly important, why push it?

We used to say that all we needed was fuel and darkness, but after Vega-31 the old days of charging forward regardless of the support assets were long gone. So the boss decided to call off the northern strikes and concentrated his attention on those strikes originating from the west of Serbia and the more-or-less permanent presence over Kosovo Province in the south. Support aircraft in the north that could be of use elsewhere were shifted south to support the other efforts. Strikers that couldn't be retargeted in flight were ordered to abort their missions and return to base. The 8th aborted while still over Hungary and began returning to Aviano. Everyone seemed to have gotten the word in time.

As far as the CAOC was concerned, the F-117s were done for the night. My only remaining task was to monitor each of the F-117s as they unmasked once safely away from the border. This task was very much a "sidelines" function, and I was paid no attention. As each pilot extended his antennas and turned on his IFF, a "signature" track would appear on the overhead display. I quietly ticked off each jet as a new signature began making its way toward home. One signature was missing. Process of elimination quickly narrowed it down to one our guys who went by the call sign Earp. It wasn't terribly unusual for a signature to be missing. A pilot might be unable to extend his antennas or turn the IFF set back on. Or maybe he'd just missed a step in the checklist. Perhaps the IFF equipment had inadvertently dumped its codes while the jet had been stealthed up or had just broken. Stranger things could happen. In any case, the northern strike had been recalled, so what was there to worry about?

As the minutes ticked by, the rest of the package began breaking radio silence to check in with AWACS for flight monitoring on their way home. Still no Earp. Occasionally, the general would toss a questioning look at me. All I could do at that point was shrug. Because of the very nature of stealth, I never really *knew* where anyone was at any given moment before they unmasked. What I knew was where they were *supposed* to be—if they were on time and following the plan. And as far as the CAOC was concerned, the plan was for my guys to be headed home.

One thought kept nagging at me, but I was initially prone to dismiss it. As time passed, I couldn't avoid the possibility any longer. I approached the general's desk to inform him of Earp's planned target and TOT. His slow nod suggested that he had been thinking along the same lines. The information was passed to the person working BDA, to keep an eye on the area. Just in case.

Sure enough, at the appointed time, the intel guy called out, "XXX source reports large explosion at. . . ." In no time at all, Earp's route and timeline was laid out on the general's desk. A half dozen officers were huddled over these bits of paper as we envisioned his route out of the target area. Then right on time, an IFF signature appeared where it was supposed to along the Hungarian border. A few moments later Earp broke radio silence and broadcast the code word that announced a successful mission. Needless to say, that was the last track coming away from the north of Serbia that anyone on the floor had to monitor. As the boss was getting up to leave he was slyly grinning as he said to no one in particular, "I'd like to hear that story someday."

I liked Earp. He was a study in contrasts. He was an A-10 Gulf War veteran, medium height, stocky, with a marine flattop haircut and a cheesy little mustache. A devout Mormon, with two notable exceptions to the culture: He was fond of good cigars and single-handedly supported about 12 percent of the entire Brazilian coffee industry. He was equally capable of quietly preaching God's will and brotherhood toward man, then going out to fine-tune an M1 Garand rifle able to drive tacks at 200 yards. I believe that he and his wife had eight children at last count, and the only inconvenience evident to them was they were still just shy of being able to field their own softball team.

His job back at Holloman was that of standards & evaluations liaison officer (SELO). In the function of SELO, he was responsible for the record keeping of the squadron pilots' check ride paperwork, currencies, and flight qualifications. This was a job for a meticulous and precise personality whose attention to detail was innate. How he managed all of that was an absolute mystery to everyone who knew him, since he was a paperwork slob. The only time the surface of his desk ever became visible was when the pile became so deep that it could no longer support its own weight and a portion would avalanche off onto the floor. Yet he would also handwrite a letter with a style that bordered on calligraphy, then actually go to the effort of sealing the letter with a gob of red wax and a signet. So learning that Earp had been off on a slightly nonstandard adventure wasn't much of a surprise.

In general there are two sorts of recalls. The first consists of a direct order not to violate a border, to egress the area immediately if you have crossed that border, and absolutely not to employ weapons except in cases of self-defense. The "self-defense" clause doesn't really apply to the F-117, but you get the drift. This is the "stop the war" recall. The second type of recall is the sort that applied that night. In this case, a lack of supporting assets such as AWACS, fighter caps, HARM shooters, EA-6B jammers, or perhaps just bad weather that, in the judgment of the CAOC, precluded a full-up strike. The war was still on, but particular aspects of a strike, or even entire pushes, might be canceled.

On a strike mission the "black line" an F-117 flies is carefully planned to provide the safest routing possible—assuming that you are going all the way to the target. To get off the line at some intermediate point is a judgment call. The pilot has to ask himself if he is safer trying to make an immediate run for a convenient friendly border and, by straying off the line, possibly blunder over threats the EWOs had deliberately routed him away from in the first place.

There is also the issue of having to remain in stealth mode while accomplishing this dash. Since we can't communicate our intentions by radio without risking being detected by direction finding–equipped adversaries, it is usually more prudent to remain silent. What inevitably happens next is our sudden arrival and unmasking in the midst of the tankers, AWACS, EA-6Bs, and other high-value assets on the far side of the border—completely unannounced and unexpected. F-15C pilots have nightmares about this kind of stuff, and in the excitement and confusion of war, itchy trigger fingers happen!

To allow for all of these variables during this second type of recall (assuming that the pilot even heard it in the first place), our doctrine allowed us some leeway. The pilot could decide for himself which was the better option for that particular situation, to get off the safe track and make a beeline for a convenient border or press on. One last factor sometimes influenced these deliberations, but this one didn't fall under the headings of safety or coordination with the supporting assets. This one fell squarely in the "Fangs out, let's be sneaky and kill something" column.

In all likelihood, an enemy would never be completely blinded. While we strove to accomplish this effect in general, and dedicated a lot of effort to accomplishing this at least temporarily during specific parts of a mission, the big picture was usually still out there to be seen to some extent. So on this particular night, the enemy was probably watching the entire NATO coalition northern strike package visibly withdrawing and working to turn the thundering herd around. And all the while our little F-117 pilot, with larceny in his heart, had quietly been left behind.

In the F-117 community, we were very careful never to call any of the non-stealth players around us "aluminum chaff"—certainly not when they could hear us. But that was exactly how we used them on occasion. The defender in battle is always going to be desperate to engage the enemy before they can inflict damage on his territory, but he has to see them first. So, if a few tiny little enemy planes (tiny on a radar scope anyway) happen to be mixed in with an absolute hoard of easy-to-see enemy fighters, bombers, and tankers

. . . which planes will draw the most attention? It's a simple case of hiding a tree in the forest, and if we happened to be only a shadow of a shadow of a tree—well, so much the better.

So imagine a Serbian radar operator's mindset that night. The enemy hoard had surged toward his border, but had then turned around and was now leaving. The defender can't go to sleep just yet. There are still hundreds of the enemy right over there. Sure, they're going away now, but they could turn back, so he'll have to watch them. In any case, they are just all so easy to watch and account for now. Without the need for communications security, all the aircraft are jabbering away on their radios while forming up into wonderfully easy to track formations. Hundreds of them! Who could look away? Besides, no one would ever dream of using an entire air force as a diversion for just one plane. Would they?

Not deliberately, of course, but sometimes opportunities present themselves. By the time the cancellation had been broadcast, our man Earp had already pushed the border and, without a good line of retreat, had elected to stay on the black line. He continued on alone over a quiet countryside, found his target, and whacked it with a couple tons of high explosive. He was the hero of the hour to us grunts in the planning cell.

One of my pet projects during this time was working on a Radrel (radio-relay tower) attack. This huge thing was about the size and approximate shape of a three-legged Eiffel Tower. It was supposedly one of the primary radio and television transmission antennas in the country. It was also built like a brick. After our trouble dropping the Doumer Bridge and other towers, we invested some extra planning effort on this one. In addition to collapsing the whole structure if possible, we planned simultaneously to hit the top cab to take out the transmitters in case the tower didn't fall. There was also a large support building just off to one side we wanted to hit.

The plan was to put a four-ship over the target with minimal spacing while attacking from different directions. One aircraft would drop a pair of GBU-27s on the base of the leg closest to the building to dig in and break up the foundation. Another jet would drop a pair of GBU-10s on that same spot a few seconds later to shear off the leg. If that failed, we had two more jets with GBU-10s. One would aim for the top of the tower to destroy the electronics and antennas in the cab, and the last would follow to complete that job or hit the support building, depending on what remained intact. I was anxious to see how it all worked out.

The news on the diplomatic front seemed a little more encouraging. Russia was being actively courted to broker some sort of compromise that would get us out of this mess, but would the Serbian national character allow it? They'd just spent the better part of a decade engaging in a bloodletting that had reduced most of Bosnia and the jewel that once was Sarajevo to rubble. And for what?

A paper ran an article around that time on the subject of Serbian humor—that it was a cross between Monty Python–type nonsense and something much more caustic. The untranslatable "Inat," as it is called, is a blend of cutting wit, defiance, fatalism, spitefulness, and irrational stubbornness. It was the comedic equivalent of a Pyrrhic victory—the idea that it was more important for your enemy to lose than for you to win. One example of Inat is a common joke the Serbs told amongst themselves: that NATO should stop shooting expensive missiles, but instead drop one large bundle of money, as they'd kill each other off fighting for it. An even better example is embodied in the traditional Serbian folktale of Zoran and Branko. I've heard several variations but they all seem to go something like this:

Zoran and Branko were poor peasants who lived on adjoining farms. They had been neighbors since childhood. Then Zoran happened to find a cow wandering loose. With this windfall, he proceeded to make a modestly better life for himself and his family by selling the milk and calves it provided. Branko was green with envy over his friend's good fortune. Then one day, purely by happenstance, Branko saves the King's child from drowning. Overcome with gratitude, the King took favor upon Branko and promised a reward. The monarch offered him anything he wanted—castles, women, riches . . . all could be his for the asking—whatever would make Branko happiest and most content. Branko thought long and carefully about this singular chance of a lifetime before making his one request.

"Kill Zoran's cow."

CHAPTER 18

No Whining
Allowed

A crew chief's joke:
What's the difference between
a fighter pilot and a jet engine? At least the
engine will stop whining when
the plane shuts down.

ON FRIDAY, APRIL 30, I went back to Aviano—home, such as it was. In the morning I briefed E.T. as my replacement and caught a ride to Aviano. I called Bets as soon as I got back, then caught up on some emails.

In the squadron I went right to work lobbying for a sortie. After weeks of dealing with bored pilots demanding more flying time, both Mauler and Flounder had developed thick skins in their roles as schedulers. Their sense of humor had evidently taken a hard turn as they immediately pointed to a handmade sign taped up over their corner of the room:

NO WANKING
ALL VIOLATORS WILL BE FINED ONE SIX-PACK
    PER OCCURRENCE
NO EXCEPTIONS
NO APPEALS

There are a few universal truths instinctively known to everyone in uniform. Two of which are never piss off the cook and never piss off your scheduler. So I began diplomatically—with little success, as they'd heard it all before. Pleading that I'd paid my dues after two weeks down at the CAOC only got a snort in reply. Even after being gone, my sortie count was still about the same as everyone else's. I considered backing off for a moment, but just couldn't do it. After all, this war wouldn't last forever, and I could always get more beer.

I did retreat before working my way up to a full case, though, and still got my name on the board for a sortie in a couple of days time.

Our reputation at the CAOC had greatly improved after the work the 8th did the night before. The Radrel tower I'd worked on was dropped in a spectacular manner, and Mauler got it all on tape. In a classic case of overkill, Fozzy's very first set of bombs broke the leg off the tower, which then toppled directly onto the support building. The cab on top was toast of course, as was the building, so the extra bombs already on their way down were just chasing the wreckage and rubble of the collapsing structures.

During that one Munk had a bit of a scare. Evidently, several SAMs he took to be SA-3s were shot at him close enough to get his attention in a big way. He was white for hours afterward. In typical fighter pilot fashion, we supported and empathized with him by posting a picture of a surprised-looking albino monkey on the wall, the caption stating that this was a picture of Munk after landing.

The next day was a day off for the entire squadron, which was good, as I slept most of it away. That evening four of us walked to a little restaurant across the street for an absolutely excellent dinner. On the news front, it appeared that the three U.S. soldiers captured from the Macedonian border the month before would be released to Jesse Jackson. With a possible ground invasion still looming, it seemed odd that the Serbs were cutting loose three prisoners to a freelance politician. Perhaps they were trying to play some sort of race card for public opinion. If so, then they really didn't understand the dynamics of U.S. culture very well. How Jesse Jackson fit into this administration's foreign policy picture was a mystery. I couldn't imagine that Clinton sent him. Jackson certainly generated a lot of publicity out of it for himself, though. In any case, I'm sure the three soldiers involved didn't care why they were being released, so long as they got back.

On Monday, May 3, we went in very early and launched well before sunset. It threw our natural vampire rhythms off terribly—but the moonlight was just too bright later in the evening. The big story of course, was turning out the lights in Belgrade—at least temporarily.

Strike aircraft from an unacknowledged unit within the coalition used "soft-kill" cluster munitions, which had been loaded with hundreds of carbon fiber spools. These things deploy and reel out to cover electrical transformer yards with acres of spider-like conductive filaments. Everything gets shorted out, but without causing significant physical damage. Afterward, the area looks like it has been "silly-stringed" to death. As much as I disliked the whole soft-kill concept, the results looked great for a few hours. The report from Brent Sadler in Belgrade went something like this: "After the air-raid sirens sounded, and heavy AAA was seen, there were no reports of explosions but the lights all suddenly went out for as far as the eye could see."

The results were more symbolic than permanent. The electricity, at least in Belgrade, was back on by morning. The Serbs had to send out hundreds of workers with brooms and rakes to clear off enough stuff to get power back online, which they were able to accomplish after only a few hours of effort. While certainly an interesting effect, the results seemed to be more of a nuisance than substantive. I thought that we should follow up with hard kills on the transformer yards after that. We were going to have to get serious about this war eventually if we wanted it to end without sending in ground troops.

I listened to a speech by British Prime Minister Tony Blair. Aspiring to the role of Churchill, perhaps, he had been the one true political leader during all of this. Unlike Clinton, who gave a good speech on the first day then absolutely disappeared, Blair had been out front and forcefully making the case for war and acknowledging his role. If it went well in the long run, Clinton would probably get back out front to claim credit, but in the meantime, Tony Blair was the only politician involved that we respected.

More locally, an F-16 from the 555th, the famous "Triple Nickel" squadron, was shot down the other day. The CSAR guys pulled the pilot out, the squadron's commander, within two hours. Those rescue guys had been amazing.

That afternoon we drove in to work at 15:00 for the flight briefing and an OG update on what we could expect in the future. We were told to expect a dramatic slowdown in our operations—to be withheld most of the time and saved for "downtown" targets and "war-winning events." To the rank and file, that mostly just sounded like we'd talked ourselves out of the bulk of the war. Everyone was frustrated at being underutilized already. Now we were going to slow down even more?

I had a sortie that night, so I put my disappointment on hold for the moment. The target mix was the usual mishmash of random stuff with only two of us going against a single point. As the briefing continued, and the preparations progressed, call after call came in withholding different targets. The ever dwindling group of players was forced to keep looking over our shoulders for an intel troop to tap us and shake their head. Every time a phone rang, the room got quiet for a moment until the person answering it would wave us on.

By step time, there were only three of the original ten lines left. As we were being processed out at the desk, another target was pulled, and only Guz and I made it out the door. A grand total of two jets were going to fight the entire northern war that night. There were myriad tankers, AWACS, escorts, and the perpetual presence over Bosnia and Kosovo, of course, but we were the only strikers left in the top half of the theater.

Two jets also constituted the designated "package minimum" required to launch anything at all. If either of us had fallen out for maintenance, weather, or any other reason, the whole thing would have been canceled . . . no pressure.

Both of us were fragged against a large isolated complex just south of the Danube River near Novi Sad. The plan was for Guz to swing down the western border between Croatia and Serbia. He would then run in toward the target to hit it from the west. His arrival would be about ten minutes before mine so that there would be a quiet period after his attacks in order for any reactive AAA fire to fade away, hopefully lulling the defenders into thinking that it had been a single strike. That was the plan anyway. While all of that was going on, I would be hugging the Romanian border on the east side of the country before swinging westward to eventually come up on the target from the south.

I was flying tail number -833 while going by the not-so-imposing call sign of Hooter-43. As soon as the engines started, I was pleased with the jet. The IR display was exceptionally sharp, and the tracker had a good smooth action. As usual, I warmed up by using the tracker to trace the outlines of buildings and vehicles that were in front of my jet. Even though I was only being fragged against a single point, I was carrying two GBU-10s for a dual-door attack. Unlike our single-bomb load-outs earlier in the war, the slower pace of operations had made economizing on weapons unnecessary.

We pulled onto the runway together for the engine run-ups. After Guz released brakes, I gave him twenty seconds to let some of the wake turbulence from his jet subside before following. At 185 knots, I rotated the nose gear off the runway, and with only a partial load of fuel the jet lifted away right at 199 knots as the overrun fell behind me. The takeoff and departure went smoothly (it was still daylight), and we were all the way to the tanker tracks over Hungary before the orange of the sunset began to fade.

After taking our fuel, we split off to our separate holding tracks to run our checks and listen to the radio chatter. There was a lot of it, and it wasn't very professional. At times it sounded like some bored young lieutenant in an AWACS had lost his copy of the plan and was running a verbal inventory over the unsecure radio. As always, I tried to give a running commentary into the tape to help with the debriefing if anything significant were to occur.

"Tape on. It's time to push out of the track, and I haven't heard a recall. Looking out to the right, in the direction of bad-guy land, it's darker than normal. Most of the lights up north are off. I can just barely see the lights of what appears to be Belgrade to the south."

A call came over our frequency: "Aircraft, Slappy, zero four three, one two nine, say call sign."

I don't like that sort of call. The guy didn't identify himself as Magic, Iron, Hooter, Grip, or anyone else who had legitimate business talking on this frequency, and he was referencing a bull's-eye, Slappy, that wasn't in that night's plan.

Someone else came on line to transmit "Reference Bat," which was our actual bull's-eye. The first guy comes right back with "Bat, zero four six, five two." This clown was showing lousy discipline. With the calls that close together, if the Serbs had an inkling of where Slappy was that night, by a little triangulation they could also know where Bat was, and vice-versa.

The point wasn't anywhere near me, so it was none of my business, other than to be annoyed. When there was no answer, the call was repeated. Eventually there was a disgusted response of "Grip zero one" by the lead of an F-15C flight, no doubt accompanied by an unspoken cursing for having their position and identification broadcast to any listening enemy for no good reason.

Clown-boy chirped right back, "Copy, Grip zero one at . . ." just in case the Serbs hadn't heard him the first time.

In the meantime, I was focusing most of my attention on a series of isolated thunderstorms along the Romanian border. In the clear air, they looked spectacular with tall columns of sharply defined clouds intermittently pulsing with purple and pink light as lightning illuminated them internally.

I certainly had no intention of going through one. The question was how close I was willing to get before I left my planned routing to circumnavigate the things. The area below was still very dark after the most recent strikes on the transformer yards a few days earlier. It was also sparsely populated, so I decided I'd stray to the east a little if needed, but it never came up. A planned jink in my flight plan arced me around the worst storm as if it had been planned that way.

The last bits of the sunset were still fading on the western horizon. That could be a small factor in silhouetting my position. But from where I was the only ones who could take advantage of that angle would be in Romania, so no worries. The skies above were clear, and I saw what had to be a shooting star. It was well over Hungary, so it was in the wrong location to be a HARM or a SAM. Quasar and Magic conducted a series of casual talks over the frequency, but at least they were using call signs. The slowness of the night seemed to be altering the entire mood of the strike.

It was awfully dark down there. There were some lights on the horizon toward the Novi Sad and Belgrade areas, but they were very dim-looking—more so than would be accounted for by distance alone. The entire northern region of Vojvodina from the Hungarian border in for fifty to sixty miles was almost completely blacked out. There were only a few isolated points of light evident. I could clearly see the outline of the southern Hungarian border as defined by the Serbian blackness. There weren't any significant lights until you looked at least as far south as Novi Sad. Beyond that, the small towns were also dark. The medium-sized and bigger towns were lit but at a very much lower than normal level. It was as if the light switch for the north had been turned off entirely and the dimmer switch for the rest of the country had been set at 30 percent.

I diverted my attention back into the cockpit for a short while to analyze a warning light. My EDTS (electronic data transfer system) had failed, but since my mission had already been programmed into the computer before takeoff, I didn't really care. If my computers were to dump, I'd be unable to reload them, but the odds of needing to do that were slight since a bad computer rarely comes back online anyway.

Minutes dragged by as I listened to others making routine calls to each other. Clown-boy must have finished his bag of popcorn and become bored again. He returned to call out, "Aircraft, Bat, zero three five, four zero, watch border, watch border." Not only was he trying to tell another flight where they were, he was broadcasting an actual location in correlation with the bull's-eye. Maybe he was a Serb trying to goad us into betraying ourselves. In any case, no one answered.

I had a reminder to myself scribbled on the flight plan to activate the fire-suppression system on this leg. "Inert is on, lights are off, VNAV, Record on, TOT-mode engaged, speed, altitude, and timing look good." I was still fifteen minutes from the target.

Clown-boy interrupted the quiet several more times over the next few minutes without being answered. Finally a very distinct response, just oozing with sarcasm, slowly came back

"That . . . is . . . Grip . . . flight . . . and . . . we . . . know . . . where . . . we . . . are . . . THANK . . . YOU!"

So much for Clown-boy.

The radio chatter quieted down for a while. There was a small fire up in the direction of Sombor. There were also the perpetually burning fires around the Novi Sad petrol refinery, but otherwise it was just quiet. Just before Guz's TOT, Clown-boy came back for one last encore and broadcast in an excited voice: "Bogey [an unknown aircraft] at Bat, XXX, XXX,"—which was our target area. Clown-boy had just called out Guz's position as he was making his attack. To make matters even more tragic-comic, the guy seemed to catch himself for just a second before asking, "Hooter four two [Guz's call sign], say position." Now he had tied a call sign to the impending attack. We responded to none of this, of course.

I caught the flash of his bombs out of the corner of my eye, then the slow-motion wave of AAA fire rising vertically up out of the ground. Streams of silver 23mm, clusters of heavier dark red bursts, then strobe-like sparkles as the self-destruct timers began to detonate at their peak altitude. The AAA fire covered the entire area from Novi Sad down the river to as far away as Batajnica and Zemun. The wave had gone up into the sky, sustained itself for about three minutes, then slowly fallen back to earth. Guz had had his fun and was already on his way home.

The high angle that the AAA had been shot at, and the altitude it was reaching, was unsettling. They seemed to have bracketed our working altitude with unusual precision—maybe Clown-boy was working for them after all. A few minutes later, AAA from around Belgrade lit up the sky before fading away after a short while. The action also stirred up the support folks. Magic, Quasar, and others kept up a good chatter on the radio. As I got closer, I could see that there were now two separate areas of AAA fire around Novi Sad.

My route took me just north of Belgrade, and pretty much directly over Batajnica airfield. My first night's target was just to my left. I was tempted to swing the DLIR in that direction to take a look, but didn't want to risk disturbing the sensors until the mission was complete. As I rolled out onto my final attack heading, I could see Novi Sad through my sensors just across the river to my north. Just long and left of my target was a large bridge spanning the river. It wasn't an OAP and only caught my attention because a missing span had taken a huge chunk out of its profile. Less than a minute out, the radio got busier as an F-16CJ flight close to me, Iron, had caught the attention of a battery of SA-6s and were defending themselves. They sound stressed, but I only had time to concentrate on my own attack. I couldn't look out for any launches.

The target was huge, like a factory complex. My specific aim point was a spot on a roofline midway up the target near the eastern edge. There were multiple large dish antennas mounted along this roofline. A spot in the dead center of this antenna array was my DMPI.

The display was clear. It looked a little different than usual because I'd chosen to use the other polarity than I normally do. The display polarity a pilot chooses is purely at his whim. It isn't unusual for a guy to cycle back and forth between the two to see which gives a better picture that night. Normally, I preferred my display to be in "black hot" because at night it made the roads appear dark against the background, so the sensor display more closely resembled our black-and-white target photos. That particular night, I'd chosen "white hot" because I thought it might help cut through any extraneous heat created by Guz's attack ten minutes earlier. Now that I was actually there, I could see that it really didn't make any difference. The surface wind was from the east and blowing the fire and smoke from his attack away from my target.

As my jet approached the drop point, I felt the rumble of both bomb bay doors opening simultaneously, followed by two good thumps as the GBU-10s fell away. Fifteen seconds from impact, I mashed down on the tracking button to hold the laser cursor on the aim point. Eight seconds from impact, the automatic firing sequence engaged, and I had an indication of good laser-ranging. As the seconds ticked away, I saw two dots of light zip up the center of the display before the huge flash-flash of the twin detonations.

Baa . . . boom!

The jet immediately went into a hard programmed turn toward the west. The border wasn't far. Over my shoulder, I saw that I'd kicked the hornet's nest again as AAA came up to meet me. The character of this fire was different than usual. Instead of randomly trying to fill the sky with fire, it was concentrated in tight bands. This is called curtain fire and is designed to create dense walls that an attacker has to fly through. The 23mm didn't quite have the right angle to reach me, but the four-shot bursts of 57mm had me wired and were air-bursting all over the 20,000- to 25,000-foot block— which, coincidentally, happened to be where I was.

For a brief panic-stricken moment I noted a warning light in my cockpit telling me that the left bomb bay door was still open. If true, then I was no longer a "stealth" fighter, but an unarmed target with a radar signature approaching that of a B-52. Faster than my hand has ever moved before, I cycled the master arm switch a few times and the light extinguished. Without the adrenaline rush, I suspected that it was just a faulty pressure switch instead of an actual stuck door, but it certainly had my full attention at the moment. Back outside I saw the AAA falling away behind me, which was just fine.

I ran for the border and settled down for a satisfying cruise home, thus completing my seventh F-117 combat sortie. I absolutely had to conclude that sneaking around on a quiet night was definitely the way to employ this jet. No big excitement, just some lone snipers creeping into enemy territory to stalk their targets. No protracted fighting, or even a warning, just calm, and then *boom*! And as soon as the shot was taken, it was all over. This is what we were meant to do.

During debrief with intel the OG specifically asked me to make an estimate of the state of electricity evident over northern and central Serbia for the intel report. My report was "About 70 percent diminished. Most of the electricity still visible was in the Belgrade and Novi Sad areas. The rural areas were almost completely dark except for a few isolated points of light."

Afterward, there was a quorum in G-Man's room as usual, but we had to move on to Woody's room around 05:00 after a noise complaint. There was talk of the medal recommendations being written up and the philosophy behind them. An air medal for everyone who had successfully flown combat missions was pretty much a given. Distinguished Flying Crosses (DFCs) were being recommended for a few significant events, such as a couple of the first-night/first-wave attacks, especially heavy ground fire, and so on. It turned out that I had already been nominated for a DFC for the Kragujevac headquarters attack, mostly because of the red time and SA-6s shot at me. This was a little ironic, since I was much more excited on other missions that weren't being recognized. The very first DFC was awarded to Charles Lindbergh for his solo flight across the Atlantic in 1927—wonderful company, assuming that any of the awards were approved.

We also talked about the medal's relevance. When you read the descriptions of the various awards, pretty much everything we did qualified. In Vietnam, Silver Stars were awarded for targets we think nothing of, like destroying aircraft on the ground. But what we consider to be routine in the stealth world wasn't routine in the past, and what may have been routine in 1944, or 1968, seems extraordinary to us. The short answer is that the rules were written for a different stage of technology, and a different level of warfare, than what exists today.

Over the next couple of days, the weather was bad over Serbia, so no new targets were hit; mine and Guz's were still the most recent strikes. The news showed our target burning for days. The Serbian media had branded the guy who hit the TV station in downtown Belgrade a war criminal (anonymously, of course). The truth is that the target had been approved by the government of every single NATO nation within the coalition.

On Wednesday, May 5, I went in at 15:30 to brief a mission. We knew it wouldn't count for anything more than practice. The weather was dismal over the AOR, and we canceled early enough to eat dinner at the tents—which was just as well, since I thought all the targets were rather inconsequential anyway.

Afterward, we used the free time for a SEAD planning session with the 555th F-16 guys and a few navy EA-6B people. That turned out to be a valuable exchange of information. A fun part occurred when the navy briefer misspoke the acronym SEAD (pronounced "seed" in the air force) as "Sea-Ad."

"What's Sea-Ad?"

I wish I'd thought of it first, but a Viper guy chimed in with "Sea-Ad is SEAD when your plane flies off of a 'Bow-At' instead of a boat."

G-Man extended his standing bounty of a case of scotch to anyone in the coalition who could pop a specific radar that had been annoying us for the past two months. The Serbs had been shuffling around what we thought was a TPS-70 mobile radar. This thing was used for long-range detection and had been a factor in our plans from the beginning, more for our support assets than for us, of course. The Serbs only radiated for an hour at any one location before breaking it down to move to another site. G-Man was after this thing in particular mostly because it had made so many close escapes. The HARM guys in the audience were in. They had been after the thing for a while anyway, but were more than willing to take G-Man's scotch if the opportunity presented itself.

The highlight of the evening was getting Hammer-34, the commander of the 555th, Fingers, to describe his adventures of getting shot down and then rescued a couple of nights earlier. He told the story well.

He and his wingman had been in the south playing cat-and-mouse with the SAMs down there when they strayed over an active site. The SAM (probably an SA-3) came up from directly below and took out his engine turning the jet into, in his words, "a very expensive glider." Then the AAA began to zero in on his stricken jet as he tried to make it to the border. In addition to trying to get closer to the border before jumping, he wanted to minimize his time hanging in the chute highlighted by the full moon, so he stretched it as far as he could before ejecting.

After coming down in a plowed field, he scooped up the parachute and the rest of his gear to make a run toward a ravine he had spotted on the way down. He must have gotten tripped up by the parachute lines or something, because he then took a header and belly-flopped on top of the stuff as he slid all the way to the bottom of the ravine. From there he collected himself enough to ditch his unwanted gear and to make radio contact with his wingman circling above.

He heard dogs in the area, so decided to leave that hole-up site and travel away from the sound of the barking. A couple of miles away, he found a more remote clearing with tall grass and brush to hunker down in. By now his adrenaline was at maximum, and every sense was supremely acute. As he slowly belly-crawled toward the center of the clearing, he froze at the sound of a rustling ahead. By moonlight he dimly saw the outline of some nocturnal hunter quietly creeping toward him.

He fumbled for his pistol, but it had been lost in the ejection. He knew it wasn't a dog—it would have barked or charged—this thing was stealthy. As he tried to draw the survival knife from his vest, the creature reared up on its hind legs above him, beady eyes glinting in the dark. (Kosovo doesn't have any wild tigers does it?) Then the *whop-whop* sound of the approaching rescue helicopter broke the stalemate and the field rat scampered off.

Later on they counted five bullet holes in the helicopter. Other than several unmanned drones, that was the second jet we'd lost in combat, though the Serbs had claimed something on the order of seventy-five aircraft so far.

My earlier guess of a 70 percent reduction in electricity across Serbia must have been on the mark, as I later read exactly that number in several different reports. I wondered if that was just a coincidence, or if I had been the original source of the estimate.

I caught a ride back to billeting with the OG and heard his take on the war, which matched everyone else's. It was now openly admitted that we hadn't started this one properly. We'd escalated so gradually that the enemy was allowed to disperse, adapt, and entrench before any real pressure could take effect. Now we'd have to open up the target set drastically to achieve any results.

If a political solution couldn't be agreed upon, this might take a while militarily. The Gulf War, at forty-three days of hostilities from start to finish, including the ground war, was over at this point, making this the longest sustained U.S. combat since Vietnam, and we only now seemed to be getting started. The good news from the CAOC was that at least we finally had a real (though still target-deficient) JIPTL to work from. So now we could *begin*.

* * *

On Friday, May 7, I actually got a long and satisfying sleep. It had taken a while to get there, but I guess I was on my long-term war footing. We'd all settled in. While the guys had accepted the idea of a long haul, there was also a feeling in the air that a political decision might soon wind this up.

The Russians had agreed with the other G8 nations on terms for a ceasefire. A compromise could be in the offing now that the Serbs couldn't count on a Russian bailout, which is what many of us thought they were holding out for all along. Milosevic hadn't agreed to anything yet, of course, and as an indicted war criminal, he really had no incentive to. In the meantime, the bombings continued.

The level of frustration back in Brussels and Washington must have been rising, since the quality of the target set being released was beginning to improve. My next target, weather permitting, was in the center of downtown Belgrade. These were places that we should have hit during the first few days of strikes, but had been off limits. On Friday night, we briefed a good set of targets—a *worthy* set. It seemed that our leaders were finally getting serious and were going to treat this like an actual war. Intel briefed another set of carbon filament ("silly-string") attacks on the transformer yards. There wasn't a guy there who wouldn't have rather just put a few tons of Tritonal into the power plants, or at least the transformer yards, and be done with it, but the politicians weren't quite there yet. Fortunately, my sub-group was carrying good old-fashioned bombs of the high-explosive variety to go downtown.

The three of us with downtown targets had planned a simultaneous attack, but I ended up adding a fifteen-second Rolex to my TOT. With another strike right across the street, the flash from whoever's bomb detonated first might blind the other. The third guy was aiming a couple of blocks away and wouldn't be a factor. We figured that fifteen seconds should be enough to allow the initial blast to subside enough to make my target more easily visible, without allowing smoke to accumulate too much. It made more sense for me to be the one to delay, since my target was upwind of the other. It might also set me up for any reactive fire, but I guess we were getting a little blasé about that.

We had another afternoon launch with a sunset refueling over the Adriatic. I pushed over the border just as it got dark. The weather over land was never predicted to be very good, but we still pressed on. Sure enough, there was a solid, though thin, undercast the entire way. The three of us headed for Belgrade had been told we'd be about ten minutes behind the strikes on the electrical yards.

My call sign was Edge-43, and I was carrying a single GBU-10. Since the target was in the city, just a single bomb was being employed to help minimize any collateral damage. Visibility above the clouds was superb, and I could see the AAA ahead of me for many miles off in the distance. I could also see a solid cloud deck stretching for many miles. That didn't look good.

Once committed to the line, I knew that I was going to fly over Belgrade regardless of the weather, but I equally knew that I wasn't going to drop once I got there. In the distance I watched a HARM shot arc down from the stratosphere into the cloud deck. The radio continuously announced AAA up where I could see red-orange and silver-white shells rising up out of the clouds. The aircraft hitting the transformer yards had woken up the bad guys (they were allowed to drop without seeing their targets), and each "impact" caused the clouds to pulse with flashes of man-made lightning.

The last few minutes prior to my IP were quiet at least. An occasional peek at the ground through small openings in the deck gave a tiny glimmer of false hope that I might be able to drop. But I knew I'd need a huge opening in the clouds in order to satisfy NCD criteria. As I futilely cast my cursors from OAP to OAP looking for a glimpse through the weather, Magic began announcing SAM activity directly ahead. The Serbs were trying comm-jamming again, and the noise initially sounded like occasional metallic blips. As the city came closer, the blips became louder and more rapid. By the time I was on my target run it was like a loud, tinny drum roll. In the background, more and more excited transmissions were being made as friendly aircraft tried to shout their way through the noise. Most calls that were understood referenced Mud-6 (indications of an SA-6's radar) at various locations all around us.

The last few seconds of my target run were frustrating as tiny little breaks in the clouds revealed buildings. But I never saw either of my OAPs or the actual target. After calling "No drop" into my tape, I turned down the cockpit lighting and saw AAA beginning to come up all around us (the other two guys on the simultaneous drop were out there somewhere, unseen, within a mile or so of me). The comm-jamming was getting uncomfortably loud.

Just then the most excited radio call of the war—that I heard, anyway—broke over the frequency. It wasn't one of our guys, so it had to come from one of the supporting F-16CJ guys. "Missile in the air! Missile in the air!" The glow had already caught my eye just off to the right. "Oh, shit!" I whispered to myself. There it was—a brilliant white-flamed rocket zorching straight up out of the clouds at my two o'clock position. The jamming noise was now painfully loud and coming out as a continuous ragged, tinny buzz. Several voices simultaneously tried to shout through the noise, but it was all just gibberish. The thing was close, and it was moving fast—really fast. I was easily within its range if it was coming for me. Just seconds away! For a few fractions of a second I waited to see in which direction it would arc. Then my jet snapped into a preprogrammed hard diving turn to the left and I lost sight of the missile. Damn! The turn wouldn't be enough to save me, and now I couldn't even see it coming. I mentally noted the distance between my right hand and the ejection handle as

I tensed up waiting for the impact. An eternity later (probably a few seconds), I realized that I'd have been hit by then if I'd been its target.

Betty, the jet's female automated warning voice, was insistently calling "Airspeed, airspeed, airspeed, . . ." The odd thought that popped into my mind was that she sounded much too calm for the situation right then. I realized that my left hand had been instinctively trying to push the throttles through the instrument panel as we dove, and the mach meter was telling me that the jet was going a touch faster than the book says is possible. I backed off the throttles a fraction, and Betty became more sociable. Within thirty seconds the comm-jamming became more sporadic, then faded away, and the only problem I had left was just some standard old AAA fire all around. We were on easy street now. There were still SAM calls, but since they weren't visibly in my face, they didn't seem very significant.

Curiously, I heard a call for an aircraft being ordered to "Exit Serbia—CAOC directs." Just that one aircraft. Not the rest of us. I'd never heard that before. Back home the three of us who had been on the attempted simultaneous drop all recounted virtually identical impressions, curses, and thoughts of impending doom at the first sight of that SAM. There is an old saying that "you had to be there to understand." Well, we all were!

Later on, when I learned that someone in our strike package (later found out to be a B-2) had accidentally bombed the Chinese Embassy, I remembered the mysterious call for that one aircraft. It was a bad situation; only hitting the Russian Embassy could have been worse. China had been adamantly opposed to this war from the beginning, not because they cared much for the Serbs (and nothing at all about the Kosovars) but as part of their long-standing objection to any power interfering with the internal events of another country (if that were to become commonplace, the light might very quickly be shined upon them).

What made the screw-up even worse was that it occurred just as it appeared there might be some progress on an agreement. Any mistake on our part encouraged Milosevic to dig in a little longer. Although perhaps we were just deluding ourselves about the possibility of an agreement happening in the first place. The old-timers from Vietnam talked about a lot of false-start peace initiatives. Oh well—our role remained to soldier on.

The guys got in some good work the next day. They dropped eight for ten, though not on especially significant targets. The GBU-27s into buildings gave the best visual results. Their delayed-action fuses were definitely the way to go. The other two guys lost bombs on NCD targets. One was just a simple no-guide. The other one probably shouldn't have been released, but it's easy to second-guess people after the fact.

The fallout from the Embassy bombing was getting ugly. Evidently we'd deliberately targeted the location thinking that it was something else. The structure that housed the Chinese Embassy had once been a logistical center within the Serbian Arms Procurement and Supply Directorate. The Embassy had moved to that address two years earlier. Though the map used to locate the intended target had been updated in 1997, most of the CIA's experienced analysts pursuing this arcane specialty had been shuffled out to pasture in 1996 when their Agency Center had been eliminated as part of a Clinton budget-cutting measure. The intended target was still actually on that same street, but a block away. Even so, the normal scrutiny that any target would have received was lacking, as it had been a "late-add" piled on in the attempt to pad out General Clark's "T2K" list, according to our intel officer. In any case, the diplomatic repercussions would be significant, and we were directed by the White House not to hit anything in Belgrade until further notice.

Sunday was a slow day. The highlight was a barbeque out on the lawn (and in the sun) down by G-Man's. Everyone brought some steaks to grill, and we had a great afternoon. I took a few pictures, and we talked about recent developments. Everyone looked tired— maybe because of our frustrations over how the war was being managed, or perhaps for the simple fact that "afternoon" was still pretty early in the day for a vampire.

Whatever anticipation existed for a quick peace, brought on by the Russians leaning toward our side of the argument, had melted away after that B-2 popped the Chinese Embassy. The fact that the strike also destroyed an illegal listening post within the embassy, and that the workers killed were all actually intelligence agents, was all pretty much irrelevant (though not without some justice).

Monday, May 10, I went in thinking that I was a spare, but was quickly moved up to a flying slot. Unfortunately, because we were so deficient in targets, this was only a training sortie. It was rather pathetic to think that the pace of this war was so very slow that we had to fly training sorties between combat missions just to maintain our landing currency and exercise the jets. It turned out to be a 2.5-hour loop over Sarajevo and Mostar doing camera attacks. We didn't even have weapons loaded. In contrast to my own expectations, my pacing and habit patterns were pretty sharp. Evidently the relatively little flying (by sortie count) we'd been doing was compensated for by its quality and intensity.

We were told again that we were being withheld for "war- winning" targets in Belgrade and Novi Sad—which meant that when it was for real we'd be in the thick of it, but doing very little else in the meantime. The toughest part for us may have been fighting the complacency of these training missions. It was easy to relax too much. I did take advantage of the opportunity to film a full instru- ment approach in order to upgrade my weather category rating. Afterward, we went to the recreation hard tents for a few beers and to watch a compilation of a "greatest hits" video: sanitized snippets from all of our successful attacks set to music.

The following night's mission went off as planned. I was on hand as a designated spare again, but none of the primary pilots fell out so I didn't get to fly. G-Man popped a bridge in order to sever a bundle of fiber-optic cables underneath. It was an NCD target that I might not have dropped on, but he'd been at this business a long time, and it worked out fine. But we were beginning to consider that perhaps we were all starting to hang it out too far in that regard.

There was a quorum afterward where we traded more stories. The latest rumor through the OG was that now, instead of getting rotated out, we'd stay for a full "remote" tour credit. A remote ranges from 181 days to a year. That would mean another three to nine months over there. Spending them all on that base might not be assured. Ramp space was becoming a premium, so there was a possibility of consolidating operations with the 9th up in Germany.

After that we had a couple more slow days. On Wednesday afternoon I went in to work on the plan for the following day. The whole pace of life was just so lazy that it was hard to reconcile that we were still at war. I wasn't scheduled to fly a primary line, but had a chance as a designated spare. It was looking like Sunday might be our last real combat for a while. After that, there were finally, and literally, no targets left. Our planning folders were empty.

Rumors involving more details of a consolidation of the squadrons in Germany and a personnel rotation began to circulate. We'd floated that idea before, but it had been shot down at the higher levels. Just getting up to Germany would be an interesting change though. I had the feeling that I might have flown my last combat sortie. If that was the case, then it was time to head home. I found myself spending more time making plans for my return than I did thinking about the mission—what sort of vacation we would have when the family got back together. That was a dangerous mindset—I needed to keep my head in the game.

By the following week it was official: we were told that we would only fly training sorties until further notice. About the only interesting bit of news was to hear that two of our O-5s might be swapping patches to the 9th to help balance out the rank distribution a little. Because I had been barely out of training before the deployment, and never got a permanent position within the squadron other than the training shop, I was near the top of the list to move. I told G-Man that I didn't have any specific objections to moving, since (without saying it out loud) I thought it would be easier to work with Mace and Haiji in the 9th than the new boss projected to take over the 8th.

After sending the guys out to fly training sorties in the rain, we gathered out on the lawn to celebrate Draft's first combat birth. His wife had just had a baby girl back home. They hadn't named her yet, which led, of course, to all sorts of helpful suggestions from the crowd: Paveway, Bang-Bang, Nobella Anvilina, and, my favorite, Aviana, were just a few of the suggestions. Draft didn't appear to be impressed.

In addition to Draft, both Tot and Reverend from the 9th had new babies waiting for them in New Mexico when we got back. Reverend's daughter would also be a dual-citizen, as he was our resident exchange officer from the Royal Air Force

Three months deployed. During the first few years in Vietnam, squadron deployments were ninety-day TDYs—so we'd be going home now. On Monday and Tuesday I flew more training routes. On Tuesday's solo flight I only saw the "ground" over what looked like an oil rig in the Adriatic. The rest of Bosnia was covered in cloud.

Later on I called back to Alamogordo to talk a while. Other than the usual stuff about things in the house that needed fixing when I returned, and the kids getting out of school soon, nothing was new. I received a small package in the mail from Bets that contained a 9th squadron T-shirt (already assuming that I'd transfer) and a few dozen pictures. The pictures were far and away the best part. The kids seemed to be growing in leaps and bounds. I missed them.

We got word that Woody had been picked up on the Hawk Board. Since the results were out and I hadn't been notified, it looked like I had at least another year at Holloman coming. After the training flight, I had a few beers with Pete and some of the others from the planning cell. Then we went to the marine bar to watch some serious gambling over a game of "4-5-6" until the sun came up. Staying awake past sunrise was never a good idea for us vampires. It throws off the clock badly. We scurried back to billeting for a day's sleep.

Thursday was yet another squadron down day—a "no-shave day" in the recent parlance. We went in earlier than normal for a commander's call in the base theater where the first of this operation's medals were awarded. The NATO medal, with a Yugoslavia bar, was awarded by G-Man to the five youngest enlisted troops in the squadron. The presentation may have been a bit premature since nothing had been officially approved yet, but it was a sure enough thing in order to justify taking care of the young troops. In the evening several of us went to a local restaurant. It appeared to be an old family estate, serving an excellent vegetable lasagna and chicken cordon bleu, all washed down with a very rich Merlot—war is hell.

Afterward, we talked about our possible consolidation at Spangdahlem and, more pointedly, about the need for a few of us to stay there with the 9th for an indeterminate period. In my automatic fighter pilot response mode, I volunteered, mostly because the war wasn't done yet. Then I spent the rest of the evening feeling guilty about what that decision would do to Bets and the kids. As it turned out, only four of us volunteered.

Friday night, Day 59 of the war, was perhaps the least satisfying one of all for me. We finally had a few combat lines, and I was up to fly a double GBU-27 attack. The target was sweet, a command bunker buried under a presidential villa just west of Belgrade. I was supposed to dig out the entrance to the bunker hidden deep beneath a smaller structure in the compound. No one made any pretense of thinking that Milosevic was actually in there, but you never knew.

I was Club-12 flying formation on Guz's wing through all sorts of nasty weather along the way, just hanging on for dear life with my eyes padlocked on a few bits of white light fading in and out of the mist. The airspace was crowded, and the tanker tracks were floating around in search of clear patches of sky. At one point the AWACS controlling us ran No. 3 and No. 4 directly on top of us at the same altitude (and in the weather), then rather nervously for a Brit, I thought, asked, "You do see them on radar, don't you?" Guz's response that we weren't equipped with radar got us a resigned reply: "Well, best get on the radio and sort it out yourselves then."

Getting killed like that seemed far more likely than getting shot down. It made for a few tense moments as lights suddenly appeared, and flashed by, before disappearing into the black just as quickly as they had appeared.

We finally got our fuel and pressed on. With all of the extra maneuvering, I was running well below my planned fuel but continued on the run. I skirted some thunderstorms along the Romanian border and thought I was going to be weathered out over my target though most of the country was only 50 percent covered.

With less than three minutes to go, I rolled out on my attack run. The cursors darted back and forth showing only bright clouds. Resignedly I taped, "Damn, damn, damn. So close too. Anyway, level attack, record, narrow, cued, MPT, master arm is on already."

I ran the sensor gain down to get a more distinct view of the cloud bank blocking my way. It appeared that it might end soon enough to allow me a view over the top in a minute or so. If I could just get past this one last bank, I might be able to get some work done.

Beyond that large bank were some low thin wisps. Just over a minute out, I got a fleeting glimpse of OAP-2—a road intersection—then it was gone. AWACS came up with "All players, possible stranger, Bull's-eye, one one zero, six zero. Possible Bogey." That was about twenty miles from where I was, so I could afford to ignore it, for a short while anyway. Forty-five seconds out, I caught a quick glimpse of OAP-1, a bend in a small river, before it quickly disappeared. With the cursors pointed toward the target, I knew that I was in roughly the right area by the road patterns. But both OAPs were gone now, and I still hadn't seen the target directly.

A wisp moved aside for a moment and there it was. This wasn't an NCD target and I thought I was close enough to risk it. A quick slew of the cursors to the left, and I mashed down on the release button to feel the two bombs fall away. Then the target was gone again.

"Come on, come on, come on." The frustration was palpable. Like a bowler trying to talk his ball toward the pins with body English, I was trying to urge the clouds out of the way. My laser was in manual mode the entire time. I should've already been on the trigger, but the target wasn't there. Then it reappeared at TTI-3. Way too late, but the bombs were already on their way, so I had to try. I manually fired the laser. The cursor wasn't steady. This was partly my fault and partly because the laser was trying to range in on the top of the cloud wisps. As it finally worked out, I could only give the bombs a few seconds of laser guidance (instead of the sixteen seconds the computer had recommended), and they never had a chance. I was too disappointed to even swear.

I had no idea where the bombs landed. In theory, a no-spot may go as far as 1.5 to 2.5 miles either long or short of the intended target. The variables depend on the release altitude and whether or not the guidance fins tucked in search of the laser spot. I was way out in the countryside, so I wasn't too worried about hurting anyone. Most guys had had several failures like this. A few guys never hit anything at all—one poor soul up at Spangdahlem was shooting zero for five. I had been luckier than most, and these were my first released bombs not to hit their target. I had a long and depressing ride back. I also desperately needed fuel, and my post-strike tanker wasn't on station yet. Ruble-91 was handy, so I bootlegged enough fuel for the flight home. I ended up logging 3.5-hours with nothing to show for it except the experience and the thought that two large, circular, and very expensive duck ponds somewhere in Serbia now owed their existence to me.

Over the next couple of days, there were no combat sorties, or even any target sets to plan toward. The only flight we got airborne was a single 0.4-hour flight for a quick maintenance check/fini-flight by Speedy. At least the Serbs were reporting that a presidential retreat was attacked, so my bombs must have fallen somewhere in the ballpark.

Tensions with China were still pretty high—both from the Embassy bombing incident, and reports that a scientist within our nuclear weapons program had been arrested for spying on China's behalf.

On Wednesday night we took over the 510th bar for a naming ceremony. The party went way too long. Before things really got going, I learned two significant bits of news. The first was that the consolidation of the squadrons had been approved and would probably occur within the next few days. Right then the plan was to send all twelve jets up to Germany to get bedded down. We weren't scheduled to fly combat sorties anyway. The question of what to do with the extra people hadn't been decided yet. In any case, I was already a volunteer to go. The next bit of news was that I was being permanently transferred to the 9th to become one of three new ADOs along with Flash and Reverend. For the naming itself, we had six people to deal with but only finished three before knocking it off.

By Friday morning, the packing had begun. It didn't take long. I did what was required for my training documents and binders, then left to pack out my room. I planned to convert my Lira back to dollars the following morning. I was on the list to fly one of the F-117s up to Germany, versus having to follow in a C-17. How long we'd have to stay there was entirely unknown at that point.

CHAPTER 19

Germany and Home

If it ever occurred to you to wonder who the world's greatest fighter pilot is, then it isn't you!

SATURDAY MORNING, MAY 29, I finished packing, settled my bills, and exchanged the last of my Lira. At the squadron we did a short briefing and checked the weather. The squadron spaces that we had been living out of for the last few months had been gutted and looked even more forlorn than when we'd first arrived back in February.

By early afternoon we had stepped, done a thorough pre-flight, and gotten the jets cranked up and ready to go. The fleet had taxied and was ready to launch when we began hearing hints over the radio that our flight plan clearance to Germany was beginning to fall apart. As we sat there, burning fuel and wasting time, a thunderstorm rolled in from over the mountains. The clearance problems were sorted out just as the weather hit.

We continued to sit there, with engines running, as the rain pounded us for a full two hours. For the first time in my career I was going to have to shut down and cancel a mission for lack of fuel before I'd even taken off. Okay, change of plans.

We taxied back to the ramp to refuel, refiled the flight plan, and headed off to grab some quick chow (we had planned to have dinner in Germany). By sunset the weather had cleared, and we launched off toward the west to enjoy a gorgeous view of the snow-covered Alps illuminated by the full moon.

The flight plan, as most in Europe seem to be, was overly complicated, and there were a few more hiccups along the way. I was on Woody's wing as No. 2 in the gaggle. A few wrong turns were made and No. 3 and No. 4 got squirted out to the front of the train. But overall it was a simple trip. No tankers were required, no AWACS did any controlling, no one was shooting at us, and nothing got blown up.

I had never been to Spangdahlem before, so, after clearing the runway, I requested taxi instructions to our assigned parking spots. Requesting "progressive taxi" turned out to be a good move on my part. Aside from it being dark, the maze of taxiways, ramps, shelters, revetments, and blind turns would otherwise have gotten me completely lost. Later on I learned that a few of the guys up there had screwed up already while taxiing. One guy had made that mistake on his first night of combat and been caught nose-in on a blind taxiway with no room to turn around, requiring the assistance of a tug.

Several of the guys from the 9th turned out to greet us as we disembarked. I quickly decided that I was going to like it here with my new squadron, other than having to start over with new procedures and (worst of all) having to "buy my name" yet again. That evening a good-sized group was sitting around Buck's room (Buck the insignificant) drinking *real* Bitburger Pils—one of the many advantages to being stationed in Germany. I got to hear some of the local frustrations. Most were centered on a particular individual within their leadership. So my volunteering to swap squadrons at the same time he was moving over to the 8th seemed like a great trade in their eyes. Even as a complete unknown, I was at least one up on the other guy simply because I wasn't him. The fact that I had volunteered to cross over, was ready to fit into their group, and showed up wearing the 9th-squadron T-shirt that Bets had mailed me didn't hurt at all.

The physical setup was outstanding. The 9th had taken over a complete squadron facility from a recently deactivated F-15 unit. The squadron building was hardened, furnished, wired, and ready to move into before they had arrived. All that was required was to turn on the lights. Billeting was a mere hundred yards or so up the hill, so they never had the transportation and vehicle issues that we had to deal with in Italy. I made a comment that this would be an outstanding time and place to install an F-117 unit in Europe permanently. My idea wasn't original in the least. Everyone nodded, as they'd been talking about that for months. I would've been among the first to volunteer.

The next morning a dozen of us rounded up some vans and made a road trip to Luxembourg. This was the Eiffel region of Germany where much of World War II's Battle of the Bulge had been fought. Bastogne was only thirty to forty miles west of the base. Traveling country to country here was like driving state to state in New England. And in a mere forty-five minutes or so we were in Luxembourg City.

We had lunch at an outdoor café on the same plaza where Patton had returned the newly liberated country to its citizens a half century previously. We ate a little and drank a lot. Fighter pilots tend to drink a lot by American standards. The 9th drank a lot by fighter pilot standards.

We toured the local English and Irish pubs. In the beginning we'd stay at a place just long enough to finish one large brew before wandering off to the next place. We only ordered multiple drinks at a single location after we'd tired of walking, sometime long after dark. That last place was many centuries old and overlooked a canal at the base of the city's citadel. Our bartender was an ex-pat Brit who had married a local girl and then settled down to make his life. He spent many hours telling stories of the local history and the small adventures his in-laws had experienced during the Nazi occupation.

Memorial Day—the peace talks were continuing without sign of any real progress, but we weren't being tasked for missions either. Milosevic had been formally indicted for war crimes by a tribunal in The Hague. Tactically, that didn't help our situation at all. While under indictment, there wasn't anything for him to gain by being cooperative. All he could do was fight it out and hope that we'd leave him in place afterward (assuming that there hadn't already been some quiet offer to do just that). The one reasonable argument for the indictment I heard at the time was that it might help sway any lingering Russian support.

All I could think was that this war would have gone so much more smoothly from the beginning if we had fought it as an actual war instead of as a political inducement. Every significant target hit up to that point could have been taken out in the first two weeks if we had been given free rein, and we would have been to that point months ago. If delivered all at once, the shock to Milosevic and his cronies would have been awe inspiring. But unfortunately, that wasn't to be.

I received my first email since the move. Bets informed me that Bob, a friend of ours from our first assignment up in Rome, New York, had died of a possible brain aneurysm at a family reunion. Bob and I had been lieutenants a million years ago while flying T-33s out of Griffiss AFB. He was my age, with a wife and two kids. I survived a dozen combat sorties over here, and with no apparent warning he collapsed while eating at a picnic—so much for rhyme or reason. He had been a passionate sailor and talked constantly about the huge boat he'd buy someday.

The next day I flew my first local sortie. It was purely for currency. We hadn't been assigned a combat line in quite a while. The toughest part of the brief was getting a handle on the convoluted ground procedures there. I had cranked up my jet and was just ready to taxi when a hydraulic line somewhere in the nose gear compartment ruptured, spraying bright red fluid everywhere. The stuff is very slippery and moderately flammable. One of the problems with a hydraulic leak is that because the system operates at 3,000 psi, when a line blows, the fluid goes everywhere. Everything gets coated so thoroughly with the stuff that it's hard to tell where the leak originated.

I only lost a little time as I hopped over to the spare aircraft and started her up. As a front line base for World War III, the shelters were randomly scattered about and the taxiways deliberately convoluted and redundant, all designed to make it harder for a Soviet strike to damage or block more than one aircraft caught on the ground at a time. The taxi plan through the shelters didn't turn out to be too bad though, as long as I carefully followed my map. This was my first day sortie since leaving New Mexico, and I had a great time touring the countryside and dealing with the professional German airspace controllers.

I wasn't on the schedule to fly the following afternoon, so a few of us stopped by the club for dinner. Back at work, I sat through a few meetings, did some studying in the vault (that never seemed to end), and introduced myself to a few more people.

Every squadron has its own personality and collection of characters. Tuna is one example. He was an A-10 pilot by training but had crossed to the F-117 several years ago. He had also done an exchange with the navy as an F-18 instructor on the east coast. It didn't take long for the subject of carrier landings to come up, to which his immediate response was that he had "*well* over one hundred"—101 to be precise.

More interesting to me was his involvement with civilian flying. He had restored Stearmans and several other small planes and at that time owned a J-3 Cub, two Beech-18s (one flyable, one in pieces), and the Lockheed Neptune I'd seen out at the Alamogordo airport. The Neptune had previously belonged to a museum in Florida and came equipped with everything needed to chase 1950s-era Russian submarines around the Atlantic. He had already stripped out several thousands of pounds of electronic gear while trying to build and install a slurry tank. He planned to get a contract with the Forest Service once he had finished converting the Neptune into a fire-bomber.

Tuna paid for these things by buying basket cases to restore and trading up at opportune times. I hadn't figured out how to swing it yet, but it made me start thinking about owning an antique plane again. It was all very impractical, but not all of us fly solely because it makes sense. For too many people being a pilot is just a job, but many of us still do it for the love of flying.

Years ago, I had visited a friend, Torch, himself an avid civilian flyer, who had been flying A-10s out of England AFB in Louisiana. He had told a story about a crazy guy down the street who was rebuilding a Stearman biplane in his driveway on base. Evidently that had been Tuna. The housing authority had tried to stop him but couldn't get any traction because they had neglected, understandably enough, to include aircraft restoration or manufacturing as a prohibited activity in their residential area, so Tuna's project got grandfathered. As soon as he was done, the housing people rewrote the regulation to specifically preclude aircraft hulks in driveways (the "Tuna Clause").

Torch's advice on buying planes had always been this: "Just do it. Life is too short not to cash out on occasion for nothing more than fun." Of course, he was single when he said that. But on the other hand, you had to wonder what Bob had been waiting for—that big boat, and any other dreams he may have had, had been put off for too long.

On Friday, pretty much everyone was at the club. It was wild, and on Saturday morning many a poor pilot was paying the price of too many collisions around the Crud table. Crud is to billiards what rugby is to lawn bowling. It is a glorious fast-paced fighter pilot game with a long and rich tradition. Legend has it that the game was first invented by the Royal Canadian Air Force in the 1950s before being imported into the U.S. Air Force by interceptor pilots from Air Defense Command. It is now a staple on every base.

Crud is played on a snooker table when available, or an ordinary pool table with the side pockets blocked by rolls of toilet paper (don't ask). There are only two balls. The cue ball is the "shooter" and is only launched by hand. The 8 ball is the "object" and may never be touched by hand. The objective is to fire the shooter to sink the object ball—thus taking a "life" from one of your opponents. If the shot misses, the next person in turn from the opposing side must run around to snatch up the shooter, position himself off one end of the table, and shoot the object ball before it stops rolling from the previous shot. If he misses or allows the object ball to stop rolling, he will have lost a life.

Two equal teams, each member possessing three "lives," compete until all members of the opposing team have lost all of their lives. Then the losing team buys everyone on the winning team a beer. There are lots of arcane rules, such as being prohibited from using proper names (call signs are fine), pointing at a person with your finger (you can only point with an elbow), and never, ever, ever, bumping into the referee or disturbing his drink. Any violation, and the offending individual will be assessed a life by the referee. Then, just to rub salt in the wound, the first person "killed off" by the ref immediately has to run off to buy that same ref another beer. At the Crud table, the referee is God—there is no appeal.

Some of the other rules that will cost a life are touching the object ball, shooting out of order, bouncing the shooter off the table, shooting from the side of the table, and pretty much whatever else the referee thinks up along the way. The game is nonstop and chaotic while still having some structure, occasionally violent (elbows are up, and no one is *ever* looking where they're running), and does in as many people for rules violations as legitimate kills. Ironically, it is good practice for fighting a war with silly ROE.

The navy has made a few half-hearted attempts to pick up the game over the years (during my time at Meridian, I always had to be the referee—mostly to explain the rules). Unfortunately, pool tables and ships don't get along well, and the game never really caught on.

Most rules are designed to minimize injuries to the lumps-and-bruises level until a certain threshold of consumption has been passed when the game may progress (or regress, depending on your point of view) to a separate set of "combat rules." Normally a defender may only block an opposing player from getting at the shooter ball, or positioning himself at an end of the table, with whatever motion he can make while both feet are planted on the floor and both hands are grounded to the table. All else is fair game. Once combat rules have been invoked, events become more kinetic. At this point the game more closely resembles hockey, without the sticks and with less regard for doing things that might actually affect which side is going to win the contest.

Crud is a great game for blowing off steam, building controlled aggression, and celebrating individual action, but I'll never understand how we get away with playing it without hurting more people each year. So, that afternoon everyone gathered their bruised bodies and heavy heads for the drive to a small village on the Mosel River for a "wine probe."

We met in the back hall of an ancient winery owned by a German friend of Stamp. Ernie was a real character and had a story for each vintage of the dozen or so different varieties of bottled white wines we tasted, then more stories about the underground cellars we visited to sample three different varieties still fermenting in their casks. Ernie told about having slept in the wine vaults as a child during World War II air raids, then more stories and samplings back upstairs for some other bottled stuff he'd forgotten before. We were going downhill fast.

The winery was a family-run business that had been in existence along the river for centuries. One of the more notable, fun, and potentially disastrous, events of the afternoon was when Ernie unexpectedly brought out the family goblet. This thing was a huge funnel-shaped crystal with a long thick stem on a golden base. There were large bubbles embedded in the crystal. Each bubble symbolized something and had a small story associated with it (though I don't remember any of them).

The goblet was etched with the family name, the crest of St. Peter, and the date it had been presented by the Austro-Hungarian Kaiser to its original owner—13 June 1728. We were all immensely honored that Ernie had brought out this irreplaceable family heirloom to show us and a bit shocked when he began to fill it with a special wine to be passed around.

When the Berlin wall had come down, Ernie had called his pilot friends at Spangdahlem to celebrate but they had been deployed on an exercise. So he called all of their wives and kids instead to come out to harvest grapes before the day was over. From those grapes, he had bottled his special "Reunification Vintage." There wasn't too much of it left, so he only opened a bottle occasionally. Ernie was now pouring his special wine into this irreplaceable antique and passing it around to thirty-three drunken strangers for a swallow. There were helping hands hovering under each pass ready to attempt a catch. Mace worried us the most.

Mace was our new squadron commander after having taken over the 9th shortly after combat operations had ended. He was a good guy, but liked to talk and was more than a little in the bag by then, as were we all. He took his turn as an occasion to lean up against a stone wall and give a long, vigorous, impromptu, and heavily slurred speech about absolutely nothing. Mace also tended to swing his arms around a lot while talking.

It was horribly fascinating to watch. Arms were gesturing about, great splashes of wine were sloshing horizontally through the air, and sparkles of light danced off the crystal in the afternoon sun as Stamp and Slammer scuttled around Mace's feet frantically swinging back and forth with cupped hands under the goblet.

So how many drunken hands *does* a treasured heavy, wet, slippery, goblet have to pass through before inevitably being dropped to shatter across an ancient stone floor? Thank God we didn't find out that day.

Meanwhile, the Kosovo peace talks seemed to have stalled again. We thought perhaps we'd be back in business soon. These cycling moods weren't good for us. False hope has no value. We needed to be either fighting or leaving. This back-and-forth stuff just didn't work.

Monday evening I flew an hour-long local training sortie. It was half during daylight and half at night. It was good practice I suppose, but we would rather have been doing something more substantial. Since the talks were progressing poorly, the initial optimism that this might be ending was fading somewhat, and we'd begun planning a combat sortie for that upcoming Wednesday. The target set wasn't anything special, more punitive and symbolic than substantial—just something designed to nudge the Serbs along in the peace talks I suppose. But at least we'd be back in the game, and my name was on the list to fly—by mistake.

Sorties were being rationed there in much the same way they were at Aviano. Evidently the 9th believed that I hadn't flown over the border recently, and the date they were using as my last combat sortie on the priority list was off by a couple of weeks. At first I wasn't inclined to disabuse them of their mistake. I really wanted to fly another sortie, especially if it might be the last of the war. But eventually the guilt about being greedy for one more finally got to me. There were people there who'd arrived late and hadn't gotten even a single mission over the border. As soon as I provided the correct date of my last mission, my name fell twenty spots on the list.

As it turned out, it didn't matter anyway. The Russians had pretty much abandoned the Serbian cause, and the talks had taken a turn for the better. A phone call from Vicenza that afternoon removed our mission from the ATO. The bombs were defused, and we used planes that hadn't been armed to fly another local training mission instead.

On Friday, June 11, 1999, the war was over. Seventy-eight days, and no U.S. infantry units had set foot on enemy soil. It was the first U.S. conflict fought entirely from the air. Though obviously not anywhere near as intense, this had also been the longest sustained U.S. military action since we left Vietnam in 1975. Thursday, June 10, was the last day of combat, as Javier Solana at NATO headquarters officially called for an end to the airstrikes. The Serbs, agreeing to even less than they could have had at the Rambouillet talks back in March, signed the surrender agreement and promptly declared victory.

Russian occupation troops (preinformed evidently) were already rolling down through Serbia from the north to a hero's welcome.

Another contingent of two hundred Russians had left their UN posts in Bosnia and were making a dash toward the Pristina airport. NATO troops would begin entering Kosovo from the south in a few days.

The Russians were being treated by the Serbs as saviors as they passed through the length of the country. They also seemed to be in an inordinate hurry to get down to Kosovo in force before we did, which caused a little concern among some of our leaders— General Clark in particular. No one outside of the White House or State Department was pretending that we'd bought ourselves anything more than another decade-long occupation. After Bosnia had burned itself out, Clinton had committed U.S. troops to that particular occupation. "One year only. Sink or swim! The deadline for troops coming home is June 1998." But, since no troops had come home in body bags, nobody had noticed that they never came home at all. Kosovo probably wouldn't be any different. But at least the bombings had stopped.

There wasn't much excitement about the war ending. I suppose we just saw it coming for too long, and while the threat was certainly real, the actual sacrifices turned out to be minimal, on our side anyway. In the meantime training continued. I got a flight and then got tagged with the job of writing medal recommendations for several people. Amongst other projects, the squadron was trying to figure out what to do for a going-away party in honor of one of their outgoing members, whom they all seemed to hate.

Later that evening, there was a gathering at Mace's room for a few loud hours. The big story of the night was Slammer's adventure at the Irish pub. They had been drinking afterburners.

Afterburners are another claimed fighter pilot tradition, but there has probably been something similar out there for centuries. The proper poison is cognac, but any flammable liquor will do. The idea is to fill a shot glass, then, in the presumably dark bar, light it with a match. (The blue flames look very impressive to the onlookers who have been sucked in.) Then you calmly contemplate the flames for a few moments before slowly lifting the drink to your lips to swallow it down in one smooth motion. Properly executed, the drink will be gone and the fire will still be burning the residual drops as you slowly lower the glass to the bar. A perfect execution will have the last flame puff out just as the glass touches the bar.

To be performed gracefully, this stunt takes some practice. Like any other activity, the more you practice the better you get, and like any other endeavor requiring alcohol, the more you imbibe the more inebriated you get. So, somewhere in the process, the line of increasing speed and competence is going to cross the line of decreasing motor skills and judgment. If you rush the job, splashes of flaming liquid are headed toward your face. If you go too slowly, the glass becomes too hot and may be dropped (bar owners generally disapprove of Molotov Cocktails in their establishments). If you inhale during the process, you'll burn your lips. Exhaling slowly is one of the tricks, but if you exhale too much, the flame will go out prematurely and require a do-over.

Slammer was good at this, but like most of us, he could get cocky when lit (so to speak) and was a little complacent. A bit of a slosh set his still-smiling face on fire momentarily. Reverend stepped up as the hero of the moment to put Slammer out with a few well-aimed slaps across the face with a wet bar rag. Even with his parts of his face a little more pink than they ought to be Slammer was still oblivious. He kept grinning and running around the room recreating the scene for us by waving his hands over his head and shouting, "I'm on fire, I'm on fire," while laughing his ass off.

Each of us has *been there, done that, got the T-shirt* to some degree or another, but the story wasn't quite over yet. As they were being ejected from the bar, some of the guys decided to kidnap an enormous ceramic duck from the lawn as a souvenir. Unfortunately, it wouldn't fit into the car, and they accidentally knocked off its head while trying to wrestle it through the door. What was left of the duck was ceremoniously propped up in the commander's room on top of the TV, proving once again that duct tape can (sort of) fix anything.

The following night, the news on TV showed the first Russian contingents from Bosnia rolling into Pristina. NATO was trying to figure out whether this was the act of an overeager commander or if the Russians were trying to steal a march on the occupation plan. We were told that General Clark was furious and had tried to order the Brits to parachute troops in to occupy the airfield first. They'd refused. Then he asked for helicopters and tanks to block the runways in order to prevent any Russian transports from landing. The British General who would command the occupation, Sir Michael Jackson (really), became a quiet hero by simply refusing to do so. Reportedly, his reply to General Clark was, "No, I'm not going to start the third world war for you." The shared occupation seemed to be progressing smoothly.

In the afternoon, the squadron held a farewell dinner at the Greek restaurant, Santorini's, for a guy departing the 9th to go over to the Sheep. The guys did an admirable job of being polite to this guy who, not understanding his audience at all, decided to forgo making the customary short speech of thanks and goodbye, and instead decided to entertain his captive audience with an extended poetry recitation.

On Monday, June 14, I flew a 1.5-hour sortie around the patch in the afternoon before finishing the bulk of five different medal recommendations for some people in the 8th. I'd been trying to shift my sleep schedule around to a little earlier but had failed miserably. The next day was much the same. I flew a 1.1-hour local sortie then went back to work in an attempt to get more writing done on the medal recommendations. The good news was that I still had until the following Wednesday to get out the rough drafts (thirteen in total, plus citations). We had a three-day weekend coming up and a few guys were going to drive to Normandy. I would've loved to have gone, but decided to hang back to get the writing done.

The following Sunday we received tasking orders for another combat mission. No one knew where that came from since nothing new was going on according to intel. A lot of atrocities were coming to light, especially in the western part of Kosovo, but the occupation troops were fully in place, so this thing was truly over. NATO had called off the war almost two weeks prior. It was widely assumed that this was saber rattling on General Clark's part. Maybe now they could fire him without it looking too bad politically.

I was walking in to work when I heard that the combat sortie had already been canceled, so I got to read up on some local standards and then briefed Nordo for an upgrade flight. I had finally gotten myself scheduled for a two-ship flight lead upgrade. It was important to get that done since back home "monsoon season" had already begun, so this might be our last chance to get night tankers until October.

Even though the best jets had been in reserve for the combat sortie, my flight went smoothly. We had a nice "pinkie" sunset, and the local German controllers did a superb job of vectoring us around some weather to rejoin on the tanker. It was short and easy, and it was probably my last landing in Germany.

A couple of days later we went in to work early for a redeployment briefing only to learn that our flight home had been canceled when it was discovered that AOS forgot to file airspace across the Atlantic for us. AOS (the organization responsible for moving aircraft around the world) didn't seem to have the sharpest people working for them right then.

Two days later we finally received the redeployment briefing, collected our flight plans and charts, then broke up for individual flight briefs. A dozen jets were to be launched in two waves the following day. I was No. 2 in the second wave of six, on Flash's wing. Each wave of six was to be allocated a string of eight KC-135 tankers—an impressive armada. The plan was for us to launch a half hour after the first wave, then join on the stacked-trail formation of tankers over England before continuing across the Atlantic. Initially we would station two F-117s on each of the last three tankers in the string. As we sucked them dry, they would peel off to return to their bases in England, or Iceland later on in the flight, and we would shuffle forward in the string to the next tanker in line.

After a rather sleepless night (I still hadn't made the shift from vampire-mode to normal hours), we had a short top-off brief—mostly just to pass on a weather update. Our baggage had already been strapped to narrow pallets called sleds, which were in turn mounted on the very same bomb racks that had until recently been carrying ordnance. Because of the expected seawater temperatures toward the Canadian coast, we were required to wear our anti-exposure suits, or "poopie-suits," under all of our normal gear. These heavy-duty all-rubber suits come in one piece and are tightly sealed at the wrists and neck. They even have rubber booties glued on at the ankles. They are heavy, stiff, and uncomfortable, chaff in all sorts of unpleasant ways, and are designed not to let moisture enter, or consequently escape, at all.

The techniques required for relieving oneself through strategically misplaced and misaligned zippers when sealed into one of these contraptions, with a survival vest over that, and a parachute harness over that, and strapped into an ejection seat, while by the way still trying to fly a jet in a formation on the wing of a KC-135 tanker over the north Atlantic, are fraught with the potential for personally embarrassing peril—or so I've heard. In any case, after twelve to fourteen hours sealed inside of one of these things, it will have earned its nickname—but, they are also absolutely essential for cold-water survival, so the griping when we have to wear them is only perfunctory.

My jet for the return flight was -803, which I'd flown on my second combat mission during that ineffective attempt to attack the MiG-21 squadron at Batajnica. She had a total of twenty-nine combat sorties to her credit. My call sign was Zesty-22, and everything went smoothly as we launched to fly over Germany and the Netherlands toward the coast. From over the Zuiderzee, that massive dike-controlled inlet to Holland, we could see the fabled 350-foot-tall chalk face of the White Cliffs of Dover in the distance as we left continental Europe behind. It was a beautiful day as we headed toward the rendezvous point over Coltishall, England, the last active Battle of Britain field.

The eight KC-135 tankers were right on time for the rejoin as we settled into our assigned places within the formation. The mass of aircraft continued on across Great Britain as our resident exchange pilot, Reverend, gave a running travelogue commentary over a secure channel of the radio.

Our flight plan included eight scheduled refueling legs across the Atlantic. AOS procedures try to ensure that at any given point over the ocean a jet always has enough fuel to divert to dry land. Otherwise, we could probably have made it with only three or four top-offs. Two of the tankers in our cell exhausted the last of the fuel they had to pass and left us for Reykjavik, Iceland.

About two-thirds of the way across, Flash's jet, having received only field repairs in Germany after being damaged previously, began venting fuel from the left wing. To comply with the divert constraints, he needed quite a few more plugs than normal and was cycling on and off the boom regularly until reaching the Canadian coast. There were a few hours where we had to tighten up on the wing as we passed through some weather. Hanging on the wing, in the clouds for hours on end, can be extremely tiring, but we were lucky and the clouds weren't too thick.

Our first indication that we were nearing the "new world" was the sight of some stray icebergs east of Newfoundland. There was also a lot of pack ice still floating off the coast of the Maritimes. The idea of a swim certainly wasn't inviting. Had any of us been forced to bail out, the only thing that was going to keep us alive for more than a few minutes was our poopie-suits.

Our flight path continued over the length of Nova Scotia to Yarmouth, near where my grandparents came from, down the coast of Maine and across Cape Cod. As I looked down at the familiar landmarks and beaches, I wondered how many of my relatives were down there at that very moment. By New York, the airspace was getting busy, so we took the last of our fuel and cut loose the remaining tankers to continue on their own way. The weather was getting pretty thick and the airspace through the Boston–New York–Washington corridor was crowded.

We had to be at our sharpest just as we were at our most tired. Breaking up for individual instrument approaches probably would have been the prudent thing to do, but one of those age-old points of pride for a fighter pilot is to look good while flying down initial. Flash did a great job herding us through the weather, complying with the rapid-fire vectors we were being given, and dealing with the fact that two of our guys had gotten lost off frequency and were just hanging on to the formation visually.

We reformed into a four-ship echelon, closely followed by a two-ship, to fly down initial at Langley AFB, home of Air Combat Command, looking absolutely great. A few of the first six jets, which had gotten a half-hour head start on us, were still beating up the pattern trying to accomplish individual instrument approaches. Unlike the first group that was still gaggling around, we taxied in as a tight line of six, paused for just a moment, then on signal simultaneously raised all six canopies and shut down our engines. We were sharp! Thus ended another 9.1 hours of flight time and eight AARs for the logbook.

I slowly unfolded my body out of its sitting position to climb down the ladder carefully on numb legs. As soon as my boots touched ground, I was greeted by the new ACC Commander, General Eberhart. He presented each of us with one of his coins (command coins have been around for years to be awarded as keepsakes in recognition for some significant act or ceremonial occasion). The 94th—World War I fighter ace Eddie Rickenbacker's old "Hat in the Ring" squadron—hosted us and provided some locker space to store our stuff after we had peeled ourselves out of our gear.

After an overnight hotel stay (and a great all-you-can-eat seafood buffet), we were prepared to leave the following morning. But by brief time it had become obvious that Flash's jet wouldn't be ready. It was continuing to leak fuel, and the specialists needed to fix it were still en route from Holloman. Since his kids were waiting for him on the ramp in New Mexico and mine were in New England at the moment, I volunteered to hang back and gave him my jet. They launched without any other problems. I called Bets later on to talk a while. She had almost flown down to Holloman to greet me off the plane as a surprise. Our reunion would have to wait a bit longer.

A couple of days later, we greeted the second group of F-117s in from Germany. There were only ten jets left. Two of the twelve had had to abort back to Spangdahlem with fuel problems. General Eberhart was out there again, and we got to talk a little about some of the lessons learned from the war. Our perspectives were pretty far apart though. I saw the problems with strategic control of the war as a flaw in the Goldwater-Nichols reorganization, since it allowed an army general to preempt a process outside of his expertise. He saw it as an opportunity to make an air force general the next SACEUR.

One area where we could agree was that the F-117 community should get some serious money for weapons upgrades in the near future, the enhanced GBU-27 in the short term and perhaps the JDAM later on to address our weather limitations.

The next morning, Tuesday, June 29, we went over the plans for our arrival show at Holloman, then packed the jets before starting. I was flying aircraft -818 on Buck's wing as No. 11 at the end of the train. The jet's fuel leak had been patched up enough for the trip home where it awaited a complete refitting. Six jets had launched initially. Our remaining five followed after a half hour. We only had to refuel twice along the way, and after a few hours we rendezvoused with the first six jets. They had been circling over the mountains in the Beaks airspace east of Alamogordo.

We gathered into a formation consisting of a trail of three three-ships in V-formation followed by our two-ship. Each three-ship was stacked exactly 0.2 miles behind the previous flight. We used the air-to-air function of the TACAN to get the spacing right. Each flight then stacked 100 feet higher than the one they were following in order to avoid the jet wash. From my vantage point as tail end Charlie, it looked wild. I wished that I'd had a camera and a free hand to take a picture.

After landing, the first guys paused along the taxiways to let everyone else get on the ground so that we could all enter the canyon at once. Our eleven jets formed a single line down the center of the canyon, then cocked off 45 degrees to the left before simultaneously shutting down. There was a tremendous crowd of people there to greet us. That was nice, since there wouldn't be any parades for us like there were for the Gulf War veterans.

As the engines wound down and the canopy rose to admit a blast of hot, flinty desert air, I sat there for a moment to reflect upon my adventure. Neither of the two guys still trying to catch up from Germany had deployed with the 8th, and since I was the last one to land, it turned out that I was (just barely) the longest deployed from the 49th. I took my time writing up the forms while sitting there in the cockpit.

Unable to delay any longer, I slowly stood to climb down the ladder from my F-117—exactly one year to the day that, as a student with the 7th, I had first climbed up.

My war was over.

Epilogue

The ultimate responsibility of every pilot is to
fulfill the dreams of his countless millions
of earthbound ancestors who could only
stare skyward . . . and wish.

I STAYED IN NEW MEXICO just long enough to hand off some paperwork to the 789th (what the conglomeration of guys left behind from the three squadrons had been calling themselves) and to arrange for leave. Bets and the kids had been staying with my in-laws in upstate New York and were waiting for me as I got off the plane in Syracuse.

My first clue that I'd have trouble sharing my experiences came quickly. I completely failed to have a successful conversation with a friend of ours who worked as a blacksmith at a local heritage village. Beyond the obvious differences in background between a fighter pilot and a blacksmith, there was a larger void.

We tried hard. I knew exactly what it was that I was trying to express. I knew what he wanted to hear, and he knew what I was trying to convey. But we lacked a common language or shared experience through which we could communicate. I had become one of those veterans unable to explain what combat was like.

The Fourth of July celebrations that year were different also. Not the celebration itself, or the patriotism, or the flag waving. All of that was still great and just as I remembered. What had changed were the fireworks. My wife noticed it first and asked why I was frowning at parts of the show when all around us were oohing and aahing at every pop, boom, and flash. I had become transfixed by just one portion of the displays. And suddenly it struck me that the silvery strobe-light flashes looked exactly like the airburst of 23mm AAA fire over Belgrade and Novi Sad. With an embarrassed chuckle, I had to shake that thought out of my head.

But life slowly evened itself out. We swam and had cookouts on the beaches of Cape Cod. For the first time in months I really slept. We were even in Rome, New York, during the 1999 Woodstock concerts but didn't make it inside, for which our then thirteen-year-old daughter will never forgive us.

Over the course of that summer the Kosovar Albanians drifted back to their farms, and it became the Kosovar Serbs' turn for exodus as they fled their farms to move north. The same injustices were still occurring—just in reverse. A mere seven weeks after the bombings were halted, General Clark was informed that he would be relieved of his command as SACEUR early, to be replaced by a USAF general.

General Clark's firing caused a short flurry of words from the media, but that quickly faded away as soon as they noticed that there were virtually no military voices raised in protest. The helicopters he had ordered to Albania never flew a single mission over the border. Two of the twenty-three crashed while attempting to train up to interdiction standards while in the field, for an accident rate in training higher than the F-117's in combat. Sadly, two crew members were killed—the only combat-related deaths within the coalition.

All told, over 37,000 sorties were flown over Yugoslavia for the loss of two jets. Both pilots were rescued. Later analysis showed that a pilot was two and half times more likely to have been shot at by a SAM during this war than over Iraq during Desert Storm. That exposure had been prolonged by the glacial pace of operations. During the first thirty days the coalition averaged only 92 strikes per day versus an average of 1,300 strikes per day during Desert Storm. We had been allowed to do less that entire first month than what was being accomplished every two or three days back then.

Milosevic was eventually arrested by his own people, but died in prison before a verdict was reached in his trial.

While at least superficially more quiet, the Kosovars continue to push for independence and the country still seethes with irreconcilable tensions, and if history has taught us anything, it probably will for a very long time to come.

That fall I honored what I saw as the lesson of Bob's death. Life can be too unpredictable not to chase after a few impractical dreams on occasion. I was determined to own a plane with character before the year was out. So in October, as part of a three-way exchange involving one of his Beech-18s, Tuna and I trekked up to Iron Mountain, Michigan, so that I could purchase a 1943 Stearman biplane. We flew this open-cockpit, fifty-six-year old, fabric-covered, no-radio bit of nostalgia for seventeen flight hours across 1,200 very chilly miles to its new home in New Mexico.

Was that a practical purchase? Not at all. Could I use it to commute anywhere? Nope. Could I fit the family in there for a trip? Not a chance. Were there more than a few twinges of buyer's remorse at the thought of what I'd gotten myself into? Sure. But when the wind was buffeting past my goggles and making the wires sing, and we flew down Main Street of some small farming village in Iowa low enough to smell the hay, drifting along at maybe eighty miles per hour, and the sound of the clattering old nine-cylinder radial engine swinging its antique wooden propeller caused a pair of kids just to dump their bicycles on the sidewalk and jump up and down waving both arms over their heads (I saw myself down there, thirty years ago), did I think it was worth it?

Absolutely.

I still do.

Appendix

The Nighthawk Series

A grand total of sixty-nine objects were created in the Nighthawk series. Of those, only sixty-six were ever intended to fly; only fifty-nine of those were intended to become operational aircraft. Due to the program being so highly classified initially, conventional tail-number identifications were not accorded. After the two Have Blue aircraft the series was identified solely by numbers, beginning with the completely arbitrary number of 777 and sequentially progressing through the number 843 for the last object built. Years later these same numbers were incorporated into the conventional tail-numbering system , which is why the year-group occasionally jumps up and down and why there were some accidental duplicate numbers allocated that actually belonged to a series of F-16s. Listed below is the complete family tree and where they are now. A single asterisk signifies an aircraft flown by the author, two asterisks were those flown by the author in combat.

Have Blue Series

XST-1, Have Blue 1001
First flight 12/1/1977; destroyed in crash 5/4/1978, Groom Lake area.

XST-2, Have Blue 1002
First flight 7/21/1978; destroyed in crash 7/11/1979, Groom Lake area.

Static Test Series

These were static test airframes for engineering stress analysis and radar cross-section testing—not intended for, or capable of, flight.

777, 778, and 779

Full Scale Development (FSD) Series (not operational)

79-0780, FSD-1
First flight 6/18/1981; Gate Guard at Nellis AFB, Nevada.

79-0781, FSD-2
First flight 9/4/1981; on display at the National Museum of the U.S. Air Force, Wright Patterson AFB, Ohio.

79-0782, FSD-3
First flight 12/18/1981; on display at Holloman AFB, New Mexico (painted as aircraft 85-0816).

79-0783, FSD-4
First flight 7/7/1982; on display at Blackbird Airpark, Palmdale, California.

79-0784, FSD-5
First flight 4/10/1982; unceremoni-
ously destroyed by a backhoe to test
destruction methods 4/26/2008.

Operational Production Series

79-0785
First (and only) flight 4/20/1982;
crashed on initial takeoff (pilot
severely injured).

80-0786 *War Pig**
First flight 7/15/1982; retired to storage
4/11/2008. First operational F-117
delivered to the USAF, and the first to
see combat. Combat missions: Panama,
1; Desert Storm, 24; Allied Force, 32.

80-0787 *Pete's Dragon*
First flight 7/20/1982; retired to
storage 10/12/2007.

80-0788**
First flight 9/8/1982; retired to storage
4/11/2008. Combat missions: Allied
Force, 44.

80-0789 *Black Magic**
First flight 10/27/1982; retired to
storage 3/13/2007. Combat missions:
Desert Storm, 31; Iraqi Freedom, 9.

80-0790 *Deadly Jester* (at first public
unveiling 1987); *Obsidian*
First flight 11/11/1982; retired to
storage 3/13/2007. Combat missions:
Desert Storm, 30.

80-0791 *Lazy Ace**
First flight 11/22/1982; retired to
storage 1/25/2008. Combat missions:
Desert Storm, 33; Allied Force, 37.

80-0792
First flight 12/9/1982; crashed
7/11/1982 (pilot killed).

81-I0793 *Tritonal Express*
First flight 1/20/1983; crashed at
Baltimore Airshow 9/14/1997 due
to in-flight breakup. The *I* in the tail
number indicates a duplicate number
assigned to another aircraft. Combat
missions: Desert Storm, 33.

81-I0794 *Delta Dawn**
First flight 3/4/1983; retired to storage
10/12/2007. Combat missions: Desert
Storm, 35; Allied Force, 29; Iraqi
Freedom, 8.

81-I0795**
First flight 6/7/1983; retired to storage
3/13/2007. Combat missions: Allied
Force, 31.

81-I0796 *Fatal Attraction**
First flight 6/16/1983; retired to
storage 1/25/2008. Combat missions:
Desert Storm, 29.

81-I0797 *Spell Bound**
First flight 8/3/1983; retired to storage
10/12/2007. Combat missions: Desert
Storm, 8.

81-I0798 *Aces and Eights**
First flight 8/25/1983; retired to
storage 10/12/2007. Combat missions:
Desert Storm, 34.

82-0799 *Midnight Rider**
First flight 12/22/1983; retired to
storage 1/31/2008. Combat missions:
Desert Storm, 21; Allied Force, 22;
Iraqi Freedom, 11.

82-0800 *Black Sheep**
First flight 11/10/1983; retired to
storage 4/22/2007. Combat missions
Allied Force, 38; Iraqi Freedom, 5.

82-0801 *Perpetrator*
First flight 12/21/1983; crashed north
of Holloman 8/4/1992. Combat
missions: Desert Storm, 38.

82-0802 *Black Magic**
First flight on 3/7/1984; retired to
storage 10/12/2007. Nicknames were
unofficial, so repeats such as this were
allowed. Combat missions: Desert
Storm, 19.

82-0803 *Unexpected Guest***
First flight 5/8/1984; retired to storage
3/23/2007. Holds the record for
number of F-117 combat missions
with a total of seventy-eight. Combat
missions: Panama, 1; Desert Storm, 33;
Allied Force, 44.

82-0804 *Rammer**
First flight 5/25/1984; retired to
storage 4/11/2008.

82-0805*
First flight 7/5/1984; retired to storage
10/12/2007. Holds the record for
number of F-117 combat missions in
a single conflict. Combat missions:
Allied Force, 50.

82-0806 *Something Wicked*
First flight 8/20/1984; shot down over
Serbia 3/27/1999, during Allied Force.
Combat missions: Desert Storm, 39;
Allied Force, 5.

83-0807 *Chickenhawk**
First flight 9/13/1984; retired to
storage 4/11/2008. Combat missions:
Desert Storm, 14; Allied Force, 43.

83-0808 *Thor**
First flight 10/23/1984; retired to
storage 1/29/2008. Combat missions:
Desert Storm, 37.

84-0809*
First flight 1/3/1985; retired to storage
4/22/2008. Combat missions: Allied
Force, 17.

84-0810 *Dark Angel**
First flight 1/18/1985; retired to
storage 1/25/2008. Combat missions:
Desert Storm, 26; Allied Force, 18.

84-0811 *Double Down**
First flight 3/8/1985; last assigned to
the 410th TS at Palmdale, California.
Combat missions: Desert Storm, 33.

84-0812 *Axel**
First flight 5/1/1985; retired to storage
1/29/2008. Holds the record for
number of F-117 combat missions
in Desert Storm. Combat missions:
Desert Storm, 42.

85-0813 *The Toxic Avenger**
First flight 6/7/1985; retired to storage
1/25/2008. Combat missions: Panama,
1; Desert Storm, 35.

85-0814 *Final Verdict**
First flight 7/26/1985; retired to
storage 4/11/2008. Combat missions:
Desert Storm, 34; Allied Force, 9.

85-0815
First flight 9/13/1985; crashed north of
Nellis 10/14/1985 (pilot killed).

85-0816 *Lone Wolf**
First flight 10/30/1985; retired to
storage 10/12/2007. Combat missions:
Panama, 1; Desert Storm, 39; Iraqi
Freedom, 8.

85-0817 *Shaba***
First flight 1/9/1986; retired to storage
3/13/2007. Combat missions: Panama,
1; Desert Storm, 18; Allied Force, 40.

85-0818 *The Overachiever**
First flight 2/11/1986; retired to
storage 6/22/2007. This was the only
jet to employ in all four conflicts.
Combat missions: Panama, 1; Desert
Storm, 38; Allied Force, 12; Iraqi
Freedom, 9.

85-0819 *Raven Beauty***
First flight 4/14/1986; retired to
storage 10/12/2007. Combat missions:
Desert Storm, 30; Allied Force, 20;
Iraqi Freedom, 5.

85-0820**
First flight 5/2/1986; retired to storage
3/23/2007. Combat missions: Allied
Force, 37.

86-0821 *Sneak Attack**
First flight 6/20/1986; retired to
storage 1/31/2008. Combat missions:
Desert Storm, 32; Allied Force, 19.

86-0822
First flight 8/18/1986; crashed south
of Zuni, New Mexico, 5/10/1995 (pilot
killed).

86-0823*
First flight 10/7/1986; retired to
storage 10/12/2007.

84-0824*
First flight 11/13/1986; retired to
storage 4/22/2008 (non-sequential
year-group markings due to numbers
being assigned after public unveiling).
Combat missions: Allied Force, 27;
Iraqi Freedom, 6.

84-0825 *Mad Max*
First flight 1/29/1987; retired to
storage 10/12/2007. Combat missions:
Desert Storm, 33; Iraqi Freedom, 6.

84-0826 *Nachtfalke**
First flight 3/2/1987; retired to storage
1/29/2008. Combat missions: Desert
Storm, 29; Allied Force, 31.

84-0827*
First flight 4/7/1987; retired to storage
10/12/2007.

84-0828 *Air Rage** (author's
assigned jet)
First flight 5/15/1987; retired to
storage 8/1/2008. Combat missions:
Allied Force, 33.

85-0829 *Avenging Angel**
First flight 7/10/1987; retired to
storage 6/22/2007. Combat missions:
Desert Storm, 23.

85-0830 *Black Assassin**
First flight 9/3/1987; retired to storage
1/25/2008. Combat missions: Desert
Storm, 31.

86-0831
First flight 10/20/1987; retired to
storage 8/11/2008. This was a Palmdale
test aircraft only.

85-0832 *Once Bitten**
First flight 12/10/1987; retired to
storage 3/13/2007. Combat missions:
Desert Storm, 30; Allied Force, 17.

85-0833 *Black Devil***
First flight 2/19/1988; retired to
storage 4/11/2008. Combat missions:
Desert Storm, 30; Allied Force, 45.

85-0834 *Necromancer**
First flown 4/29/1988; retired to
storage 1/31/2008. Combat missions:
Panama, 1; Desert Storm, 34; Iraqi
Freedom, 6.

85-0835 *The Dragon*
First flight 6/30/1988; retired to
storage 3/13/2007. Combat missions:
Desert Storm, 26.

85-0836 *Christine**
First flight 9/21/1988; retired to
storage 1/31/2008. Combat missions:
Desert Storm, 39.

86-0837 *Habu II*
First flight 12/8/1988; retired to
storage 1/31/2008. Combat missions:
Desert Storm, 31.

86-0838 *Magic Hammer**
First flight 3/17/1989; retired to
storage 10/12/2007. Combat missions:
Desert Storm, 36.

86-0839 *Midnight Reaper**
First flight 6/14/1989; retired to
storage 1/25/2008. Combat missions:
Desert Storm, 39.

86-0840 *Black Widow**
First flight 9/12/1989; retired to
storage 4/11/2008. Combat missions:
Desert Storm, 32.

88-0841 *Mystic Warrior**
First flight 12/7/1989; retired to
storage 8/1/2008. Combat missions:
Desert Storm, 18.

88-0842 *It's Hammer Time***
First flight 3/13/1990; retired to
storage 1/29/2008. Combat missions:
Desert Storm, 33; Allied Force, 23;
Iraqi Freedom, 9.

88-0843 *Affectionately Christine**
First flight 5/11/1990; retired to
storage 4/22/2008. This was the last
F-117 delivered. Combat missions:
Desert Storm, 33; Allied Force, 37.

Glossary

AAA	Anti-Aircraft Artillery, also called Triple-A
AAR	Air-to-Air Refueling
ACC	Air Combat Command
AETC	Air Education and Training Command
AFMSS	Air Force Mission Support System (a computer system used to plan combat missions)
ATO	Air Tasking Order
AWACS	Airborne Warning and Control System (a Boeing-707 with a radar disk on top)
BDA	Bomb Damage Assessment
Berm	A protective mound of dirt surrounding a potential target
Betty	Nickname for the aircraft computer's automated female voice
Boldface	A series of emergency procedures committed to memory
Block-50	F-16 fitted with an HTS pod and HARM missiles, also called CJ's
BOQ	Bachelor Officer's Quarters, or Qs for short

BUFF	B-52 Bomber (Big Ugly Fat Fellow)
CALCM	Conventional Air Launched Cruise Missile
CAOC	Combined Air Operations Center
CAP	Combat Air Patrol
CBU	Cluster Bomb Unit
CSAR	Combat Search and Rescue
Dash-1	An aircraft's systems and operation manual
DARPA	Defense Advanced Research Projects Agency
DLIR	Downward-Looking Infrared
DMPI	Desired Munition Point of Impact (pronounced *dimpy*)
ECM	Electronic Counter Measures
ECS	Electronic Combat Squadron
EDTM	Electronic Data Transfer Module (an F-117's portable hard-drive)
EW	Electronic Warfare
EWO	Electronics Warfare Operator
Feet-wet	Flying over a coastline toward the sea, the opposite of Feet-dry
FLIR	Forward-Looking Infrared
GBU	Guided Bomb Unit
Go	A "go" is a wave of sorties within a scheduling block
GPS	Global Positioning System
HARM	High-Speed Anti-Radiation Missiles
HAS	Hardened Aircraft Shelters
HTS	HARM Targeting System
HUD	Heads-Up Display
ILS	Instrument Landing System
INS	Inertial Navigation System
IP	Instructor Pilot, or Initial Point
IR	Infrared
IRADS	Infrared Acquisition and Designation System

JDAM	Joint Direct Attack Munition (a GPS-guided bomb)
JIPTL	Joint Integrated Prioritized Target List
LANTIRN	Low-Altitude Navigation and Targeting Infrared for Night
LGB	Laser-Guided Bomb
MAAP	Master Aerial Attack Plan
MIL	Or Mil-power, 100 percent engine thrust without afterburner
NAS	Naval Air Station
NATO	North Atlantic Treaty Organization
NVGs	Night Vision Goggles (sometimes called Nogs)
OCIP	Offensive Capability Improvement Program (replaced by RNIP)
OG	Operations Group Commander
ORE	Operational Readiness Exercise
ORI	Operational Readiness Inspection
PAARS	Pilot-Activated Automatic Recovery System
PGM	Precision-Guided Munitions
RAF	Royal Air Force
Radrel	Radio Relay (a transmission tower)
RAM	Radar-Absorbent/Attenuating Material
RCS	Radar Cross-Section
RLG	Ring-Laser-Gyro
RNIP	Ring-Laser-Gyro Navigation Improvement Program
ROE	Rules of Engagement
Rolex	The act of pushing back an attack a fixed amount of time
RTU	Replacement Training Unit
SACEUR	Supreme Allied Commander Europe
SAM	Surface-to-Air Missile
SEAD	Suppression of Enemy Air Defenses
SIGINT	Signals Intelligence

SOF	Supervisor of Flying
Sortie	A single flight by an aircraft
TAC	Tactical Air Command
TDY	Temporary duty to another location
TLAM	Tomahawk Land-Attack Missiles
TOT	Time Over Target
TTG	Time To Go before a bomb release
TTI	Time To Impact of that bomb
SD	Sensor Display (also called the attack display)
UFC	Upfront Control panel
VFR	Visual Flight Rules

Bibliography

Ambrose, Stephen E. *Band of Brothers*. New York: Simon & Schuster, 1992.

Bowden, Mark. *Black Hawk Down*. New York: Atlantic Monthly Press, 1999.

Campbell, Greg. *The Road to Kosovo: A Balkan Diary*. Boulder, CO: Westview Press, 1999.

Cobleigh, Ed. *War for the Hell of it: A Fighter Pilot's View of Vietnam*. New York: Berkley Publishing Group, 2005.

Davies, Steve. *Red Eagles: America's Secret MiGs*. United Kingdom: Osprey Publishing, 2008.

De Botton, David. *F-111A in SEA*. F-111.net, 2006.

Gerolymatos, Andre. *The Balkan Wars*. New York: Basic Books, 2002.

Halberstam, David. *War in a Time of Peace: Bush, Clinton and the Generals*. New York: Scribner, 2001.

Henneman, Greg. *Fighting 49ers: The History of the 49th Fighter Wing*. Holloman AFB, New Mexico: 49th History Office, 2005.

Ignatieff, Michael. *Virtual War: Kosovo and Beyond*. New York: Metropolitan Books, 2000.

Lambeth, Benjamin S. *NATO's Air War for Kosovo: A Strategic and Operational Assessment*. RAND, 2001.

Peebles, Curtis. *Dark Eagles: A History of Top Secret U.S. Aircraft*

Programs. Novato, CA, Presidio Press, 1995.

Rasimus, Ed. *Palace Cobra: A Fighter Pilot in the Vietnam Air War.* New York: St. Martin's Press, 2006.

Rich, Ben R. & Janos, Leo. *Skunk Works.* New York: Back Bay Books/ Little Brown and Company, 1994.

Ryan, Craig. *The Pre-Astronauts: Manned Ballooning on the Threshold of Space.* Annapolis, MD: Naval Institute Press, 1995.

Simpson, Ross W. *Stealth Down.* Charleston: Narwhal Press, 2002.

Strachan, Hew. *The First World War.* New York: Viking, 2003.

Thompson, Warren E. *Bandits over Baghdad.* North Branch, MN: Specialty Press, 2000.